EDWARDIAN PLAYS

Edwardian Plays

EDITED AND WITH AN INTRODUCTION BY

GERALD WEALES

A MERMAID DRAMABOOK

HILL AND WANG · NEW YORK

Manufactured in the United States of America by
The Colonial Press, Inc., Clinton, Massachusetts

CONTENTS

	Page
Introduction	vii
LOAVES AND FISHES	I
A Satire in Four Acts	
by W. Somerset Maugham	
THE RETURN OF THE PRODIGAL	78
A Comedy in Four Acts	
by St. John Hankin	
GETTING MARRIED	137
A Disquisitory Play	
by Bernard Shaw	
MID-CHANNEL	221
by Arthur Wing Pinero	
THE MADRAS HOUSE	319
A Comedy in Four Acts	
by Harley Granville-Barker	
Notes	429

INTRODUCTION

"At the time, it looked like going on forever," says Colonel Redfern in John Osborne's *Look Back in Anger*. "When I think of it now, it seems like a dream. If only it could have gone on forever." The Colonel's *it* is the period before World War I, the Edwardian years—partly historical, partly fictional —that have become the nostalgic equipment of English writers —even the young and supposedly angry ones—who need a time of comparative calm and certainty against which to place their own confusion and that which surrounds them. In those days, the myth says, a man knew who he was; so Phoebe, in *The Entertainer,* can say of Billy Rice, the music-hall variation on Osborne's sentimentalized colonel, "He's just a has-been, I suppose. Still—it's better to be a has-been than a never-was." This evocation of the Edwardian past seems little more than a literary device with Osborne, who, after all, was born years after World War I had broken open the neat Edwardian world; it comes more naturally to a writer like J. B. Priestley, who, twenty years before *Look Back in Anger,* was recalling the years of his childhood and adolescence when, in *Time and the Conways,* he contrasted the good times of the Edwardian days with the brittle and empty thirties.

Within the invention of Osborne and the reminiscence of Priestley, there is a kind of truth, but their backward looks tell us as much about the England of the fifties and the thirties as of the first decade of the century. There *was* something safe, almost sealed about the Edwardian period. World War I did bring it to an end. This is nowhere more obvious than in the work of Bernard Shaw: contrast the tough optimism of *Major Barbara* (1905) and the despair of *Too True to Be Good* (1931), where the Shaw life force can scarcely find breathing room. *Heartbreak House,* which he began writing in 1913 and finished six years later, is Shaw's pained funeral speech over the dead years of innocence and inconsequence. But his dissection of what Mazzini Dunn calls "what is best in our English culture," the "advanced, unprejudiced, frank, humane, unconventional, democratic, free-thinking" people who failed to prevent the war, is as unfair to the Edwardians (to the Shaw of a few years earlier) as is Osborne's portrait of Colonel Redfern.

The period was not so complacent and content as the Osborne longing suggests, nor was it so facile and false as the Shaw disappointment insists. The quality of the years between 1900 and 1914 (Edward VII reigned from 1901 to 1910) is a bit difficult to define because no era is quite so neat as historians like to pretend. If the general feel of the period was one of expectation—the optimistic assumption that if intelligence were brought to bear, the problems of society could be solved—the nineteenth-century idea of inevitable progress was already doubted. Even Shaw, whose mystical turn of mind allowed him to find a religious metaphor in biology, said again and again that his evolutionary will did not insist on man as the instrument. Harley Granville-Barker* and particularly St. John Hankin, among the playwrights, mixed their hope for the future (including the future of the theatre) with doubt of a kind. Although Granville-Barker frees Philip Madras of the Madras House and points him toward the County Council, allows him to turn his attention from the making of dresses to the remaking of society, the playwright knows, as Philip does, that he will have "to do dull, hard work over drains and disinfectants," because "That's how these great spiritual revolutions work out in practice, to begin with." If Granville-Barker displays an affectionate irony which colors the activity of his characters, Hankin's plays suggest a strange mixture of reformism and pessimism; Eustace, for instance, in *The Return of the Prodigal,* sounds like a Shavian gone sour.

It would be a mistake to overemphasize the pessimistic undertones in Hankin. His wryness, which at times approaches cynicism (the result, perhaps, of having two idols—Wilde and Shaw), is a variation on the honest doubt of the period. It was this doubt that was responsible for the tendency, on- and off-stage, to hold society up to the light to search out flaws. Such examinations, however, went on in an atmosphere that always suggested that something was about to happen (it was, after all, a new century), although no one expected that the happening would be a world war. It is not surprising that such a period should have been full of beginnings. Joyce, Forster, Lawrence, Yeats, all started to write during the Edwardian years, although we tend to think of these men as writers of the twenties.

The Edwardian era was a time of theatrical beginnings, too. The theatre of this period is rather different from the rest

* It was not until after World War I that Granville Barker, apparently at the genteel insistence of his second wife, changed his name to Harley Granville-Barker. Although the hyphenated form is used in most reference books, the playwright, director, and actor of the Edwardian years is more correctly Granville Barker, and it is that name that will be found in all the source material and most of the critical and biographical works about the period.

of Edwardian literature. Drama did not, like poetry and the novel, move on to a new richness after the war. Although the theatrical practitioners of the Edwardian years considered themselves pioneers—as their endless talk of endowed theatre, art theatre, repertory theatre, national theatre indicates—the period, in retrospect, has become one of achievement. This is not simply because modern drama at last became domesticated in England with the full acceptance of Shaw, who had to put up such a hard fight in the nineties; it is because the period produced at least one other first-rate dramatist, Harley Granville-Barker, and a comparatively large number of playwrights —John Galsworthy, St. John Hankin, James M. Barrie, W. Somerset Maugham, Arnold Bennett—whose best work still has vitality and value. This description is a restrained one, at least insofar as I have not demanded that the reader step with me across the Irish Sea where we could pick up Yeats and Lady Gregory and, most important, John Millington Synge, who, next to Shaw, is the greatest of the English-language playwrights of this time. No editor in his right mind is going to tout a selection of plays as sure winners in the race for literary greatness, for play fanciers can sometimes read and the evidence lies just beyond the introduction. I can probably find as many faults per act in the plays that follow as any other reader can (even in *The Madras House*, which I am convinced is one of the best plays to come out of England), but I doubt that any other span of seven years in the modern English theatre can turn up five plays which, when they are pushing sixty, will be as lively as these still are.

Despite the occasionally dated social references (divorce reform in *Getting Married*, the living-in system in *The Madras House*), any of these plays could be put on successfully today (I am speaking aesthetically, not economically), and most of them—*Mid-Channel* is the exception—would sound as modern in tone and idea as a large number of Broadway and West End productions of the current season. *The Madras House* and, somewhat less fully, *Getting Married* present a whole range of attitudes toward sex and marriage that are as contemporary as they are Edwardian. Some of the surface concerns of Canon Spratte, Maugham's charming schemer, may seem a little old-fashioned, but his goals (status and money) are current enough and his machinations are familiar to anyone who has watched a professional on the make; it is possible, of course, that a generation that does not know the Bible might miss the real bite of the Maugham title, *Loaves and Fishes*. The returning prodigal in Hankin's play, who uses his avowed incapacity for any kind of work to blackmail his father into supporting him, might have become a popular hero a few years ago when the Beats, in their haphazard search for cultural heroes, latched on to con men as different in quality as W. C. Fields and Major Hoople. It was this possible reading of *The Return of the Prodigal,* I suspect, that made Bernard Shaw so dislike the play that (as with *The Importance of Being Earnest* ten years earlier) he failed to embrace it for those things (from the wonderfully comic entrance of Eustace at the end of Act One to the social commentary implicit in the family's scramble for position) which he would ordinarily have admired.

There was greater variety in the Edwardian theatre than these five plays suggest. There were the musical comedies, particularly those produced by George Edwardes, who had invented the Gaiety Girl years earlier—*San Toy,* for instance, and *The Merry Widow.* There were the matinée-idol shows like those in which Lewis Waller swashed and buckled. There were the fragile West End comedies of R. C. Carton and Captain Marshall. There were the plays of Stephen Phillips, whose *Paolo and Francesca* (1902) was wrongly supposed to have brought poetry back to the English stage. There were still the overstuffed Shakespearean productions of Beerbohm Tree and other aspirants to the buskins of Sir Henry Irving, although Granville-Barker's production of *The Two Gentlemen of Verona* in 1904 began to show managers how to take out some of the stuffing. Theatre, however, is not always the same as drama. The best of the Edwardian playwrights were those who took part in or—like Pinero and Barrie—allowed themselves to be influenced by the chief theatrical movement of the period, which, as Granville-Barker complained (*The English Review,* July, 1910), was "sometimes called—by the people who don't like it—the Advanced Theatre, sometimes even the Intellectual Theatre; and that is one of the most abusive epithets that one Englishman can fling at another." Granville-Barker suggested the phrase "Normal Drama" to describe the kind of play that he wanted to see take over the English theatre, the kind that he himself wrote. The renascence of drama that John Galsworthy celebrated in "Some Platitudes Concerning Drama" (*Fortnightly Review,* December, 1909) was real enough, but the "new spirit" that he saw sweeping the theatre was new only in the sense that it described the feeling of ferment and excitement that the playwrights of the period shared. What the playwrights were about, of course, was the old business of the dramatist. Whether they worked in comedy (like Shaw) or in the social play (like Galsworthy), they were intent on a theatre which had some connection to the psychological and social life of its creators and its audience, which is another way of saying, with Barker, that they believed "that the art of the theatre may be taken seriously."

The most important vehicles for the new theatre were the Stage Society and the Granville-Barker–J. E. Vedrenne seasons at the Court Theatre, 1904-1907. Although the first was not a commercial venture and the second was never a financial success, what they did was to take the English theatre, at least its most serious wing, out of the hands of Pinero and Henry Arthur Jones, who had been under attack from Shaw in his theatre criticism in the *Saturday Review* a decade earlier when he insisted that they (particularly Pinero) represented the most obvious kind of popular playwright masking as serious dramatist. The change in theatrical tastes can be seen in *Mid-Channel*. Although Pinero deals with a favorite theme of his (the double standard) and passes his usual judgment on the erring woman (death after dishonor), Zoe is more complicated and more vulgar than his earlier put-upon heroines, and the play, although it telescopes its punch lines, is wonderfully restrained by comparison with his successes of the nineties, *The Second Mrs. Tanqueray* and *The Notorious Mrs. Ebbsmith*.

There was experimental theatre in London in the days when Paula Tanqueray and Agnes Ebbsmith were walking big in the West End and, ironically, Pinero and Jones were among the people who gave their support to J. T. Grein's Independent Theatre. Grein's venture began with the famous production of Ibsen's *Ghosts* (1891) that brought him such vituperation from the London critics, and it was Ibsen— *John Gabriel Borkman,* this time—that initiated (1897) the New Century Theatre, organized by William Archer, who was not only the translator of Ibsen but the man who supposedly talked Shaw into becoming a playwright. Although both of these groups produced new English playwrights (Grein introduced Shaw with *Widower's Houses*), and although both the Stage Society and the Court seasons produced Ibsen, it was the later groups that did most toward emphasizing homegrown modern drama. There were many direct connections between the early groups and the Edwardians, almost as though each group grew out of the preceding one. Gilbert Murray, for instance, who had been one of Grein's supporters, was for a time on the Council of Management of the Stage Society, and his Euripides translations were produced both by the Society and by Granville-Barker and Vedrenne.

Although *The Return of the Prodigal,* which was done at

the Court, is the only play in this volume to have been produced by either of the two main experimental groups, the playwrights—with the exception of Pinero—were very much involved with both the Stage Society and the Court management. Shaw, who was frequently produced by both groups, was Chairman of the Producing Committee during the first season of the Stage Society and was a financial backer, a not very silent partner of Granville-Barker and Vedrenne at the Court. Granville-Barker made his debut both as playwright (*The Marrying of Ann Leete* was the first of his plays written without a collaborator to reach production) and as director with the Stage Society, where he also acted regularly; as co-manager, director, playwright, and actor he was almost synonymous with the Court. Both Hankin (*The Two Mrs. Wetherbys*) and Maugham (*A Man of Honour*) were first introduced to audiences through the Stage Society. All of Hankin's full-length plays were produced by one of the two groups, but Maugham's connection with the experimental theatre ended after the production of his first play. In *The Summing Up*, in which he speaks harshly of Granville-Barker, who played the lead in *A Man of Honour* and who must have made him feel uncomfortable at rehearsals (both men were in their twenties then), Maugham has a few funny paragraphs in which he tells how, after his Stage Society experience, he set out in cold blood to write a successful comedy, one that would bring him money. His first try was *Loaves and Fishes*, of which he says: "No manager would consider it; it was thought impossible that a play that held a clergyman up to ridicule would be tolerated." By 1907, he had achieved his goal, he had three plays running simultaneously in the West End and he had become as innocuous as the rest of the writers of popular fluff. He says, somewhat pompously, "If I had continued to write plays as bitter as *A Man of Honour* or as sardonic as *Loaves and Fishes* I should never have been given the opportunity of producing certain pieces to which not even the most severe have refused praise." Presumably, he means the best of his later comedies, plays like *The Circle*; but insofar as their reception was not due to their quality (and the twenty years that passed between *A Man of Honour* and them), it lies not with the fact that Maugham was the author of *Mrs. Dot*, but with the success of the kind of theatrical organization of which Maugham speaks so slightingly. The Stage Society and the Granville-Barker–Vedrenne management did the job of the experimental theatre everywhere—toughened the commercial theatre by making the once outrageous quite acceptable. While they performed that service in London, the

Abbey Theatre was doing the same thing in Dublin as was A. E. F. Horniman's repertory company in Manchester; by 1914 and the end of the Edwardians, the new drama was firmly fixed in England, was, in fact, ready to become a commercial cliché in its own right, ready to be blown over by the next experimental wind.

The plays of the period—as those in this collection indicate —share certain characteristics. Setting, for one thing. The five plays in this volume, like so many of their time, take place in middle- or upper-class households. If we put aside the special difficulties of Eustace in *The Return of the Prodigal* and Canon Spratte in *Loaves and Fishes*, only in *The Madras House*—in the case of the Brigstocks—is a serious economic problem hinted at. Plays with working-class protagonists were being written elsewhere in the British Isles—among the Manchester school (Stanley Houghton's *Hindle Wakes*), in Wales (J. O. Francis's *Change*) and in Ireland (St. John Ervine's *John Ferguson*), but even these were much more concerned with the conflict between generations, a subject familiar enough in middle-class surroundings, than with the problems that were to come in later working-class plays. Sometimes the London playwrights did deal with the struggles of the workingman, but in John Galsworthy's *Strife*, for instance, the meeting of the Board of Directors is more convincing than the gathering of the workers. Although Shaw was able to draw believable workers or loafers, as in the shelter scene in *Major Barbara*, his attack on poverty is voiced best through the mouth of the millionaire Andrew Undershaft, and that play is really about the spiritual salvation of Barbara, who expects to have to forgive God "as becomes a woman of my rank." Insofar as the playwrights attacked the economic structure of society, they did so as middle-class intellectuals (there are strong Fabian allegiances here and not only in the case of Shaw). Edward, in Granville-Barker's *The Voysey Inheritance*, can accept his father's legacy of swindling since property is theft, and Eustace, in *The Return of the Prodigal*, can equate his living off his father with his father's living off the workers. Insofar as the playwrights defended the structure of society, they worked as Barrie did in *The Admirable Crichton*, in terms of below and above stairs or else, as with Maugham's portrait of the Christian socialist and his crusading sister in *Loaves and Fishes*, by depicting dedication as bad manners.

Although serious political and economic concerns are implicit in much of the work of the Edwardian theatre, specific

social themes—position in society, the family, sex and marriage—are more likely to be explicit. The great tragedy for
the Pinero heroine in the nineties (and for the Wilde heroine,
too, although Wilde was a bit more tongue-in-cheek about it)
is that she should commit an indiscretion that would keep her
from being invited to the right homes, that she should be shut
out of the narrow society of fashionable London. In the
Edwardian theatre, the plight of the uninvited could no longer
be taken seriously. The hatchet work on fashionable society,
begun by Wilde with such characters as the Duchess of Ber-
wick in *Lady Windermere's Fan* and Lady Bracknell in *The
Importance of Being Earnest*, was continued, particularly by
St. John Hankin, whose Lady Faringford in *The Return of
the Prodigal* and the Countess of Remenham in *The Cassilis
Engagement* may have been less comic but were no less blunt
than the Wilde originals. The climber is still around, but he
is no longer a satiric butt because he is trying to get out of
his station; he is treated comically or nastily (the Jacksons
in *The Return of the Prodigal* are more than just funny),
because the playwrights have come to believe that once he
gets to the top of the ladder he will find nothing there. There
are a few exceptions. Pinero can still suggest that one of the
difficulties with the Blundell marriage in *Mid-Channel* is that
they have pushed too hard for position, but even Maugham,
whose fastidiousness keeps him from playing quite fair with
the Railings, makes hash of Canon Spratte's nonsense about
family. Shaw, in *Getting Married*, comes at the pretention of
position from all angles: the recurring business of costume
(Boxer's uniform, Collins's alderman's robes); the greengrocer's disquisition on rank; the passion of St. John Hotchkiss, the declared snob, for the coal merchant's wife. He even
slips into fantasy on the subject, as in this exchange between
Boxer and Hotchkiss:

The General. And pray, sir, on what ground do you dare allege
that Major Billiter is not a gentleman?

Hotchkiss. By an infallible sign: one of those trifles that stamp
a man. He eats rice pudding with a spoon.

The General. Confound you, *I* eat rice pudding with a spoon.
Now!

Hotchkiss. Oh, so do I, frequently. But there are ways of doing
these things. Billiter's way was unmistakable.

So much for the Victorian gentleman and his good opinion.

The English family, which had the support and the example
of the late good queen, comes off no better. Hugh, the failed
artist son in Granville-Barker's *The Voysey Inheritance,*

describes his brother Trenchard, who broke with the family, as having escaped "From tyranny! . . from hyprocrisy! . . from boredom! . . from his Happy English Home!" Although the Voyseys, with the stultifying atmosphere of affection and restraint that has made victims of all of the children except Trenchard, is the harshest family portrait on the Edwardian stage, there is a good runner-up in the Huxtables in *The Madras House*, where the domineering mother and the too-provident father have made spinsters of the six daughters. In that play, too, there is the terrible whine of Amelia Madras which shows graphically how lucky Constantine was to escape her. Violet, in *The Return of the Prodigal*, is another of the family-made spinsters, like Honor Voysey and the Huxtable girls, and so is Hester, in Hankin's *The Last of the De Mullins*, who finds herself a little envious of her sister Janet, an unmarried mother. Although the families that Shaw puts on stage tend to be cheerfully drawn, he does suggest, with less venom than Granville-Barker and Hankin, the destructiveness of the dominated family (think of what Lady Britomart has made of her children other than the tough Major Barbara), and he occasionally describes comically what, in fact, would be a little horrifying—the off-stage Mrs. Collins in *Getting Married*, whose intense mother love made the children run away. Even in *Loaves and Fishes*, the personable Canon Spratte has made a cipher of his son.

If the family on the Edwardian stage is not the warming shelter it was once taken to be, the marriage that leads to it is no longer the inevitable happy ending. Two of Hankin's plays—*The Charity That Began at Home* and *The Cassilis Engagement*—are comedies not about boy gets girl, but about how boy and girl avoid what is almost certain to be a disastrous marriage. In his preface to *Three Plays with Happy Endings*, which contained *Charity*, *Cassilis*, and *The Return of the Prodigal* (in which Eustace does not get Stella), Hankin attacked the dramatic critics who "leave all sense of reality outside and judge what they see there by some purely artificial standard which they would never dream of applying to the fortunes of themselves or their friends." As the Hankin quote implies, the playwrights were beginning to accept as artists what they accepted as men, that marriage is a more complicated process than popular drama has suggested. Not only was marriage the traditional reward for the juveniles, it was a safe and sure thing unless, as in the melodramas, it smashed on the rock of grand passion. Among the serious Edwardian playwrights, that dramatic cliché was pretty much passed over; even Pinero in *Mid-Channel* suggests that it is boredom that drives Zoe to infidelity. Not that the Edwardians did not have clichés of their own. Janet De Mullin and Marion Yates are New Women, who choose to have babies without the entanglement of husbands, putting into action the program that Lesbia Grantham puts into words in *Getting Married*, a system that will let the woman experience motherhood without becoming trapped in a marriage contract which can only be broken through adultery or the hypocritical pretense to it. It is understandable that the playwrights should have been interested in the problem of divorce, although, as Langdon Mitchell's *The New York Idea* indicates, in America the more liberal divorce laws led to a different kind of divorce comedy. Although *Getting Married* is quite specific in its dealing with English divorce law, it goes beyond the limits of that subject and ends by presenting a wide range of attitudes toward marriage and sex. *The Madras House* does the same thing with less fun, perhaps, but with far greater incisiveness.

My brief discussion would seem to indicate that the experimental theatre of the Edwardian period was largely a matter of subject and attitude, a shift from the conventional ideas of the nineties to a greater concern with and a broader understanding of social problems. In general, that is true. Still, as two of the plays in this volume indicate, there was also experimentation in form. The Hankin and Maugham plays are reasonably conventional comedies that depend for the most part on situation (the Canon's discovery that Mrs. Fitzgerald will have no money if she marries him) or stereotypical character (Hankin's mindless doctor) for their laughter and for their satirical effect. *Mid-Channel* is the standard Pinero melodrama, carefully plotted (too carefully perhaps: the speed with which Leonard gets himself engaged to Ethel) and too neatly wrapped in the ribbon that gives the fatal ending its look of pathos. At the beginning of Act One, Zoe says, "You'll see, when I put an end to myself, it will be in the winter time," and, at the end, after she has jumped, the *raisonneur* gets as curtain line, "She told me once it would be in the *winter* time—!" Unfortunately, he is not onstage during Zoe's first speech. Some of the younger dramatists failed to avoid this kind of finger-pointing obviousness, as the work of John Galsworthy indicates; in *Strife*, for instance, he breaks both the industrialist and the union leader after three acts of struggle, only to tag on the easy irony of Tench's "D'you know, sir—these terms, they're the *very same* we drew up together, you and I, and put to both sides before the fight began?"

Getting Married and *The Madras House* are much more interesting in form. The immediately obvious thing about the Shaw play, as his note at the beginning indicates, is that it is written without act or scene breaks—a return, he suggests, to the unity of time and place that the Greeks observed. The Greek analogy is not very useful, but Shaw is right that certain subjects demand continual playing, as Strindberg discovered almost twenty years earlier in *Creditors*. The impressive thing about *Getting Married* is that it is, as his description indicates, "a disquisitory play." Insofar as conventional action is concerned, the two young people do decide, first, not to get married and, then, to get married, but they and their indecision are only the occasion for a single, long conversation which is organized so that participants may take part, withdraw, return without breaking the flow of the whole piece. Shaw's business as a playwright is simply to see that the right kind of character is onstage, confronted with his necessary opponent, so that a particular attitude can be expressed.

It is customary, in discussing Shaw and Granville-Barker, to point out how much the younger man was influenced by the older, but, in the case of *Getting Married*, it is almost as though Shaw had set out to write a Granville-Barker play. Unlike Shaw, Granville-Barker was never particularly interested in plot. All of his plays are organized thematically; he might be describing his own work in *On Dramatic Method*, when he says of *Measure for Measure* that "the impersonal central subject is the chief matter." Thus in *The Voysey Inheritance* he plays with the idea of inheritance (financial, familial, societal), and in *Waste* he chronicles many kinds of social and personal waste. *The Madras House* is the best example of this technique in operation, however, for here the plot has almost disappeared. All that happens is that Philip Madras sells the dress business, but that is hardly what the play is about. Granville-Barker sets up four scenes, only vaguely connected by the presence of Philip, in which he exposes the audience to a wide variety of attitudes toward sex and suggests how those attitudes are formed through personal psychology, conventional expectation, economic pressure and on and on. It is one of the subtlest examinations of sex in the English theatre, one that—alas for the success of the play —made and makes great demands on an audience conditioned to think of sex in terms of melodrama or the open zipper.

All decades tend to become stereotypes to the ones that follow. The Edwardians, unfortunately, have become tamer and primmer and less intellectual in retrospect. Perhaps these plays will help to modify that stereotype. If so, that is an incidental good; the plays are collected here for their own sakes, which is to say for the pleasure of the reader.

LOAVES AND FISHES
A Satire in Four Acts

by
W. SOMERSET MAUGHAM

Reprinted by permission of W. Somerset Maugham, A. P. Watt &
Son, and William Heinemann Ltd.

All applications for permission to perform this play must be made
to A. P. Watt & Son, Hastings House, 10 Norfolk Street, Strand,
London W.C.2, England.

CHARACTERS

THE HON. AND REV. CANON THEODORE SPRATTE, *Vicar of St. Gregory's, South Kensington*
THE EARL SPRATTE
THE REV. LIONEL SPRATTE
LORD WROXHAM
BERTRAM RAILING
PONSONBY
MRS. FITZGERALD
LADY SOPHIA SPRATTE
WINIFRED SPRATTE
GWENDOLEN DURANT
MRS. RAILING
LOUISE RAILING

SCENE: The drawing room at ST. GREGORY'S VICARAGE throughout.

LOAVES AND FISHES

ACT ONE

SCENE—*The drawing room at St. Gregory's Vicarage. It is large and handsome. The furniture follows the fashion of the moment. It is luxurious, elegant, and costly. Prominently placed is a full-length portrait of the first Earl Spratte, Lord High Chancellor of England. The drawing room opens into another room at the back and is separated from it by an archway. There are doors right and left.*

LADY SOPHIA *is lying on a sofa, reading the* Fortnightly Review. *She is a handsome, well-groomed woman of a determined appearance. She cultivates a light irony, and it pleases her sometimes to be sarcastic. She is fifty years of age. Tea things are set out on a table.* PONSONBY *is a butler of the most impressive appearance. He joins the self-confidence of a member of Parliament to the somber dignity of a mute at a very expensive funeral.* PONSONBY *brings in a teapot and a kettle. He lights the spirit lamp.* LADY SOPHIA *continues to read and* PONSONBY, *having done his duty, retires. In a moment* LIONEL *comes in. This is* CANON SPRATTE'S *son and curate, and* LADY SOPHIA'S *nephew. He is a tall young man, languid and fair-haired. He is dressed as little like a clergyman as is decent.* LIONEL *looks at* LADY SOPHIA *and at the teakettle.*

LIONEL. Is tea ready, Aunt Sophia?

Lady Sophia [*putting down her magazine*]. It looks suspiciously like it, Lionel.

During the next speeches she makes the tea.

Lionel. What a regiment of cups, are you expecting a crowd?

Lady Sophia. I'm not. I dare say Ponsonby is.

Lionel. I sometimes wonder if Ponsonby invites the people who come here. He's generally the only person who knows they're expected.

Lady Sophia. If he does I can only say that his circle of acquaintance is rather mixed.

Lionel. Is Father in?

Lady Sophia. I shouldn't think so. He's probably discussing the simple life at the tea table of a dowager marchioness.

Lionel. I say, I am glad to get my tea.

Lady Sophia. Have you been busy today?

Lionel. No, not very.

3

Lady Sophia. You must be glad you're paid by time and not by the piece.

Lionel. I say, I think the Governor ought to give me a rise. He couldn't get anyone else for the money.

Lady Sophia. Your father has always underpaid his curates on principle. He thinks it keeps them out of temptation.

Lionel. The Governor doesn't seem to realize that laying up treasure in heaven won't help you to pay a tailor's bill.

Lady Sophia. But you don't look as if you were in any want of clothes.

Lionel. I'm not. That's why I've got a tailor's bill.

CANON SPRATTE *comes in. He is a tall, very handsome man, with a fine head of curly white hair; clean-shaven, dignified, and very bland. He knows he is a good-looking and successful man. His clothes fit admirably.*

Canon. Is tea ready?

Lady Sophia. You are not going to honor us with your company, Theodore?

Canon [*smiling*]. If you have no objection, my dear. Has Mrs. Fitzgerald arrived?

Lady Sophia. Mrs. Fitzgerald?

Canon. You've not forgotten that she comes today?

Lady Sophia. Oh dear, oh dear. . . . Do ring, Lionel, will you?

Canon. Really, Sophia!

Lionel [*touching the bell*]. Is she coming to stay?

Canon. She's having her house done up, and it wasn't quite ready, so Sophia very kindly asked her to stay here till she was able to move in.

Lady Sophia. How lucky you reminded me, Theodore.

Canon. I'm used to reminding you, my dear Sophia.

Lady Sophia. You bear your cross with such gallantry, Theodore, it would be a pity to deprive you of it.

Enter PONSONBY.

Lady Sophia. Ponsonby, Mrs. Fitzgerald is coming here today. Will you see that rooms are got ready.

Ponsonby. I've already seen to it, my lady.

Lady Sophia. Oh, you knew she was coming?

Ponsonby. I saw it in this morning's *Post*, my lady.

[*Exit.*

Canon. How clever the newspapers are. They know everything.

Lionel. I've not seen Mrs. Fitzgerald since her husband died.

Canon. She must be out of mourning by now.

Lady Sophia. I imagine that depends on how mourning became her.

Lionel. Is she well-off?

Canon. I understand that her husband left her everything he had. It was the least he could do considering how much longer he lived than anyone expected.

Lady Sophia. It's a way rich old husbands have.

Lionel. Did she marry him for his money?

Canon. Certainly not. Mrs. Fitzgerald's a charming woman and incapable of doing anything of the sort. She married him *with* his money.

Lionel. Have you had a busy day, Governor?

Canon. I always have a busy day, my boy. By the way, you won't forget those two funerals tomorrow, will you?

Lionel. Oh no, rather not.

Lady Sophia. Do I know the corpses?

Canon [*rather shocked*]. My dear, you have a way of expressing yourself. . . . [*With a twinkle.*] As a matter of fact I believe one of them is our own fishmonger.

Lady Sophia [*with deep satisfaction*]. Ah, I thought the fish had been very inferior the last few days.

PONSONBY *enters to announce* MRS. FITZGERALD. *She is a tall, handsome woman of thirty-five. She is beautifully dressed. There is a suggestion of half-mourning about the costume, but, as* LADY SOPHIA *suspected would be the case, it appears to be worn for aesthetic reasons rather than as a mark of lamentation.* MRS. FITZGERALD *gives the impression of a woman keenly alive to her own advantages, self-confident and full of humor.*

Exit PONSONBY.

Ponsonby. Mrs. Fitzgerald.

She goes up to LADY SOPHIA *and kisses her.*

Mrs. Fitzgerald. At last! I've had such a tiring journey.

Lady Sophia. I am glad to see you, Mary.

Mrs. Fitzgerald. My dear Sophia, it's so kind of you to let me come and stay here for a couple of days.

Canon. I hope the slowness of the British workman will force you to give us at least a week of your charming society.

Mrs. Fitzgerald [*shaking hands with him*]. If I thought that, I'd send my washing.

Canon. I implore you to risk it.

Mrs. Fitzgerald [*as he holds her hand*]. It always makes me feel ten years younger to see you, dear Canon.

Canon. Ah, don't say that, or I shall feel like a father to you. Look how white my hair is growing.

Mrs. Fitzgerald [*with a smile*]. It suits you.

Lady Sophia [*smiling*]. My dear Mary, don't start flirting with him the moment you come.

Mrs. Fitzgerald [*gaily*]. I can't help it. The Canon calls forth all my baser instincts.

Canon. Ah, you only say that because you think my advancing years make me quite safe.

Mrs. Fitzgerald. Oh, I don't know about that. Handsome men are never so dangerous as when their hair is just turning gray.

Canon. Do you remember Lionel? He's my curate at St. Gregory's, you know.

Mrs. Fitzgerald. I'm sure you've grown since I saw you last.

Lionel. Only in grace then.

Canon. I must tell you that Lionel is seriously thinking of getting married.

Lionel [*turning scarlet*]. I, Father? What are you talking about?

Canon. A little bird has whispered to me that Master Cupid has been busy with you, Lionel. Come, come, you must have no secrets from your old father.

Lionel. I really don't know what you mean.

Canon. Are you going to deny that you have cast a—a favorable eye upon Miss Gwendolen Durant.

Lady Sophia. Gwendolen?

Lionel [*embarrassed*]. I like her very much, Father, but I've not said anything to her. I have no reason to believe that she cares for me.

Canon. Good heavens, that's not the way to make love, my boy. When I was your age I never asked if there were reasons why a young woman should care for me. It's a foolish lover who prates of his own unworthiness.

Lionel. But I've not altogether made up my mind.

Canon. Well then, make it up, my boy, for it's high time you were married. Don't forget that an old and honored name depends on you. Your uncle is unlikely to marry now. Your duty is to provide a male child to inherit the title, and I'm assured the Durants run to boys.

Mrs. Fitzgerald [*amused*]. My dear Canon, you think of everything.

Lionel [*taking out his watch*]. I must be getting along. I've got several things to do.

Canon. Remember what I've told you, Lionel. Faint heart never won fair lady.

Lionel. You needn't pull my leg, Father. [*Exit.*

Mrs. Fitzgerald. You've driven the poor boy away.

Canon. I'm not altogether satisfied with Lionel. He's so phlegmatic. He's not half the man his father is.

Mrs. Fitzgerald [*smiling*]. Tell me more about Miss Durant. She's not the brewer's daughter, is she?

Canon [*rather apologetically*]. We live in a different world from that of my boyhood. Everyone has a finger in some commercial pie nowadays.

Mrs. Fitzgerald. Then she is the brewer's daughter?

Canon. I don't deny it for a moment.

Lady Sophia. I shouldn't have thought it was a match entirely after your own heart, Theodore.

Canon. My dear, I don't want you to think me cynical, but there are very nice girls *and* very nice girls, and the very nice girls with sixty or seventy thousand pounds of their own do not grow on every gooseberry bush.

Enter PONSONBY.

Ponsonby [*to* LADY SOPHIA]. You're wanted on the telephone, my lady.

Lady Sophia. Oh, very well.

She gets up and goes out.

Canon. You'll have an opportunity of seeing for yourself what you think of the young lady. I've asked Winnie to bring her in to tea.

Mrs. Fitzgerald. Oh, do talk to me about Winnie.

Canon. I'd much sooner talk to you about you.

Mrs. Fitzgerald. My dear friend, we've known one another much too long.

Canon. What has that got to do with it?

Mrs. Fitzgerald. You want to flatter me, and for flattery to be pleasing one must be convinced at least for a moment that it's sincere.

Canon. I never flatter and I'm always sincere.

Mrs. Fitzgerald. I've never concealed from you my belief that you're the most desperate humbug I've ever known.

Canon. You put me at my ease at once.

Mrs. Fitzgerald. Still, if you really insist, you may make it.

Canon. What?

Mrs. Fitzgerald. The compliment that's on the tip of your tongue.

Canon [*promptly*]. I think you grow handsomer every day.

Mrs. Fitzgerald. You have a way of coming straight to the

point that's very comforting to a widow-lady who's not quite, quite so young as she was.

Canon. With such a clever woman as you it would be only a waste of time to beat about the bush.

Mrs. Fitzgerald [*throwing up her hands*]. Oh, do take care, or you'll overdo it.

Canon. My dear lady, I'm only just getting into my stride.

Mrs. Fitzgerald. Then how fortunate that Sophia is just coming back.

LADY SOPHIA *enters the room as* MRS. FITZGERALD *says the words.*

Lady Sophia. Winnie has just telephoned to say she's bringing Mr. Railing back to tea.

Mrs. Fitzgerald. Who is Mr. Railing?

Lady Sophia. Oh, he's Theodore's latest discovery.

Canon. He's a mighty clever young man, and I think he'll be very useful to me.

Lady Sophia. Your actions are always governed by such unselfish motives, Theodore.

Canon. God helps those who help themselves, Sophia.

Mrs. Fitzgerald. In that case the Almighty must be kept uncommonly busy.

Canon. Mr. Railing is by way of being a Christian-Socialist. He fought a seat for the Labor Party at the last election, but he didn't get in. I think he has a future, and I feel it my duty to give him some encouragement. Nowadays, when socialism is rapidly becoming a power in the land, when it is spreading branches into every stratum of society, it behooves us to rally it to the church.

Lady Sophia [*in tones of mild remonstrance*]. Theodore, we're quite alone.

Canon [*ignoring the interruption*]. I pride myself above all things on being abreast of the times. Every movement that savors of advance will find in me an enthusiastic supporter. My father, the late Lord Chancellor of England [*with a wave of his arm toward the portrait*], was one of the first to perceive the coming strength of the people. And I am proud to know that my family has ever identified itself with the future. Advance has always been our watchword. Advance and progress.

During this speech LORD SPRATTE *has come in and listened silently. He is a tall, stout, smart man of fifty odd. He is very well dressed in a rather horsy way.*

Lord Spratte. You speak as if we'd come over with the Conquest, Theodore.

Canon [*with a magnificent flourish*]. Behold the head of the family, Thomas, Second Earl Spratte of Beachcombe, Viscount Rallington and Baron Spratte in the United Kingdom of Great Britain and Ireland.

Lord Spratte [*shaking hands with* MRS. FITZGERALD]. Shut it, Theodore.

Canon. And pray have you never looked up the name of Spratte in Burke or Debrett?

Lord Spratte. Frequently. I find the peerage excellent readin' to fall back on when there's nothin' in the sportin' papers. It's my favorite work of fiction. But it's no bloomin' good, Theodore. A man with the name of Spratte didn't have ancestors at the Battle of Hastings.

Canon. My father, the greatest lawyer of his age, implicitly believed in the family tree.

Lord Spratte. He must have been a pretty innocent old buffer to do that. I never met anyone else who would. And upon my word I don't know why a man called Spratte *should* have ancestors called Montmorency.

Canon. I should have thought that even in your brief stay at Oxford, you learned enough natural history to know that every man must have a father.

Lord Spratte. Theodore, if a man called Spratte had a father called Montmorency the less said about it the better. I may be particular, but it don't sound moral to me.

Canon. Your facetiousness is misplaced, Thomas, and the taste of it is doubtful. The connection at which you are pleased to sneer is perfectly clear and perfectly honorable. In 1631 Aubrey de Montmorency married . . .

Lady Sophia. Oh, Theodore, Theodore, not again.

PONSONBY *brings in the* Westminster Gazette *and hands it to the* CANON.

Ponsonby. The evening paper, sir.

Canon. Ah, thank you.

Lord Spratte. Oh, Theodore, I've got some news that'll simply make you chortle. The Bishop of Colchester died this morning.

Canon. Thomas, pray express yourself with more seemliness. [*Looking at the paper.*] Tut, tut, tut—very sad. But, after all, he's been out of health for a long time. It's a happy release.

Lady Sophia. I met him once. I thought him a very brilliant man.

Canon. The Bishop of Colchester? My dear Sophia! Well, of course, I don't want to say anything against him now he's dead, poor man, but between ourselves, if the truth must be told, he was nothing more than a doddering old imbecile. And a man of no family.

Mrs. Fitzgerald. I wonder who'll succeed him.

Lord Spratte. You'd look rather a toff in leggin's, Theodore. [*To* LADY SOPHIA.] Wouldn't he?

Lady Sophia. My dear Tommy, I've not seen his legs for forty years.

Canon. It's really quite providential that the poor old man should die on the very day that I'm going to meet Lady Patricia Pears at dinner.

Lord Spratte. Who on earth is she?

Canon. Good heavens, why don't you study your peerage? She's the aunt by marriage of the second wife of the Prime Minister's youngest son. And all the ecclesiastical patronage is in her hands.

Lord Spratte. I hope you will accept no bishopric until you've made quite sure that the golf links are all right.

Canon [*ironically*]. I'll tell the Prime Minister that an eighteen-hole course is a *sine qua non* of my elevation to the episcopacy.

A ring is heard at the front door.

Lady Sophia. I dare say that's Winnie. She ought to be here by now.

Lord Spratte. Where has she been?

Canon. She went to a temperance meeting to hear our friend Mr. Railing speak.

Mrs. Fitzgerald. That sounds exhilarating.

Lord Spratte. I say, what's the matter with Winnie? She sent me a book the other day called *The Future of Socialism*. It looked devilish instructive.

Lady Sophia. Did you read it?

Lord Spratte. I avoid instruction.

Canon. That is painfully obvious from your conversation.

WINNIE *comes in with* GWENDOLEN DURANT *and* BERTRAM RAILING. WINNIE *is a pretty, fair girl of one and twenty, very fashionably gowned. She is pink and white and virginal.* GWENDOLEN *is a little taller, more languid, but something of the same type. She is a year or two older.* BERTRAM RAILING *is in everything a marked contrast to the two girls. He has the obvious, flaunting good looks which attract women. He is dark, with fine eyes, young, and of a romantic appearance. He wears his very fine hair much too long. His blue serge suit hangs about him comfortably, and though it is obviously ready-made, he looks more like a Greek god in it than any modern young man should dream of looking. His red tie is carelessly tied. He is not at all bashful at finding himself among strangers, but is apt to look upon them with a certain superciliousness.*

Winnie. We're simply dying for tea. Oh, Mrs. Fitzgerald!

There are general greetings. WINNIE *kisses* MRS. FITZGERALD *and her uncle* LORD SPRATTE. GWENDOLEN *shakes hands with* LADY SOPHIA.

Gwendolen. I can only stay a moment. It's so late.

Winnie [*to* RAILING]. D'you know my uncle?

Lord Spratte [*shaking hands with* RAILING]. How d'you do!

Canon. I'm delighted to see you, Mr. Railing. So sorry I couldn't come to your meeting. I had to lunch with Lady de Capit to meet the Princess of Wartburg-Hochstein. A clergyman's time is really never his own.

Lord Spratte. People so often forget that even princesses have spiritual difficulties.

Canon [*to* MRS. FITZGERALD]. You must let me introduce Mr. Railing to you.

Mrs. Fitzgerald. How d'you do?

Canon. Mr. Railing is the author of that much discussed book, *The Future of Socialism.*

Mrs. Fitzgerald. I'm afraid it sounds as if it were too deep for me.

Railing. The Duchess of St. Ermyns told me she found it as exciting as a novel.

Canon. And was your meeting a success?

Winnie [*eagerly*]. You should have seen the audience, Papa. While Mr. Railing spoke you could have heard a pin drop, and afterward there was such a storm of applause I thought the roof was coming down.

Railing. They were all very kind and appreciative.

Canon. It's wonderful how people are carried away by real eloquence. You must come and hear me preach.

Railing. I should like to very much.

Canon. Advance and progress have ever been my watchword. My family has always been in the vanguard when there has been any movement for the advantage of the working classes.

Lord Spratte. From the days of the Montmorencys down to our father the late Lord Chancellor of England.

Canon. As my brother appositely reminds me, my ancestor, Aubrey de Montmorency, was killed while fighting for the freedom of the people in the year 1642. And his second son, Roger de Montmorency, from whom we are directly descended [LADY SOPHIA *coughs significantly, but the* CANON *proceeds firmly*] was beheaded by James II for resisting the tyranny of that popish and despotic sovereign.

Lady Sophia. Gwendolen is waiting for a semicolon to make her escape, Theodore.

Canon [*taking* GWENDOLEN's *hand*]. Must we lose you already? I've not had a chance of saying a word to you.

Gwendolen. Papa is speaking at the Licensed Victuallers tonight, and he wants me to hear his speech.

Canon. It's charming of you to have given us at least a glimpse of you.

Gwendolen. You always say such nice things, Canon.

Canon. Only to nice people.

Gwendolen [*to* RAILING]. Good-by, I enjoyed your lecture so much.

Railing. I hope it was convincing.

Gwendolen. Oh, it didn't convince me because I make my living out of alcohol. But Papa says the moderate drinker pays much better than the habitual drunkard.

Railing. It's the moderate drinker we want to convert. The habitual drunkard we can deal with by act of Parliament.

Gwendolen. I wonder you didn't insist on coming here in an omnibus instead of Papa's new limousine. Good-by.

Railing [*as she goes out*]. I see that we've just lost one of our most ardent champions in the cause of temperance.

Canon. Ah, yes. The Bishop of Colchester. I knew him well. Charming fellow.

Railing. He'll be a great loss.

Canon. Oh, a great loss. I was deeply distressed when I heard of the sad event.

Lord Spratte. I noticed that you kept your emotion well under control, Theodore.

Canon [*ignoring the interruption*]. I was just telling Sophia what a brilliant man he was.

Railing. There's a rumor that you are going to succeed him, Canon Spratte.

Canon. I? It would require a great deal to tear me away from St. Gregory's. Where did you hear that?

Railing. Two or three people have mentioned it to me.

Canon. Really, really! Fancy anyone thinking of it.

Railing. I don't know what they would do without you here.

Canon. Of course, no man is indispensable in this world.

Lord Spratte. Theodore, you're too modest.

Canon. And I don't know that I consider myself fit to take so large and so important a see as that of Colchester.

Mrs. Fitzgerald [*getting up*]. I think I'd like to go to my room. I'm rather tired.

Canon. Forty winks, dear lady? You've had a long journey, haven't you? And yet you look as fresh as paint.

Mrs. Fitzgerald [*with a smile, rubbing her cheek*]. It doesn't rub off.

Lady Sophia. I will show you the way, shall I?

Mrs. Fitzgerald. D'you mind? [*Shaking hands with* RAIL-ING.] Good-by. I shall make a point of reading your book.

Railing. That's very kind of you.

With a nod at LORD SPRATTE *she goes out, accompanied by* LADY SOPHIA. *The* CANON *catches* RAILING'S *glance at the Lord Chancellor's portrait.*

Canon. Ah, I see that you are admiring Millais' portrait of my father. Fine old fellow, wasn't he? Come and let me show you Sargent's portrait of myself. It's in here.

Railing. I should like to see it very much.

They go into the inner room, but remain in sight.

The CANON *is seen gesticulating as he points out the merits of the picture.* LORD SPRATTE *and* WINNIE *are left by themselves.*

Winnie. What d'you think of Mr. Railing?

Lord Spratte. He smells of the only sort of spirit which I've never acquired a taste for.

Winnie. What on earth d'you mean?

Lord Spratte. Public spirit.

Winnie [*with an impatient shrug of the shoulders*]. I wanted your serious opinion.

Lord Spratte. He's the sort of chap that has statistics scribbled all over his shirt cuffs. And I shouldn't be surprised if his shirt cuffs took off.

Winnie. I don't see why a man's cuffs shouldn't take off just as much as a woman's hair.

Lord Spratte. I do. The auburn switch is a tribute to the superiority of my sex. It points to a pathetic desire on the part of lovely woman to make herself pleasing in my sight. The removable shirt cuff indicates merely an economy in washing.

Winnie. I think he's the most wonderful man I've ever seen in my life.

Lord Spratte. Do you, by George! Have you told your papa?

Winnie [*defiantly*]. No. But I mean to.

Lord Spratte. I wonder what you mean by that?

Winnie. You all think I'm a child. You none of you seem to understand I'm a grown woman.

Lord Spratte. I notice your sex generally claims to be misunderstood when it has a mind to do something foolish.

Winnie. Why shouldn't his cuffs take off?

Lord Spratte. My dear, there's no reason at all. Nor have I ever been able to discover why you shouldn't eat peas with a knife or assassinate your grandmother. But I notice there is a prejudice against these things.

Winnie. If you heard him speak, you wouldn't think of anything so trivial.

Lord Spratte. Am I wrong in thinking when he's excited or nervous he's not quite secure on his aitches?

Winnie. He's the greatest gentleman I've ever known.

PONSONBY *enters and meets the* CANON *and* RAILING *as they come out of the back drawing room.*

Ponsonby. Lord Wroxham has arrived, sir.

Canon. Oh! [*He gives* RAILING *a glance, evidently wishing him out of the way.*] Have you shown him into the library?

Ponsonby. Yes, sir.

Canon. Well . . . ask him to wait just one moment.

Ponsonby. Very good, sir.

RAILING, *seeing that the* CANON *is occupied, holds out his hand. The* CANON *seizes it with relief.*

Railing. I think I'll be getting along.

Canon. What, must you go already? Well, well, I dare say you're busy.

Railing [*shaking hands with* LORD SPRATTE]. Good-by.

Canon [*bustling him*]. You must come and see us again soon. I want to have a long talk with you. Oh, Ponsonby.

The CANON *goes to* PONSONBY *and speaks in an undertone.* LORD SPRATTE *takes up the evening paper as a pretext and watches* RAILING *who goes over to say good-by to* WINNIE.

Winnie. Good-by. You see they're not so terrible.

Railing. They're very kind.

Winnie. I know they'll all like you. I shall see you tomorrow, shan't I?

Railing. I shall think of nothing else till then.

Winnie. I must tell you again how grateful I am for all you've done for me.

Railing. I haven't done anything for you.

Winnie. I want to help you in your work. I want to work with you.

Railing. If I spoke well today it was because I felt that your eyes were upon me.

Winnie. Good-by.

As RAILING *goes out, the* CANON *again cordially shakes hands with him.*

Canon. Good-by, good-by. Mind you come and hear me preach. Ah, here is Sophia.

LADY SOPHIA *comes in.*

Canon. Mr. Railing refuses to waste any more of his time on us. I was just telling him he must come and hear me preach.

Lady Sophia [*with a smile and a handshake*]. Oh, yes.

Canon. You haven't heard me preach for a long time, Thomas.

RAILING *goes out.*

Lord Spratte. My dear Theodore, I never hear you do anything else.

Canon. That's not your own, Thomas.

Lord Spratte. In these socialistic days I look upon it as affectation only to make my own jokes.

Canon. That's an intelligent fellow, I like him very much. Remarkably brilliant, isn't he, Sophia?

Lady Sophia. My dear Theodore, how could I judge? You never let him get a word in. He seemed an intelligent listener.

Canon. Sophia, I may have faults, but no one has ever accused me of usurping more than my fair share of the conversation. I dare say he was a little shy.

Lady Sophia. I dare say.

Canon [*turning to his daughter*]. Oh, Winnie, I wonder if you'd mind fetching me the *Times*. It's in the library.

Winnie. Certainly. [*She walks towards the door and stops suddenly.*] Didn't Ponsonby say Harry Wroxham was there?

Canon [*smiling*]. He did.

Winnie. But . . .

Canon. Unless I'm greatly mistaken, he's waiting there to see you.

Winnie. Me, Papa? What on earth does he want?

Canon [*going toward her and putting his arm round her shoulder*]. He will tell you that himself, my love.

Winnie [*shrinking back*]. But I can't see him. I don't want to.

Canon [*leading her to the door*]. My dear, you must. I can quite understand that you should feel a certain bashfulness . . .

Winnie [*interrupting*]. But Papa, I must speak to you first. I want to explain.

Canon [*good-humoredly*]. There's nothing to explain, my dear. I know all about it. And you need not be nervous. You go with my full approval.

Winnie. For goodness' sake, let me speak.

Canon. Come, come, my dear. You must pluck up courage. It's nothing very terrible; go downstairs like a good girl, and I dare say you'll bring Lord Wroxham up with you. [*He opens the door and all but pushes her out. When he comes back, he is rubbing his hands and laughing.*] A little maidenly modesty. Very charming. Very pretty. It's a lovely sight, my dear Sophia, the pure, fresh, rosy English girl, suffused in the blushes of virginal innocence.

Lady Sophia. Fiddlesticks, Theodore.

Canon [*good-humoredly*]. You're a cynic, my dear. It's a grave fault of which I should recommend you to correct yourself.

Lady Sophia [*bridling*]. I beg you not to preach to me, Theodore.

Canon. No man is a prophet in his own country. No man is a hero to his valet.

Lord Spratte. I feel that you could preach a moving sermon on that topic, Theodore.

Canon. Thomas, I wish to speak to you in your official capacity, if I may call it. As the head of the family . . .

Lord Spratte [*interrupting*]. My dear Theodore, merely by courtesy. I am unworthy . . .

Canon. That fact is sufficiently patent without your recalling it. But I should be obliged if at this moment, when the affairs of our house are at stake, you would adopt such sobriety and decorum as you are capable of.

Lord Spratte. By Jupiter, I wish I'd got my coronation robes on.

Lady Sophia. Go on, Theodore, don't keep us waiting.

Canon. Well, you will both of you be gratified to hear that Lord Wroxham has asked my permission to pay his addresses to Winnie.

Lord Spratte. What did you say, Theodore—not 'alf?

Canon [*freezing*]. I informed him that I had no objection to him as a son-in-law, and I inquired into his circumstances.

Lord Spratte. What blooming cheek, when everyone knows he's got twenty thousand a year.

Canon [*taking no notice of his brother*]. And finally I imparted to him my conviction that Winnie looked upon him with sincere affection.

Lord Spratte. You are a downy old bird, Theodore.

Canon. I did not expect that you would treat the matter with decorum, Thomas. And it is only from a strong sense of duty toward you as the head of my house that I requested your presence.

Lord Spratte [*not at all abashed*]. Shut it, Theodore. You know very well that Wroxham can just about wipe his boots with the likes of us. There's a deuce of a difference between the twenty-first Lord Wroxham with half a county to his back and the second Earl Spratte.

Canon [*with great dignity*]. I should like you to understand once for all, Thomas, that I very much object to the sneering manner which you are pleased to affect with regard to our family. I am proud to be the son of the late Lord Chancellor of England, and the grandson of a distinguished banker.

Lady Sophia. Fiddlesticks, Theodore. You know quite well that our grandfather was a bill-broker, and rather a seedy one at that.

Canon. He was nothing of the sort. He was a most polished and accomplished gentleman.

Lady Sophia. I remember him quite well. At home we always asked him to dinner the day after a party to eat up the scraps. I'm sure it never occurred to anyone that he was a distinguished banker until he was safely dead and buried.

Lord Spratte. It's carried for bill-broking. And my belief is that the old chap did a bit of usury as well. It's no good stuffin' people, Theodore, they don't believe us.

Lady Sophia [*much amused*]. And what about the bill-broker's papa, Theodore?

Lord Spratte. That's where the Montmorencys come in.

Canon [*with much dignity*]. I confess that I'm not quite certain what my great-grandfather was. But I know he was a gentleman.

Lady Sophia. My dear, I've always had a sneaking sort of idea that he was a greengrocer.

Lord Spratte. Ah, that beats the Montmorencys, by Jove!

The ancestral greengrocer goin' out to wait at dinner parties in Bedford Square, and havin' a sly drink at the old sherry when no one was looking.

Canon. I hope, Thomas, that you will have the good sense and the decorum to keep these observations from Wroxham. He's very sensitive on these matters.

Lord Spratte. By the way, what would you say if Winnie refused him?

Canon. What! Nonsense! Why should she? He's a very eligible young man, and he has my full approval.

Lord Spratte. Supposin' she should take it into her head to marry that socialist johnny?

Canon. Young Railing? Absurd.

Lord Spratte. D'you think it's absurd, Sophia?

Lady Sophia [*with a shrug of the shoulders*]. She's her father's daughter.

Canon. My daughter knows what is due to herself and to her family. She may be young, but she has a sense of dignity which I should be pleased to see in you. Remember our motto; *malo mori quam fedari:* I prefer to die than to be disgraced.

Lord Spratte. I always think we were overcharged for that.

Canon. Of course, a fine sentiment merely excited your ribaldry.

Lord Spratte. My dear Theodore, I've got the receipt among the family papers.

Lady Sophia. I well remember the discussion between our father and mother when we were fixing up our coat of arms. Mother thought our crest should be a lion couchant, but Father said, by George, madam, I should never have been made Lord Chancellor if I hadn't made my party sit up. I'll have a lion rampant and damn the College of Heralds.

Canon. I see no point in that story at all, Sophia. Our coat of arms is just as genuine as that of half the great families in England.

Lady Sophia [*smiling*]. Oh, just. I'm quite aware of that.

WINNIE *comes in. She is pale and unhappy. The* CANON *goes towards her and takes her in his arms.*

Canon. Ah, my child, my child . . . but where is Lord Wroxham? Why haven't you brought him upstairs with you?

Winnie [*disengaging herself*]. Papa, Harry Wroxham has asked me to marry him.

Canon. He did it with my full approval.

Winnie. And I—I had to say—I refused him, Papa.

Canon [*starting back*]. What! You're joking. Oh, it's a mistake. I won't have it. Where is he? [*He goes toward the door.*]

Winnie [*quickly*]. Papa, what are you doing? He's gone.

Canon [*coming back firmly*]. I suppose you're joking, Winnie. I am quite bewildered with all this humor.

Winnie. I'm already engaged to be married, Papa.

Canon. You . . . ? And to whom, pray?

Winnie. I'm engaged to Bertram Railing.

Canon. Good Lord! [LORD SPRATTE *smothers a little chuckle. The* CANON *turns on him angrily.*] I think we shall proceed in this matter better without your presence. I regret that I cannot expect from you either assistance or sympathy or any of the feelings to be awaited in a nobleman or a gentleman. I shall be grateful if you will take your departure.

Lord Spratte [*good-humoredly.*] All right, Theodore. I don't want you to wash your dirty linen before me. Good-by, Sophia. [*He kisses* LADY SOPHIA. *The* CANON *turns angrily away as his brother goes toward him to shake hands.* LORD SPRATTE, *with a smile, goes to* WINNIE *and puts his hand on her shoulder.*] Never mind, Winnie, old girl, you marry the man you want to, and don't be jockeyed into takin' anyone else. I'll always back you up in anythin' unreasonable.

Winnie. It isn't unreasonable.

Lord Spratte. By the way, don't let him wear a frock coat at the wedding. I think his legs are a little too short. He'd look stumpy.

Winnie. D'you suppose he cares what he wears? He has a soul above clothes.

Lord Spratte. I gathered by the look of them that he had that sort of soul. [*To the* CANON.] Am I keeping you?

Canon. I can't expect you to believe that my time is any more valuable than yours.

Lord Spratte. Well, so long. I hope you'll have a very jolly half hour.

He goes out.

Canon. Now what does all this mean, Winnie. . . . Am I to understand that you are serious?

Winnie. Quite.

Canon. The whole thing is preposterous. Do you mean seriously to tell me that you're engaged to a penniless, unknown scribbler?

Winnie. It's most unfair to call him that, Father, after *The Future of Socialism.*

Canon. Any fool can write a book. It takes a wise man not

to. A man whom no one knows anything about. A rogue and a vagabond.

Winnie. Papa, you said yourself he was a man of great intellect. You said you very much admired him.

Canon. That proves only that I have good manners. When a mother shows me her baby, I say it's a beautiful child. I don't think it's a beautiful child. I think it's a very ugly child. I can't tell one baby from another, but I assure her it's the very image of its father. That's just common politeness. . . . How long has this absurd business been going on?

Winnie. I became engaged to him yesterday.

Canon. You perceive, Sophia, that I was not consulted in this.

Lady Sophia [*mildly*]. Don't be ridiculous, Theodore.

Winnie. Oh, don't you understand, Father? You can't imagine what he's done for me. He's taught me everything I know. He's made me what I am.

Canon. How long have you enjoyed the privilege of his acquaintance?

Winnie. Six weeks.

Canon. Fancy.

Winnie. I was a fool. I was just the same as any other girl. I was happy for a week if I got a hat that suited me. And then I met him and everything was changed. He found me a foolish doll, and he's made me into a woman. I'm so proud and so grateful to him. He's the first real man I've ever known.

Canon. I should like to know what you find in him that you cannot find in Wroxham or in—or in your father.

Winnie. I don't love Harry Wroxham.

Canon. Fiddlededee. A girl of your age doesn't know what love is.

Winnie. Harry Wroxham wants his wife to be a slave, a plaything when he's tired or bored. I want to be a man's companion. I want to work with my husband.

Canon. I'm surprised and shocked to hear you have such ideas, Winnie. I thought you were more modest.

Winnie. You won't understand, Papa. Don't you see that I have a life of my own, and I must live it in my own way.

Canon. You're hopelessly behind the times, my poor girl. The new woman is as extinct as the dodo. Your ideas are not only silly but middle-class. They fill me with disgust.

Winnie. You're making me dreadfully unhappy, Papa.

Canon. Don't be absurd. I cannot make you marry Lord Wroxham. Far be it from me to attempt to force your affections. I confess it's a great disappointment. However I accept it as the will of Providence, and I shall do my best to bear it. But I'm quite sure it's not the will of Providence that you should marry Mr. Bertram Railing. The man's nothing better than a fortune hunter.

Winnie. That's not true, Father.

Lady Sophia [*good-humoredly*]. I don't think you ought to contradict your father so flatly, my dear. It's not done.

Winnie. He's got no right to abuse the man I love more than the whole world.

Canon. You're talking nonsense. I think you're a very disobedient and unaffectionate girl.

Winnie. After all, it's my business alone. It's my happiness that is concerned.

Canon. How selfish you are. You don't consider my happiness.

Winnie. I've made up my mind to marry Bertram. I'm over twenty-one, and I'm my own mistress.

Canon. What d'you mean by that, Winnie?

Winnie. If you won't give me your consent, I shall marry without.

The CANON *is thunderstruck. He walks up and down indignantly.*

Canon. And this is the return I get for all the affection I have lavished upon my children. I've sacrificed myself to their every whim for years. And this is my reward.

Lady Sophia [*to* WINNIE]. And do you know anything about this young man? Has he anything to live on?

Winnie. We shall work hard, both of us. With what he earns and the little I have from my mother we can live like kings.

Canon. In a flat at West Kensington, I suppose, or in a villa at Hornsey Rise.

Winnie. With the man I love, I'd live in a hovel.

Canon. People often think that till they try it.

Lady Sophia. Of course, it's a delicate question with that kind of person, but had he a father, or did he just grow?

Winnie [*defiantly*]. His father died many years ago, he was first mate on a collier trading from Newcastle.

Lady Sophia. That, I should imagine, as a profession was neither lucrative nor clean.

Canon. At least it's something to be thankful for that his relatives are dead.

Winnie. He has a mother and sister.

Canon. And who are they, I should like to know?

Winnie. I don't know and I don't care. He has told me already that his mother is not a very highly educated woman.

Canon. Where does she live?

Winnie. They have a little house in Peckham.

Canon. Revolting. I wish to hear nothing more about it.

He walks towards the door, but WINNIE *stops him.*

Winnie. Papa, don't go. Don't be angry with me. You do love me, and I love you, next to Bertram, better than anyone in the world.

Canon. If you love me, Winnie, I don't know how you can cause me such pain. I must leave you to your own reflections. I think you ungrateful, disobedient, and unkind. And it's only from regard to your sex and out of respect to the memory of your dead mother, that I don't say as well that I consider you stupid and vulgar. I beg you to go to your room. [*Without a word* WINNIE *goes out.*] How sharper than a serpent's tooth. [*He savagely kicks the evening paper which* LORD SPRATTE *has dropped on the floor. He looks at it and picks it up*]. Sophia, I wish you'd take down a note to Wilson for me.

Lady Sophia [*sitting at the desk*]. Who is Wilson?

Canon. He's a newspaper man. He does the clerical intelligence for two or three very important papers.

Lady Sophia. Oh!

Canon. My dear Mr. Wilson. I wish you would announce in your valuable journal that there is no truth in the rumor that I have been offered the vacant bishopric of Colchester. In these days of self-advertisement, I suppose it is too much to ask that people should keep silent on the positions to which they expect themselves or their friends to be elevated. But I cannot help thinking such a proceeding would be more decorous and more discreet. Yours most cordially.

Lady Sophia [*leaning back with a smile*]. You are rather a downy old bird, Theodore, aren't you?

Canon. I don't know what you mean, Sophia.

Curtain.

ACT TWO

The scene is the same as in the preceding act, the drawing room at St. Gregory's Vicarage.

LADY SOPHIA *is writing letters at a bureau.* CANON SPRATTE

enters, bland as ever, spruce and alert, with a newspaper in his hand.

CANON. Well, Sophia?

Lady Sophia [rising]. Oh, of course, I've not seen you today.

The CANON *kisses her on the cheek.*

Canon. I've been lunching at the Athenaeum, and find everyone is expecting me to go to Colchester. Did you see the notice in this morning's paper?

Lady Sophia. I've not had time to read it yet.

Canon. I wish you took more interest in me. It's extraordinary that when there's anything about me in the paper, everyone sees it but my own family.

Lady Sophia [good-humoredly]. Please tell me what it is.

Canon [reading]. "There is no truth in the rumor that Canon Spratte, Vicar of St. Gregory's, South Kensington, has been appointed to the vacant bishopric of Colchester."

Lady Sophia [dryly]. It will certainly remind those in power that there is no more excellent candidate.

Canon. My dear Sophia, I honestly don't think anyone would call me a vain man, but I cannot think myself unsuitable for the position. I'm sure you will be the last to deny that my parentage gives me certain claims upon my country.

Lady Sophia [with a dry smile]. Which I suppose you took care to point out to Lady Patricia when you met her at dinner?

Canon. Oh, no, I was discretion itself. I merely explained in the course of conversation how important it was that the bishops should be imbued with conservative principles.

Lady Sophia. And d'you think she swallowed the bait?

Canon. My dear, I wish you would not express yourself quite so brutally.

Lady Sophia [leaning back and looking at him critically]. I often wonder if you humbug yourself as much as you humbug other people.

Canon. Upon my soul, I don't know what you mean. I have always done my duty in that state of life in which it has pleased a merciful Providence to place me. And if I say so without vanity, I have done it with pleasure to myself and with profit to mankind.

Lady Sophia. D'you remember our old nurse, Theodore?

Canon. Her affection is one of the most charming recollections of my childhood.

Lady Sophia. I always think she must have been an excellent judge of character. I remember how frequently she used to say: "Master Theodore, self-praise is no recommendation."

Canon. You certainly have the oddest memories, my dear. Now, I remember how frequently she used to remark: "Miss Sophia, your nose wants blowing."

Lady Sophia [*bridling*]. She was a woman of no education, Theodore.

Canon. That is precisely what your reminiscence led me to believe.

Lady Sophia. Humph!

Enter LORD SPRATTE *and* MRS. FITZGERALD.

Canon. Ah, dear lady, this is an unexpected pleasure. I thought you were out.

Mrs. Fitzgerald. I got bored with my shopping, and as I was walking home through the park, I found Lord Spratte, so I brought him back with me to keep him out of mischief.

Lord Spratte. I've reached an age when I can only get into mischief with an infinite deal of trouble, and when I've succeeded I find the game hardly worth the candle.

Lady Sophia [*to* LORD SPRATTE]. Theodore turned you out of the house very unceremoniously the other day, Tom.

Canon. I hope you bear no malice.

Lord Spratte. Not in the least, Theodore. I not only have a Christian disposition, but you have an excellent cook.

Lady Sophia. Winnie seems determined to marry Mr. Railing.

Mrs. Fitzgerald. You know, I can't help thinking it very romantic. It reminds me of that poem of dear Lord Tennyson's.

Canon. Dear Lord Tennyson hadn't a marriageable daughter.

Mrs. Fitzgerald. When two young things are fond of one another, don't you think it's best to let them marry, whatever the disadvantages?

Lady Sophia. The man isn't even a gentleman.

Mrs. Fitzgerald. But we have it dinned into our ears that kind hearts are more than coronets.

Canon. Yes, but we all know that they're nothing of the sort.

Lord Spratte. What are you going to do, Theodore?

Canon. I promise you that Winnie shall break her foolish engagement with this ridiculous counterjumper, and what's more I promise you she shall marry Wroxham.

Mrs. Fitzgerald [smiling]. You'll need some very skillful diplomacy to achieve all that.

Canon. People must get up early in the morning if they want to get the better of Theodore Spratte.

Lady Sophia. What is your idea, Theodore?

Canon. My dear, I rack my brains. I can't think of anything. It's monstrous that she should refuse Wroxham. He's got everything that a girl can want to make her happy. He's got the highest principles.

Lord Spratte. And a very comfortable income.

Canon. Though he's quite young he has acquired a respected and assured position in the House of Lords.

Lord Spratte. It's lucky we don't all take ourselves so seriously, or we should have got long ago the only order the British people seem at all generous with nowadays.

Mrs. Fitzgerald. What is that?

Lord Spratte. The order of the boot.

MRS. FITZGERALD *gives a ripple of laughter.*

Canon. Oh, don't laugh at him. Don't encourage him in this criminal flippancy. [*To* LORD SPRATTE.] It's such as you who've brought the Upper House into discredit.

Lord Spratte. Such as I, my dear Theodore? Why, I've been proppin' up the old place for years by the simple method of systematically avoiding it.

Canon. Indeed!

Lord Spratte. As long as we kept to shootin', huntin', and fishin', no one interfered with us. I went to the House of Lords the other day—

Canon. You surprise me.

Lord Spratte. Oh, it was quite accidental. I had to go to Westminster on business.

Canon. Wonders will never cease.

Lord Spratte. I had to see a terrier that a man wanted to sell. Well, I had a new topper on and no umbrella, an' of course it began to rain. "By Jupiter," I said, "I'm hanged if I won't go and legislate for ten minutes." Well, I walked in, and somebody asked who the dickens I was. Upon my word, I was almost ashamed to say. Spratte's a very awkward name to give to a policeman. It sounds like a practical joke.

Canon. A rose by any other name would smell as sweet.

Lord Spratte. Well, they let me in after a bit, and I found twenty old buffers lyin' about on red benches. Good Lord, I said, who *are* their tailors? I listened to a funny old thing who was mumblin' away in his beard for a bit, and then I said to myself: Shall I stay here and listen to this twaddle or shall I get my hat wet? Suddenly, I had an inspiration. By Jupiter, I thought, I'll take a taxi.

Canon. Your levity grows more marked every day, Thomas. I used to hope it was due chiefly to the exuberance of youth, but it seems that increasing years bring you no sense of your responsibilities.

Lord Spratte. It shows what a charmin' nature I have, to stand bein' ragged by my younger brother. What price primogeniture now?

Canon. You forget that it's my name as well as yours that you drag through the dust.

Lord Spratte. The name of Spratte?

Canon. It was borne by the late Lord Chancellor of England.

Lord Spratte. Oh, Theodore, don't drag him in again. I'm just about sick of him. It's been the curse of my life to be the son of an eminent man. After all, it was only by a beastly job that they stuck him on that silly old woolsack.

Canon. Have you never heard the maxim: *De mortuis nil nisi bonum?*

Lord Spratte. That means, don't pull an old buffer's leg when he's kicked the bucket.

Canon [*impatiently*]. You have no sense of decorum, no seemliness, no dignity.

Lord Spratte. The fact is, I don't feel important enough. I can't stand all these gewgaws. I don't want the silly title with its sham coat of arms and its bogus pedigree. And those ridiculous ermine robes. The very thought of them gives me goose flesh. I should have been right enough if I'd been just plain Tom Spratte. I might have made a fairly good horse dealer, and if I hadn't brains enough for that, I could always have gone into Parliament. I'd have been a capital First Lord of the Admiralty, because I can't tell a man-o'-war from a coal barge.

A bell is heard and the CANON *gives a start.*

Canon. Oh! What's that?

Mrs. Fitzgerald. My dear Canon, what a state your nerves are in.

Canon. It's the front door.

Mrs. Fitzgerald. Do you always jump out of your skin when there's a ring at the bell?

Lord Spratte. If it's an importunate creditor let me see him, Theodore. I'm used to dealing with the beast.

Canon. For goodness' sake be serious, Thomas.

Lady Sophia. What *is* the matter, Theodore?

Canon. Don't you know that every bell may be a message from the Prime Minister? A note or a telegram. How do I know? But at all events, the offer of the vacant bishopric. The last time there was a vacancy he practically assured me that I should have the next.

Lady Sophia. He's probably done the same to half the schoolmasters in England.

Canon. Nonsense! Who is there that could take it? They've none of them half the claims that I have. Besides, it's a ridiculous system altogether to give a bishopric to Tom Noddy because he's taught Latin verses to a parcel of stupid schoolboys. As the youngest son of the late Lord Chancellor of England, I think I may expect something from my country. I have a presentiment that Colchester will be offered to me.

Lord Spratte. In that case I have a presentiment that you will accept it.

Mrs. Fitzgerald [*smiling*]. I think you're the most ambitious man I've ever known.

Canon. And if I am? Ambition, says the Swan of Avon, is the last infirmity of noble minds. But what is the use of ambition now? I should have lived four centuries ago when a bishop might hold the destinies of Europe in the hollow of his hand. I feel in me the power to do great things. Sometimes I sit in my chair and I can hardly bear my inaction. Good heavens, what is there for me to do? To preach sermons to a fashionable crowd, to preside on committees, to go to dinner parties in Mayfair. I've come into the world too late. I hear Ponsonby on the stairs.

Half unconsciously, as the door opens and PONSONBY *enters, he throws himself into such an attitude as a man may adopt when he expects a message from the Prime Minister.*

Ponsonby. Miss Durant.

The CANON's *mouth outlines the word "Damn!", but he recovers himself at once and goes forward to meet* GWENDOLEN *with his usual gallant friendliness.*

Canon. Ah, this *is* a pleasant surprise.

Gwendolen [*shaking hands with* LADY SOPHIA]. How d'you do.

She gives her hands to the CANON *who holds them during the conversation.*

Canon. How nice of you to come and see us.

Gwendolen. I came to fetch Winnie.

Canon. You break my heart. I was flattering myself that you'd come to see me.

Gwendolen [*smiling*]. That would be dreadfully forward.

Canon. Why are you blushing?

Gwendolen. Why are you holding my hands?

Canon. At my age it's of no consequence.

Gwendolen. I think you're the youngest man I've ever known in my life.

Canon. Ah, why don't we live in the eighteenth century so that I might fall on one knee and kiss your hand in gratitude for that pretty speech.

Lady Sophia. Don't believe a word he says, Gwendolen. Theodore has a peculiar talent for deluding our sex.

Gwendolen. He has a peculiar talent for making himself agreeable.

Canon. I belong to the old school, which put a lovely woman on a gilded pedestal and worshiped the ground she trod on.

Lord Spratte. Excuse me, but if she was on a gilded pedestal, surely she wasn't treading on the ground.

Canon. You have no poetry in your soul, Thomas.

LORD SPRATTE *has shaken hands with* MRS. FITZGERALD.

Mrs. Fitzgerald. Are you going?

Lord Spratte. I prefer my family in homeopathic doses.
                                                    [*Exit.*

Gwendolen. You know you're going to be Bishop of Colchester, don't you?

Canon. My dear child, that is not a subject upon which I allow my thoughts to dwell. I will not conceal from you that, as the youngest surviving son of the late Lord Chancellor, I think I have some claim upon my country. But in these matters there is so much ignoble wire-pulling, so much backstairs influence to which my character is not suited and to which I could never bring myself to descend.

Gwendolen. Papa says it's all settled. I told him to use his influence. And you've got the liquor interest solid.

Canon. When the Church and the Licensed Victuallers stand shoulder to shoulder, not all the powers of Satan can avail against them.

Gwendolen. I wonder where Winnie is.

Lady Sophia. She's certain to be in soon. She went down to Peckham.

Canon [*quickly*]. Where?

Lady Sophia. Mr. Railing has taken her down to see his mother and sister.

Canon. Why wasn't I told of this, Sophia?

Lady Sophia. I suppose because Winnie knew perfectly well that you wouldn't approve.

Canon. Listen.

The CANON'S *exclamation is preceded by a ring at the bell, followed by a second and third in rapid succession.*

Gwendolen. What is it?

Canon. It's someone at the door.

Mrs. Fitzgerald. Someone apparently in a great hurry.

The CANON *throws himself in the attitude of a man awaiting the call of his country. The door is flung open and* LIONEL *comes quickly in. This time* CANON SPRATTE *is unable to conceal his vexation.*

Canon. Oh, it's only you. I don't know why on earth you ring the bell as though the house were on fire.

Lionel. I say, Father, have you heard about Colchester?

Canon. Heard what?

For a moment he is uncertain whether to be elated or disappointed.

Lionel. It's announced that Dr. Gray, the headmaster of Harbin has been appointed.

Canon. Impossible!

Lionel. It's in the *Westminster.*

Canon. The *Westminster* is a radical paper and would say anything. It can't be true. I make the best of my fellow men and I cannot bring myself to believe that the Prime Minister can be so wicked and foolish.

Gwendolen. I am so sorry.

Canon [*recovering himself, with a gallant smile*]. Oh, my dear child, you mustn't let my affairs worry you.

Gwendolen. I don't think I'll wait for Winnie after all.

Canon. Lionel will take you down to your car. Good-by, dear child. It's been like a ray of spring sunshine to see you.

Gwendolen. Good-by.

She goes out accompanied by LIONEL.

Canon. Sophia, you must go and call on Lady Patricia.

Lady Sophia. I?

Canon. You must find out what all this means. I can't believe it. It's preposterous.

Mrs. Fitzgerald. But who is Dr. Gray?

Canon. A man of no family. I cannot think the government would be so crassly idiotic as to give an important bishopric to a man of Gray's powers. Powers? They're not powers; he's the most ordinary and stupid man I've ever known. He's stupider than a churchwarden.

Lady Sophia. My dear Theodore, do keep calm.

Canon. How can I keep calm when I see such an odious job about to be perpetrated? And then the government expects me to support it. How can any right-minded man support such corrupt and ignoble practices?

Lady Sophia. I'll go and put on my hat.

Canon. I thank heaven that I'm not a vain man. I may have faults—we all have faults.

Lady Sophia [*at the door*]. We do.   [*Exit.*

Canon. But no one has ever accused me of vanity. But this, I will confess: I don't think I should have been out of place in that responsible position. I have been mixed up with public affairs, I may say, all my life; I am used to responsibility and authority.

Mrs. Fitzgerald. I'm afraid you're quite upset. Don't you think a glass of sherry would do you good?

Canon. Oh, my dear lady, at this moment—at this moment, I cannot think of sherry.

Mrs. Fitzgerald. It would keep you up.

Canon. I could almost say that I will never drink sherry again.

Mrs. Fitzgerald. My poor Canon, I feel so sorry for you.

Canon [*taking her hands*]. Thank you, my dear, for sympathizing with me. I have often felt that you really understood me. It's a dreadful thing to be surrounded by persons who don't appreciate you. They say that no man is a prophet in his own country, and I have experienced that, too. I am surrounded by cynical laughter and by flippant vulgarity. I don't want to say anything against Sophia. I dare say she does her best. But she has not the delicacy of sentiment necessary to understand a character like mine. Ah, you should have known my wife. She was an angel—loving, obedient, respectful, self-effacing. She was all that a wife should be. She was taken from me. I shall never get over it. [Mrs. Fitzgerald *tries to disengage her hands*.] What is the matter?

Mrs. Fitzgerald. Nothing, except that you've been holding my hands quite long enough.

Canon. Why shouldn't I hold them? We're old friends.

Mrs. Fitzgerald. I want to scratch my nose.

Canon. Such a pretty nose.

Mrs. Fitzgerald. You really mustn't say things like that to me.

Canon. At such a moment anything I say is pardonable.

Mrs. Fitzgerald. Will you give me possession of my hands, or must I scream for help?

Canon. You talk as if we were perfect strangers, and heaven knows how many years it is since we first met.

Mrs. Fitzgerald. That's just it. Heaven knows that we're both of us quite old enough to have learnt how to behave ourselves.

Canon. Nothing is so untruthful as anno Domini. You don't look a day more than eighteen, and I'm sure I feel barely twenty-two.

Mrs. Fitzgerald [*laughing*]. How *can* you talk such nonsense!

Canon. You think I'm joking, but I'm deadly serious.

Mrs. Fitzgerald. Then there's no possible excuse for you.

Canon. Does it mean nothing to you that the springtime is smiling in the street and all the birds are quivering with song?

Mrs. Fitzgerald. What do you think Lionel would say if he heard you?

Canon. Lionel is wisely occupied with his own affairs. I sent him downstairs with Gwendolen, and if he's half the man his father is, he'll propose to her before she reaches her carriage.

Mrs. Fitzgerald. Perhaps poor Lionel doesn't know how.

Canon. It's so easy that I wonder how men ever remain bachelors. This modern jewelry is so charming that you can hardly help admiring the lovely ring that adorns a lady's finger. And that leads you inevitably to take her hand.

He takes Mrs. Fitzgerald's *hand, but she withdraws it.*

Mrs. Fitzgerald. I gather your meaning without your actually giving an example.

Canon. Why are you so unkind to me?

Mrs. Fitzgerald. I don't know how far you're going.

Canon [*with an imitation of a bus conductor*]. All the way, madam, all the way.

Mrs. Fitzgerald. How lucky I'm bringing my visit to an end tomorrow.

Canon. I couldn't bear to think of your going so soon, if it weren't for the hope that I might induce you to come back for good.

Mrs. Fitzgerald. Do my ears deceive me, or is this a proposal of marriage that I'm listening to?

Canon. It's a proposal of marriage.

Mrs. Fitzgerald. Take it back quickly, in case I accept.

Canon. I insist on your accepting.

Mrs. Fitzgerald. Then I'm quite sure you're not yourself today, and I shall refuse without further delay.

Canon. As if I should take such a flippant answer as that.

Mrs. Fitzgerald. You're really the most unexpected person I ever knew. Why on earth d'you want to marry me?

Canon. Look in your glass, dear friend, it will tell you a hundred good reasons.

Mrs. Fitzgerald. And what d'you think your children would say to it?

Canon. My children are making their own homes and I shall be left alone.

Mrs. Fitzgerald. You've forgotten Sophia.

Canon. Sophia can shave her head and go into a nunnery.

Mrs. Fitzgerald. Sophia would like that, wouldn't she? [*He leans forward and is just about to kiss her, when she draws back. With assumed surprise.*] What are you going to do?

Canon [*smiling*]. I was going to kiss you.

Mrs. Fitzgerald. Oh, but I haven't accepted you.

Canon. I never take a refusal.

Mrs. Fitzgerald. That must complicate a proposal of marriage wonderfully.

Canon. I shall inform Sophia that you've promised to marry me.

Mrs. Fitzgerald. I shall inform her that I've done nothing of the sort.

Canon. I cannot imagine why you hesitate.

Mrs. Fitzgerald. I'm not sure that I feel equal to the responsibilities of a clergyman's wife.

Canon. You may be quite certain that I didn't venture to make you this proposal till I was fully convinced that your duty as well as mine pointed to our union.

Mrs. Fitzgerald. I don't think I could marry anyone from a sense of duty.

Canon [*flatteringly*]. I know you too well to think that you would ever turn a deaf ear to the dictation of your conscience.

Mrs. Fitzgerald. My conscience is very well regulated. It never ventures to dictate anything that would be disagreeable to me.

Canon. Then I can only hope it will come to you after a certain amount of reflection, that it would be not only right that you should marry me, but also agreeable.

Mrs. Fitzgerald. You have evidently the highest opinion of my understanding, dear Canon.

Canon. Won't you call me Theodore?

Mrs. Fitzgerald. I really couldn't; it sounds so familiar.

Canon. Perhaps you would care to go to your room?

Mrs. Fitzgerald. Why?

Canon. I thought you might like a few moments of solitude to think it over.

Mrs. Fitzgerald. You're so thoughtful.

Canon. That, if I may say so, is the least of my virtues.

Mrs. Fitzgerald [*demurely*]. I will retire to the privacy of my bedchamber.

She goes out.

CANON SPRATTE *walks toward another door. Passing a looking glass, he stops and runs his fingers through his hair. He takes a little comb from his pocket and arranges it with nicety. His face assumes a look of anxiety as he realizes that his trousers are a little too long. He unbuttons his waistcoat and hoists his braces.*

Canon [*with deep conviction*]. What a leg for a gaiter! [WINNIE *comes in, pale and tired. The* CANON *gives a slight start as sees her, and then watches her walk rather wearily across the room. She sinks into a chair and begins moodily to tear off her gloves. It is plain that she is cross and wretched.*] You've returned safely from the wilds of Peckham. I trust you encountered no savage beasts in those unfrequented parts?

Winnie [*her answer is almost a groan*]. None.

The CANON *pricks up his ears. The idea dawns on him that the visit to* BERTRAM RAILING's *family has not been altogether a success.*

Canon [*watching her keenly*]. I hope you enjoyed yourself, darling. You're very pale.

Winnie. I have rather a headache.

Canon. You don't often have headaches. . . . And did your prospective mother-in-law take you to her bosom?

Winnie. She was very kind.

Canon [*very blandly*]. I imagine she was not exactly— polished.

Winnie. I didn't expect her to be.

Canon. But, of course, to you such things as that are nothing. True disinterestedness is such a beautiful thing, and in this world, alas! so rare. By the way, what is the address of your—of the young man you're walking out with?

Winnie [*defiantly*]. Asquith Villas, Gladstone Road, Peckham.

Canon. And Mrs. Railing, I think you said, was the widow of a coal heaver?

Winnie. Her husband was first mate on a collier.

Canon. Does she smack of the briny, my dear—or does she smack of Peckham Rye? [*He breaks into song.*]

> For I'm no sailor bold,
> And I've never been upon the sea,
> And if I fall therein,
> It's a fact I couldn't swim,
> And quickly at the bottom I should be.

My dear, how uncommunicative you are, and I'm dying with curiosity. Tell me all about Miss Railing. Aitchless, I presume?

Winnie [*almost breaking down*]. Oh, Papa, how can you!

Canon. My dear, I have no doubt that they are rough diamonds. But you mustn't be discouraged at that, you must make the best of things.

Winnie. It's charming of you to give me good advice.

Canon. Remember that externals are not everything. I'm sure that the Railings are very worthy people. It is doubtless possible to eat peas with a knife, and yet to have an excellent heart. I should imagine that your—[*He hesitates and then assumes a cockney accent.*] bloke, was devoted to his mother and sister. Those sort of people always are. One's less desirable relations are such patterns of affection. They're always talking of the beauty of a united family. But I have no doubt that you will soon accustom yourself to their little eccentricities of diction, to their superficial vulgarities of manner. Kind hearts are more than coronets and simple faith than Norman blood.

Winnie. Father, I've given my solemn promise to Bertram, and I'd sooner die than break it.

The CANON *walks up and down the room. Suddenly he determines to do what has been hovering in his mind since he saw* WINNIE's *state upon returning from Peckham.*

Canon. My darling, nothing shall stand between you and my great affection. If your heart is set upon marrying this young man—I withdraw my opposition.

Winnie [*springs up and looks at him*]. Father!

Canon. I have come to the conclusion that it is wrong and even wicked for a parent to attempt to influence his children's matrimonial choice. Their youth and inexperience naturally make them so much more capable of judging for themselves.

Before WINNIE *has got over her astonishment, in which there is ever so slight a suspicion of dismay, the door is opened by* PONSONBY.

Ponsonby. Lord Wroxham.

LORD WROXHAM *enters. He is a young man with no particular distinction of appearance. He is dark, with a small mustache, and he wears pince-nez. No one would look twice at him. He is not the least good-looking, but he is well dressed and of gentlemanly appearance.* CANON SPRATTE *is, as usual, master of the situation, and, as* WROXHAM *comes in, he goes up to him with cordiality but with every appearance of being in a great hurry.*

Canon. Ah, my dear fellow, how nice of you to come! The very man I wanted to see. But you must excuse me one moment. A clergyman's time is never his own, you know, never for a moment. There's a poor woman waiting to see me downstairs; she's lost her first husband and she's looking everywhere for number two and she can't find him. I shall only be five minutes.

Before WROXHAM *can utter a word,* CANON SPRATTE *has swept out, singing gaily, "For I'm no sailor bold."*

For a moment WINNIE *and* WROXHAM *look at one another in silence.*

Wroxham. You're not angry with me for coming, Winnie?
Winnie. Good heavens, why should I be? We've been friends for ages. It would be absurd if we never saw one another again because—because of the other day. You know I'm always glad to see you.
Wroxham. I couldn't take your answer as final.
Winnie [*hurriedly*]. Oh, don't, please!
Wroxham. I don't want to bother you and make you miserable, but don't you care for me at all? Don't you think that after a time you might get to like me?
Winnie. I told you the other day it was impossible.
Wroxham. Oh, I know. But then I couldn't say what I wanted to. I couldn't understand. Like a fool, I thought you cared for me. I was so awfully keen on you that it seemed impossible I should be nothing to you at all.
Winnie. Please don't say anything more. It's so kind of you, and I don't know how to thank you, but I can't marry you.
Wroxham. I want to say this. I shall never care for anyone else. If by any chance you should ever change your mind, you'd find me—waiting for you, don't you know. Of

course, I don't want any promise, or encouragement, or anything of that sort, but I'd just like you to know that you can always count on me.

Winnie. I didn't know you were so kind. I misjudged you. I thought you treated me like a fool. I'm sorry. Don't be wretched because I can't marry you. I'm not worth troubling about.

She gives him her hand, and he, holding it, looks into her eyes.

Wroxham. Is anything the matter?

Winnie [*trying to smile, blushing to the roots of her hair*]. No, what should be?

Wroxham. You look so—so unlike yourself.

Winnie. I've got rather a headache. There's really nothing else . . . Oh, there's Father.

They hear him gaily singing outside, and WINNIE *quickly slips out of the room by another door as he comes in. He goes towards* WROXHAM *with all his affability.*

Canon. I hope I haven't kept you waiting. Has Winnie left you? Where are the child's manners?

Wroxham. I've been talking to her. I don't think I quite understand her.

Canon. My dear fellow, don't be misled by woman's complaint that she's misunderstood, into thinking she's complex. Woman's the obvious and a powder puff, horse sense and a high-heeled shoe.

Wroxham. I'm not quite sure I know what that means.

Canon. Neither am I, but it sounds so well, I shall probably say it again.

Wroxham. I thought she'd been crying when I came in.

Canon. All women cry when they have nothing better to do. It's the only inexpensive form of amusement they have.

Wroxham. I asked her to marry me, Canon Spratte.

Canon. And of course she refused. No nice girl accepts a man the first three times she asks her.

Wroxham. Winnie is so different from other girls.

Canon. Every man thinks the girl he wants to marry different from every other. But she's not. All women are pretty much of a muchness, and that is why, on the whole, they make tolerable wives and mothers. No, my dear Wroxham, you have my full approval, and you have my assurance that Winnie undoubtedly cares for you. What more can you want? Hammer away, my dear sir, hammer away. The proper manner to deal with a woman is to ask her in season and out of season. Worry her as a terrier worries a bone. Insist on marrying her, and sooner or later she'll say yes, and think herself a prodigious fool for not having done so before.

Wroxham. You're very encouraging.

Canon. Believe me, there are few men who have more experience in the management of the sex than I.

Wroxham [*with a rather rueful smile*]. You speak as if you'd conducted with success a harem of more than common dimensions.

Canon. I confess that has not been among my experiences, but if the occasion arose, I have no doubt of my capacity to deal satisfactorily with the situation.

Wroxham. Good-by.

Canon. Good-by, my dear fellow. You must come and see us again in a day or two. I think it not impossible that you will find dear Winnie in a very different state of mind. Good-by.

Wroxham. Good-by, and thanks awfully.

They shake hands and LORD WROXHAM *goes out.*

CANON SPRATTE *walks up and down in high good humor, rubbing his hands.*

Canon [*singing*]. For I'm no sailor bold,
    And I've never been upon the sea,
     And if I fell therein,
     It's a fact I couldn't swim,
    And quickly at the bottom I should be.

[*He sits down at a desk, and with a smile on his face writes a short note. He puts it into an envelope and addresses it.*] "Asquite Villas, Gladstone Road, Peckham. [*Just as he has fastened the envelope* MRS. FITZGERALD *comes in. The* CANON *springs to his feet and goes towards her with outstretched hands.*] You come in like a ray of spring sunshine.

Mrs. Fitzgerald. You've already said that to Gwendolen Durant today.

Canon. Have I? The difference between a great man and a little one is that the great man never hesitates to repeat himself.

Mrs. Fitzgerald. I've been thinking over your very flattering proposal, dear Canon.

Canon. And you have good news for me. I see it in your smiling eyes.

Mrs. Fitzgerald. I wonder if you meant it quite seriously.

Canon. Of course I meant it, every word of it, with all my heart. Do you think I'm a boy, not to know my own mind?

Mrs. Fitzgerald. I think you're a very susceptible man, and you're sometimes carried away by the fire of your own eloquence.

Canon. It was no sudden whim on my part. Ah, why can't I make you believe that love may spring up in a man's heart even though his hair is strewn with silver? I tell you I'm passionately devoted to you, and I insist on marrying you.

Mrs. Fitzgerald. Don't say such things. You make my heart go pitapat, pitapat, pitapat.

Canon. We'll have a dozen bishops to marry us, and Tom shall lend us Beachcombe for our honeymoon. Or would you prefer Homburg and the Italian lakes?

Mrs. Fitzgerald. You go so quickly. You positively take my breath away.

Canon. You see, I have no time to lose.

Mrs. Fitzgerald. Then let us talk business.

Canon [*with a fine gesture of distaste*]. Why should we? You know I'm not mercenary. Let us pretend that no tiresome maters have to be discussed. We can leave it all to our solicitors.

Mrs. Fitzgerald. But it's very important.

Canon. Nonsense! Nothing's important except that you're the most charming woman in the world. I'm a lucky dog to have got hold of you. We'll never grow older than we are now. We'll only grow younger year by year. When will you make me the happiest man in London?

Mrs. Fitzgerald. For heaven's sake, sit down quietly and let me get a word in.

Canon. I won't give you a moment's peace till you've fixed the day.

Mrs. Fitzgerald. Heavens, what a man it is! You shall fix the day yourself.

Canon. I said so. Worry her as a terrier worries a bone. Hammer away, my dear sir, hammer away!

Mrs. Fitzgerald. You shall fix the day yourself after I've told you what I've been vainly trying to say for the last ten minutes.

Canon. Shall we say six weeks from now? That will bring us to the end of the season, and I can safely leave Lionel to preach to a regiment of empty pews.

Mrs. Fitzgerald. For goodness' sake, let me speak.

Canon. What an obstinate woman! Well, speak on. It shall never be said that I hesitated to give way to your smallest whim.

Mrs. Fitzgerald. What I wanted to tell you is that I have an income of five thousand a year.

Canon. I cannot bear these gross and sordid details. Of course, it shall be settled absolutely upon you. What more is there to be said?

Mrs. Fitzgerald. Only that it ceases on the day I marry again.

The CANON'S *face suddenly falls. There is the briefest possible pause.*

Canon. All of it?

Mrs. Fitzgerald. Every penny. My husband was a very generous man, but he had apparently no desire to provide for the wants of his successor.

CANON SPRATTE *struggles to master his very pardonable emotion. He finds some difficulty in breathing. The room on a sudden seems extraordinarily stuffy.*

Canon. I'm very glad. You will be more precious to me with the thought that I alone am providing for you. It will sustain me in my work to think that you are—if I may say so—dependent upon me.

Mrs. Fitzgerald. Do you realize that I shall be so penniless, you will even have to provide the clothes for my back, and my very fare when I take the tube?

Canon. I shall look upon it as an enviable privilege.

Mrs. Fitzgerald. I was a little afraid you might not love me solely for myself, but every word you say proves that I was wrong.

Canon. If I hesitated for a moment, to ask you to marry me, it was only because your greater income might have cast suspicion on the purity of my motives.

Mrs. Fitzgerald. You have a noble character, Theodore. You may kiss me.

She puts forward her cheek, and he, grimly, with rage, disappointment, and mortification in his heart, does his duty.

Curtain.

ACT THREE

The scene is the same as in the preceding acts.

The room is empty when the curtain rises, but in a moment CANON SPRATTE *comes in. He rings the bell,* PONSONBY *enters.*

CANON. Is Mr. Lionel in, Ponsonby?

Ponsonby. I'll find out, sir.

Canon [*as* PONSONBY *is leaving the room*]. And you might ask her ladyship if she'd be good enough to come to the drawing room.

Ponsonby. Very good, sir.   [*Exit.*

After an interval LADY SOPHIA *comes in with* MRS. FITZGERALD.

Canon. I hope I've not disturbed you.

Lady Sophia. We were wondering if you were in.

Mrs. Fitzgerald. I wanted to say good-by to you. I should have been so disappointed if I'd gone without seeing you.

Canon. You don't mean to say you're leaving us?

Mrs. Fitzgerald. My train starts in an hour.

Canon. This is extraordinarily sudden.

Mrs. Fitzgerald. It isn't really. You only asked me to stay till Friday.

Canon. But didn't Sophia insist on your stopping over the week end?

Mrs. Fitzgerald [*smiling*]. I can't honestly say she did.

Lady Sophia [*with a chuckle*]. My dear, your washing came home last night.

Canon [*to* MRS. FITZGERALD]. It's too bad of you. Oh, Sophia, I wanted to tell you that I'm expecting Mrs. and Miss Railing to tea today.

Lady Sophia. Winnie told me you'd consented to her engagement.

Canon [*chaffing her*]. It must be a match after your own heart, my dear. You have always affected to look down upon our family. You must be pleased that the descendant of your ancestral greengrocer should form an alliance with the near connection of a coal heaver. They pair like chalk and cheese.

Mrs. Fitzgerald. And when are they to be married?

Canon. They're not to be married.

Mrs. Fitzgerald. My head is beginning to swim.

Canon. Winnie is going to marry Lord Wroxham.

Lady Sophia. And d'you think the best way to bring that about is to let her be engaged to somebody else?

Canon. My dear Sophia, have you ever known me to make a mistake yet?

Lady Sophia. Frequently. Though I'm bound to say I've never known you to acknowledge it.

Canon. It comes to the same thing. Like a typical Englishman, I never know when I'm beaten.

Lady Sophia. Good heavens, what a man it is! One can't even remark that it's a fine day without your extracting a compliment from it. Master Theodore, self-praise is no recommendation.

Canon. Miss Sophia, your nose wants blowing.

Lady Sophia [*stiffly*]. That, I think, is rather vulgar, Theodore.

Mrs. Fitzgerald. Do explain yourself, Canon.

Canon. Well, I flatter myself . . .

Lady Sophia. You frequently do, my dear.

Canon. I flatter myself that I know my daughter's character. Now, I am convinced that if I had put my foot down, Winnie would have gone off and married the man there and then. But I know the Spratte character inside out. We are a family of marked idiosyncrasies.

Lady Sophia. Inherited from the Montmorencys, I suppose.

Canon. I have no doubt. You will remember in our father the firmness and decision of which I speak.

Lady Sophia. I remember that he was as obstinate as a pig.

Canon. My dear, I do not want to rebuke you, but I really must ask you not to make these unseemly remarks. If you are incapable of recognizing the respect due to your father, I would have you recollect that he was also Lord Chancellor of England.

Lady Sophia. Do you ever give me the chance to forget it?

Mrs. Fitzgerald [*smiling*]. But what exactly has that to do with Winnie?

Canon. I was about to observe that whatever my faults, when I make up my mind that a thing is right, no power on earth can prevent me from doing it. Now, I do not wish to be offensive, but I cannot help perceiving that the firmness which, if I may say it without vanity, is so marked a characteristic in me, is apt in other members of our family to degenerate into something which the uncharitable may well call obstinacy.

Lady Sophia. Upon my word, Theodore, it's fortunate you told me you had no wish to be offensive.

Canon. Please don't interrupt. Now, I am dealing with Winnie as the Irishman deals with the pig he is taking to market. He pulls the way he doesn't want to go, and the pig quite happily goes the other.

Mrs. Fitzgerald. Even now I'm afraid I don't quite understand.

Canon. When Winnie said she would marry Mr. Railing, she didn't reckon on Mr. Railing's mamma, and she didn't reckon on Mr. Railing's sister. In such cases the man has often educated himself into something that passes muster, and your sex has no great skill in discerning a gentleman from the spurious article. But the women! My dear lady, I tell you Winnie won't like them at all.

Mrs. Fitzgerald. The more repulsive his relations are, the more her pride will force Winnie to keep her promise.

Canon. We shall see.

Mrs. Fitzgerald. Like all great plans it has a certain effective obviousness about it.

Lady Sophia. Are you quite sure it's honest, Theodore?

Canon. My dear Sophia, what *do* you mean?

Lady Sophia. It seems to me a little underhand.

Canon. My dear, I do not wish to remind you that I am a clergyman, though occasionally you seem strangely oblivious of the fact. But I should like to point out to you that it's unlikely, to say the least of it, that a man of my position in the church should do anything dishonest or underhand.

Lady Sophia [*with a little smile*]. My dear brother, if as Vicar of St. Gregory's and Canon of Tercanbury, you assure me that you are acting like a Christian and a gentleman—of course, I haven't the temerity to say anything further.

Canon. You may set your mind at rest. You can be quite sure that whatever I do is right.

Mrs. Fitzgerald. Upon my word, you're a very extraordinary man, Canon.

Canon. That, madam, is a fact which had not entirely escaped my observation. By the way, Sophia, I wonder if you'd ring up Thomas and ask him to look in.

Lady Sophia. I'll tell Ponsonby to telephone.

Canon. Do it yourself, there's a dear. Ponsonby's growing so stupid, and I'm particularly anxious Thomas should come this afternoon.

Lady Sophia [*with a little smile*]. You *are* a troublesome creation.

She goes out.

Canon. I haven't the remotest desire to see Thomas, but

that was the only way I could think to get poor Sophia out of the light.

Mrs. Fitzgerald. And why did you want to do that?

Canon. So that I might be alone with you.

Mrs. Fitzgerald. That's very flattering.

Canon. I'm going to scold you for leaving us so suddenly. Have you no regard for my feelings?

Mrs. Fitzgerald. That's precisely why I'm leaving you.

Canon. I've not had a moment alone with you since you promised to be my wife.

Mrs. Fitzgerald. When I think of the long companionship of married life, I'm convinced that engaged persons should see as little of one another as they can.

Canon. I believe you said you were thinking of going to Ascot.

Mrs. Fitzgerald. That was my intention.

Canon. Of course, I have no right to preach to you, but— isn't it a little worldly?

Mrs. Fitzgerald. I *am* a little worldly.

Canon. I'm afraid you'll have to abandon many little luxuries when you're mistress of my humble vicarage. There'll be no little visits to Ascot then.

Mrs. Fitzgerald. I'm not cynical. I believe devoutly in love in a cottage.

Canon. I understand people often do till they try it. I'm afraid we shan't be able to afford a carriage.

Mrs. Fitzgerald. I'm beginning to think a Bath chair fulfills all my aspirations.

Canon. And will you think me very unkind if I suggest that you must do without a maid?

Mrs. Fitzgerald. I'm sure it will amuse me immensely to darn my own stockings.

Canon. Are you fond of district visiting?

Mrs. Fitzgerald. I love to interfere with other people's concerns, and it's only the poor who can't actively resent it.

Canon [*with a show of frankness*]. I don't know whether you realize that I'm full of faults.

Mrs. Fitzgerald. You would be very tedious without.

Canon. You'll find me impatient and exacting, ill-tempered and overbearing. I'm anxious that you should know the worst before it's too late.

Mrs. Fitzgerald. It's so charming of you to tell me. Now I can confess without a qualm that I'm quarrelsome and vain, extravagant and untruthful.

Canon. They say that mutual confidence is the best foundation for a happy marriage.

Mrs. Fitzgerald. I don't think our married life will be devoid of incident.

Canon [*reflecting*]. I knew a man a little while ago who told me that he'd never spent such a moment of dismay as when he saw his engagement announced in the *Morning Post*.

Mrs. Fitzgerald. I knew a woman who when she read hers, cried: "Talk of tarpon."

Canon. I don't know what she meant.

Mrs. Fitzgerald. She meant he was a difficult fish to catch, but she'd landed him at last.

Canon [*stiffly*]. I don't think your friend can have been a very nice person.

Mrs. Fitzgerald. She was a widow, and as you have the best reasons for knowing, they're always dangerous. . . . Have you told Sophia that we're engaged?

Canon. No, I haven't yet.

Mrs. Fitzgerald. Oh!

Canon. I thought it would be rather a joke if we made a secret of it for a little while.

Mrs. Fitzgerald. You have a very keen sense of humor.

Canon. Of course, if you wish me to, I'll cry it from the housetops at once.

Mrs. Fitzgerald. That would be both unbecoming and dangerous.

Canon. You see, the date of our marriage is necessarily uncertain.

Mrs. Fitzgerald. Is it?

Canon [*feeling his way*]. I don't think we went into that question, did we?

Mrs. Fitzgerald. Surely you asked me if I could be ready in six weeks.

Canon. How stupid of me to forget! Of course I did. My memory is so bad, it's really quite time they made me a bishop.

Mrs. Fitzgerald. But of course it would be indecent if I showed the least eagerness to succumb to your fascinations. It's right and proper that Amaryllis should display a retiring disposition.

Canon. While Corydon is ardent and will hear of no delay.

Mrs. Fitzgerald. I don't know if the world was topsy-turvy then, or if it's topsy-turvy now.

Canon. I will be perfectly frank with you. I will not attempt to conceal from you that what you told me yesterday about—the subject is infinitely distasteful to me.

Mrs. Fitzgerald. About my husband's will?

Canon. Exactly. . . . It *has* made some alteration in the matter. It would be insincere to deny it. Not in my feelings, of course.

Mrs. Fitzgerald. I know you too well to suspect that.

Canon. Your poverty can only make my love the greater.

Mrs. Fitzgerald. You know, Theodore, I'm almost glad that I shall have no money. It delights me to think that I shall owe nothing to a living soul but you—and a certain number of tradesmen. I wish now I'd paid ready money for everything.

Canon. I hope you're not heavily in debt?

Mrs. Fitzgerald. Oh, six or seven hundred pounds at the utmost.

Canon. I can quite believe that what I'm going to say is liable to misconstruction. But I know how sympathetic you are. That's what first drew me toward you. I can trust you to understand me. I would give the whole world rather than you should think me mercenary.

Mrs. Fitzgerald. I'm quite certain that you'll say nothing without the best of motives, Theodore.

Canon. Yesterday I asked you to marry me as quickly as possible. Would you think it very odd if today I asked you to wait?

Mrs. Fitzgerald. I should think it very wise.

Canon. After all, my first duty is to you, isn't it?

Mrs. Fitzgerald [*earnestly*]. I know very well that there's no thought for yourself in anything you say.

Canon. I can't ask you to face poverty with me. You're too unused to it. I've tried to persuade myself, but I can't. It would be sheer selfishness on my part if I yielded to my own inclinations.

Mrs. Fitzgerald. I think you're too, too generous.

Canon. I dare say you know my income is not very large.

Mrs. Fitzgerald. I looked it out in the clergy list.

Canon. I shall have to spend a good deal on Winnie's trousseau, and I have every belief that Lionel will—bring it off with Gwendolen Durant. It's true she's got sixty thousand pounds, but in common decency I must make him some sort of allowance.

Mrs. Fitzgerald. You certainly have a great many expenses.

Canon. In a year or two all sorts of things may happen. It's true that they've given Colchester to a trumpery headmaster, but, after all, more than one of the bishops is very old and doddering. I have a good deal of influence at headquarters.

Mrs. Fitzgerald. Already you look every inch a bishop.

Canon. I know I'm asking a good deal, but would you very much mind waiting a year or two for me?

Mrs. Fitzgerald. Are you certain you wouldn't prefer not to be bound by an engagement?

Canon. Surely you have not so poor an opinion of me as to think I am capable of abandoning our projected union because you're not so rich as I thought.

Mrs. Fitzgerald. My dear friend, has it ever occurred to you that there are two sorts of love? There's one that's like the sweet pea: a young thing falls in love with another young thing, and their foolish heads are turned; so they marry, and have seventeen children, and live miserably ever after. Then there's another sort of love that's like the eating pea: a well-bred person not without means, falls in love with another well-bred person, whose circumstances are adequate. His passion is perfectly sincere, but he'd have no difficulty in restraining it within safe limits unless the lady had a large enough income to prevent marriage from being inconvenient. The sweet pea is very delightful and we all admire it, but the eating pea is both practical and sustaining.

Canon. Your simile leaves me unmoved.

Mrs. Fitzgerald. Remember that you're a young man and two or three years makes no difference to you, but in three years I shall be at least five years older than I am now. I'm afraid that is one of the unjustices of fate that votes for women will not be able to remedy.

Canon. My dear friend, I am attached to no passing charms of your person, but rather to the enduring qualities of your mind.

Mrs. Fitzgerald. Don't say that; it's how a man always tries to console a thoroughly plain woman.

Canon. I should be the last to deny that your personal attractions are considerable.

Mrs. Fitzgerald [*with a little bob*]. Thank you, sir.

There is a moment's pause, while he wavers uncertainly. She watches him with serious face but with brightly twinkling eyes.

Mrs. Fitzgerald. Shall we forget that the other day you murmured in my shell-like ear various things which you didn't quite mean?

Canon. I should be contemptible if I asked you to give me back my word.

Mrs. Fitzgerald. It's no sacrifice when I think of your future. I see already those shapely calves encased in the gaiters episcopal.

Canon. You'd despise me all your life if I—accepted your suggestion.

She looks at him for a moment, enjoying his embarrassment.
At last she cannot restrain a chuckle.

Mrs. Fitzgerald. My dear man, do you suppose for a moment that I had any intention of marrying you?

Canon [*astounded*]. I beg your pardon.

Mrs. Fitzgerald. Nothing would have induced me to do it. If I let you think so for four and twenty hours it was from pure devilry.

Canon. D'you mean to say you've been playing with me all the time?

Mrs. Fitzgerald. I rather liked you. And it's always nice to be proposed to.

Canon. You likened the two sorts of love just now to the sweet pea and the eating pea. I don't want to seem discourteous, but your emotion reminds me chiefly of the scarlet runner.

Mrs. Fitzgerald. Let us forget all about it. You're perfectly free, and there's no need whatever for you to marry me. Let us be friends. You're charming as a friend, but as a husband you'd be quite unsufferable. And don't flirt any more with widow ladies. They're dreadfully dangerous. Good-by. I've had such a jolly time.

Canon [*very stiffly*]. It rejoices me to hear it. [MRS. FITZGERALD *goes out.* CANON SPRATTE *draws a long breath of relief. It has been an awkward quarter of an hour, but it is over, and he is free. The door is opened and* WINNIE *comes in.*] There you are. I was wondering what on earth had become of you.

Winnie. I wrote to Bertram and told him you consented to our engagement.

Canon. He must be in the seventh heaven of delight.

Winnie. I've just had a note from him. He's coming round.

Canon. I'm pleased to see you looking so happy, darling. [LADY SOPHIA *comes into the room as he says these words and he turns to her.*] Our children, Sophia, are often a sore trial to us, but we must take the rough with the smooth. At times also they give us a great deal of self-satisfaction.

Winnie. I'm afraid Aunt Sophia isn't very pleased.

Lady Sophia. My dear, if you love him, and your father approves, I don't think there's anything more to be said. I suppose he'll go into Parliament, and I dare say it's not a bad thing he's a radical. I don't think they want clever young men on our side, they want them rich.

Canon. I dare say we shall be able to get him made something or other.

Lady Sophia. It doesn't seem to matter much whether you're a radical or a Tory; when there's a job going, you take it.

Enter PONSONBY, *followed by* BERTRAM RAILING.

Ponsonby. Mr. Railing.   [*Exit.*

Canon. We were just talking of you.

Railing. I want you to know how grateful I am for . . .

Canon [*interrupting*]. Not a word, my dear fellow.

Railing. I wanted to speak to you before, but Winnie wouldn't let me.

Canon. All's well that ends well, my dear fellow. Sophia, I have something to say to you. Come into the next room for a minute, will you?

The CANON *and* LADY SOPHIA *go into the inner drawing room.*

BERTRAM *stretches out his hands.*

Railing. Well?

Winnie. Well?

Railing. What a discreet man your father is.

He draws her towards him, but she slightly resists.

Winnie. Take care.

Railing. What d'you think your father took Lady Sophia away for?

Winnie. They seem less put out than I expected.

Railing. I'm so tremendously happy. Sit down.

They seat themselves and he tries to put his arm round her waist. She draws away from him.

Winnie. Please don't.

Railing [*surprised*]. Why on earth not?

Winnie. I should feel such a fool if someone came in.

Railing. But if we're engaged what does it matter? Why, when my sister Louise was engaged we used to leave the front room for them, and when anyone had to go in they gave the door a good old rattle.

Winnie. Your sister isn't married is she?

Railing. Oh, no, she broke it off. He wasn't quite up to her mark. She's an advanced radical and a suffragist, you know. And he was rather an ordinary young fellow. He was a solicitor's clerk. Louise is very brainy and he hadn't the remotest ideas about art or anything like that. He wouldn't go and see a play unless he was sure it would make him laugh.

Winnie. I rather like being amused at the theatre myself.

Railing. Oh, we'll get you out of that. The drama is destined to something nobler than to entertain.

Winnie. Bertram, I wish you'd tell me, do your cuffs take off?

Railing. What on earth makes you ask that?

Winnie. I was wondering.

Railing. As a matter of fact, they do. It's an awfully ingenious plan. [*He pulls up his sleeve and shows the arrangement which he describes.*] You see, they button on, and you turn them round—it's only the edges that have got dirty—and it looks as if you had a clean shirt on. It saves no end of washing.

Winnie. I thought men wore a clean shirt every day.

Railing. Only on account of the cuffs.

Winnie. I wish you'd ask Uncle Tom to give you an introduction to his tailor. I'm sure he'd be delighted.

Railing. Why, what's wrong with the clothes I've got on?

Winnie. They're very nice, but I don't think they're so nice as Uncle Tom's.

Railing. I expect he goes to somebody in Savile Row. I could never afford that.

Winnie. But you wouldn't have to pay. Uncle Tom never pays his tailor. Men don't.

Railing. But I've never owed a penny in my life. That's one thing that mother taught me from the beginning: "Pay as you go," she said. It's one of the best things I ever learned. I bought this suit in the city off the nail.

Winnie. But you couldn't be married in a ready-made suit, Bertram.

Railing. Good gracious me, why not? I'm going to be married in the very suit I've got on. I'll put on a clean shirt if you like.

Winnie. Aunt Sophia said you'd probably go into Parliament after we were married.

Railing. I've got the offer of a Labor seat at the next election. A safe one this time.

Winnie [*tentatively*]. Papa says he'll be able to get you made something.

Railing. What d'you mean?

Winnie. There always are jobs, aren't there, and Papa has a lot of influence with the government.

Railing. But d'you think I'd consent to be made anything?

Winnie. But don't you want to get on? You wouldn't be content to remain a scrubby journalist all your life, would you?

Railing [*kneeling down beside her*]. Oh, my darling, don't you understand? I'm nothing. I'm only an instrument and I'm proud to be an instrument. Whether I'm poor or rich what does it matter? [*He takes her hands and his voice grows extraordinarily caressing.*] In the few years of my life I want to work for my fellows. I want you to work with me. I don't offer you ease and comfort. I offer you poverty and hardship and the weary, weary round of every day. I want you to know the misery of this horrible civilization of ours. The injustice, the cruelty. [*She hangs her head.*] You ask me if I want to get on. And I think of those long processions of the workless. And I see fear in their eyes, the fear of the horrible tomorrow, cold and hungry and hopeless. D'you know that all through the winter nights the bobby walks up and down the embankment to prevent the poor homeless wretches from sleeping in case they freeze to death?

Winnie. Oh, don't, don't.

Railing. I wonder if you ever think of the Nazarene who was the friend of the poor, the outcast, and the leper. Sometimes in a common lodginghouse I see a carpenter out of work, and I wonder. . . . Sometimes I think He looks at me through the eyes of a mason carrying his hod, and sometimes He speaks to me in the humility of the scavenger who sweeps the streets.

Winnie. You make me feel such a cad.

Railing. I don't want to do that.

Winnie. I'm so ashamed. Oh, teach me to be more worthy of you, Bertram.

She bends down and he kisses her on the lips. At the moment CANON SPRATTE *is heard singing.*

Canon.   For I'm no sailor bold.
            And I've never been upon the sea.

[*He comes in joyously.*] Your uncle has just driven up, Winnie.

PONSONBY *comes in and announces* LORD SPRATTE, *who follows on his heels.*

Ponsonby. Lord Spratte.   [*Exit.*

Lord Spratte. How d'you do?

Canon. You remember Mr. Railing, don't you?

Lord Spratte [*shaking hands with him*]. I hear that I have to congratulate you.

Railing. It's very kind of you.

Canon. Sophia will be down in one moment. This is a family party. I've invited you too, Tom.

Lord Spratte. Oh, Lord!

Canon. I don't know why you should say that. I can imagine nothing more charming, nothing more beautiful, and nothing more entertaining.

Lord Spratte. And I always thought you *such* an imaginative fellow.

Winnie. You're not expecting anyone else, Papa?

Canon. I consider it my duty to be as cordial as possible to your future relations, Winnie. I have asked Mrs. Railing to bring her daughter to tea today.

There is a slight pause of embarrassment.

Railing. I owe a great deal to my mother, Canon Spratte. My father died when I was a lad, and it's only by her strength of will and sheer hard work that I've done anything at all.

Canon. I am very anxious to make her acquaintance.

Enter LADY SOPHIA.

Lady Sophia. I've just seen Mrs. Fitzgerald safely off the premises. [*To* LORD SPRATTE.] She wished me to say good-by to you.

Lord Spratte. Nice woman.

Canon. A charming woman. A little worldly perhaps. But a charming woman.

PONSONBY *comes in.*

Ponsonby. Mrs. and Miss Railing.

MRS. RAILING *is short and stout, with a red face and gray hair rather tightly drawn. She wears a shabby crepe bonnet a little on one side, and a black old-fashioned mantle, cotton gloves, and she carries a gloomy and masculine umbrella.* LOUISE RAILING *wears a pince-nez, a sailor hat, and a white blouse with a leather belt and a plain black skirt. She is a determined young woman. She is not only quick to take offense, but she is positively on the lookout for it.*

Canon [*going toward them cordially*]. How d'you do. Mrs. Railing?

Mrs. Railing. Nicely, thank you.

Canon [*to* LOUISE]. How d'you do?

Louise. Quite well, thank you. Hello, Bertram.

Railing. Hello, Louise.

Mrs. Railing. You didn't expect to see us this afternoon, Bertie, I lay.

Lady Sophia. Won't you sit down. Tea will be in in one minute.

Canon. Let me introduce you to my sister, Lady Sophia Spratte . . . Miss Railing, my sister.

Louise. I'm really Miss Louise Railing, you know.

Mrs. Railing. I 'ave two daughters, my lord. But the elder one, Florrie, ain't quite right in her 'ead, and we 'ad to shut her up in a lunatic asylum.

Railing. It was the result of an accident.

Canon. Very sad. Very sad. It's so fortunate you were able to come. In the season one has so many engagements.

Louise. I thought you people in the West End never did anything.

Canon [*smiling*]. The West End has a bad reputation in Peckham Rye.

Louise. Well, I don't know that I can say extra much for the people of Peckham Rye either.

Railing. There's no public spirit amongst them.

Louise. And yet we do all we can. The Radical Association tries to stir them up. We give meetings every week, but they won't come to them.

Lady Sophia. I wonder at that.

Canon. And do you share your brother's talent for oratory?

Louise. Oh, I say a few words now and then.

Mrs. Railing. You should 'ear 'er talk.

Railing. Louise is one of the best speakers in South London.

Louise. Well, I hold with women taking part in everything. I'm a radical from top to toe. I can't stand the sort of woman who sits at home and does nothing but read novels and go to balls. There's an immense field for woman's activities.

Railing. Immense.

Louise. And who thinks now that women are inferior to men?

Mrs. Railing. Ain't she a marvel?

Louise [*remonstrating*]. Ma.

Mrs. Railing. She says I always praise 'er in front of people . . . but I can't 'elp it. You should see all the prizes and certificates she's got. Oh, I am proud of 'er, I can tell you.

Louise. Ma, don't go on like that always. It makes people think I'm a child.

Mrs. Railing. Well, Louie, I can't 'elp it. You are a marvel and there's no denying it. Tell 'em about the gold medal you won.

Lord Spratte. I wish you would. I always respect people with gold medals.

Louise [*smiling*]. Go on with you.

Mrs. Railing. Well, Louie, you are obstinate. She 'as been—ever since she was a child.

PONSONBY *brings in the tea things.* MRS. RAILING *looks round the room, and the* CANON *sees her eyes rest on the portrait of the first Lord Spratte.*

Canon. That is my father, the late Lord Chancellor of England.

Mrs. Railing. It's a very 'andsome frame.

Lord Spratte [*with a guffaw*]. He is plain, isn't he?

Mrs. Railing. Oh, I didn't mean it like that. I would never take such a liberty.

Lord Spratte. Now you can't honestly say he was a beauty.

Canon. Thomas, remember he was my father.

Mrs. Railing. Now I come to look at 'im I don't think he's so bad looking after all.

Lord Spratte. In the family we think he's the very image of my brother Theodore.

Mrs. Railing. Well, now you mention it I do see a likeness.

Canon. My brother is quite a humorist.

He gives MRS. RAILING *a cup of tea and she stirs it meditatingly.*

Mrs. Railing [*to* LADY SOPHIA]. Nice neighborhood, this.

Lady Sophia. South Kensington? It's the least unpleasant of all the suburbs.

Canon. My dear, I cannot allow South Kensington to be called a suburb. It's the very center of London.

Lady Sophia. It always reminds me of the Hamlet who was funny without being vulgar. South Kensington is Bayswater without being funny.

Mrs. Railing. Peckham's a nice neighborhood. You get such a nice class of people there.

Lady Sophia. So I should think.

Mrs. Railing. We've got such a pretty little 'ouse in the Gladstone Road. Of course we 'aven't got electric light, but we've got a lovely bathroom. When we moved in Louie said to me, "Ma," she said, "I can't wait till Saturday, I'm going to 'ave a bath tonight." Bertie takes one every morning.

Canon. Does he indeed?

Mrs. Railing. Yes, and 'e says he couldn't do without it. If he doesn't 'ave it, 'e's uncomfortable all day.

Railing. Mother.

Mrs. Railing. Things 'ave changed since I was a girl. Why, nobody thought of 'aving all these baths then. Now, only the other day I was talking to Mr. Smithers, the builder. You know who I mean, Bertie, don't you?

Railing. Yes, Mother.

Mrs. Railing. And he said to me, "Lor', Mrs. Railing," says he, "people are getting that fussy, if you built 'em a house without a bathroom they wouldn't so much as look at it."

Canon. They say that cleanliness is next to godliness.

Mrs. Railing. There's no denying that, but one 'as to be careful. I've known a rare lot of people catch their death of cold all through 'aving a bath when they wasn't feeling very well.

LORD SPRATTE *has given* LOUISE RAILING *a cup of tea and hands her the sugar.*

Louise. Thanks. No sugar. I think it's weak.

Canon. What, the tea? I'm so sorry.

Mrs. Railing. Oh, Louie, how can you say such a thing. They will think you're rude. You mustn't expect such a strong cup of tea as you get at 'ome. Not the Queen of England could make a better cup of tea than this.

Louise. I didn't mean that, Ma. I meant taking sugar was weak. I won't approve of hydrocarbons.

Lord Spratte. Rough on the hydrocarbons, ain't it?

Mrs. Railing. Don't mind 'er, my lord. It's only one of 'er fads. They're full of them, Bertie and Louie are. Sometimes they just about give me the 'ump. I can tell you.

Louise. Ma, do mind what you're saying.

Mrs. Railing. Well, you do, Louie—that is Louise. She don't like me to call her Louie. She says it's so common. You know, me lord, my children was christened Bertram and Louise; but we've always called them Bertie and Louie, and I can't get out of the 'abit of it now. But, lor' when your children grow up and get on in the world they want to turn everything upside down. Now what do you think Bertie wants me to do?

Canon. I can't imagine.

Mrs. Railing. Well, would you believe it, he wants me to take the pledge.

Railing. Mother!

Mrs. Railing. Well, look 'ere, me lord, what I say is, I'm an 'ard workin' woman, and what with the work I do, I want my little drop of beer now and then. The Captain—my 'usband, that is—'ad a little bit put by, but I 'ad to work to make both ends meet when I was left a widow, I can tell you. And I've given my children a thorough good education.

Canon. You have reason to be proud of them. I don't suppose my little girl has half the knowledge of Miss Louise.

Louise. That's your fault. Blame nobody but yourself for that. That's because you've not educated her properly. I hold with the higher education of women. I always have. But there's no education in the West End. I always said so. Now, if I had charge of your daughter for six months I could make a different woman of her.

Mrs. Railing. Ain't she wonderful. I can sit listening to 'er talking for hours at a time.

Canon. Except on the subject of teetotalism?

Mrs. Railing [*with a hearty laugh*]. You're right there, me lord. What I say is, I'm an 'ard working woman. . . .

Canon. And you want your little drop of beer, I know, I know. I was discussing that matter the other day with the lady who does me the honor to clean out my church, and she expressed herself in the same manner. But she rather favored spirits, I understand.

Mrs. Railing. Oh, I never take spirits.

Canon. What, never?

Mrs. Railing [*her face beaming*]. Well, 'ardly ever.

Canon. Capital! Capital!

Mrs. Railing. Now don't you laugh at me. The fact is, I sometimes 'ave a little drop in my tea.

Canon. Bless me, why didn't you say so? Winnie, you really ought to have told me. . . . Ring the bell, will you?

Mrs. Railing. Oh, I didn't mean it like that, me lord.

Canon. My dear lady. What is it you take? Rum?

Mrs. Railing [*making a face*]. Oh, I can't bear it.

Canon. Whisky?

Mrs. Railing. Oh, no, me lord. I wouldn't touch it if I was paid.

Canon. Gin?

Mrs. Railing [*with a broad smile*]. Call it white satin, me lord.

Canon. White satin?

Mrs. Railing. It's a funny thing now, but rum never 'as agreed with me. An' it's wholesome stuff, you know.

Canon. I have no doubt.

Mrs. Railing. The last time I 'ad a little drop—oh, I was queer. Now, my friend, Mrs. Cooper, can't touch anything else.

Canon. Come, come, that's very strange.

Mrs. Railing. You don't know Mrs. Cooper, do you? Oh, she's such a nice woman. And she's got such a dear little 'ouse in Shepherd's Bush.

Canon. A salubrious neighborhood, I believe.

Mrs. Railing. Oh, yes, the tube 'as made a great difference to it. You ought to know Mrs. Cooper. Oh, she's a nice woman and a thorough lady. No one can say a word against 'er, I don't care who it is.

Louise. Ma!

Mrs. Railing. Well, they do say she takes a little drop too much now and then. But I've never seen 'er with more than she could carry.

Canon. Really!

Mrs. Railing. Oh, I don't approve of taking more than you can carry. My motto is strict moderation. But as Mrs. Cooper was saying to me only the other day, "Mrs. Railing," she said, "with all the trouble I've gone through, I tell you, speaking as one lady to another, I don't know what I should do without a little drop of rum." And she 'as 'ad a rare lot of trouble. There's no denying it.

Canon. Poor soul, poor soul!

Mrs. Railing. Oh, a rare lot of trouble. Now, you know it's funny 'ow people differ. Mrs. Cooper said to me, "Mrs. Railing," she said, "I give you my word of honor I can't touch white satin. It 'as such an effect on me that I don't know whether I'm standing on my head or on me 'eels." So I said to 'er, "Mrs. Cooper," I said, "you're quite right not to touch it." Now wasn't I right, me lord.

Canon. Oh, perfectly! I think you gave her the soundest possible advice.

Enter PONSONBY.

Canon. Ponsonby, have we any—white satin in the house?

Mrs. Railing. I 'ave 'eard it called satinette.

PONSONBY'S *fishlike eyes travel slowly from the* CANON *to the stout lady, and he blinks when he catches sight of the rakish cock of her crepe bonnet.*

Ponsonby. White satin, sir? I'll inquire.

Canon [*unmoved*]. Or satinette? [PONSONBY *looks at the* CANON *with an air of perplexity.*] Perhaps Ponsonby does not quite understand. I mean, have we any gin in the house?

Ponsonby. Gin, sir? No, sir.

Canon. Is there none in the servants' hall?

Ponsonby. Oh, no, sir.

Canon. How careless of me. You ought to have reminded

me that there was no gin in the house, Sophia. Well, Ponsonby, will you go and get sixpenny worth at the nearest public house?

Mrs. Railing. Oh, no, don't send out for it. I could never forgive myself.

Canon. But I assure you it's no trouble at all. And I should very much like to taste it.

Mrs. Railing. Oh, well then, threepenny worth is ample.

Railing. You're very much better without it, Mother.

Canon. Come, come, you mustn't grudge your mother a little treat now and then.

Mrs. Railing. And it's a real treat for me, I can tell you.

Canon. Threepenny worth of gin, Ponsonby.

Ponsonby. Yes, sir.   [*Exit.*

Mrs. Railing. You don't 'ave to go far in London to find a public 'ouse, do you?

Lord Spratte. The only reason for which I inhabit the metropolis.

Louise [*pouncing on him*]. May I ask if you have ever studied the teetotal question?

Lord Spratte. Not I!

Louise. And you're a hereditary legislator?

Lord Spratte. At the moment.

Louise. I should just like to have a few words with you about the House of Lords. I'm a radical and a Home Ruler. The House of Lords must go.

Lord Spratte. Bless you, I'll part from it without a tear.

Louise. I've been looking for this opportunity for some time. Will you be so good as to tell me what moral right you have to rule over me?

Lord Spratte [*deprecatingly*]. My dear lady, if I rule over you it is entirely unawares.

Louise. I'm not concerned with you personally. To you as an individual I am absolutely indifferent.

Lord Spratte. Don't say that. Why should you ruthlessly crush my self-esteem?

Louise. I wish to discuss the matter with you as a member of a privileged class. Now, so far as I can see, you are utterly ignorant of all the great social questions of the day.

Lord Spratte. Utterly.

Louise. Can you give me three reasons in favor of protection?

Lord Spratte. I confess I can't, but then I happen to be a free trader.

Louise. What do you know about the housing of the working classes?

Lord Spratte. Nothing.

Louise. What do you know about secondary education?

Lord Spratte. Nothing.

Louise. What do you know about the taxation of ground rents?

Lord Spratte. Nothing.

Louise. And yet you are a member of the Upper Chamber. Just because you're a lord you have power to legislate over millions of people with ten times more knowledge, more ability, and more education than yourself.

Canon. Capital. Capital. You rub it in. A good straight talking to is just what he wants.

Mrs. Railing. When you once get Louie going, not wild horses will stop her.

Louise. And how do you spend your time I should like to know. Do you study the questions of the hour?

Lady Sophia and Canon. No.

Louise. Do you attempt to fit yourself for the task entrusted to you by the anachronism of a past age?

Lady Sophia and Canon. No.

Lord Spratte. I wish you'd put that umbrella down, it makes me quite nervous.

Louise [*angrily throwing her umbrella on the floor*]. I'll be bound you spend your days in every form of degrading pursuit. At race meetings, billiards, and gambling.

Canon. Capital, capital!

Lord Spratte. In point of fact, I'm much too poor to gamble, I always get rheumatism at race meetings, and I've never played billiards in my life.

Canon. You *are* a radical, aren't you?

Louise. I should like you to know that a radical government poured filthy muck down my nostrils for three days in Pentonville prison.

PONSONBY *comes in, bearing a large tray and small liqueur bottle.*

Canon. Ah, here is the gin.

Mrs. Railing. Oh, me lord, don't call it gin. It sounds so vulgar. When my poor 'usband was alive I used to say to 'im, "Captain, I won't have it called gin in my 'ouse." I always used to call my 'usband the captain, although he was only first mate. I wish you could 'ave seen 'im. If anyone 'ad said to me, "Mrs. Railing, put your 'and on a fine, 'andsome, 'ealthy man," I should 'ave put my 'and on James Samuel Railing. And would you believe it, before he was thirty-five he was dead.

Canon. How very sad.

Mrs. Railing. Oh, and he was a dreadful sight before the end. You should have seen his legs.

Louise. Ma.

Mrs. Railing. Leave me alone, Louie; you're always naggin'.

Louise. No, I'm not, Ma.

Mrs. Railing. Don't contradict, Louie. I won't 'ave it.

Canon. Won't you have a little more—white satin?

Mrs. Railing. No, thank you, me lord. I don't think I could stand it. You made the first dose rather strong and we've got to get home, you know.

Louise. I think we ought to be trotting, Ma.

Mrs. Railing. P'raps we ought. We've got a long way to go.

Louise. We'd better take the train, Ma.

Mrs. Railing. Oh, let's go in a bus, my dear. I like riding in buses, the conductors are so good-looking and such gentlemen. Why, the other day I got into conversation with the conductor, and would you believe it, he made me drink a drop of beer with 'im at the end of the journey. Oh, he was a nice young man.

Railing. You oughtn't to have done that, Mother.

Mrs. Railing. Well, my dear, so 'e was. And 'e's none the worse for being a bus conductor. They earn very good money, and he told me he was a married man, so I don't see no 'arm in it.

Louise. Come on, Ma, or we shall never get off.

Mrs. Railing. Well, good-by, me lord, and thank you.

Canon. So kind of you to come all this way. We've thoroughly enjoyed your visit.

There are general farewells and the RAILINGS *go out.*

For a moment there is a complete silence. LADY SOPHIA, SPRATTE, *and the* CANON *look at* WINNIE. *She stares straight in front of her.*

Canon [*softly*]. For I'm no sailor bold.
    And I've never been upon the sea,
      And if I fell therein,
      It's a fact I couldn't swim,
    And quickly at the bottom I should be.

With a sudden stifled sob WINNIE *goes quickly out of the room.*

Lady Sophia. You brute, Theodore.

Canon. Sophia, just write a note to Wroxham and ask him to come to tea tomorrow.

Curtain.

ACT FOUR

The scene is the same as in the preceding acts.

When the curtain rises LIONEL *is discovered sitting in an armchair with his feet on the chimney piece. He is reading a book. The* CANON *comes in and rings the bell.*

CANON. You seem to be taking things easily, Lionel.

Lionel. I'm doing my little best not to get overtired.

Canon. What is the book on which you have been improving your mind?

Lionel. Oh, it's a detective story. It came from Mudie's the other day.

PONSONBY *enters.*

Canon. Has Lord Wroxham been here today, Ponsonby?

Ponsonby. No, sir.

Canon. That's strange. I rather thought he was coming to tea. Is Miss Winnie at home?

Ponsonby. Yes, sir.

Canon. All right. That'll do.

Ponsonby. Very good, sir.   [*Exit.*

Canon. I ran up against the Bishop at the Athenaeum after lunch today.

Lionel. Did you?

Canon. There's been no confirmation of that announcement that Gray had been appointed to Colchester.

Lionel. I wonder if there's been some hitch.

Canon. I shouldn't be altogether surprised if Gray refused. When a man is still young and vigorous I can imagine no position with greater opportunities for good than the head-mastership of a great public school.

Lionel [*yawning*]. Yes, Father.

Canon. I wish to goodness you wouldn't yawn when I talk to you, Lionel.

Lionel. Sorry, Governor.

Canon. Most people find my conversation entertaining rather than otherwise. You've done nothing all day . . .

Lionel. I took a wedding this afternoon.

Canon. I haven't been at all satisfied with you of late, Lionel. You seem to show no keenness in your work. You're so phlegmatic. Now that the armies of dissent surround us on every side we must be up and doing, my dear boy. You take things too easily. You haven't got any push. Now look at me. Surely I give you an example of energy and strenuousness which you would do well to follow.

Lionel. I don't know what you've got to complain about in particular.

Canon. Good heavens, surely you can occupy your time better than by reading trashy novels. If you have nothing better to do why don't you take down a volume of sermons and see whether you can't improve yours a little. I assure you there's room for it.

Lionel. Reading sermons isn't a very cheerful occupation, Father.

Canon. They're not written with the object of making you laugh through a horse collar. And there's something else I wish to speak to you about.

Lionel. I suppose it's best to get it all over at once.

Canon. I want to know for good and all what you propose to do about Gwendolen. I think you've shilly-shallied long enough.

Lionel. What are you talking about now, Father?

Canon. Good Lord, man, you're not a perfect idiot. We've discussed your marriage *ad nauseam.* I want to know what your intentions are.

Lionel. I thought it was only one's prospective mother-in-law who asked one that.

Canon. It's not fair to the girl to keep her dangling in this fashion. Are you going to marry her or not?

Lionel. Well, Father, there's no hurry about it.

Canon. On the contrary, there's the greatest possible hurry.

Lionel. Why?

Canon. I have every reason to believe that someone else is thinking of proposing to her.

Lionel. Who?

Canon. I prefer not to say.

Lionel [*rather sulkily*]. Well, I don't think she cares two-pence about me. Lately when I've seen her she's talked of nothing but you.

Canon [*smiling*]. There *are* less diverting topics of conversation.

Lionel. One can have too much of a good thing.

Canon. Well, I warn you candidly. If you don't look sharp someone else will step in and cut you out.

Lionel. I shan't break my heart, Father.

Canon. I don't know what the young men of the present day are coming to. They have no enterprise. Gwendolen is one of the most charming girls I have ever met. She's extremely pretty, her fortune is considerable, and she has a thoroughly nice nature. Anyhow, I've done my duty and you mustn't be surprised whatever happens.

Lionel. You're not thinking of marrying her yourself, Governor?

Canon [*with some asperity*]. And would you have anything to say against my doing so?

Lionel. Well, she's a good deal younger than you.

Canon. Let me tell you, my boy, that a man of fifty is in the very flower of his age. I flatter myself there are few men of your years who have half the vigor and energy that I have.

Lionel [*looking at his watch*]. Well, I think I'll go and dress for dinner.

Canon [*sarcastically, still rather ruffled*]. Do. It generally takes you an hour and a half.

Exit LIONEL.

CANON SPRATTE *touches the bell. He walks to the window and looks out.* PONSONBY *comes in.*

Canon. Oh, Ponsonby, Lady Sophia is at home to no one but Lord Wroxham.

Ponson. Very good, sir.

Canon [*as* PONSONBY *is leaving the room*]. Oh, and—when his lordship has been here a moment or two, I wish you to call me away.

Ponsonby. Very good, sir.

As PONSONBY *leaves the room he winks solemnly at the portrait of the first Earl Spratte.*

Enter WINNIE.

Canon. Well, darling, what have you been doing this afternoon?

Winnie. I haven't been doing anything. I've been resting.

Canon. Dear me, did you have a very strenuous morning?

Winnie. No, I didn't do anything this morning.

Canon. How is Mr. Railing today?

Winnie. I've not seen him. He was too busy. But he's coming round for a few minutes before dinner on his way to some meeting he's going to speak at.

PONSONBY *comes in and announces* WROXHAM, *who enters immediately afterward.*

Ponsonby. Lord Wroxham.

Canon. Ah, my dear boy, I'm so pleased to see you.

Wroxham [*giving his hand to* WINNIE]. You must think me a dreadful bore. I'm always coming.

Canon. Nonsense. We're always delighted to see you. I want you to look upon the vicarage as your second home.

Wroxham. Lady Sophia very kindly asked me to tea, but I couldn't get away. I thought you wouldn't mind if I looked in for half a minute on my way home. My mother wanted to know if Winnie would come to the opera with us tomorrow.

Canon. I'm sure she'll be delighted.

Winnie. It's very kind of you to think of me.

Enter PONSONBY.

Ponsonby. There's a party wishes to see you, sir, if it wouldn't be troubling you.

Canon. Tut, tut, tut. I can't see anybody at this hour. I'm just going to dress for dinner.

Ponsonby. The party said she'd look upon it as a great favor if you could spare her five minutes.

Canon. Oh, well, I suppose I shall have to go down. [*To* WROXHAM.] I must ask you to excuse me for a few minutes.

Wroxham. Oh, pray don't mind me.

Canon. It's really too tiresome.

He goes out, followed by PONSONBY.

Wroxham. What a piece of luck!

Winnie. Why?

Wroxham. I so seldom get a chance of speaking to you. [WINNIE *does not reply, but, in a certain embarrassment, pulls to pieces a marguerite.*] What does it come to?

Winnie [*with a smile, holding out the flower with one petal still remaining on it*]. He loves me not.

Wroxham. It's not true. He loves you passionately. He always will. Don't be angry with me for saying so.

Winnie. I'm not angry. I think I like it.

Wroxham. Winnie!

Winnie. I'm so miserable. I want someone so badly to care for me.

Wroxham. Why don't you tell me what's the matter? I may be able to do something.

Winnie. It is kind of you to be nice to me. You're so much nicer than I ever thought you.

Wroxham. Winnie, won't you say you love me?

Winnie. Do you remember when I first saw you? You came with Lionel from Eton to spend a week with us. And you used to get so angry when I beat you at tennis.

Wroxham. Oh, you never did—except when I let you.

Winnie. You used to punt me up the river, and I remember how frightened I was when you fell in.

Wroxham. Oh, you fibber. You shrieked and roared with laughter.

Winnie [*with a sigh*]. I'm so tired. I've had such an exhausting day.

She sits down and he seats himself beside her.

Wroxham. What ripping days those were. And I was so unhappy. You used to make me frightfully jealous by talking to other little boys.

Winnie. I wonder when you first began to like me.

Wroxham. I've never liked you. I've loved you always.

Winnie. Even when I wore a pigtail and square-toed boots?

Wroxham. Always. And I always shall.

Winnie. Harry, you don't think my mind wants widening, do you? And you don't think my character stands in need of strengthening?

Wroxham [*surprised*]. No. Why?

Winnie. Oh, I only wanted to know.

Wroxham. Winnie, you didn't mean it when you said you couldn't love me?

Winnie. I don't quite remember. I don't think I could have.

Wroxham. Winnie. You're going to marry me? Oh, Winnie.

Winnie. I'll do anything to make you happy.

Blushing, she turns her lips to him, and he kisses her passionately. The CANON's *voice is heard outside.*

Canon. La donna è mobile. Tra-la-la-la-la-la.

He comes in and gives a slight start when he sees the young couple sitting together on the sofa.

Canon. Hello, I thought you must have gone. I was detained longer than I expected.

Wroxham [*to* WINNIE]. May I tell him?

Winnie [*smiling*]. Yes.

Wroxham. Canon Spratte, I want to tell you that Winnie has just promised to be my wife.

Canon. What! Capital! Capital! My dear fellow, I'm delighted to hear it. My dear child! [*He opens his arms and* WINNIE *hides her face in his bosom. He kisses her affection-*

ately, then shakes hands with WROXHAM.] I knew she was devoted to you, my boy. Trust me for knowing a woman's character.

Winnie [*with a laugh, stretching out her hand to* WROXHAM]. Papa's wonderful.

Wroxham. You've made me very happy.

Canon. Now, my dear boy, you must go and tell Sophia. You'll find her in her boudoir.

Wroxham. I?

Canon. You know she's rather touchy. I think you ought to tell her yourself.

Wroxham. And Winnie?

Canon. Winnie and I will follow you in a minute.

Wroxham. I go like a lamb to the slaughter.

He goes, with a smile to WINNIE, *and she kisses her fingers to him as he disappears through the inner room.*

CANON SPRATTE *looks at his daughter with an expression of great amusement. She turns away and, still standing, begins to turn over the pages of a book.*

Canon. Would it be indiscreet, dear Winnie, to inquire when you broke off your engagement with Mr. Railing?

Winnie [*looking up*]. I haven't broken it off.

Canon [*in tones of mild interrogation*]. And do you intend to marry them both?

Winnie. Oh, Papa, you must help me. I'm simply distracted.

Canon. Do I understand that the fact that Mrs. Railing drops her aitches and drinks gin, while her daughter is bumptious and vulgar, has had any effect upon your attachment to Mr. Bertram Railing?

Winnie. D'you think I'm an awful snob, Father?

Canon. Of course you're a snob, my dear, but I would not have you anything else. I do not share the vulgar contempt for the most valuable quality of the Anglo-Saxon race. Snobbishness has made us not only a great nation, but a Christian nation, for snobbishness is no more than a desire to improve our position, first in this world and then in the next. I cannot help thinking that if I had possessed a particle of it myself I should not now be languishing in obscurity.

Winnie [*going on with her own reflections*]. I've made such a fool of myself. He took me unawares, and I thought for a moment that I could live his life. But I'm frightened of him.

Canon [*gravely*]. One thing I insist upon knowing, Winnie. Which do you honestly prefer?

WINNIE *hesitates for a moment. Then she gives a little stifled sob.*

Winnie. That's just it. I love them both.

Canon [*astounded*]. What!

Winnie. When I'm with one I think he's so much nicer than the other.

Canon [*much annoyed*]. Really, Winnie, you can't shilly-shally in this way.

Winnie. When I see Bertram I'm simply carried away. I'm filled with high and noble thoughts. But I can't live up to his ideal. He doesn't love the woman I am, he loves the woman I may become. You see, Bertram's a hero.

Canon [*irritably*]. Fiddlededee! He's a journalist.

Winnie. But Harry doesn't want me any different from what I am. He loves me for myself. He doesn't think I have any faults . . .

Canon [*interrupting*]. Really, Winnie, I don't think it's quite nice for a girl of your age to analyze her feelings in this way. I hate people who can't make up their minds.

Winnie. Oh, but I know quite well which I want to marry.

Canon [*relenting*]. Oh, well, I suppose that is the chief thing.

Winnie. You will get me out of the scrape, Father?

Canon. You see, your poor old father is still some use after all. What do you wish me to do, my child?

Winnie. When Bertram comes, I want you to tell him it's all a mistake and I can't marry him.

Canon. He won't take it from me.

Winnie. I daren't see him again. I should be so ashamed.

PONSONBY *comes in.*

Ponsonby. Mr. Railing, sir. I said her ladyship was not at home . . .

Canon [*interrupting* PONSONBY's *explanations*]. Oh, yes, ask him to come up.

Ponsonby. Very good, sir.   [*Exit.*

Canon [*to* WINNIE, *quickly*]. Wait in the next room.

WINNIE *slips out of the room just before* RAILING *enters it.*

Ponsonby. Mr. Railing.

The CANON *goes up to him with every appearance of cordiality.* RAILING *has in his hands a bunch of roses. He puts them down.*

Canon. How d'you do. How good of you to look in so late, dear Railing.

Railing. Winnie told me she'd be at home this afternoon.

Canon. Of course, I didn't flatter myself you'd come to see me, but it so happens that I've been wanting to have a little chat with you.

Railing. I'm at your service.

Canon [*gaily*]. It's a very serious step that you young folks are taking.

Railing. Then we're wise to take it with a light heart.

Canon. Ha, ha—capital. Now, I should have thought you were both very young to be married.

Railing. I'm twenty-five, sir, and Winnie is twenty-one.

Canon. I need not tell you that I have the highest esteem for you personally, and the sincerest admiration for your talents. But we live in an age when talent is not always rewarded according to its merits, and I am curious to know upon what you propose to live.

Railing. I make about two hundred and fifty a year, and Winnie has about a hundred and fifty from her mother.

Canon. You're very well informed.

Railing. Winnie told me.

Canon. Obviously. I didn't for a moment suppose that you had examined the will at Somerset House. And do you imagine that Winnie will be content to live on four hundred a year?

Railing. It's three times as much as my mother ever had.

Canon [*very politely*]. What has that got to do with it?

Railing. Do you think your daughter cares two straws for the gewgaws and the tawdry trappings of society?

Canon. I think my daughter is human, Mr. Railing, and although it may surprise you I will confess that I think an electric brougham essential to her happiness.

Railing. I know Winnie, and I love her. You think she's a doll and a fool. She was. I've made her into a woman of flesh and blood. She's a real woman now and she loathes all the shams and the shallowness of society.

Canon. She told you that, did she? Upon my word, we Sprattes *have* a sense of humor.

Railing. Thank God, she knows now how narrow this little circle is of idle, selfish people. She wants to work. She wants to labor with her fellow men, shoulder to shoulder, fighting the good fight.

Canon. And do you think, my dear young man, that it would ever have occurred to Winnie that the world was hollow and foolish if you had a wart on the tip of your tongue or a squint in your eye?

Railing. You believe that all people are bad.

Canon. On the contrary, I'm so charitable as to think them merely foolish.

Railing [*beginning to lose his temper*]. What are you driving at? Why don't you say it out like a man instead of beating about the bush?

Canon. My dear Mr. Railing, I must beg you to observe the conventions of polite society. It is clearly my duty to inquire into the circumstances of any young man who proposes to marry my daughter.

Railing. I distrusted you when I heard you agreed to our engagement. I knew you despised me. I knew that all your flattery was humbug.

Canon [*blandly*]. I am sure that when you are calmer you will regret some of the expressions that you have seen fit to use. But I will tell you at once that I bear you absolutely no ill will on their account.

Railing. I'm much obliged to you but I'm not aware that I've used any expression which I'm in the least likely to regret.

Canon. Then if I may say so, as a man much older than yourself, and as a clergyman, you show both your want of Christian charity and your ignorance of social amenities.

Railing. D'you want me to understand that you withdraw the consent which you gave two days ago?

Canon. It has come to my knowledge that your eldest sister is in a lunatic asylum. I need not tell you that I regret this misfortune, but my views on the subject are very decided.

Railing [*interrupting*]. That's absurd. Florrie had an accident when she was a child. She fell downstairs, and since then she's been . . .

Canon. Not quite right in her head as your mother expressed it, Mr. Railing, I should like you to observe, however, that every child falls downstairs, and the entire human race is not so imbecile as to need the restraint of a lunatic asylum.

Railing. The fact remains that Winnie loves me.

Canon. Are you quite sure of that?

Railing. As sure as I am of my own name and my own life.

Canon. Well, it is my painful duty to inform you that you are mistaken. Winnie recognizes that she misjudged the strength of her affection.

Railing. Rot!

Canon. She has asked me to tell you that she finds she does not care for you enough to marry you. She regrets the unhappiness that she has caused and begs you to release her.

Railing. It's not true.

Canon. On my honor as a gentleman, I have told you the exact truth.

Railing. Then let her tell me so herself.

Canon. I think it would be better for both of you if you did not meet again.

Railing. I must see her. I won't go till I see her. I tell you I won't go.

The CANON *hesitates for a moment, then shrugs his shoulders. He goes to the inner room, opens the door, and calls.*

Canon. Winnie. [*There is a moment's pause and then* WINNIE *enters.*] I wished to spare you both a painful scene, but Mr. Railing insists on seeing you.

Railing. It's not true, Winnie?

Winnie. I'm very sorry.

Railing [*to* CANON SPRATTE]. Please leave us alone . . . [*As he sees that the* CANON *is about to refuse.*] Surely you can't grudge me that.

Canon. I'll wait in the next room.

He goes into the inner drawing room.

RAILING *catches sight of the roses he brought with him and hands them to* WINNIE.

Railing. I brought you some flowers, Winnie.

Winnie. It's very kind of you.

He looks at her for a moment. She keeps her eyes averted.

Railing. The other day you said you loved me better than anyone in the whole world. What have they done to turn you against me?

Winnie. No one has done anything.

Railing. And yet, suddenly, with nothing to explain it you send your father to say you've made a mistake.

Winnie. I'm awfully sorry for all the pain I've caused you.

Railing. Are you afraid because I'm poor and nobody in particular? But you knew that before. How can you sacrifice all that we planned so joyfully, the life of labor shoulder to shoulder and the fine struggle for our fellows.

Winnie. I should hate it.

Railing. Winnie!

Winnie. Oh, Bertram, try to understand. I want you to see that we made a dreadful mistake. Thank heaven we discovered it before it was too late. I'm not made for the life you want me to lead. I should be utterly out of it.

Railing. But why? Why?

Winnie. It was only a pose when I enthused about labor and temperance. I wanted you to think me clever and original. I don't like the poor. I don't want to have anything to do with them. I dare say poverty and crime are very dreadful, but I want to shut my eyes and forget them. I hate grime and dirt. I think the slums are horrible. Can't you see how awful it would be if we married? I should only hamper you, and we'd both be utterly wretched.

Railing. Your father said an electric brougham was essential to your happiness. You can't mind whether you go on foot or in a gaudy carriage. Life is so full and there's so much to do. What can it matter so long as we do our duty?

Winnie. But I don't want to do my duty. I want to be happy.

Railing. Have you no care for humanity?

Winnie. Humanity? I'm awfully sorry, but I think I cared less for humanity after you showed me how your cuffs took off.

Railing. Oh! How can you be so flippant! You're all the same, all of you, trivial, petty, frivolous.

Winnie. It's not just one act of heroism that it needs. It's strength to be heroic day after day in a dull, sordid fashion. And there can never be any escape from it. One has to make up one's mind that it'll last forever. I see myself living in a shabby house in a horrid pokey street, and having Socialists to high tea. And I could almost scream.

Railing. It's all so small.

Winnie. It's all very fine for you to talk. You've been brought up without luxury, and of course you don't miss it. You think it's very easy for me to do housework and mend linen as your mother does, but d'you think it's any easier than it would be for you who've worked with your brains to mend roads from morning till night?

Before he can answer WROXHAM's *voice is heard in the inner room, and immediately afterward he comes in impetuously, followed by the* CANON.

Wroxham. Oh, there you are, Canon. Where's Winnie . . . I've done the deed, Winnie. I told her and we fell upon one another's necks. [*Seeing* RAILING.] Oh, I'm sorry. I thought you were alone. Why, it's Mr. Railing. How d'you do?

Railing [*shaking hands*]. How d'you do?

Canon. I had no idea that you knew one another.

Wroxham. Oh, yes. I was chairman at a meeting Mr. Railing

spoke at the other day. By the way, I've been reading your book.

Canon. Yes, it's a capital book. I've always thought so, my dear Railing. I'm proud to say I was among the first to discern its striking merit.

Wroxham [*to* WINNIE]. I say, Lady Sophia wants to take you to her bosom. She's awfully bucked.

RAILING *gives a slight start and looks sharply at* WROXHAM.

Canon. I remember you told us how deeply it had impressed the Duchess of St. Ermyns. I'm sure you'll be glad to hear that the Princess of Wartburg-Hochstein found it most readable.

RAILING *takes no notice, but watches* WINNIE *and* WROXHAM *suspiciously.* WROXHAM *has gone up to* WINNIE *and is smiling at her happily.*

Wroxham. Lady Sophia has asked me to dine. I must bolt off and dress.

Canon. Oh, yes, yes! We shall be delighted to have you. [*Looking at his watch.*] It must be getting late. I don't want to hurry you, but our cook is a great stickler for punctuality. What do you make the time, Mr. Railing?

Railing. Five minutes to eight.

Canon. Dear me, I had no idea it was so late.

Wroxham. Oh, it'll only take me ten minutes to get my things on . . . what are you going to wear tonight, Winnie? I want to bring you some roses.

Winnie. Yes, do—red ones. I have no flowers to wear.

Railing. Have you already forgotten mine?

Winnie. Oh!

Canon [*coming to the rescue*]. No, no. Of course she hasn't. But yours are so beautiful it would be a pity to wear them. They die so quickly. We must have them put in water, darling.

Wroxham [*smiling at the* CANON'S *deftness*]. You must come in to Lady Sophia for just one moment. You know what people are on these occasions.

Canon. Yes, go along, both of you. And I shall finish what I had to say to Mr. Railing. [*To* RAILING.] So sorry to delay you, my dear friend. You must be in a hurry to get off.

Railing. My business is with Winnie. Lord Wroxham won't mind waiting a moment or two.

Canon. Perhaps you'll continue your conversation some other time, Mr. Railing. I'm afraid it's getting very late.

Railing. Do you wish me to explain the circumstances to Lord Wroxham?

Canon. Oh, I think that's quite unnecessary. Come, come, Mr. Railing, don't be childish. In this world we must all bow to the inevitable.

Wroxham. You're all very mysterious.

Winnie [*rather frightened*]. Let's go into the others. I have nothing more to say to Mr. Railing.

Railing. But I have a great deal more to say to you. [*To* Lord Wroxham.] Please leave us alone. I'm sorry to appear rude.

Canon. I think you had better leave us, Wroxham. I will explain all this nonsense to you later.

Railing. You call it nonsense, do you?

Wroxham. Very well. I'll go home and dress. My mother will be so pleased.

He goes out.

Canon. Upon my word, Mr. Railing, your behavior is very extraordinary. I think after all I've done for you I have the right to expect a little gratitude.

Railing *in perplexity looks after* Lord Wroxham.

Railing. What did he mean by all those things he said? Why should he bring you flowers . . . ? Oh!

The truth dawns upon him, and he stalks toward the door as if he is going to follow Wroxham. Canon Spratte *gets in the way.*

Canon. Where are you going? I think you forget yourself, Mr. Railing.

Railing [*turning to* Winnie]. Are you engaged to Lord Wroxham, too?

Canon. I consider that a very impertinent question.

Railing. For heaven's sake let me alone. [*To* Winnie.] Tell me. I insist on your answering.

Canon. Upon my word, this is too much. I really wonder why I don't kick you downstairs.

Railing. Perhaps because I'm a working man and horny-handed.

Canon. It evidently hasn't occurred to you that the manners of Peckham Rye are not altogether suited to South Kensington.

Railing [*to* Winnie]. Are you engaged to that man?

Winnie [*after a moment's hesitation*]. I need make no secret of it.

Railing. That's why you threw me over. You got an offer that was too good to refuse.

Canon. Really, Mr. Railing. I cannot allow you to insult my daughter. You will have the goodness to go, or I shall have to call the servants.

Railing. What do you think Lord Wroxham would say if I told him that at the very moment your daughter accepted him she was engaged to me?

Canon [*with a thin smile*]. I should consider myself justified under the circumstances in denying the accuracy of your statement.

Railing [*looks at her for a moment with all the scorn he can command*]. Oh, what an escape I've had! I might have degraded myself so far as to marry a lady.

He flounces out of the room and slams the door behind him.

Canon. How stagy. How abominably stagy.

Winnie. How vulgar.

Canon. I hope this will be a warning and a lesson to you, my child. You see what comes of disobeying your parents, and setting yourself irreligiously against their better judgment. Never forget that you almost made it necessary for your father to tell a lie.

Winnie [*nervous and ill at ease*]. Oughtn't I to make a clean breast of it, Papa?

Canon. To Wroxham? I forbid you to do anything of the sort. And I hope you have been sufficiently punished for your willful disobedience to obey me now. Wroxham is very susceptible and it's your duty to give him no anxiety. And whatever you do, don't begin your married life by confessing everything to your husband. One can never tell the whole truth and it leads to endless deception.

Winnie. But suppose he finds out?

Canon [*infinitely relieved*]. Oh, is that all? I thought it was the voice of conscience, and it's only the fear of detection. Leave it to me. I'll tell him all that's necessary for him to know. And now, darling, we must both go and dress.

Winnie. All right, Father.

She gives him a kiss and runs off.

He is just going to follow when PONSONBY *enters to announce* GWENDOLEN DURANT. *She comes in. She is in evening dress.*

Ponsonby. Miss Durant. [*Exit.*

Gwendolen [*with girlish impulsiveness*]. Oh, don't be angry with me. I know I'm much too early.

Canon [*gallantly*]. You're never too early.

Gwendolen. I thought dinner was at eight, and when Ponsonby told me it was at a quarter past, the car had gone so I couldn't go away again.

Canon. I look upon it as a merciful dispensation of Providence. I shall have five minutes of your society without anyone to interfere.

Gwendolen. Oh, but you mustn't let me bother you. I've sent up to ask Winnie if I can go and sit with her while she's dressing.

Canon. I refuse to be dismissed so cavalierly. I insist first of all on telling you how perfectly ravishing you look tonight.

Gwendolen. I always put on my best frock when I come here.

Canon. I wish I could think you did it because of a middle-aged clerical gentleman with rapidly silvering hair.

Gwendolen. I like you to think me pretty.

Canon [*smiling*]. Do you?

Gwendolen. When I'm looking my best you always tell me so, and, of course, I try to look my best.

Canon. You make me regret more than ever that I'm not twenty-five.

Gwendolen. Why?

Canon. Because if I were I should promptly ask you to marry me.

Gwendolen. If you were I should probably refuse you.

Canon. I wonder what you mean by that?

Gwendolen. It's almost distressingly clear.

Canon. Gwendolen!

Gwendolen. I wonder if Winnie would mind my going up to her room.

Canon. I suppose it never struck you that I took more than common pleasure in your conversation.

Gwendolen. I only know that I've never met anyone who's so delightful to talk to as you.

Canon. My heart has remained as young as ever, but I'm fifty, Gwendolen. Fifty!

Gwendolen. I never asked myself what your age was. I never felt that you were any older than I.

Canon. Gwendolen, by your side I feel as young as the summer morning. What can the years matter when I have the spirit of a boy? I admire you and I love you. Don't think me too absurd.

Gwendolen. I don't think you at all absurd.

Canon. Gwendolen, will you be my wife?

Gwendolen [*smiling*]. What about Lionel?

Canon. Oh, Lionel can go to the dickens.

She stretches out her hands and he takes them and kisses them.

Gwendolen. Now you really must go and dress and I'll go and talk to Winnie.

Canon. You've made me the happiest of men. [*He opens the door for her and she goes out. He takes out his watch and looks at it.*] I say, I shall have to look sharp.

PONSONBY *shows in* LORD SPRATTE *and immediately retires.*

Ponsonby. Lord Spratte.

Lord Spratte. Hello, Theodore, you're not dressed yet.

Canon. Have you heard the news, Tom?

Lord Spratte. I passed Wroxham as I was strolling along here and he stopped his car and told me. He seems as pleased as Punch.

LADY SOPHIA *comes in, magnificent in her evening gown.*

Lady Sophia. Aren't you going to dress, Theodore? You'll be dreadfully late.

Canon. I've had a busy afternoon.

Lady Sophia [*to* LORD SPRATTE]. What do you think of Winnie's new engagement?

Lord Spratte. I think it's cost me a pony.

Lady Sophia. How is that?

Lord Spratte. I bet Mrs. Fitzgerald a pony that Theodore wouldn't work it.

Canon. She deserved to win. She believed in me. She knows that when I make up my mind to do a thing I do it.

Lord Spratte. Nonsense. She merely thinks you a more unscrupulous ruffian than I do.

Canon. Ha, ha! You may have your little joke, Tom. The fact remains that Mrs. Fitzgerald is one of the most charming women I know. If it weren't for that ridiculous will of her husband's I should insist on your marrying her. She's just the sort of wife you want.

Lord Spratte. What ridiculous will?

Canon. Well, it apparently contains a proviso, most unjust to any young woman, whereby she loses every penny of her income on her remarriage.

Lady Sophia. Have you been asking Mrs. Fitzgerald to marry you, Theodore?

Canon. My dear, what on earth makes you ask that?

Lady Sophia. She thinks quite rightly that a widow with five thousand a year is a lunatic if she marries again. She confided to me a long time ago that when her admirers grew inconveniently attentive she gave them to understand that she only retained her income while she was a widow. And the effect on their passion was nothing short of miraculous.

Canon. D'you mean to say it's not true?

Lady Sophia. Not a word of it. I've seen the will myself.

The CANON, *flabbergasted, is at a loss for words.*

Lord Spratte [*with a shout*]. Theodore, you've been done in the eye. Oh, Theodore, Theodore. A crafty old bird like you.

He begins to laugh. He rolls from side to side. He roars with laughter. LADY SOPHIA *catches the infection and goes into peal upon peal of merriment.* CANON SPRATTE *is furious.*

Canon. Be quiet. Be quiet. [*They stop, gasping, and the* CANON *seizes the opportunity to get in an explanation.*] Mrs. Fitzgerald is a most estimable person, and I should be the last to say anything against her. But I can't think for a moment that she has the stability of character or the sense of decorum which are absolutely essential to a clergyman's wife.

LORD SPRATTE *can no longer restrain himself and bursts out again into long and loud guffaws.* LIONEL *comes in dressed for dinner.*

Lionel. Hello, what's the matter?

Canon [*furiously*]. Can't you see? Your uncle has made a joke and he's quite overcome by it.

Lionel. Hello, you're not dressed yet, Governor.

Canon. Good heavens, Lionel, I know I'm not dressed. D'you think I'm a perfect imbecile? PONSONBY *comes in. The* CANON *does not immediately see that he has a telegram on a small salver. Impatiently.*] Yes, what is it? Oh, a telegram. [*He opens it and starts back with a cry, then sinks on to a chair with a gasp, putting his hand to his heart.*]

Lionel. Father, what's the matter?

Canon. Get me a glass of sherry. I'm quite upset.

Lionel [*to the butler*]. Hurry up, Ponsonby.

PONSONBY *goes out.*

Lord Spratte. What's the matter, Theodore?

Canon [*pulling himself together*]. Sophia. Sophia, you will be gratified to learn that the government has offered me the vacant bishopric of Colchester.

Lord Spratte. Oh, I am glad, Theodore.

Lady Sophia. So Doctor Gray refused it after all.

Canon. He never had it offered him. I am not the man, Sophia, to come as a second thought. And that being so, I shall not delay, I shall not consider the matter, but accept as it is offered me, frankly and by telegram.

Lord Spratte. I congratulate you.

PONSONBY *comes in during the last two speeches and pours out a glass of sherry for the* CANON.

Canon [*as he takes it*]. Ponsonby, I'm a bishop.

Ponsonby. I'm very glad to hear it, my lord.

CANON SPRATTE *smiles with gratification as he hears the title.*

Canon. Ponsonby.

Ponsonby. Yes, my lord?

Canon. Nothing. That'll do, Ponsonby; you can go.

Ponsonby. Very good, my lord.

Canon. Now, I really can go and dress for dinner . . . oh, Lionel, just take down a short notice for me, will you?

Lady Sophia. Theodore, you know how sensitive our cook is. She always gets drunk if we don't sit down punctually.

Canon. I cannot say I think it nice of you to dwell in this manner on your carnal appetites, Sophia. I should have thought at this juncture your mind would be attuned to higher things.

Lady Sophia. Fiddlesticks, Theodore.

Canon. Sophia, I have long felt that you do not treat me with proper respect. I cannot permit you any longer to act toward me with this mixture of indecent frivolity and vulgar cynicism. My position is radically altered. Are you ready, Lionel? We are authorized to announce that a marriage has been arranged between Lord Wroxham of Castle Tanker, and Winifred, only daughter of the Honorable—spell that in full, Lionel—and Reverend Canon Spratte, bishop-elect of Colchester; better known as the . . .

Lionel. Better known as the—yes?

Canon. You're very dull, Lionel. Better known as the popular and brilliant Vicar of St. Gregory's, South Kensington. Now put it in an envelope and address it to the editor of the *Morning Post.*

GWENDOLEN *enters.*

Gwendolen. Winnie wants me to tell you that she'll be ready in two minutes.

Canon. You were making very merry over me just now, Thomas. Allow me to inform you that I have asked Miss Gwendolen Durant to marry me and she has done me the great honor to accept.

THE RETURN OF THE PRODIGAL
A Comedy in Four Acts

by
ST. JOHN HANKIN

CHARACTERS

SAMUEL JACKSON, *of Jackson, Hartopp and Jackson, cloth-makers*

MARIA, *his wife*

HENRY, *their oldest son, partner in the firm*

EUSTACE, *their second son, the ne'er-do-well*

VIOLET, *their daughter*

SIR JOHN FARINGFORD, BART, *a local magnate*

LADY FARINGFORD, *his wife*

STELLA FARINGFORD, *their daughter*

DR. GLAISHER, *the local medical man*

RECTOR, *the Reverend Cyril Pratt*

MRS. PRATT, *his wife*

BAINES, *butler at the Jacksons'*

TWO FOOTMEN

The action of the play takes place at Chedleigh Court, the Jacksons' house in Gloucestershire. Chedleigh, as everybody knows, has long been famous for its cloth mills.

THE RETURN OF THE PRODIGAL

ACT ONE

The Jacksons' drawing room, a handsome room, suggests opulence rather than taste. Not vulgar, but not distinguished. Too full of furniture, pictures, knickknacks, chair covers, plants in pots. Too full of everything. There is a door; a fireplace, with a rather elaborate overmantel of wood painted white; a sofa, which sticks out square from wall; a screen with a piece of drapery sloping over it; an open upright Dutch writing table with a front which lets down flat; two windows with curtains drawn; a writing table with a chair in front of it; a grand piano; and a small table by side of piano. On the piano itself are large pots of plants in flower, photograph frames, and other inappropriate things. Below piano, between it and footlights and therefore mainly screening the player from the audience, is a palm or two in tall pots. Near this is a settee holding two. There are also plants in the fireplace, as it is summer and that is the Jacksons' conception of the proper way to adorn a fireplace and a suitable place for growing plants. Easy chairs are all over the place. The room is lighted by electricity but when the curtain rises only a few of the lights are turned on.

When the curtain rises the stage is empty. Then door opens and enter LADY FARINGFORD, *her daughter* STELLA, MRS. PRATT, VIOLET JACKSON, *and, after an interval,* MRS. JACKSON.

MRS. JACKSON [*without, in her loud, cheery voice*]. You won't stay too long over your cigars will you, Samuel? [*Entering.*] I always notice the gentlemen stay far too long in the dining room unless they're specially told not to. Now Lady Faringford, where will you sit? Try this sofa.

Lady Faringford [*sitting in corner of sofa farthest from fireplace*]. Thank you.

Mrs. Jackson. That's right. Mrs. Pratt, where shall I put you? No, don't go there. That's such a long way off. Come here. [*Drags up armchair near* LADY FARINGFORD *with hospitable inelegance.* MRS. PRATT *sits.*] Are you all right, Stella?

Stella [*who has taken place on settee*]. Quite, thanks, Mrs. Jackson.

Violet. Where will you go, Mother?

Mrs. Jackson. I'm going to sit here. Wait till I turn on some more light. [*Goes to door and does so.*] That's better!

81

MRS. JACKSON *takes seat by* LADY FARINGFORD. VIOLET *sits
by* STELLA *and quietly begins to knit.*

Lady Faringford. I do envy you your electric light, Mrs.
Jackson. Lamps are so troublesome. The servants are always
setting themselves on fire with them.

Mrs. Jackson [*comfortably*]. It *is* convenient, isn't it.

Lady Faringford. How long have you had it?

Mrs. Jackson. Only about eighteen months. We had it
brought here at the same time that they were putting it in at
the mill. It seemed a pity not to, as it was so close. And
now I don't know what we should do without it.

Mrs. Pratt. I saw it was all on at the mill as we passed
tonight.

STELLA *rises and goes up.*

Mrs. Jackson. Yes. They can work much later now it's
been put in. That was Henry's idea. It was almost impossible
to work overtime profitably before on account of the light.
Now the mill often works night and day when there's a pressure.

Stella. Surely the workmen must sleep sometimes?

Mrs. Jackson. They have different sets of workmen I
believe. But you must ask Henry. He knows all about it.

Lady Faringford. Mr. Jackson seems pretty cheerful about
his election prospects.

Mrs. Jackson. Yes. I do hope he'll get in. It will be such
an amusement for him.

STELLA *at top table.*

Mrs. Pratt. It would certainly be most regrettable if Mr.
Ling were elected. He is a dissenter. The Rector says a
clergyman should have no politics but I say a clergyman with
no politics is never made a bishop.

Lady Faringford. I trust the Rector will not allow Mr. Ling
to use the parish room for any of his meetings.

Mrs. Pratt. I'm afraid he will. He says he can't make distinctions between the two parties. If he lends the room to one
he must lend it to the other.

Lady Faringford. Then he had better lend it to neither.
That will answer the purpose quite well. For Mr. Jackson can
easily hire some place for his meetings while Mr. Ling cannot. It is such a comfort that all the rich people about here
are Conservatives. [STELLA *at table.*] But I believe the same
thing may be noticed in other parts of the country. It almost seems like a special providence.

Mrs. Jackson. I hope Sir John thinks my husband will get in?

Lady Faringford. Oh, yes, I think so. It's unfortunate that Mr. Ling is so popular. Only with quite vulgar people no doubt, Nonconformists and so forth. But even they have votes unfortunately. Still Mr. Jackson employs a large number of people and they will vote for him of course—or what's the use of being an employer? And if he is sufficiently liberal with his subscriptions . . .

Mrs. Jackson. I believe my husband subscribes to everything.

Lady Faringford. Then I'm sure he'll get in. It's a pity he won't have the Illingtons' support, by the way. [*Enter* BAINES and FOOTMAN. *The* FOOTMAN *first, carrying tray with five empty cups, then butler with tray with coffee, cream, and sugar.*] They have a great deal of influence in their part of the county.

Mrs. Pratt [*horrified*]. Surely Sir James hasn't turned radical?

Lady Faringford. No, no. Not so bad as *that!* But I hear he's quite ruined. His racing stable has cost him a fortune in the last few years and he's never won a single race. Braden will be to let in the autumn.

Mrs. Jackson. Poor Sir James. He will feel parting with the place dreadfully.

Lady Faringford. It's his own fault. He ought never to have made that absurd marriage. Mary Illington—she was Mary Tremayne, you know—one of the Wiltshire Tremaynes—hadn't a sixpence. What will become of that boy of theirs at Eton I can't think. They'll never be able to pay his school bills.

Mrs. Jackson. Public schools *are* dreadfully expensive, aren't they? I remember when Eustace, my second boy, was at Harrow—Henry was never at a public school—his bills were terribly high.

Mrs. Pratt. I wonder whom we shall have at Braden. I do hope they will be Church people. The Scalebys [STELLA *by her mother*], who took Astley Park, play tennis on Sundays and seem to me to be little better than heathens. It sets such a bad example.

Lady Faringford. The county is changing sadly. Half the old houses have changed hands and the new people are usually quite dreadful. If this sort of things goes on there won't be a single person fit to speak to within twenty miles.

Pause.

Stella [*to* VIOLET]. What are you working at?

Violet. A pair of socks for old Allen. I always give him a pair for his birthday. That's about a month from now.

Mrs. Pratt. I hope you and Mrs. Jackson have got a lot of things ready for the Mission Room Fund Bazaar, Violet? We want to clear off our debt and if possible have something in hand as well.

Violet. Oh, yes. I've done some things and so has Mother. I'll send them up in a day or two.

Mrs. Pratt. And thank *you* so much, Lady Faringford, for the embroidered tea cloth you sent. It is *sure* to sell!

Lady Faringford. Let us hope so. It's extremely ugly. I bought it at the Kettlewell sale of work last year intending to give it to my poor sister Adelaide. But afterward I hadn't the heart. So I sent it to your bazaar instead.

Pause.

Mrs. Jackson. Vi dear, won't you play us something?

Stella. Do Vi. We never have any music at the Hall now Fraulein Schmidt has gone.

Violet. Very well, if you'd really like it.

VIOLET *moves to piano with* STELLA.

Lady Faringford [*to* MRS. JACKSON]. You remember her? She was Stella's governess. Quite an intelligent good creature. But I dare say you never met her. She never used to come down to dinner.

VIOLET *begins to hunt through music.*

Lady Faringford. I always think German governesses so much more satisfactory than English. You see there's never any question about having to treat *them* as ladies. And then they're always so plain. That's a great advantage. And German is such a useful language, far more useful for a young girl than French. There are so many more books she can be allowed to read in it. French can be learned later—and should be in my opinion.

Mrs. Pratt. I quite agree with you Lady Faringford. But the Rector is less strict in these matters. He allowed my girls to begin French directly they went to school, at Miss Thursby's. But I'm bound to say they never seem to have learned any. So perhaps it did no harm.

Mrs. Jackson. Yes, I have always heard Miss Thursby's was an excellent school.

VIOLET, *having finished her search, puts a piece of music on piano and begins to play the second movement of Beethoven's twenty-seventh sonata.*

Enter BAINES.

She stops.

Baines [*going up to* MRS. PRATT]. If you please, madam, Simmonds is here asking if you could see him. They sent him on from the rectory.

Mrs. Pratt. Simmonds? Did he say his business?

Baines [*coughs discreetly*]. Something about Mrs. Simmonds, I think, madam.

Mrs. Pratt. Of course. I remember. I will come in a moment. [*Rising.*] You'll excuse me won't you, dear Mrs. Jackson? It's Mrs. Simmonds. Foolish woman, she's had another baby. Her husband is in the hall. I shall probably have to run over to the rectory for some things for her.

Mrs. Jackson [*rising at once*]. Oh, no, you mustn't do that. I am sure we have everything necessary here, soup and jelly and flannel and anything else you think wise. And of course they will want some money. I had better come and see Simmonds with you. Then we can tell the housekeeper to put the things together for him.

Mrs. Pratt. But it's giving you so much trouble.

Mrs. Jackson. Not in the least. It's no trouble. And I can't have you running away and leaving us before the Rector has finished his cigar. That would never do.

Violet [*rising*]. Can I do anything, Mother?

Mrs. Jackson. No, dear. I can manage quite well. You stay here and entertain Lady Faringford and Stella. We shan't be five minutes.

Exeunt MRS. JACKSON *and* MRS. PRATT, *shown out by* BAINES.

Violet. Poor Mrs. Simmonds. I do hope the baby will be all right.

Lady Faringford. I have no doubt it will. When people have far more children already than is either convenient or necessary, their babies always exhibit extraordinary vitality. Nothing seems to kill them. But you were going to play to us, dear.

VIOLET *goes to piano again and begins to play. After a few moments* LADY FARINGFORD *beckons to* STELLA, *who rises, crosses, and sits by her mother.* LADY FARINGFORD *begins to talk under cover of the music.*

Lady Faringford. By the way, Stella, how are things going between you and Henry?

Stella [*who has been absorbed in the music, turns to* LADY FARINGFORD *quickly*]. What do you mean, Mother?

Lady Faringford. Has he asked you to marry him yet?

Stella. No.

Lady Faringford. Strange! I thought he would have done so before now. I have given him several opportunities.

Stella. Mother!

Lady Faringford. He is going to, I suppose?

Stella. I don't know.

Lady Faringford. Nonsense, child. Of course you do. A girl always knows when a man wants to propose to her, unless she is perfectly idiotic. He will certainly propose if you give him proper encouragement. And when he does you will accept him.

Stella [*thoughtfully*]. I'm not sure.

Lady Faringford. Not sure? Why not? You like him, don't you? [*Three or four loud chords on piano.*] I can't think who invented music after dinner. One can hardly hear oneself speak. As I was saying, you like him?

Stella. Oh, yes. I like him.

Lady Faringford. Then of course you will accept him. When a man proposes to a girl and she likes him and he is well off and otherwise eligible she should always accept him.

Stella. But [*Hesitates.*] I don't love him, Mother.

Lady Faringford. My dear, you must not expect impossibilities. Love matches aren't very common among people of our class. And they're by no means always successful either. Quite the contrary. If you marry a man you like you may come to love him—in time. But if you marry a man you love you may easily come to loathe him.

Pause.

Stella [*sighs*]. Well I suppose I shall have to marry him in the end.

Lady Faringford. Of course you will. And I'm sure you might do a great deal worse. The Jacksons are really very well off. The business has grown enormously in the past few years. What can be keeping Mrs. Jackson so long? Since she left this room she has had time to pauperize the entire village.

Stella. It will take a little time to get the things together, I suppose, for poor Mrs. Simmonds.

Lady Faringford. As to being in love, that is a thing to which people attach far too much importance. Of course, the Jacksons are parvenus. But everybody one meets nowadays is either a parvenu or a pauper. And really girls are so numerous just now they can't afford to be as particular as they were. Henry is the only son.

Stella. No, Mother. There's Eustace.

Lady Faringford. I don't count Eustace. He went away years ago—to one of the colonies I believe—and doubtless came to a bad end. Probably he's dead by now.

Stella. Mother! How can you say such terrible things!

Lady Faringford. Nonsense. Of course he's dead. And a very good thing too. Really what a noise our good Violet is making —. If he weren't dead, one would have heard something of him. That sort of young man always makes himself felt by his relations as long as the breath's in his body.

Stella. But if he's abroad . . .

Lady Faringford. Then he would write—for money. People in the colonies always do write for money. You don't remember him do you?

Stella. Hardly at all. I've seen him of course.

Lady Faringford. Ah. He was a handsome fellow. Clever too. But a thorough detrimental. It's just as well he went to the colonies. No, my dear, you can't do better than accept Henry. He'll be quite a rich man some day and he's really very fairly presentable. And his father will get into Parliament. Not that that means anything nowadays. [*Door opens. Men's voices without.*] Here he is.

Enter SIR JOHN FARINGFORD, *a little bald, The* RECTOR, *a little gray,* MR. JACKSON, *very portly and pompous, and* HENRY, *his son.*

MR. JACKSON. Hello, all alone, Lady Faringford? What's become of Maria—and Mrs. Pratt?

Violet [*rising from piano*]. Simmonds came to ask if he could see Mrs. Pratt. Mrs. Simmonds is ill. Mother and Mrs. Pratt are putting some things together for him to take to her.

Lady Faringford. Your daughter has been entertaining us with her charming music while Mrs. Jackson was away. What was that little piece you were playing, dear?

Violet. A sonata of Beethoven, Lady Faringford.

Lady Faringford. Indeed? Very pretty.

The Rector. You are going to play at our next parish concert I hope, Miss Jackson?

Violet. Yes. Mrs. Pratt and I have been getting out the program.

Sir John. Miss Jackson is a tower of strength in the musical line. Stella hardly plays a note. I always tell my wife it's the result of having had a German governess. How can you expect a child to learn music in German?

Lady Faringford [*rising*]. I believe all modern music is written in German. It certainly sounds like it.

LADY FARINGFORD *goes upstage, sits, and begins to talk to* MR. JACKSON. *The* RECTOR *talks to* VIOLET *on sofa with* SIR JOHN. HENRY *sits down by* STELLA.

Henry. I hope you haven't been dull, Miss Faringford, while my mother has been out of the room. It's shocking of her to leave her guests in this way.

Stella. Not at all. Vi has been playing to us. It has been delightful.

Henry. You're very fond of music, aren't you?

Stella. Yes. It's curious. When I was a child they made me learn, of course, but I didn't care a bit about it. I was awfully troublesome over my lessons, I remember. So I made nothing of it. And now, when I'd give anything to be able to play, I can't.

Henry. Why don't you take it up again?

Stella. I do try sometimes. Sometimes I set to work and practice feverishly for a whole week. But it doesn't last.

Henry. You should persevere.

Stella. I know. But I don't. I suppose I'm lazy. But that's like me. I want to do things. I see I *ought* to do them. But somehow they don't get done. I expect you can't understand that?

Henry. I'm afraid I can't. If I want a thing I take the necessary steps to get it. That's what "wanting" means with me.

Stella [*thoughtfully*]. And do you always get it?

Henry. Generally. A man can generally get a thing in the end if he gives his mind to it.

Stella. Most people wouldn't say that.

Henry. That's because most people don't know what they want. Instead of fixing their mind on one thing, and being determined to get it, they keep aiming first at one thing and then at another. So of course they don't get anything. They don't deserve to.

Stella. Most people don't *aim* at all. They simply take what comes.

Henry. Surely *you* don't do that?

Stella. I believe I do. [*Laughing.*] You see there's really not room for more than one *will* in any family. In our family it's Mamma's. Mamma always knows what she wants—like you. The worst of it is she doesn't always know what *we* want.

Henry. I see. What happens then?

Stella. Oh, Mamma wins. We struggle a little sometimes, Papa and I. But she gets her way in the end. [*A pause.*]

Henry. Miss Faringford, there's something I want to say to you.

Stella. That sounds very serious.

Henry. It is serious to me. It's something I've wanted to tell you for a long time.

Stella [*rising nervously*]. Well, don't tell it me tonight. Later on perhaps. I don't think I want to hear about serious things tonight.

Door opens—enter MRS. JACKSON *and* MRS PRATT, *a little later.*

Henry [*rising also*]. When may I tell it to you?

Stella. I don't know. Sometime, perhaps. But not now. [LADY FARINGFORD *enters.*] Here's your mother come back with Mrs. Pratt.

Mrs. Jackson. Lady Faringford, what will you think of me for leaving you so long. But the housekeeper was out. She had gone down to the village, to see her niece who is ill. So Mrs. Pratt and I had to put the things together for Simmonds ourselves. Mrs. Simmonds has another baby, Samuel. [*Sits.*]

Mrs. Pratt. The poor are terribly thoughtless in these matters. That makes her sixth. I'm bound to say poor Simmonds seemed quite conscious of his folly.

Lady Faringford. That at least is satisfactory. But I have no hope that it will affect his future conduct. He will go on having children—at the usual intervals—until he dies. And then they will come on the parish.

Mrs. Jackson. But is Simmonds going to die? He said nothing about it. But of course he was rather flurried.

Mr. Jackson. I hope you sent whatever was necessary, Maria?

Mrs. Pratt. Far more. I really had to interfere to prevent Mrs. Jackson from emptying her store cupboard.

Rector. Well, well, I dare say poor Mrs. Simmonds will find a use for everything.

Mrs. Jackson. No doubt. And besides with an election in prospect . . .

Sir John. Exactly. It can do no harm.

Mrs. Jackson. By the way, Sir John, as chairman of my election committee, there's a point on which I want your advice. The local branch of the Independent Order of Good Templars wrote to me ten days ago asking for a subscription. So I sent five guineas.

MRS. JACKSON *rises and goes to* MRS. PRATT *at table.*

Sir John. Quite right. The temperance vote must be reckoned with in this Division.

Mr. Jackson. Just so. But the Good Templars published the fact in the local newspaper.

Sir John. Well, that's what you wanted, wasn't it?

Mr. Jackson. Ye-es. No doubt. But I forgot that the secretary of the local branch of the Licensed Victuallers Association would be sure to see the paragraph and write to me for an explanation.

Sir John. I see. Did he?

Mr. Jackson. Yes.

Sir John. Ah! What did you do?

Mr. Jackson. I was in some doubt. But Sims, my agent, told me the Licensed Victuallers had a benevolent fund or something. So I sent ten guineas to that. That seemed the best way out of the difficulty.

Sir John. Much the best, much the best. [*Trying to escape.*]

Mr. Jackson [*detaining him*]. But that's not the end of the matter. For now the Good Templars have written to ask if I am prepared to support any legislation designed to combat the evil of the drink traffic. And the Licensed Victuallers want to know if I will pledge myself to oppose any bill which aims at the reduction of the sale of intoxicating liquors.

Sir John. Hum! They rather had you there!

Mr. Jackson. Yes. . . . However, I think I've got out of it all right. I've written a letter to the Licensed Victuallers to say I'm not in favor of unduly restricting the sale of liquor in the interests of temperance propaganda. And I've written another to the Good Templars saying that I'm quite in favor of temperance propaganda providing it doesn't unduly restrict the sale of intoxicating liquor. I think that meets the case?

Sir John. I see. Running with the hare and hunting with the hounds in fact? Quite right. And now we really must be saying good night. [*To* LADY FARINGFORD.] Come, my dear. It's time we were going.

Mrs. Jackson. Oh, you mustn't go yet. It's quite early.

Lady Faringford. We are early people. [*Rises.*] We really must go. Stella, my dear, we must be putting on our things.

Henry. I'll ask if your carriage is round. [*Rings.*]

Lady Faringford. If you will be so good. I told the coachman ten. I do hope it's stopped raining. I believe the farmers want it but it's so bad for the horses.

Enter BAINES.

Henry. Lady Faringford's carriage.

Baines. It's at the door, sir.

Henry. Very well.

Lady Faringford. Good night then, Mrs. Jackson. Such a *pleasant* evening. Come, Stella.

MRS. JACKSON *by* RECTOR.

General adieux. The FARINGFORDS *and* STELLA *go out escorted by* HENRY *and* MR. JACKSON.

Mrs. Pratt. I think *we* ought to be going too.

Mrs. Jackson. No. No. You mustn't run away like that. I've not had a moment to speak to the Rector. And I'm sure Vi will want to talk to you about the next concert. Sit down again, Mrs. Pratt. [MRS. JACKSON, *at sofa. Re-enter* HENRY *and* MR. JACKSON.] What sort of a night is it, Samuel? *Has* it stopped raining?

HENRY *goes to* VIOLET.

Mr. Jackson. Yes, it's not raining now. But it's very dark.

Rector. The moon's full too. But I suppose there's too much cloud about.

Mrs. Jackson. I do hope it will be lighter before you have to go home. It's such a dark road from here to the rectory.

Rector. We have a lantern. We always bring it when we go out at night. We don't trust the moon. She's fickle, Mrs. Jackson, like all her sex.

Mrs. Jackson. Rector, if you talk like that I shall scold you. And so will Mrs. Pratt.

Sudden noise of footsteps outside. Then door opens and enter BAINES, *rather flurried.*

Baines [*a little breathless*]. If you please, sir . . .

Mr. Jackson. Well, what is it, Baines?

Baines. If you please, sir, it's Mr. Eustace. [MR. JACKSON *turns sharp round.*] He was lying just by the front door.

Mr. Jackson. Mr. Eustace?

Mrs. Jackson [*jumping up*]. Eustace!

Baines. Yes, sir. Yes, madam. Thomas saw him just as he was coming in after shutting the front gate. The moon came out for a moment and he saw him. He's fainted, sir. At least I think so.

MRS. JACKSON *moves across as* VIOLET *meets her.*

Mrs. Jackson. I must go to him.
Mr. Jackson. No. Not you, Maria. I'll go.

The door opens.

Baines. I think they're bringing him in here, sir.

Enter the TWO FOOTMEN *carrying a draggled and disheveled body by the shoulders and the heels.*

Pause. VIOLET *moves the armchair which is taken by* HENRY. *The* RECTOR *and* VIOLET *move the sofa to receive the body.*

MRS. PRATT *by piano,* MRS. JACKSON *by body's head—all standing by the sofa.*

Mrs. Jackson. Oh, my poor boy! My poor dear boy! [*Rushes to him.*]
Violet. Wait a minute. Put him here.
Mrs. Jackson. Oh, he's dead! He's dead! I know he's dead.
Violet [*immediately*]. Hush, Mother. Some brandy, quick, Baines. And some cold water. I think he's only fainted. [*Puts cushion under his head and opens shirt at neck.*]
Rector. Poor fellow.
Mrs. Pratt. Oh, Mrs. Jackson. Your sofa! It will be utterly ruined.
Mrs. Jackson [*bending over him*]. Oh, I wish they'd be quick with the brandy. Henry, go at once for Dr. Glaisher.
Rector. Let *me* go. We pass his house anyway. And we mustn't stay any longer. We should only be in the way here. Come, my dear.

Enter BAINES *with brandy and jug of water.*

Mrs. Pratt. Good-by, dear Mrs. Jackson. No. You mustn't stir. And I do hope he'll be all right soon. We'll send Dr. Glaisher round at once.
Rector. Good-by. [*To* HENRY.] Don't come with me, my dear fellow. Baines can find my things. Stay and look after your brother.

Exeunt MR. *and* MRS. PRATT *and* BAINES.

Meantime MRS. JACKSON *has been trying to force some brandy between clenched teeth of the patient.*

Violet. Your handkerchief, Henry. Quick.

HENRY *gives it. She dips it in jug, wrings it out, and puts it over patient's forehead by way of bandage.*

Mrs. Jackson. He doesn't stir.

Mr. Jackson. I can feel his heart beating a little, I think. But I'm not sure.

Mrs. Jackson [*lamentably*]. Oh, will he *never* come round! I *wish* Dr. Glaisher would come. If he were to die!

Violet [*soothing her*]. Hush, Mother! He's only fainted. Didn't you hear Father say he could feel his heart beating?

Mrs. Jackson. Isn't there anything else we could do? My salts!

Violet [*rising*]. I'll get them, Mother.

Mrs. Jackson. They're on my dressing table. [*Exit* VIOLET *hurriedly.*] No, I remember, I had them in the library this morning. I'll go and look. Or was it the breakfast room? I'm not sure. Oh, dear, oh, dear, poor darling Eustace!

Exit in burst of tears.

Mr. Jackson. She'll never find them. You go, Henry, and help her. Try the breakfast room.

Exeunt all save MR. JACKSON *and* EUSTACE.

After MR. JACKSON *has fidgeted round his son for a minute or so in helpless and grotesque efforts to restore his son to consciousness* VIOLET's *voice is heard through door which is left open.*

Violet [*without*]. Father!

Mr. Jackson [*going to door, hurriedly*]. Yes, yes, what *is* it?

Enter VIOLET.

Violet. Have you your keys? Mother thinks she may have left her salts on your desk in the library and it's locked.

Mr. Jackson. Tsk! Here they are. [VIOLET, *going.*] I'd better come or you'll disturb all my papers.

Exeunt MR. JACKSON *and* VIOLET.

The stage is left empty for a moment of all save the man on the sofa. Presently EUSTACE *raises himself cautiously, looks round, then finding no one there takes off head bandage and wrings it out, listens again, then sits up and puts feet to ground, picks up a book with conspicuous red cover, on which he has been lying, glances at it, reads title,* Hester's Escape, *makes face, hears sound without, hurriedly puts feet up again on couch, replaces bandage, and lays his head back on pillow just as* MRS. JACKSON *re-enters with* HENRY.

Mrs. Jackson [piteously]. They're *not* in the library. Where *can* I have put them?

Henry. The others will find them. Violet is looking in your bedroom. She always finds things. And the governor is in the breakfast room. They'll be here in a moment.

Enter VIOLET *with salts in her hand, followed at a short interval by* MR. JACKSON.

Mrs. Jackson. Thanks, dear. [*Holds the salts tremulously to patient's nose, but forgetting to take out stopper, kneeling by his side.*] Where were they? [*Kneels by sofa.*]

Violet. In the dining room, on the writing table.

Mrs. Jackson, Oh, yes, I remember. I had them there at lunchtime. I *knew* I had put them somewhere.

Henry [irritably]. My dear Mother, there's no use holding those salts to his nose unless you take the stopper out.

MRS. JACKSON *fumbles with stopper. Patient stirs slightly and turns away his head.*

Mrs. Jackson. He's coming round. He moved a little. Try him with some more brandy.

MRS. JACKSON *puts down salts and takes up brandy which she pours into patient's mouth. He makes elaborate business of coming round, gives a sigh, opens his eyes, then raises himself and looks round.*

Eustace. Is that you, Mother?

Mrs. Jackson. Yes, dear, yes.

Eustace. Where am I?

Mrs. Jackson. At home, dear. Your own home. Oh, he's not dead! He's not dead! [*Embraces him, sobbing passionately.*]

ACT TWO

The breakfast room at the Jacksons'. In the middle of stage, the breakfast table, which is round and would hold about six people. It is fully laid with cloth, tea and coffee things, toast, dishes, etc. There is a fireplace; leather-covered armchairs; large French window at back through which is seen garden. The windows are open as it is a bright summer day. There is a door; a sideboard on which stand fruit, some spare plates, etc., also a box of cigars and a box of cigarettes. On either side of the window are bookcases. Near sideboard, a writing table. When the curtain rises MR. JACKSON *sits at table.* HENRY *on left,* VIOLET *on the side farthest from footlights. She has the coffee, etc., in front of her.* MR. JACKSON *is faced by bacon dishes. They all go on eating their breakfasts for half a minute after curtain has risen.* HENRY *is reading a newspaper propped up by his side.* VIOLET *is reading letters.*

HENRY [*handing cup*]. More coffee, please, Violet. [*To* MR. JACKSON.] Wenhams have failed, Father.

Mr. Jackson. It's only what we expected, isn't it?

Henry. Yes. Forty thousand they say here. But of course it's only a guess. No one can know till the accounts are made up.

Mr. Jackson. They've been shaky for some time. [*Enter* MRS. JACKSON.] Well, how is he?

Mrs. Jackson. Much better. He looks quite a different person.

Mr. Jackson. Did he eat any breakfast?

Mrs. Jackson. He hasn't had any yet. At least only a cup of tea. He says he'd rather come down. He's getting up now.

Violet. Didn't Dr. Glaisher say he was to stay in bed?

Mrs. Jackson. Yes. But if he wants to come down I don't think it can do any harm. He can lie down on the sofa till lunch if he feels tired.

Mr. Jackson. What time is Glaisher coming?

Violet. Half past ten, he said.

Henry. Has Eustace explained how he came to be lying in the drive in that state? Last night we could get nothing out of him.

Mrs. Jackson. No wonder. He was dazed, poor boy. He had walked all the way from London and had had nothing to eat.

Henry. How was it he was in London? He was sent to Australia.

Mrs. Jackson. He *had* been in Australia. He worked his passage home.

Mr. Jackson. His money is all gone, I suppose—the thousand pounds I gave him?

Mrs. Jackson. I don't know, Samuel. I didn't ask.

Mr. Jackson. Humph! . . . [*Pause.*] I'll trouble you for the toast please, Henry.

Henry. I suppose we'd better make inquiries about Wenhams, Father. It might be worth our while to buy the mill if it goes cheap. Then we could run it and ours together.

Mr. Jackson. Just so. Will you see to that?

HENRY *nods.*

Mrs. Jackson. I've got a letter to Aunt Isabel to send by the early post. I ought to have written it last night. Will you put it into the box for me, Samuel, as you go to the mill? [*Goes to writing table and sits.*]

Mr. Jackson. Certainly, my dear.

Henry. Very tiresome, Eustace turning up in that disreputable condition last night. What will Stella think?

Mr. Jackson. It's lucky the Faringfords had gone before he was brought in.

Henry. The Pratts hadn't. Mrs. Pratt will have told the entire village before lunchtime.

Violet. I don't see why we should mind if she does. There's nothing to be ashamed of. [*Rises and reads letter by fireplace.*]

Henry [*impatiently*]. Well, we won't discuss it. [*Returns to his paper.*]

Mrs. Jackson [*moving nearer* HENRY *to get paper*]. By the way, Henry, did you say anything to Stella last night?

Henry [*hesitates*]. No.

Mrs. Jackson. I thought you were going to.

Henry. I was. In fact I did begin. But she didn't let me finish. I suppose she didn't understand what I was going to say.

Mr. Jackson. Don't put it off too long. There may be an election any day now and the Faringford influence means a great deal.

Henry. You've got Faringford's influence already. He's chairman of your committee.

Mr. Jackson. That's true. Still, he'll take more trouble when

I'm one of the family, so to speak. Yes, I shouldn't put it off if I were you.

Henry. Very well, Father.

Mr. Jackson. Of course, Faringford is as poor as Job. The estate's mortgaged up to the hilt. And anything there is after he and Lady Faringford go out of the coach—if there is anything—will go to the son. Stella won't have a sixpence. Still they're good people, position in the county and all that. And *you'll* have enough money for both.

Henry. Yes. Especially if we get hold of Wenhams' mill. I'm sure I could make a good thing out of it. We'd put in turbines as we did here, get new machinery, and double our output.

Mr. Jackson. How are the turbines working by the way?

Henry. All right. And they'll go still better when the new sluices are done. [*Rising.*] Well, I shall go over to the mill now. Are you coming?

Mr. Jackson. In a moment. [*Finishes his coffee and rises.*]

Exit HENRY.

Violet. Shall I get your hat and stick, Father?

Mr. Jackson. Do dear. [*Exit* VIOLET.] Is your letter ready, Maria?

Mrs. Jackson. Just done. [*Fastens it up, rising.*] You won't forget it, will you?

Re-enter HENRY *with hat.*

Mr. Jackson. No. Or if I do Henry will remind me.

Mrs. Jackson [*to* HENRY]. Won't you wait and see Eustace before you go, Henry? He'll be down in a moment.

Henry. It doesn't matter. I shall see him soon enough. Coming, Father?   [*Exit.*

Mrs. Jackson. I think Henry might have stayed to see Eustace before he started.

Mr. Jackson. I dare say he'll be over in the course of the morning.

VIOLET *re-entering.*

Violet. Here's your hat and stick, Father.

Mr. Jackson. That's a good girl. [*Kisses her.*] Good-by. I shall be in for lunch.   [*Exit.*

Mrs. Jackson [*going to bacon dish and lifting cover*]. We must order some more bacon. Or do you think Eustace had better have an egg?

Violet. Shall I go up and ask him?

Mrs. Jackson. Do dear. And I wonder if you'd see cook at the same time and ask her if she's wanting anything. I have to go into the village.

Violet. Very well, Mother.

Exit VIOLET. MRS. JACKSON *takes away plates to sideboard, clears a place for* EUSTACE *where* HENRY *sat, and lays for him.*

Baines [*announcing*]. Dr. Glaisher.

Enter DR. GLAISHER.

Mrs. Jackson [*shaking hands*]. Oh, Doctor. Good morning. [*To* BAINES.] Tell Mr. Eustace Dr. Glaisher is here.

Exit BAINES.

Dr. Glaisher [*brisk and professional*]. Well, how does he seem? Going on well?

Mrs. Jackson. Quite well, I think.

Dr. Glaisher. Did he have a good night?

Mrs. Jackson. Excellent, he says.

Dr. Glaisher. Ah. Just so. Shall I go up to him?

Mrs. Jackson. He's coming down for breakfast. He'll be here in a moment.

Dr. Glaisher. Coming down, is he? [*By fireplace.*] Come, that looks satisfactory. Still we must be careful. No over-fatigue. His condition last night gave cause for considerable anxiety. Indeed I may say that if I had not fortunately been sent for at once and applied the necessary remedies there was distinct danger of collapse, um! distinct danger.

Mrs. Jackson. Oh, Doctor!

Enter EUSTACE, *very fresh and genial in an admirable suit of clothes.*

Dr. Glaisher. Ah, here he is.

Eustace. Good morning, Mother. [*Kisses her.*] Hello, Doctor. Come to see me?

Dr. Glaisher [*shaking hands*]. Well, and how are we this morning?

Eustace. Getting on all right, I think. A bit limp and washed out perhaps.

Dr. Glaisher. Just so. The temperature normal? No fever? [*Touches forehead.*] That's right. Pulse. [*Feels it.*] A little irregular, perhaps. But nothing serious. Excitement due to overfatigue no doubt. Now, let me see your tongue. [*Does so.*] Just so. As I should have expected. Just as I should have expected, dear Mrs. Jackson. Appetite not very good, I suppose?

Eustace. Er—not very.

Dr. Glaisher. Just so. Just so. [*Nods sagaciously.*]

Eustace [*gaily*]. Not dead yet, eh, Doctor? [*Sits on arm of chair.*]

Mrs. Jackson. My dear!

Dr. Glaisher [*with heavy geniality*]. We shall pull you through. Oh, we shall pull you through. But you must take care of yourself for a few days. No excitement! No over-fatigue. The system wants *tone* a little, wants *tone.*

Eustace. I see. I'm to take it easy, in fact, for a bit, eh?

Dr. Glaisher. Just so.

Eustace. I won't forget. I say what clever beggars you doctors are! You feel a fellow's pulse and look at his tongue and you know *all* about him at once. Don't you?

Dr. Glaisher [*pleased*]. Not *all* perhaps. But there are indications, symptoms, which the professional man can interpret . . .

Eustace [*interrupting*]. Quite extraordinary. I say, what do you think of these clothes? Not *bad,* are they? They're Henry's. But *I* chose them—out of his drawers. Poor old Henry!

Mrs. Jackson. How naughty of you, Eustace. I'm sure Henry won't like it.

Eustace. Of course he won't, Mother dear. Nobody does like his clothes being worn by someone else. But I must wear something you know. I can't come down to breakfast in a suit of pajamas. Besides they're Henry's pajamas.

Mrs. Jackson. But I told Thomas specially to put out an old suit of your father's for you. Didn't he do it?

Eustace. Yes. But I can't wear the governor's clothes, you know. We haven't the same figure. I say I'd better ring for breakfast. [*Does so.*]

Mrs. Jackson. Have you ordered it, dear? I sent Vi up to ask whether you'd like bacon or eggs.

Eustace. Yes. Violet asked me. I said bacon *and* eggs. [*Enter* VIOLET.] Hello, Vi, you're just in time to pour out my coffee.

Dr. Glaisher [*shakes hands with* VIOLET]. Well, I must be off to my other patients. [*To* MRS. JACKSON.] Good-by, Mrs. Jackson. He is going on well, quite as well as can be expected, that is. There are no fresh symptoms of an unfavorable character. But you must keep him quiet for a few days. There are signs of nervousness about him, a sort of suppressed excitement which I don't like. The system wants *tone,* decidedly wants tone. I'll send him up a mixture to take. He has evidently been through some strain lately. I knew that directly I saw him last night. You can't deceive a doctor!

FOOTMAN *brings in breakfast—rack of toast on table, coffee and rolls on sideboard, clears table of dirty plates, etc., so as to leave only a manageable quantity of "business" for* BAINES *when latter has to clear the table later.*

Mrs. Jackson [*anxiously*]. But you don't think there's anything *serious* the matter?

Dr. Glaisher. No! no! Let us hope not. The general constitution is sound enough, not overstrong perhaps, but sound. And with youth on his side—let me see, how old is he?

Mrs. Jackson. Nine and twenty.

Dr. Glaisher. Just so. Just so. Well, good morning. [*To* EUSTACE.] Good morning. And remember, quiet, perfectly quiet. I'll look in again tomorrow morning and see how he's getting on.

Eustace [*nods*]. Good-by! [*Goes toward breakfast table.*] DR. GLAISHER *shakes hands with* VIOLET *and goes out.* VIOLET *seats herself at table to pour out* EUSTACE'S *coffee.* MRS. JACKSON *sits by* EUSTACE.] Mother, I think *I* must become a doctor. It's the only profession I know of which seems to require no knowledge whatever, and it's the sort of thing I should do rather well. [*Begins his breakfast.*]

Exit FOOTMAN.

Mrs. Jackson. I dare say, my dear. You must speak to your father about it. . . . [*Sitting.*] And now you must tell us *all* about yourself. What have you been doing all this time? And why have you never written?

Eustace. There was nothing to tell you—that you'd have liked to hear.

Mrs. Jackson. My dear, of course we should have liked to hear everything about you.

Eustace. I doubt it. No news is good news. I bet the governor thought that—and Henry.

Mrs. Jackson. No, no, dear. I assure you your father was quite anxious when we never heard—at first.

Eustace. Ah well, if the governor was so anxious to know how I was, he shouldn't have packed me off to Australia. I never could endure writing letters.

Violet. Still you might have sent us word. It would have been kinder to Mother.

Down to fire and sits front of table.

Eustace [*laying his hand on his mother's as it lies on the arm of her chair*]. Poor Mother. I suppose I was a brute. But I've not been very prosperous these five years, and as I'd nothing pleasant to say, I thought I wouldn't write.

Mrs. Jackson. But what became of your money, dear? The thousand pounds your father gave you?

Eustace. I lost it.

Mrs. Jackson. Lost it?

Eustace. Part of it went in a sheep farm. I suppose I was a bad farmer. Anyhow the sheep died. The other part I put in a gold mine. I suppose I wasn't much of a miner. Anyhow there was no gold in it. I was in the mounted police for a time. That was in Natal. It wasn't bad but it didn't lead to anything. So I cleared out. I've been in a bank in Hong Kong. I've driven a cable car in San Francisco, I've been a steward on a liner, I've been an actor, and I've been a journalist. I've tried my hand at most things in fact. At one time I played in an orchestra.

Mrs. Jackson. You were always so fond of music.

Eustace [*dryly*]. Yes, I played the triangle—and took a whack at the big drum between times.

Violet. How absurd you are!

Eustace. Finally, I came home. That was when my experience as a steward came in. I worked my passage as one— if you can call it work! I was sick all the time.

Mrs. Jackson. How dreadful!

Eustace. It was—for the passengers.

Violet. How long ago was that?

Eustace. Only about a month. Since then I've been in London picking up a living one way or another. At last, when I found myself at the end of my tether, I started to walk here. And here I am.

Mrs. Jackson. My dear boy! You must have found it terribly muddy!

Eustace. I did. But life always is rather muddy, isn't it? At least that's my experience.

Mrs. Jackson. But weren't you *very* tired?

Eustace. I was tired, of course. Give me some more coffee, Vi. [*She does so.*] Well, how have you all been at home? How's the governor?

Mrs. Jackson. He's been very well, on the whole. His lumbago was rather troublesome at the end of last year. Otherwise he's been all right.

Eustace. Does he stick to business as close as ever?

Mrs. Jackson. Not quite. You see Henry's a partner now. The firm is Jackson, Hartopp and Jackson, and *he* takes a good deal of work off your father's shoulders. Henry is an excellent man of business. [EUSTACE *nods.*] Your father gives more of his time to public affairs now. He's a magistrate and been on the County Council for the last three years. And now he's standing for Parliament.

Eustace. The family's looking up in the world. The business is flourishing, then?

Mrs. Jackson. Oh, yes. They've put in all new machinery in the last three years. And they've got turbines instead of the old water wheels. That was Henry's idea. And now they can turn out a cheaper cloth than any of the mills round here.

Eustace. Cheaper? The governor used to despise cheap cloth.

Mrs. Jackson. Yes, but Henry said it was no use making cloth that would last a lifetime if people only wanted it to last twelve months. So he got over new machines—from America. And now they don't make any *good* cloth at all and your father has trebled his income.

Eustace. Bravo, Henry.

Mrs. Jackson [*rises*]. And now I really must go down to the village and do my shopping. Have you got cook's list, Vi?

To side table for cigarettes, then nearer to bell.

Violet. Yes, Mother. But I'm coming, too. I promised Mrs. Pratt I'd call at the vicarage before twelve to arrange about the next Mothers' Meeting.

Mrs. Jackson [*to* EUSTACE]. You'll find the paper there dear, and some cigarettes unless you think you oughtn't to smoke. I'll ring for them to clear away. And remember, dear, Dr. Glaisher said you were to keep *quite* quiet. [*Kisses him.*]

Eustace. All right, Mother. I'll remember. [*Still at table.* MRS. JACKSON *and* VIOLET *go out.* EUSTACE *shuts the door. The smile dies out of his face and he gives a perceptible yawn. Then he goes and chooses a cigarette, lights it in leisurely fashion. Takes up paper. Selects chair near fireplace, sits down, and begins to read. Enter* BAINES.] You can clear away, Baines.

Baines. Thank you, sir. [*Pause, clearing away.*] I hope

you're feeling better this morning, sir? [*Goes on clearing table throughout this scene.*]

Eustace. Thanks Baines, the doctor thinks I'm getting on all right.

Baines. Narrow escape you had last night, sir. Thomas says the carriage wheels must have gone within a foot of your head.

Eustace. Thomas is a—I mean does he say that?

Baines. Curious thing we shouldn't have seen you, sir. We must have been that close. But it was a very dark night except when the moon was out. Then it was as bright as day almost. That was how he came to see you, sir.

Eustace. Oh that was it, was it?

Baines. Yes, sir. You see Thomas had just shut the gate after the carriage drove away and the moon happened to come out . . .

Eustace [*bored*]. Quite so. Whose carriage was it by the way?

Baines. Sir John Faringford's, sir.

Eustace. Well if one's head is to be driven over, it may as well be by a member of the aristocracy, eh Baines!

Baines. Certainly, sir.

Eustace. Sir John often dine here nowadays?

Baines. Yes, sir. And Lady Faringford, and Miss Stella.

Eustace. Miss Stella?

Baines. Their daughter, sir. I dare say you wouldn't remember her. Only came out about a year ago. [*Pause.*]

Eustace. So my father is standing for Parliament, is he?

Baines. Yes, sir.

Eustace. Will he get in?

Baines. It's thought so, sir.

Eustace. By the way, which side is he on?

Baines [*puzzled*]. I beg pardon, sir?

Eustace. Which side? Liberal or Conservative?

Baines. Conservative of course, sir. All the people round here are Conservative. All the gentry, that is.

Eustace. More respectable, eh Baines?

Baines. Yes, sir. [BAINES, *who has tray in his hand, hears bell, has a moment of indecision, then puts tray down on table.*] Excuse me, sir.   [*Exit.*

EUSTACE *goes back to his paper. A moment later* BAINES *returns and looks about on writing table.*

Eustace. What is it, Baines? Do you want anything?

Baines. If you please, sir, Miss Faringford has called for a book Miss Violet promised to lend her. [*Continues to search.*]

Eustace [*after pause*]. Have you found it?

Baines. No, sir.

Eustace [*putting down paper on other armchair, bored and rising*]. I'd better see her. [*Goes out.* BAINES *folds tablecloth and puts it away in sideboard drawer. Is just about to go out carrying tray when* STELLA *enters followed by* EUSTACE. *Draws back to let them pass as they enter.*] Come in, Miss Faringford. Perhaps I can find the book for you. What was it like?

Enter STELLA.

Stella. It was just an ordinary-looking novel. With a bright red cover. Called *Hester's Escape*.

Over by writing table.

Eustace. Hester's Escape. I seem to remember the name. [*Turns round and faces her for the first time. Pause. Is obviously struck by the fact that she is a very pretty girl.*] But Vi will know where it is. You'd better wait till she comes in. Sit down. She'll be back directly.

Stella [*sitting in armchair by the fireplace*]. Are you sure?

Eustace. Quite! [*Turns round chair at breakfast table in front of fireplace and sits in it. Exit* BAINES.] You won't mind an untidy room, will you? I'm afraid I breakfasted late.

Stella. I wonder you are down at all.

Eustace [*sits*]. Oh, I'm all right.

Stella. Are you sure you ought to talk? People who have been ill ought to be quiet, oughtn't they?

Eustace. There's really nothing the matter with me.

Stella. That's not what Mrs. Pratt told me. I met her in the village as I was coming here.

Eustace. Ah, yes. She was present of course when I made my dramatic entry. Did she tell you about it? I hope it went off well.

Stella. You frightened everyone terribly, if that's what you mean. Mrs. Pratt says you looked dreadful. She thought you were going to die.

Eustace. Quite a thrilling experience for her. She ought to be very much obliged to me.

Stella. How can you joke about it! You might really have died, you know. But when people have traveled all over the world as you have, and endured hardship and danger, I suppose death doesn't seem so terrible to them as it does to us who stay at home.

Eustace. I suppose not. They get used to it.

Stella. Have you often been in great danger, really great I mean?

Eustace. I was at Singapore when the plague was there.

Stella. How awful.

Eustace. Yes. It wasn't pleasant.

Stella. I can't think how anyone can stay in England when he might go out and see the world. If I were a man I would go abroad and visit strange countries and have wonderful adventures as you have done, not waste my life in a dull little village like Chedleigh.

Eustace. My dear Miss Faringford, the whole world is a dull little village like Chedleigh, and I've wasted my life in it.

Enter BAINES.

Baines. If you please, sir, the Rector has called to ask how you are.

Eustace. Oh, bother. Say I'm very much obliged and I'm all right.

Baines. He said he would like to see you if you felt well enough, sir.

Eustace. Ah! wait a minute. [*Thinks.*] Will you say I'm not well at all and quite unfit to see him this morning.

Baines. Very well, sir. [*Exit.*

Stella [*rising*]. And now I must go. I'm only tiring you. I expect you oughtn't to talk.

Eustace. But I assure you . . .

Stella. And as you're quite unfit to see visitors . . .

Eustace. I'm quite unfit to see the Rector. That's quite a different thing. I'm perfectly up to seeing you. Besides, Violet should be here directly, now. Sit down again.

Stella [*hesitating*]. I don't think I *ought* to stay.

Eustace. I'm sure you ought. One should visit the sick you know.

Stella [*with a laugh*]. You don't seem quite able to make up your mind whether you are ill or well.

Eustace. No. I vary. I find it more convenient. [*Enter* BAINES. *Irritably.*] Well, what is it *now*, Baines?

Baines. Lady Faringford.

Enter LADY FARINGFORD. EUSTACE *rises.*

Stella [*rising*]. Mamma!

Lady Faringford [*ignoring her*]. Mr. Eustace Jackson, is it not? How do you do? [*Shakes hands frigidly.*] I heard in the

village of your sudden return and stopped the carriage to ask
how you were. As the servant told me you were downstairs I
thought I would come in for a moment.

Eustace. Very kind of you, Lady Faringford.

Lady Faringford [*severely*]. You hardly appear as ill as I
expected.

Eustace. I hope the disappointment is an agreeable one?

Lady Faringford. No disappointments are agreeable, sir.
And pray what are *you* doing here, Stella?

Eustace. Miss Faringford called for a book my sister lent
her last night, *Hester's Escape.* I persuaded her to come in
and sit down till Violet returned.

Lady Faringford. You are expecting her soon?

Eustace. Every moment.

Lady Faringford. Ah. Then I don't think we can wait.

Eustace. But Miss Faringford's book. She mustn't go away
without it. Sit down for a moment while I see if I can find
it. [*To* STELLA.] A bright red cover I think you said. [*Looks
round the room for it.*]

Lady Faringford [*icily*]. Pray don't trouble, Mr. Jackson.

Eustace. Hester's Escape? I'm sure I've seen it somewhere.
[*Thinks a moment.*] I know. It was in the drawing room,
last night. Excuse me for a moment. I'll go and get it.

                                                    [*Exit.*

Lady Faringford [*sitting down, sternly*]. Really Stella,
I'm surprised at you.

Stella. What is it, Mamma?

Lady Faringford. You know perfectly well. How long have
you been here?

Stella [*sulkily*]. I don't know . . . about ten minutes, perhaps.

Lady Faringford. Do you make a habit of paying morning
calls upon young men without a chaperon?

Stella. No, Mamma.

Lady Faringford. Then I hope you will not begin to do so.

Stella. I came to call for a book which Vi promised to lend
me. Vi was out and Mr. Jackson very kindly asked me to
come in and wait. What harm is there in that?

Lady Faringford. There is every harm. Understand, please,
that Mr. Eustace Jackson is not a suitable acquaintance for
you.

Stella. He is Henry's brother. You have no objection to my
knowing Henry.

Lady Faringford. That is quite different. Henry has a large income and excellent prospects. He is a man whom any young girl may be allowed to know. Eustace is a mere ne'er-do-well.

Stella. Am I never to speak to anyone who isn't rich? The Du Cranes aren't rich or the Vere-Anstruthers. Yet we know them. We aren't rich ourselves if it comes to that.

Lady Faringford. That has nothing to do with it. The Du Cranes and poor George Anstruther are gentlepeople. The Jacksons are tradesmen.

Stella. I think people make far too much fuss about being "gentlepeople."

Lady Faringford. Then I hope you won't say so. I don't like this pernicious modern jargon about shopkeepers and gentlefolk being much the same. There's far too much truth in it to be agreeable.

Stella. If it's true why shouldn't we say it?

Lady Faringford. Because we have everything to lose by doing so. We were born into this world with what is called position. Owing to that position we are received everywhere, flattered, made much of. Though we are poor, rich people are eager to invite us to their houses and marry our daughters. So much the better for us. But if we began telling people that position was all moonshine, family an antiquated superstition, and many duchesses far less like ladies than their maids, the world would ultimately discover that what we were saying was perfectly true. Whereupon we should lose the very comfortable niche in the social system which we at present enjoy and—who knows?—might actually be reduced in the end to doing something useful for our living like other people. No, no, my dear, rank and birth and the peerage may be all nonsense, but it isn't *our* business to say so. Leave that to vulgar people who have something to gain by it. *Noblesse oblige!*

Enter EUSTACE, *with the book in his hand.*

Eustace. Here is the book, Miss Faringford. I hope you haven't had to wait too long. It was in the drawing room as I thought, but it had got put away under some papers.

Stella. Thank you so much.

Lady Faringford [*rising, icily*]. Good-by, Mr. Jackson.

Stella. Good-by. Give my love to Violet. [*Shakes hands.*]

Exeunt LADY FARINGFORD *and* STELLA *escorted by* EUSTACE. *After a moment enter* HENRY *by window. He has some papers with him which he has brought from the mill. He takes off hat, puts papers on table, up, is about to write letter when re-enter* EUSTACE.

Eustace [*after moment strolls to* HENRY.] Hello, Henry. Where did you spring from?

They shake hands.

Henry. From the mill. I came across the lawn. We had a short cut made through the shrubbery and a gate put three years ago. It's quicker.

Eustace. One of *your* improvements, eh?

Henry. Yes. [EUSTACE *laughs.*] You're amused?

Eustace. It's so like you, having a path made so as to get to your work quicker.

Henry. Yes. I'm not an idler.

Eustace. Quite so. And *I* am, you mean?

EUSTACE *sits.*

Henry [*shrugs*]. I didn't say so.

Eustace. You wanted to spare my feelings, no doubt. Very thoughtful of you. [*A pause.*]

Henry. Is your mother in?

Eustace. I believe not. . . . By the way, I've been borrowing some of your clothes. Not a bad fit, are they? It's lucky we're so much the same size.

Henry [*grimly*]. Very!

Eustace. It's particularly lucky as I've been entertaining visitors on behalf of the family.

Henry. Indeed?

Eustace. Yes. One of them a very charming visitor.

Henry. Who was that?

Eustace. Miss Faringford.

Henry. Stella?

Eustace. Yes. Very nice girl altogether. She was here quite a long time while I told her my adventures—or as much of them as I thought suitable. Then unhappily her mother turned up. Rather an awful woman that.

Henry. What did Stella come for?

Eustace. Not to inquire after me, if that's what you mean. Miss Faringford came for a book Vi had lent her, *Hester's Escape*. She's certainly a very pretty girl. And a nice one.

Henry [*stiffly*]. I may as well tell you I intend to marry Stella Faringford.

Eustace. Indeed. [*Pause.*] Have you asked her yet?

Henry. No.

Eustace. Then I wouldn't be too sure, if I were you. Perhaps she won't have you.

Henry [*rising after silence*]. Oh, by the way, how are you?

Eustace. I'm all right, thanks.

Henry [*irritably*]. How on earth did you come to be lying in the drive in that way last night?

Eustace [*airily*]. Exhaustion, my dear chap. Cold and exposure! Hunger. You know the kind of thing.

Henry. Cold? Why it's the height of summer.

Eustace. Heat, then.

Henry. But how did you manage to *get* here? That's what *I* want to know. You were supposed to be in Australia.

Eustace [*beginning to laugh*]. I'll tell you. [*Sits on table.*] Only you must promise not to give me away. [HENRY *turns.*] I was awfully hard up and awfully sick of finding jobs and losing them and at last I began to long for a proper dinner, properly served, and a decent suit of clothes. Like these. I thought of writing to the governor. But that would have been no good. He'd have sent me some good advice and the mater would have sent a fiver and in a fortnight things would have been as bad as ever. At last I thought of a dramatic coup. The prodigal's return! The fatted calf. A father softened, a mother in tears. The virtuous elder brother scowling in the background. So I came here. Back to the old home, you know. At the front door I selected a convenient spot and lay down in an elaborate faint. Excuse the pun. I chose the moment just after the Faringford's carriage had gone. I knew the footman would have to come in after shutting the gate and I intended to kick his leg and groan in an impressive manner. Anything to attract attention. Fortunately the moon came out just at the right moment so the fool couldn't help spotting me. He called Baines who recognized me in a moment. They were very sympathetic! I expect they thought I was drunk. The lower classes are always sympathetic to intoxication. I was borne into the drawing room. The wandering sheep returned to the fold, the exile home again. Tableau! Most pathetic!

Henry [*disgusted*]. And so you *walked* all the way from London to Chedleigh in order to play off a heartless practical joke.

Eustace. Walked? Nonsense. I came by train. [*Walks across followed by* HENRY.]

Henry. But you told Vi you walked.

Eustace. I said I *started* to walk. I only got as far as the station.

Henry [*angrily*]. It was unpardonable. The mater was awfully upset. So was the governor.

Eustace. That was the idea. There's nothing like a sudden

shock to bring out anyone's real feelings. The governor had
no idea how fond he was of me until he saw me apparently
dead and unlikely to give him further trouble. And by the
time I came round he'd forgotten the cause of his sudden
affection—or perhaps he's never realized it—and was genuinely glad to see me. Psychologically, it was most interesting.

EUSTACE *goes up to window.*

Henry. It was extremely undignified and quite unnecessary.
If you had simply come up to the front door and rung the
bell you would have been received just as readily.

Eustace. I doubt it. In fact, I doubt if I should have been
received at all. I might possibly have been given a bed for
the night, but only on the distinct understanding that I left
early the next morning. Whereas now nobody talks of my
going. A poor invalid. In the doctor's hands! Perfect quiet
essential! No. My plan was best.

HENRY *moves up to* EUSTACE *and past him to fire.*

Henry. Why didn't that fool Glaisher see through you?

Eustace. Doctors never see through their patients. It's not
what they're paid for and it's contrary to professional eti-
quette. [HENRY *makes exclamation of disgust.*] Besides,
Glaisher's an ass, I'm glad to say.

Henry [*fuming*]. It would serve you right if I told the
governor the whole story.

· *Eustace.* I dare say. But you won't. [*Takes out chair.*] It
wouldn't be cricket. Besides, I only told you on condition
you kept it to yourself. [*Sits.*]

Henry [*exasperated*]. So I'm to be made a partner in your
fraud. The thing's a swindle and I've got to take a share in it.

Eustace. Swindle? Not a bit. [*Sits.*] You've lent a hand,
without intending it, to reuniting a happy family circle.
Smoothed the way for the prodigal's return. A very beautiful
trait in your character.

Henry [*grumpy*]. What I don't understand is *why* you
told me all this. Why in heaven's name didn't you keep the
whole discreditable story to yourself?

Eustace. The fact is, I was pretty sure you'd find me out.
The governor's a perfect owl but you've got brains—of a kind.
You can see a thing when it's straight before your nose. So I
thought I'd let you into the secret from the start just to keep
your mouth shut.

Henry [*exclamation of impatience*]. And what are you going to do now you *are* at home?

Eustace. Do, my dear chap? Why nothing.

ACT THREE

The lawn at Chedleigh Court. Ten days have passed since Act Two. It is a Saturday and the time is after luncheon. The house itself, with its French windows onto the lawn, is on the right of stage. The back represents the garden with paddock beyond bounded by stream on which stands the mill, a picturesque old Tudor structure of gray stone. The garden is also supposed to stretch away into the wings and there is a path leading off to the mill. The other entrance is through the French windows from house. When the curtain rises EUSTACE *is discovered in new gray flannel suit in a hammock, swinging indolently. There is a wicker table and three or four wicker garden chairs with bright red cushions. In one of these* HENRY *is seated, reading a newspaper.* EUSTACE *has cup of coffee in his hand.* HENRY *has one on table beside him. Presently* EUSTACE *drinks some, looking with indolent amusement at his brother absorbed in his newspaper.*

EUSTACE. Not bad coffee, this. [*Finishes it and begins to perform acrobatic feat of putting cup and saucer on ground without breaking them.*]

Henry [*looking up*]. I dare say. [*Takes some.*] You'll drop that cup.

Eustace. I think not. [*Puts it successfully on ground.*]

Henry. If you leave it there someone's sure to put his foot in it.

Eustace. I'll risk it.

Henry. Bah! [*Rises and puts* EUSTACE'S *cup on table.*]

Eustace. Thanks, old man. Perhaps it *is* safer there. [HENRY *grunts again and returns to his newspaper.* EUSTACE *gets cigarette out of pocket and lights it indolently.*] Anything exciting in the paper? Any convulsions in wool?

Henry. No.

Eustace. Where's the governor? He generally comes home to luncheon on Saturdays, doesn't he?

Henry. He's lunching at the Wilmingtons' with the mater. He'll be back soon. There's a meeting of his election committee at four.

Eustace. Where?

Henry. Here.

Eustace. Will he get in?

Henry. Faringford thinks so. But it'll be a close thing. A very little might turn the scale either way.

Eustace. Cost him a good deal, I suppose?

Henry. Pretty well.

Eustace. *Panem et circenses,* bread and circuses. That's the Tory prescription, isn't it? Particularly circuses.

Henry. I dare say.

Servant [*ushering* DR. GLAISHER *from French windows*]. Dr. Glaisher to see you, sir. [*Removes cups and exits.*]

Eustace. How do you do, Doctor. [*Shaking hands.*] I'm following your prescription, you see. Rest! Rest! There's nothing like it.

Dr. Glaisher. Just so. I really came for your father's committee. I thought it was to be at three o'clock. But your man tells me it's not till four. So I thought I'd like to look at my patient. Well, and how are we today?

HENRY *watches this scene with mingled rage and disgust to* EUSTACE's *huge delight.*

Eustace. Going on all right, thanks. Still a little limp perhaps.

Dr. Glaisher. Just so. The temperature normal? No fever? That's right. [*Feels pulse.*] Pulse? [*Pause.*] Quite regular. Now the tongue. Just so. [*To* HENRY.] As I should have expected. Just as I should have expected. Appetite still good?

Eustace. Excellent, thanks.

Dr. Glaisher. You're still taking your glass of port at eleven? Just so, oh you'll soon be all right.

Eustace. Thanks to *you,* Doctor.

Dr. Glaisher. Not at all. *Not* at all. [*To* HENRY.] He'll soon be himself again now. System still wants tone a little, wants tone. I'll send him round some of that mixture. Otherwise he's all right.

HENRY *grunts.*

Eustace. And you'll look in again in a day or two [HENRY *rises and goes up.*] just to see how I am, won't you, Doctor?

Dr. Glaisher. Certainly, if you wish it. And now I must

be off. I have a couple of patients near here whom I could see in the next half-hour and be back again by four. Good-by. Good-by. Don't disturb yourself, pray. [*Fusses off.*]

Henry [*savagely*]. Ass!

Eustace. My dear chap!

Henry. Old Glaisher is a perfect noodle.

Eustace. Naturally. How much does a little country doctor make hereabout? Four hundred a year? Say four hundred and fifty. You can't expect a first-rate intellect for that. 'Tisn't the market rate.

Henry. I don't expect an absolute idiot.

Eustace. Glaisher doesn't *know* anything of course, but his manner is magnificently impressive. After he's talked to me for five minutes, felt my pulse, and looked at my tongue I almost begin to wonder whether I'm not really ill after all. That's a great gift for a doctor!

Henry. You're perfectly well. Any fool can see that merely by looking at you. And old Glaisher goes on with his mixture and his glass of port at eleven. Bah! [EUSTACE *laughs.*] And you encourage him. How many visits has he paid you?

Eustace. I don't know. Seven or eight.

Henry. And every one of them completely unnecessary.

Eustace. Completely unnecessary for me, but very useful to old Glaisher, considering they mean half a guinea apiece to him.

Henry. Which the governor pays.

Eustace. Which the governor pays, as you say. That's why I do it. Somebody must keep old Glaisher going or what would become of all the little Glaishers? Here's the governor with piles of money to throw away on Parliamentary elections and similar tomfoolery. Why shouldn't I divert some of it to old Glaisher. I like the little man.

Henry. You're awfully generous—with other people's money.

Eustace. I am. Whose money are *you* generous with? [HENRY *goes upstage. He snorts with disapproval. Enter from garden,* MR. *and* MRS. JACKSON *in outdoor things, as from a luncheon party.*] Morning, Father. [*Enter* MRS. JACKSON.] I've not seen you before today. You went out before I got down.

Mr. Jackson [*gruffly, sitting down*]. Good morning.

MRS. JACKSON, *having kissed* EUSTACE, *sits.*

Eustace. Morning, Mummy. [*To* MR. JACKSON.] By the way, you've just missed one of your election committee.

Mr. Jackson [*alarmed*]. Not Sir John? It's only half past three.

Eustace. No—only little Glaisher. He said he was too early. However, as *you* weren't there he came and had a look at *me.*

Mrs. Jackson. What did he say, dear?

Eustace. Said I was getting on all right. He's coming to have another look at me in a day or two.

Mr. Jackson. When does he think you'll be well enough to get to work again?

Eustace. I don't know. I didn't ask him.

Mrs. Jackson. Oh, Samuel, it's too soon to think of that *yet!* [Mrs. JACKSON *sits at table.*] The poor boy's only convalescent. Wait till Dr. Glaisher has stopped his visits.

Snort from HENRY.

Eustace. My dear Henry, what extraordinary noises you make. It's a terrible habit. You should see someone about it. Why not consult Glaisher?

HENRY *goes up angrily.*

Mr. Jackson [*to his wife*]. As you please, dear. Still I *should* like to know what Eustace intends to do when he *is* well enough. I'm bound to say he looks perfectly well.

Eustace [*blandly*]. Appearances are so deceptive, Father.

Enter VIOLET *from house. She has some work in her hands.*

Violet. Got back, Mother dear? [*Kisses her.*] Enjoyed your lunch?

Mrs. Jackson. Very much. It was quite a large party.

Violet [*sitting down*]. What did you talk about?

Mrs. Jackson. About your father's election, principally. They say Parliament may dissolve any day now. What are you making, dear?

Violet. Handkerchiefs. I promised Eustace I'd work some initials for him.

Goes upstage and sits.

Mr. Jackson [*returning doggedly to his subject*]. Perhaps you will be good enough to tell me what your plans are, Eustace.

Eustace. I haven't any plans, Father.

Mr. Jackson. You haven't any?

Mrs. Jackson. Eustace said the other day he thought he would like to be a doctor.

Mr. Jackson. A doctor! Nonsense.

Mrs. Jackson. Well, I only tell you what he said.

Eustace. My remark was not intended to be taken literally. I don't seriously propose to enter the medical profession.

Mr. Jackson [*irritably*]. Do you seriously propose anything?

Eustace. No, Father. I don't know that I do.

Mr. Jackson [*meditatively*]. I might perhaps find you a place in the office.

Henry [*down to table firmly*]. No, Father! *I* object to that.

Violet. Henry!

Henry. Yes, I do. I object to the office being used as a dumping ground for incompetents.

Mrs. Jackson. Henry! Your own brother!

Henry. I can't help that. I don't see why the firm should be expected to pay a salary to someone who's no earthly use merely because he's my brother.

Mr. Jackson. Still, we might try him.

Henry. My dear Father, why not face the truth? You know what Eustace is. We got him into Jenkins' office. He made nothing of it. Then he was in the Gloucester and Wiltshire Bank. No use there. He tried farming. Same result. Finally you gave him a thousand pounds to settle in Australia. That was five years ago and here he is back again without a sixpence.

Mrs. Jackson. Eustace has been very unlucky.

Henry [*impatiently*]. What has luck got to do with it? Eustace doesn't *work*. That's what's the matter with *him*.

Mrs. Jackson. Still, if he had another chance.

Henry. My dear Mother, you always believe people ought to have another chance. It's a little mania with you. Eustace has had dozens of chances. He's made a mess of every one of them. You know that as well as I do.

Mr. Jackson. Yes. There's no use hiding it from ourselves.

Henry. Not the least—as we can't hide it from anyone else.

Mr. Jackson [*after a pause*]. Well, Eustace, what do *you* think? [*Goes upstage.*]

Eustace [*airily*]. I? Oh, I agree with Henry. [*Lights another cigarette.*]

Mr. Jackson. You *what?*

Eustace. I agree with Henry. I think he's diagnosed the case with great accuracy. Henry ought to have been a doctor too!

Mr. Jackson [*getting up angrily and making an oration*]. Now look here, Eustace. I've had enough of this. You seem to imagine because you've been ill [EUSTACE *grins at* HENRY.] and come home in rags, nothing more in the way of work is to be expected of you. You're to loll about in a hammock smoking cigarettes and taking not the smallest interest in any plans that are suggested for your future. Henry says the reason you've always been a failure is that you don't work and you say you agree with him. Very well. What I have to tell you is I'm not going to have you loafing away your time here. I disapprove of loafing on principle. Both as a public man and as a private man I disapprove of it. There's far too much of it in England today. That's where the Germans are ahead of us. Young men who ought to be at business or in the professions idle away their time and live on their parents. That won't do for *me*. I insist upon your getting something to do at once and doing it. I insist upon it. If you don't . . .

During the last sentence of this impassioned oration SIR JOHN *and* LADY FARINGFORD *and* STELLA *enter, shown in by* BAINES.

Baines. Sir John and Lady Faringford, Miss Faringford.

Instant change of front on the part of the whole family. MR. JACKSON *stops short in the midst of his eloquence and hurriedly substitutes a glassy smile for the irascible sternness which accompanied his speech.* MRS. JACKSON *and the others who had listened in uncomfortable silence hastily assume the conventional simper of politeness as they rise to receive their guests. The only person who remains quite self-possessed is* EUSTACE *though he too smiles slightly as he gets out of hammock.*

Eustace [*aside to* HENRY]. Poor old governor! Stemmed in full tide.

General greetings.

Mrs. Jackson. Dear Lady Faringford. How nice of you to come! Stella, my dear. [*Shakes hands with her and* SIR JOHN.]

Lady Faringford [*meeting her and then stage chattering to* VIOLET]. As Sir John was due at your father's committee at four, Stella and I thought we would drive him down.

Mrs. Jackson. You'll stay and have some tea now you're here, of course!

Lady Faringford. Thank you. Tea *would* be very pleasant.

Stella. How do you do? [*Shaking hands with* HENRY.] And how is the invalid? Getting on well?

Henry [*grimly*]. Excellently.

HENRY *stands behind her.*

Stella. That's right. [*Shakes hands with* EUSTACE. *To* HENRY.] He really looks better, doesn't he? Dr. Glaisher says it's been a wonderful recovery.

Henry. I suppose he does.

Stella [*to* MR. JACKSON]. How glad you must be to have him home again.

Mr. Jackson [*with ghastly attempt at effusion*]. It's a great pleasure of course.

Stella. It must be so sad for parents when their children go away from them. But I suppose sons *will* go away sometimes, however hard their parents try to keep them. Won't they?

Mr. Jackson. That does happen sometimes, er, unquestionably. [*More briskly.*] And anyhow young men can't stay at home always, my dear Miss Faringford. They have their own way to make in the world.

Stella. And so the parents *have* to let them go. It seems hard. But then when they come back it must be delightful.

Eustace. It is.

Sir John. Hadn't we better be going in, Jackson? I shan't be able to stay very long. I have to meet my agent at five-fifteen sharp, to see about some fences.

Mr. Jackson [*looks at watch*]. It's barely four yet. We'd better wait a minute or two. Glaisher will arrive directly and then we can get to work.

EUSTACE, *taking advantage of* MR. JACKSON'S *speaking to* SIR JOHN, *moves towards* STELLA.

Sir John. Ling's advertised to speak at Maytree, I see, tomorrow week.

Mr. Jackson. Is he? At Maytree? That's rather out of his country.

Sir John. Yes. He doesn't go down so well in the villages. Thank heaven agriculture is still Conservative! They go to his meetings though.

Stella. Mr. Ling is such a good speaker they say.

Eustace. My father is a good speaker, too, when he's roused, Miss Faringford. You should have heard him ten minutes ago.

Sir John. What was he speaking on?

Eustace [*airily*]. The unemployed.

MR. JACKSON *scowls at him.*

Sir John. I congratulate you, Jackson. It isn't all sons who are so appreciative of their fathers' efforts. *My* son never listens to *me!*

MR. JACKSON *smiles a sickly smile.*

Baines [*announcing*]. Dr. Glaisher.

EUSTACE *and* STELLA *move away.* HENRY *follows them and tries to join them without success.*

Mr. Jackson. Ah, here you are, Doctor. I began to think you weren't coming.

Mrs. Jackson [*shaking hands*]. Good afternoon. Why didn't you bring Mrs. Glaisher? She and I and Lady Faringford could have entertained each other while you were all at your committee.

Dr. Glaisher. She would have enjoyed it of all things. But I left her at home with the children. Tommy has the whooping cough just now and requires a lot of nursing.

Mrs. Jackson. Poor little chap. I hope he'll be better soon.

Mr. Jackson [*looking at watch*]. Well, well. I'm afraid we ought to go in. Come, Sir John. Are you ready, Doctor? Shall I lead the way? [*Fusses off importantly.*] Come, Henry.

Sir John. By all means.

Mrs. Jackson [*calling after him*]. As you are going, would you mind ringing the bell, Samuel, and telling Baines to bring tea out here.

Mr. Jackson. Very well, my dear.

Exit HENRY *by lower door. Exeunt* MR. JACKSON, SIR JOHN, *and* DOCTOR. EUSTACE, *having lifted up the hammock for* VIOLET *and* STELLA, *listens politely to them.*

Lady Faringford [*at center table with* MRS. JACKSON]. I do hope your husband will be elected, Mrs. Jackson. Mr. Ling has the most dreadful opinions about land—and indeed about everything else I'm told. But that is of less importance.

Mrs. Jackson. Indeed?

Lady Faringford. Oh, yes. Only a year ago at a meeting of the Parish Council he made a speech attacking Sir John quite violently about one of his cottages. It was let to young Barrett, quite a respectable, hard-working man—who afterward died of pneumonia. Mr. Ling declared the cottage was damp and not fit for anyone to live in. So ridiculous of him! As if *all* cottages were not damp. The absurd part of it was that afterward, when Mrs. Barrett was left a widow and Sir John gave her notice because she couldn't pay her rent and he wanted to convert the cottage into pigsties, Mr. Ling was equally indignant and seemed to think we ought to find Mrs. Barrett another house. I don't think he can be quite right in his head.

EUSTACE *goes upstage as* BAINES *and* FOOTMAN *bring out tea on large tray and put it on table.*

Violet [*rising*]. Shall I make the tea, Mother?
Mrs. Jackson. If you please, dear.

STELLA *down right,* EUSTACE *stands by her.*

Eustace. What do *you* think about damp cottages, Miss Faringford? Do *you* think they ought to be left standing in order that the laborer may live in them—and have pneumonia? Or be pulled down in order that the laborer may have nowhere to live at all?

VIOLET *helps* LADY FARINGFORD *to tea.*

Stella [*sits*]. I don't know. I think it's dreadful there should be damp cottages anywhere.
Eustace. That would never do. There must be good cottages and bad cottages in order that the strong may get the good cottages and the weak the bad.
Stella. You mean in order that the strong may have the bad cottages and the weak the good. They need them more.
Violet. Mother.
Eustace. That would be quite unscientific. No, the strong must have the good cottages in order that they may grow stronger, and the weak must have the bad cottages in order that they may die off. Survival of the fittest, you know.
Stella. How horrible.
Eustace. Yes, but how necessary!
Lady Faringford. Come over here, Stella. You have the sun on your face there.
Stella [*rising unwillingly*]. Very well, Mamma.
Lady Faringford. By the way, Mrs. Jackson, have you heard about poor Miss Higgs, who used to keep the school at Little Chedleigh and play the harmonium so badly on Sundays? You remember her? Quite a good creature, knew all kinds of subjects, and never expected one to take any notice of her. So of course one never did. Well, two years ago . . . [*To* EUSTACE *who offers her cake.*] no, thank you . . . an Aunt died and left her a little money and Miss Higgs retired and went to live in Gloucester. One of those unattractive houses near the canal. But she seems to have been quite incapable of managing money. Put it into a gold mine, I be-

lieve, or gave it to her solicitor to invest—which comes to the same thing—and lost every penny.

Mrs. Jackson. Oh. *Poor* Miss Higgs. What a sad thing.

Lady Faringford. Fortunately she was so affected by her loss that she drowned herself in the canal at the bottom of her garden. Otherwise I'm afraid some sort of a subscription would have had to be got up for her.

EUSTACE *gets another cup of tea from* VIOLET *and takes advantage of the move to stand by* STELLA. *He at once begins to talk to her in dumb show.*

Violet. I liked Miss Higgs very much, Lady Faringford.

From this point LADY FARINGFORD *keeps watching* STELLA *out of the corner of her eye and showing by her manner her annoyance at* EUSTACE's *marked attentions to her daughter.* MRS. JACKSON *and* VIOLET *are completely unconscious of this byplay.*

Lady Faringford. So did quite a number of people, I'm told. She was quite a good creature, as I said, much superior to the young woman who has succeeded her at Little Chedleigh. [*Takes tea from* VIOLET.] I wanted them to give the place to my maid Dawkins who is getting rather past her work and really could have taught everything that is necessary or wholesome for the lower orders to learn, though I daresay she would have had some difficulty with the harmonium—at first. However they preferred to get down a young person from London with the most elaborate qualifications. So highly educated in fact that I hear she can't *teach* at all.

Mrs. Jackson. How very awkward.

Lady Faringford. It is indeed. [*Here* EUSTACE *sits by* STELLA. *Takes his tea from* VIOLET.] Stella!

Stella. Yes, Mamma.

Lady Faringford. Say good-by to Mrs. Jackson, my dear. We really must be going [*rising also*]. Shall I let Sir John know you are ready?

Lady Faringford. Pray don't trouble. We can pick him up as we go through the house. Good-by, Mrs. Jackson. [*To* EUSTACE, *shaking hands.*] Good-by. When do you go back to Australia? *Quite* soon, I hope. Come Stella.

Stella [*shaking hands*]. Good-by, Mrs. Jackson.

Exeunt LADY FARINGFORD *and* STELLA, *escorted by* VIOLET. *A pause,* EUSTACE *sits at table indolently.*

Eustace. Clever woman, that.

Mrs. Jackson. Is she, dear? I hadn't noticed. [MRS. JACK-SON *sits at table.*]

Eustace. Yes. We're all of us selfish. But most of us make an effort to conceal the fact. With the result that we are always being asked to do something for somebody and having to invent elaborate excuses for not doing it. And that makes us very unpopular. For everyone hates asking for anything— unless he gets it. But Lady Faringford proclaims her selfishness so openly that no one ever dreams of asking her to do things. It would be tempting providence. With the result that I expect she's quite a popular woman.

Mrs. Jackson. I'm so glad you like Lady Faringford, dear. Your father has the highest opinion of her.

Eustace. The governor never could see an inch before his nose.

Mrs. Jackson. Can't he, dear? He has never said anything about it.

Eustace [*affectionately*]. Dear Mother! [VIOLET *returns.*] Seen the gorgon safely off the premises?

Violet [*laughing*]. Yes—and Sir John.

Mrs. Jackson. The committee was over then?

Violet. It is now—as Lady Faringford insisted on carrying off the chairman. Here's Father.

Enter MR. JACKSON *and* HENRY, *followed by* BAINES *with letters on salver.* BAINES *hands letters, three to* MR. JACKSON, *two to* MRS. JACKSON, *one to* VIOLET; HENRY *sits.*

Baines. Shall I take away, madam?

Mrs. Jackson. Wait a moment. [*To* MR. JACKSON.] Will you have any tea, Samuel?

Mr. Jackson [*opening long envelope and reading papers*]. No. We had some indoors.

Mrs. Jackson [*to* BAINES]. Yes, you can take away. [*To* MR. JACKSON.] Did you have a successful meeting? [BAINES *and* FOOTMAN *take away tea.*]

Mr. Jackson [*standing by table, reading still*]. Eh? Oh, yes.

Mrs. Jackson [*to* HENRY]. What a pity Sir John had to go.

Henry [*by his father*]. It didn't matter. We'd pretty nearly got through our business. [MRS. JACKSON *opens letter and becomes absorbed in its contents.*]

Mr. Jackson [*handing papers to* HENRY]. You'd better look through these. They're from Fisher & Thompson. It's about Wenhams' mill. The sale is next week.

Henry [*nods*]. Very well.

Mr. Jackson [*sits at table*]. Now, Eustace, I want to have a serious talk with you.

Eustace. Not *again*, Father!

Mr. Jackson [*puzzled*]. What do you mean?

Eustace. Couldn't you put it off till tomorrow? I'm hardly well enough to talk seriously twice in one day.

VIOLET *comes down to chair.*

Mr. Jackson. Nonsense, sir. You're perfectly well. Glaisher says there's no longer the slightest cause for anxiety.

Eustace. Traitor!

Mr. Jackson. What, sir?

Eustace. Nothing, Father.

Mr. Jackson. As I told you before tea, I'm not going to have you idling away your time here. The question is what are we to do?

Eustace. Just so, Father.

Mr. Jackson. I mean what are *you* to do? [*Pause, no remark from* EUSTACE]. Lady Faringford said as she went away you ought to go back to Australia. She said it was a thousand pities for any young man *not* to go to Australia.

Mrs. Jackson. Eustace was just saying how clever Lady Faringford was when you came out.

Mr. Jackson. I'm glad to hear it. Well what do you think?

Eustace. About Australia?

Mr. Jackson. Yes.

Eustace. I don't think anything about it.

Mr. Jackson. Would you like to go out there again?

Eustace. No, I shouldn't. I've been there once. It was an utter failure.

Mr. Jackson. You were a failure, you mean.

Eustace. As you please. Anyway it was no good and I had to work as a navvy on the railway. I don't propose to do that again.

Henry [*looking up*]. Other people do well in Australia.

Eustace. Other people do well in England. Or rather the same people do well in both.

Mr. Jackson [*peevishly*]. What *do* you mean?

Eustace. Simply that the kind of qualities which make for success in one country make for success in another. It's just as easy to fail in Sydney as in London. I've done it and I know.

Mrs. Jackson [*who has just opened her second letter*]. A letter from Janet. She is going to be at Gloucester next week and would like to come over to see us on Friday. We aren't going out on that day are we, Violet? [MR. JACKSON, *impatient at this interruption, opens one of the letters in his hand and glances at it.*]

Violet. No, Mother.

Mrs. Jackson. That will do then. She'd better come to luncheon. [*Rises.*] I'll write and tell her at once before I forget.

Violet. Shall I do it, Mother?

Mrs. Jackson. No, dear. I can manage it.

Exit to house.

Mr. Jackson [*who has opened one letter and glanced at it opens second*]. Well! [*Strikes table with clenched fist.*]

Violet. What is it, Father?

Mr. Jackson. What's the meaning of this, I wonder! Barton must be out of his senses.

Violet. Barton?

Mr. Jackson. Yes, Barton, the tailor. Why does he send me in a bill like this? [HENRY *goes to* MR. JACKSON.] Twenty-five pounds. And I've had nothing from him since Easter. Listen to this. One lounge suit four guineas, one dress suit eight guineas, one flannel suit three pounds ten, another lounge suit four guineas. One frock coat and waistcoat four guineas, one pair of trousers one guinea. Total twenty-five pounds eleven.

Eustace. They're mine, Father.

Mr. Jackson. What, sir!

Eustace. Some clothes I ordered. I told him to send the bill to you. That's all right, isn't it?

Mr. Jackson [*exploding*]. All right! Certainly not, sir. It's very far from all right. It's a great liberty.

Eustace. My dear Father, the bill must be sent in to somebody.

Mr. Jackson. And why not to you, pray?

Eustace. What would be the good of that, Father? I've nothing to pay it with.

Mr. Jackson [*fuming*]. Then you shouldn't have ordered the things.

Eustace. But I must wear something. I couldn't go on wearing Henry's things indefinitely. It's hard on *him!* [HENRY *snorts.*] My dear Henry!

HENRY *goes up.*

Mr. Jackson. But what's become of all the clothes you had? You must have had *some* clothes.

Eustace [*shrugs*]. They're in London—and in rags.

Mr. Jackson. Now look here, Eustace. I'm not going to have this. I'm not going to have a son of mine running up bills here.

Eustace. All right, Father. I'm quite willing to pay for the things—if you give me the money.

Mr. Jackson. I shall *not* give you the money, sir. If you want money, you must earn it.

Eustace. That doesn't take us very far.

Mr. Jackson. You'll disgrace me. [MR. JACKSON *rises and invokes the heavens.*] That's what will happen. I insist on your paying Barton and giving me your word of honor never to get anything on credit here again. [*Thrusts bill into* EUSTACE's *hand, then tramps about angrily.*]

Eustace. I've no objection. I don't run up tailors' bills for pleasure. I'd just as soon pay ready money as you would. Only I haven't got it. Give me twenty pounds—no, twenty-five pounds eleven—and I'll pay Barton tomorrow.

Mr. Jackson. I decline to give you money. I decline. Your request is impudent.

Eustace. Let's keep our tempers, Father.

Mr. Jackson. What, sir?

Eustace. I suggested we should keep our tempers. That's all.

Mr. Jackson. This is intolerable. I disown you, sir. I disown you.

Violet. Father!

Mr. Jackson. Be silent, Violet. [*To* EUSTACE.] I'll have nothing more to do with you. I'll pay this debt to Barton and any others you may have incurred since you came back. After that I've done with you. Leave my house at once.

Eustace [*rising, very calm and first putting chair in its place then speaking with ominous distinctness*]. Very well, Father. I'll go if you wish it. [*Movement for* MR. JACKSON.] But I warn you, if I do go, it will be to the nearest work-house!

Mr. Jackson [*fuming*]. That's your affair. It has nothing to do with me. [*Turns away.*]

Eustace. I question that. It rather knocks your election prospects on the head, I fancy.

Mr. Jackson [*swinging round*]. Eh? What?

Eustace. You don't seriously suppose if I do this *you'll* be returned for Parliament? If you do, you don't know the British electorate. This is going to be a scandal, a scandal worth five hundred votes to the other side. And the last man's majority was only fifty. Oh no, my dear Father, if it comes out

that the son of the rich Conservative candidate is in the local
workhouse, good-by to your chances in *this* constituency.

Henry. You wouldn't dare!

Eustace. Dare? Nonsense. What have I to lose?

Henry. But this is infamous. It's blackmail.

Eustace. Call it what you like. It's what I propose to do if
you force me to it.

Violet. Eustace! You couldn't be so wicked!

Eustace. My dear Vi, have I any choice? Here am I absolutely penniless. The governor flies into a rage because I
order some clothes from his tailor and turns me into the
street. What am I to do? I've no profession, no business I
can turn my hand to. I might take to manual labor, break
stones on the road. But that would only bring equal discredit
on this highly respectable family. In England, sons of wealthy
cloth manufacturers don't work with their hands. Besides I
don't like work. So there's nothing left but to beg. If I beg in
the street, the police will take me up. Therefore I must beg
from my relations. If they refuse me, I must go on the
parish.

Henry. Father, this is monstrous. I wouldn't submit to it,
if I were you. If he wants to prevent your election, let him.
I advise you to refuse. [*Down by table.*]

Eustace. All right. But it knocks *your* prospects on the
head too, my dear Henry, social advancement and love's
young dream, you know. Miss Faringford won't marry you if
this happens. Her mother won't let her. You're not so rich as
all that. And if her mother would, Stella wouldn't. Stella
rather likes me. In fact I think she likes me better than she
does you at present. I'm not absolutely certain she wouldn't
marry me if I asked her.

Henry. Lady Faringford would forbid her.

Eustace. Perhaps we shouldn't consult her. Anyhow if you
leave me to eat skilly in Chedleigh Workhouse, Stella won't
accept you. I lay you ten to one on it. [*A pause. Gong rings.*]
Well, what do you say? [*Long silence,* MR. JACKSON *obviously
not knowing what to do.* HENRY *equally uncomfortable.*]
Nothing? [*Still silence.*] *You,* Henry, *you're* full of resource.
What do *you* think? [*Still silence. With a shrug.*] Well, first
gong's gone. *I shall* go and dress for dinner. [*Strolls off.*]

HENRY *snorts.*

ACT FOUR

The drawing room at Chedleigh as in Act One. Occasional table near sofa. When curtain rises MRS. JACKSON *and* VIOLET *are discovered.* VIOLET *is playing softly at piano,* MRS. JACKSON *sitting by fireplace nodding over a piece of work of some kind. Presently enter* EUSTACE. VIOLET *stops playing, closes piano, and later takes up handkerchief she is working for* EUSTACE. EUSTACE *strolls to his mother.*

MRS. JACKSON [*waking up, drowsily*]. Is that you, Eustace? Where's your father?

Eustace. In the library with Henry.

Mrs. Jackson. Talking business?

Eustace [*nods*]. Yes.

Mrs. Jackson. Can you see the time, Vi?

Violet [*sitting by fireplace*]. Nearly ten, Mother dear.

Mrs. Jackson. So late! They must be discussing something very important.

Eustace [*grimly*]. They are.

Mrs. Jackson. Have they been long in the library?

Eustace. They went directly you and Vi left the table.

Mrs. Jackson. And you've been alone in the dining room all that time? Why didn't you come in to us?

Eustace. I thought they might want to consult me.

Mrs. Jackson. About business? I'm so glad. I'm sure you would be most useful in the business if you tried, though Henry doesn't think so.

Eustace. Are you, Mother?

Mrs. Jackson. Of course. Why not? Henry is. And you always learned your lessons far quicker than Henry when you were a boy.

Eustace [*laying hand on her shoulder*]. Flatterer!

Mrs. Jackson [*putting work into work basket*]. Well, I don't think I'll stay up any longer. [*Rises.*] And I do hope Henry won't keep your father up too late. It can't be good for him. [*Kisses* EUSTACE.] Good night, dear. Sleep well. Are you coming, Violet? [*Kisses her.*]

Violet. Directly, Mother.

Eustace *holds door open for her to go out. Then comes slowly down and sits in chair by* Violet *at table.*

Eustace. Dear old mother. She's not clever, but for real goodness of heart I don't know her equal.

Violet [*impatiently*]. Clever! I'm sick of cleverness. What's the good of it? You're *clever*. What has it done for you?

Eustace. Kept me out of prison. That's always something. [Violet *makes gesture of protest.*] Oh, yes, it has. There have been times when I was so hard up I felt I would do anything, *anything,* just for a square meal. If I had been a stupid man I should have done it. I should have robbed a till or forged a check, and that would have been the end of me. Fortunately I'd brains enough to realize that that kind of thing always gets found out. So here I am, still a blameless member of society. [Violet *says nothing, but goes on working. Pause.*] The mater hasn't been told?

Violet. About what happened before dinner? No.

Eustace. I'm glad of that.

Violet. Why?

Eustace. My dear Vi, I'm not absolutely inhuman. Because I'm fond of her, of course, and don't like giving her pain.

Violet. She'll have to know sooner or later.

Eustace. Then I'd rather it was later, in fact when I'm not here. If anybody has got to suffer on my account, I'd rather not see it.

Violet. And you call Lady Faringford selfish!

Eustace [*carelessly*]. Yes. It's a quality I particularly dislike—in others. [*Pause.*]

Violet. I can't understand you. As a boy you were so different. You were kind and affectionate and thoughtful for others.

Eustace [*shrugs*]. I dare say.

Violet. And now . . . ! Think what you have made of your life! You had good abilities. You might have done almost anything if you had only tried. You might have been a successful, honorable man with an assured position and a record you could be proud of. You might . . .

Eustace [*putting his fingers in his ears*]. Stop, Vi. Stop, I tell you. I won't listen to you.

Violet [*surprised*]. Why not?

Eustace [*doggedly*]. Because I won't. All that is over. What's past is past. I have to live my life now. Do you suppose it would make it any easier for me to grizzle over wasted opportunities? No! As each year passes I turn over the page and forget it.

Violet [*wondering*]. And do you never look back?

Eustace [*with a slight shiver*]. Never! If I did I should have drowned myself long ago.

Violet [*with horror*]. Eustace!

Eustace. Oh, my dear Vi, it's all very well for you to preach, but you don't understand. It's easy enough for you living comfortably here at home working for your bazaars and visiting your old women. Your life slips away in a quiet round of small duties, paying calls with the mater, pouring out the governor's coffee. One day just like another. You've no anxieties, no temptations. The lines have fallen to you in pleasant places. And you think you can sit in judgment on me!

Violet [*quietly*]. You think my life happier than yours then?

Eustace. Isn't it?

Violet. No. *Your* life is your own. You can do as you please with it, use it or waste it as you think best. You are free. I am not. You think, because I stay quietly at home doing the duty that lies nearest me and not crying out against fate, therefore I've nothing more to wish for! Would *you* be happy, do you suppose, if you were in my case? I live here down in Chedleigh from year's end to year's end. Mother never leaves home. She doesn't care to pay visits. So I cannot either. I may sometimes get away for a few days, a week, perhaps, but very seldom. And as Mother grows older, I shall go less. Soon people will give up asking me when they find I always refuse. And so I shall be left here alone with no friends, no real companionship, merely one of the family obliged to know the people they know, visit the people they visit, not a grown woman with interests of her own and a life to order as she pleases.

Eustace. But you'll marry . . .

Violet. Marry! What chance have I of marrying now? When we hadn't so much money and Henry and Father weren't so set on taking a position in the county, there was some chance for me. Now there is none. It's all very well for Henry. He is a partner in the firm. He will be a very rich man. He can marry Stella Faringford. Oh, we are to be great people! But you don't find Sir John Faringford's son proposing to *me!* No! He wants a girl of his own class or else an heiress, not a manufacturer's daughter with a few thousand pounds. So the great people won't marry me and I mustn't marry the little people. Father wouldn't like it. He hardly lets Mother ask them to the house nowadays. And so the years go by and my youth with them, and I know it will be like this always, always.

Eustace. Poor old Vi! And I thought you were quite contented with your bazaars and your old women. Why don't you speak to the mater?

Violet [*resuming her work*]. What's the use? Mother wouldn't understand. She married when she was twenty-one. She doesn't know what it is for a girl to go on living at home long after she's grown up and ought to have a house of her own. So I stay on here knitting socks for old Allen and working *your* handkerchiefs and here I shall stay till Mother and Father are both dead. . . . And then it will be too late.

Eustace. Poor old Vi! . . . [*A pause.*] Do you know you make me feel rather mean? Henry and the governor I can stand up to. They're very much like me. We belong to the predatory type. Only they're more successful than I am. They live on their workpeople. I propose to live on them. We're birds of a feather. But you're different. I suppose you get it from the mater.

Violet. Why are you so bitter against your father?

Eustace. Am I?

Violet. Yes. Just now. And this afternoon.

Eustace [*shrugs*]. Oh that . . . ! Well the fact is I wanted to bring things to a head. I feel I can't stay here. I must get away.

Violet. Why?

Eustace. For lots of reasons. I can't stand this place—I've outgrown it I suppose. [*Pause.*] And then there's Stella. . . .

Violet. Stella?

Eustace. Yes. If I were here much longer I might be falling in love with Stella. [*Walks over to* VIOLET *and stands by her.*] And that wouldn't be fair to Henry. After all he was first in the field. And it wouldn't be fair to her either. I'm not fit to marry a girl like that. No. I must get away.

Violet. Poor Eustace.

Eustace. Oh, you needn't pity me. I shall get along somehow. My life hasn't been successful. It hasn't even been honorable. But it's been devilish interesting.

Enter MR. JACKSON *and* HENRY.

Mr. Jackson. You here, Vi? I thought you'd have gone to bed. Your mother went long ago, I expect?

Violet. Only a few minutes.

Mr. Jackson. Well run away now, dear. It's late.

Violet. Very well, Father. [*Gathers up her things and rises.*]

Good night. [*Kisses him.*] Good night, Henry. Good night, Eustace.

Eustace [*taking her hand*]. Good night, Vi. And good-by. [*Holds open door for her.*]

She kisses him and exits.

While VIOLET *has been getting her things together* MR. JACK- SON *has been showing obvious signs of nervous impatience. Even* HENRY *has fidgeted. When* VIOLET *has gone* EUSTACE *sits on settee.*

Eustace. Well?

Mr. Jackson. Ahem! We have been in consultation, your brother and I, as to the right course to adopt with regard to you.

Eustace [*nods*]. So I supposed.

HENRY *sits in chair at top table.*

Mr. Jackson. After the extraordinary and undutiful attitude you took up this afternoon, I might naturally have declined all further relations with you. But . . .

Eustace [*matter of fact*]. But as that course might prove almost as disagreeable for yourself as it would for me, you naturally thought better of it. Let's get on.

Mr. Jackson [*rearing under this touch of the spur, but mas- tering himself*]. I might point out to you that we, your mother and I, have never failed in our duty by you. We have been indulgent parents. You were sent to a first-rate school. Nothing was spared that could make you a prosperous and successful man. But I won't speak of that.

Eustace [*dryly*]. Thanks, Father.

Mr. Jackson [*running on*]. I might point out that we have given you a score of good chances for establishing yourself in a satisfactory position and you have failed to profit by them. I might remind you that since you returned to this roof . . .

Eustace [*impatiently*]. My dear Father, I thought you were going to leave that part out? And I do wish you wouldn't begin talking about your *roof*. When people refer to their *roof*, I always know they're going to suggest something quite un- practical. In ordinary times they don't soar above the ceiling. But in moments of fervor, off goes the roof! Let's come to the point.

Mr. Jackson [*collecting himself again*]. I will do so at once. Your brother and I feel that little as you have deserved this consideration at my hands and wholly as you have forfeited all claim to further assistance both by your past failures and by your conduct this afternoon, you should yet be given one more chance.

During the latter part of this speech and the beginning of the next, EUSTACE *insensibly begins to beat time to his father's impassioned antithesis.*

Eustace. Come, that's satisfactory.

Mr. Jackson. Five years ago when, after repeated failures on your part, after paying your debts more than once and finding you openings again and again, I sent you to Australia, I gave you a thousand pounds to make a career for yourself. I told you that was the last sum of money you would have from me during my lifetime. What may or may not come to you after my death is another matter. And I gave it you on the express stipulation that if you lost or squandered it, you were not to write for more.

Eustace. I kept that stipulation.

Mr. Jackson. That is so. I now propose to do again what I did five years ago. I propose to send you back to Australia with a thousand pounds.

Henry [*looking up from book, which he has been appearing to read*]. To be paid to you *after* your arrival there.

Mr. Jackson. Quite so. I will send the thousand pounds, less the cost of your passage, to an agent to be paid to you on your landing. In return you are to promise not to come back to this country without my express permission. I think you will agree with me that the course I am taking is a kinder one than you deserve. Few fathers would do as much. I might have named a smaller sum. But I prefer to err on the generous side.

Eustace [*nodding*]. Quite so. And what do you propose that I should do with a thousand pounds?

Mr. Jackson. That is for you to decide. You might start in business.

Eustace. I've tried that.

Mr. Jackson. Sheep farming.

Eustace. I've tried that.

Mr. Jackson. Gold mining.

Eustace. I've tried that.

Mr. Jackson. Well, well, any line which you think offers you a favorable opening.

Eustace [*insinuatingly*]. And which line is that?

Mr. Jackson [*irritably*]. *I* don't know.

Eustace. No more do I. [*Pause.*] No, Father, it would be

absurd for me to accept your offer, because it isn't practical.
It would only be throwing your money away. It would do
me no good, and cause you heartfelt distress.

Mr. Jackson. Nonsense. Other young fellows go out to Australia with less than a thousand pounds and make fortunes,
far less. Why shouldn't you?

Eustace. Why indeed? However we must keep to the point.
They make fortunes. *I* don't.

Mr. Jackson [*exasperated*]. In fact, they're active and
energetic, you're useless and worthless. Where other people
by thrift and enterprise and steady application make money,
you only lose it.

Eustace. Exactly. I lose it. And doubtless for lack of the
qualities you mention. What then? Granted I am all you say,
how does that help us? Here I am, alive, and requiring food
at the customary intervals. Who is going to give it me?
[HENRY *snorts.*] Really, Henry!

Mr. Jackson [*hotly*]. That is to say you *want* to go through
life sponging on your family instead of working for your living like an honest man.

Eustace [*getting annoyed, rises and goes to his father*].
Look here, Father, hadn't we better drop all that stuff about
wanting to sponge on one's family and the rest of it. Nobody
wants to sponge on other people. The idea's preposterous.
We all *want* to be prosperous and highly respected members
of society like you and Henry, with more money than we
know what to do with, with a seat in Parliament and a wife
out of the baronetage. That's what we *want!* And if we
haven't the luck or the brains or the energy to get it, you
needn't call us names. You don't suppose I *prefer* losing
money to making it, do you? You don't suppose if I had my
choice I should drift about the world adding up accounts in a
filthy Hong Kong bank or playing steward on a filthier ocean
liner? You can't be so ridiculous. [HENRY *comes down.*] I'm
good for nothing, as you say. I've no push, no initiative, no
staying power. I shall never be anything but a failure. But
don't imagine I *like* it! You seem to think you've a terrible
grievance because I'm a ne'er-do-well and come to you for
money, but the real grievance is mine.

Henry [*tartly*]. If you don't like coming on your family for
money, you needn't do it.

Eustace [*impatiently*]. It's not what I do but what I am
that is the difficulty. What does it matter what one *does?* It's
done and then it's over and one can forget it. The real tragedy
is what one *is.* Because one can't escape from that. It's always

there, the bundle of passions, weaknesses, stupidities, that one calls character, waiting to trip one up. Look at the governor, that pillar of rectitude and business ability! Do you suppose *he* could be like me if he tried. Of course not. Nor could I be like him.

Mr. Jackson. Have you no will?

Eustace. No. Have you? Have we any of us? [*Sits.*] Aren't we just the creatures of our upbringing, of circumstance, of our physical constitution? We are launched on the stream at our birth. Some of us can swim against the current. Those who can't, it washes away.

There is a pause. HENRY *looks sullen,* MR. JACKSON *puzzled.* EUSTACE, *who has grown rather heated, regains his composure.*

Mr. Jackson. Well, what's to be done with you?

Eustace. I'm afraid you'll have to keep me. You're my father, you know. You've brought into the world a worthless and useless human being. I think those were *your* adjectives? You're responsible.

Mr. Jackson. Is that any reason why I should support you?

Eustace. No, Father. Frankly I don't think it is. I think your sensible course would be to put me quietly out of this wicked world or hire someone else to do so. I'm a bad egg. I shall never hatch into anything that will do you the smallest credit. Your sensible course is to destroy me. But you daren't do that. Social convention won't allow you; the law would make a fuss. Indeed the law won't even allow me to put an end to myself and save you the trouble. I should be rescued, very wet and draggled, from the muddy waters of the Ched by the solitary policeman, who seems to have nothing else to do but to stand about rescuing people who had much better be left to drown. I should be hauled before the magistrates—you're a magistrate yourself now, Father. You'd be there—I should be given a solemn lecture and then "handed over to my friends"—that's you again, Father—who would undertake to look after me in future. And I only hope you would be able to conceal your annoyance at my rescue from the prying eyes of your brother justices!

Mr. Jackson. You've no right to say that. You've no right to suggest that I wish you were dead.

Eustace [*genially*]. Of course, you do. You want me to go to Australia where you'll never hear of me again, where in fact I shall be dead to you. What's the difference? [*A pause.*]

Mr. Jackson. Well, I won't argue with you. The question is what do you propose?

Eustace [*after a moment's thought*]. In the circumstances, I think your wisest course will be to make me an allowance, say three hundred a year, paid quarterly. Then I'll go away and live quietly in London and you'll be rid of me.

Mr. Jackson [*angry again*]. I refuse, sir, I refuse absolutely. The suggestion is utterly shameless.

Eustace. I dare say. But it's perfectly sensible. I appeal to Henry.

Henry. Father, I think you'd better do as he says. If you gave him a thousand pounds as we intended, he'd only lose it. Better make him an allowance. Then you can always stop it if he doesn't behave himself. It's a shameless proposal, as you say, but it's practical.

Eustace. Bravo, Henry, I always said you had brains. That's exactly it. Shameless but eminently practical.

Mr. Jackson [*grumbling*]. What I can't see is why I should allow you this money. [HENRY *turns away annoyed and sits.*] Here's Henry who's perfectly satisfactory and has never caused me a moment's anxiety. I don't give *him* money. Whereas you, who have never caused me anything else, expect me to keep you for the remainder of your life.

Eustace. It is unreasonable, isn't it. But we live in a humanitarian age. We coddle the sick and we keep alive the imbecile. We shall soon come to pensioning the idle and the dissolute. You're only a little in advance of the times. England is covered with hospitals for the incurably diseased and asylums for the incurably mad. If a tenth of the money were spent on putting such people out of the world and the rest were used in preventing the healthy people from falling sick and the sane people from starving, we should be a wholesomer nation.

Mr. Jackson [*after a pause*]. Well, if Henry thinks so, I suppose I must give you an allowance. But I won't go beyond two hundred.

Eustace. I can't keep out of debt on two hundred.

Mr. Jackson. Two hundred and fifty then.

Eustace [*persuasively*]. Three hundred.

Mr. Jackson. Two hundred and fifty. Not a penny more. [*Breaking out again.*] Why, I'd starve before I consented to sponge on my family as you are doing.

Eustace [*quietly*]. Ah. You evidently don't know much about starving, Father! If you write a check for my first quarter now, I can catch the eleven-fifteen up.

Mr. Jackson. You can't go tonight. You're not packed. And you'll want to say good-by to your mother.

Eustace. I think not. As I'm to go, it had better be as suddenly as I came. It saves such a lot of explanations. You can send my things after me to London.

Mr. Jackson [*a pause*]. Very well. I'll go and write you a check.   [*Exit.*

A long pause.

Henry [*bitterly*]. Well, you've got what you wanted.

Eustace [*airily*]. Thanks to you, my dear fellow.

Henry. What a sordid plot it has been! To make your way into this house by a trick with the deliberate intention of blackmailing your own father.

Eustace. You're wrong. The blackmail as you call it was an afterthought. When I made my way into this house in the way you so accurately describe, my designs went no further than getting some decent food and a house over my head for a few days. But when I got here and found you all so infernally prosperous, the governor flinging money about over getting into Parliament, you intending to marry Faringford's daughter, I thought I'd put in for a share of the plunder.

Henry [*disgusted*]. Well, you've succeeded, succeeded because you've neither honor nor conscience about you.

Eustace. No. I've succeeded because you're a snob and the governor's a snob, and that put you both in my power. I might have been as poor and as unscrupulous as you please without getting a halfpenny out of either of you. Luckily the governor's political ambitions and your social ambitions gave me the pull over you and I used it.

Henry [*rises and goes towards* EUSTACE]. Faugh! [*Fiercely.*] You understand of course that if you are to have this allowance it is on the express condition that you give up all thoughts of Miss Faringford, give them up absolutely.

Eustace. By all means. What should *I* be about, marrying a penniless girl like Stella.

Henry. There's nothing you won't do for money! Even to giving up the girl you pretend to care for.

Eustace [*shrugs*]. I dare say. Besides, what would Stella be about marrying a penniless devil like me?

Another silence.

Henry [*breaking out*]. And the best of it is if this story ever gets about, *you'll* get all the sympathy! Ne'er-do-wells always do. The governor and I would be despised as a couple of stony-hearted wretches with no bowels of compassion who grudged money to a necessitous brother while you would be called a lighthearted devil-may-care chap who is nobody's enemy but his own!

Eustace. Well, I think I'd change places with you. After all, you're pretty comfortable here. And you'll marry Stella, damn you.

HENRY *is silent. Pause.*

Enter MR. JACKSON *with check in his hand.*

Mr. Jackson. Here's your check.

Eustace [*looks at it*]. Fours into two hundred and fifty. Sixty-two pounds ten. Thanks, Father. [*Holds out hand.*] Good-by. [MR. JACKSON *hesitates.*] You may as well. After all I'm your son. And if I'm a sweep, it's your fault!

Mr. Jackson [*takes his hand*]. Good-by. [*Hesitates—moves to fireplace.* EUSTACE *turns to go.*] You may write occasionally, just to let us know how you are.

Eustace [*smiles grimly, then hands back check*]. Make it three hundred, Father—and I won't write. [MR. JACKSON *is about to protest angrily, then recognizing the uselessness of that proceeding, says nothing, but waves check contemptuously away.* EUSTACE, *still smiling, pockets it.*] No? Well have it your own way. Good-by. Good-by, Henry. [*Nods to him without offering to shake hands.*]

Exit. MR. JACKSON *turns toward fireplace and leans head on mantelpiece with a sigh.*

GETTING MARRIED
A Disquisitory Play
by
BERNARD SHAW

CHARACTERS

THE BISHOP OF CHELSEA, *unofficially Alfred Bridgenorth*
MRS. BRIDGENORTH
WILLIAM COLLINS, *the greengrocer*
GENERAL BRIDGENORTH
LESBIA GRANTHAM
REGINALD BRIDGENORTH
LEO BRIDGENORTH
ST. JOHN HOTCHKISS
CECIL SYKES
EDITH BRIDGENORTH
SOAMES
THE BEADLE
MRS. GEORGE

GETTING MARRIED

On a fine morning in the spring of 1908 the Norman kitchen in the palace of THE BISHOP OF CHELSEA *looks very spacious and clean and handsome and healthy.*

THE BISHOP *is lucky enough to have a XII century palace. The palace itself has been lucky enough to escape being carved up into XV century Gothic, or shaved into XVIII century ashlar, or "restored" by a XIX century builder and a Victorian architect with a deep sense of the umbrella-like gentlemanliness of XIV century vaulting. The present occupant, A. Chelsea, unofficially Alfred Bridgenorth, appreciates Norman work. He has, by adroit complaints of the discomfort of the place, induced the Ecclesiastical Commissioners to give him some money to spend on it; and with this he has got rid of the wall papers, the paint, the partitions, the exquisitely planed and moulded casings with which the Victorian cabinet-makers enclosed and hid the huge black beams of hewn oak, and of all the other expedients of his predecessors to make themselves feel at home and respectable in a Norman fortress. It is a house built to last for ever. The walls and beams are big enough to carry the tower of Babel, as if the builders, anticipating our modern ideas and instinctively defying them, had resolved to shew how much material they could lavish on a house built for the glory of God, instead of keeping a competitive eye on the advantage of sending in the lowest tender, and scientifically calculating how little material would be enough to prevent the whole affair from tumbling down by its own weight.*

The kitchen is THE BISHOP'S *favorite room. This is not at all because he is a man of humble mind; but because the kitchen is one of the finest rooms in the house.* THE BISHOP *has neither the income nor the appetite to have his cooking done there. The windows, high up in the wall, look north and south. The north window is the largest; and if we look into the kitchen through it we see facing us the south wall with small Norman windows and an open door near the corner to the left. Through this door we have a glimpse of the garden, and of a garden chair in the sunshine. In the right-hand corner is an entrance to a vaulted circular chamber with a winding stair leading up through a tower to the upper floors of the palace. In the wall to our right is the immense fireplace, with its huge spit like a baby crane, and a collection of old iron and brass instruments which pass as the original furniture of the fire, though as a matter of fact they have been picked up from time to time by* THE BISHOP *at secondhand shops. In the near end of the left-hand wall a small Norman door gives access to* THE BISHOP'S *study, formerly a scullery. Farther along, a great oak chest stands against the wall. Across the middle of the kitchen is a big timber table surrounded by eleven stout rush-bottomed chairs: four on the far side, three on the near side, and two at each end. There is a big chair with railed back and sides on the hearth. On the floor is a drugget of thick fibre matting. The only other piece of furniture is a clock with a wooden dial about as large as the bottom of a washtub, the weights, chains, and pendulum being of corresponding magnitude; but* THE BISHOP *has long since abandoned the attempt to keep it going. It hangs above the oak chest.*

The kitchen is occupied at present by THE BISHOP'S *lady,* MRS. BRIDGENORTH, *who is talking to* MR. WILLIAM COLLINS, *the greengrocer. He is in evening dress, though it is early forenoon.* MRS. BRIDGENORTH *is a quiet happy-looking woman of fifty or thereabouts, placid, gentle, and humorous, with delicate features and fine grey hair with many white threads. She is dressed as for some festivity; but she is taking things easily as she sits in the big chair by the hearth, reading* The Times.

COLLINS *is an elderly man with a rather youthful waist. His muttonchop whiskers have a coquettish touch of Dundreary at their lower ends. He is an affable man, with those perfect manners which can be acquired only in keeping a shop for the sale of necessaries of life to ladies whose social position is so unquestionable that they are not anxious about it. He is a reassuring man, with a vigilant grey eye, and the power of saying anything he likes to you without offence, because his tone always implies that he does it with your kind permission. Withal by no means servile: rather gallant and compassionate, but never without a conscientious recognition, on public grounds, of social distinctions. He is at the oak chest counting a pile of napkins.*

MRS. BRIDGENORTH *reads placidly:* COLLINS *counts: a blackbird sings in the garden.* MRS. BRIDGENORTH *puts* The Times *down in her lap and considers* COLLINS *for a moment.*

MRS. BRIDGENORTH. Do you never feel nervous on these occasions, Collins?

Collins. Lord bless you, no, maam. It would be a joke, after marrying five of your daughters, if I was to get nervous over marrying the last of them.

Mrs. Bridgenorth. I have always said you were a wonderful man, Collins.

Collins [*almost blushing*]. Oh, maam!

Mrs. Bridgenorth. Yes. I never could arrange anything—a wedding or even a dinner—without some hitch or other.

Collins. Why should you give yourself the trouble, maam? Send for the greengrocer, maam: thats the secret of easy housekeeping. Bless you, it's his business. It pays him and you, let alone the pleasure in a house like this. [Mrs. BRIDGE-NORTH *bows in acknowledgment of the compliment.*] They joke about the greengrocer, just as they joke about the mother-in-law. But they cant get on without both.

Mrs. Bridgenorth. What a bond between us, Collins!

Collins. Bless you, maam, theres all sorts of bonds between all sorts of people. You are a very affable lady, maam, for a Bishop's lady. I have known Bishops' ladies that would fairly provoke you to up and cheek them; but nobody would ever forget himself and his place with you, maam.

Mrs. Bridgenorth. Collins: you are a flatterer. You will superintend the breakfast yourself as usual, of course, wont you?

Collins. Yes, yes, bless you, maam, of course. I always do. Them fashionable caterers send down such people as I never did set eyes on. Dukes you would take them for. You see the relatives shaking hands with them and asking them about the family—actually ladies saying "Where have we met before?" and all sorts of confusion. Thats my secret in business, maam. You can always spot me as the greengrocer. It's a fortune to me in these days, when you cant hardly tell who anyone is or isnt. [*He goes out through the tower, and immediately returns for a moment to announce.*] The General, maam.

Mrs. BRIDGENORTH *rises to receive her brother-in-law, who enters resplendent in full-dress uniform, with many medals and orders.* GENERAL BRIDGENORTH *is a well set up man of fifty, with large brave nostrils, an iron mouth, faithful dog's eyes, and much natural simplicity and dignity of character. He is ignorant, stupid, and prejudiced, having been carefully trained to be so; and it is not always possible to be patient with him when his unquestionably good intentions become actively mischievous; but one blames society, not himself, for this. He would be no worse a man than* COLLINS, *had he enjoyed* COLLINS's *social opportunities. He comes to the hearth, where* MRS. BRIDGENORTH *is standing with her back to the fireplace.*

Mrs. Bridgenorth. Good morning, Boxer. [*They shake hands.*] Another niece to give away. This is the last of them.

The General [*very gloomy*]. Yes, Alice. Nothing for the old warrior uncle to do but give away brides to luckier men than himself. Has—[*He chokes.*] has your sister come yet?

Mrs. Bridgenorth. Why do you always call Lesbia my sister? Dont you know that it annoys her more than any of the rest of your tricks?

The General. Tricks! Ha! Well, I'll try to break myself off it; but I think she might bear with me in a little thing like that. She knows that her name sticks in my throat. Better call her your sister than try to call her L—[*He almost breaks down.*] L— well, call her by her name and make a fool of myself by crying. [*He sits down at the near end of the table.*]

Mrs. Bridgenorth [*going to him and rallying him*]. Oh come, Boxer! Really, really! We are no longer boys and girls. You cant keep up a broken heart all your life. It must be nearly twenty years since she refused you. And you know that it's not because she dislikes you, but only that she's not a marrying woman.

The General. It's no use. I love her still. And I cant help telling her so whenever we meet, though I know it makes her avoid me. [*He all but weeps.*]

Mrs. Bridgenorth. What does she say when you tell her?

The General. Only that she wonders when I am going to grow out of it. I know now that I shall never grow out of it.

Mrs. Bridgenorth. Perhaps you would if you married her. I believe youre better as you are, Boxer.

The General. I'm a miserable man. I'm really sorry to be a ridiculous old bore, Alice; but when I come to this house for a wedding—to these scenes—to—to—recollections of the past—always to give the bride to somebody else, and never to have my bride given to me—[*He rises abruptly.*] May I go into the garden and smoke it off?

Mrs. Bridgenorth. Do, Boxer.

COLLINS *returns with the wedding cake.*

Mrs. Bridgenorth. Oh, heres the cake. I believe it's the same one we had for Florence's wedding.

The General. I cant bear it [*He hurries out through the garden door.*]

Collins [*putting the cake on the table*]. Well, look at that, maam! Aint it odd that after all the weddings he's given away at, the General cant stand the sight of a wedding cake yet. It always seems to give him the same shock.

Mrs. Bridgenorth. Well, it's his last shock. You have married the whole family now, Collins. [*She takes up* The Times *again and resumes her seat.*]

Collins. Except your sister, maam. A fine character of a lady, maam, is Miss Grantham. I have an ambition to arrange her wedding breakfast.

Mrs. Bridgenorth. She wont marry, Collins.

Collins. Bless you, maam, they all say that. You and me said it, I'll lay. I did, anyhow.

Mrs. Bridgenorth. No: marriage came natural to me. I should have thought it did to you too.

Collins [*pensive*]. No, maam: it didnt come natural. My wife had to break me into it. It came natural to her: she's what you might call a regular old hen. Always wants to have her family within sight of her. Wouldnt go to bed unless she knew they was all safe at home and the door locked, and the lights out. Always wants her luggage in the carriage with her. Always goes and makes the engine driver promise her to be careful. She's a born wife and mother, maam. Thats why my children all ran away from home.

Mrs. Bridgenorth. Did you ever feel inclined to run away, Collins?

Collins. Oh yes maam, yes: very often. But when it came to the point I couldnt bear to hurt her feelings. She's a sensitive, affectionate, anxious soul; and she was never brought up to know what freedom is to some people. You see, family life is all the life she knows: she's like a bird born in a cage, that would die if you let it loose in the woods. When I thought how little it was to a man of my easy temper to put up with her, and how deep it would hurt her to think it was because I didnt care for her, I always put off running away til next time; and so in the end I never ran away at all. I daresay it was good for me to be took such care of; but it cut me off from all my old friends something dreadful, maam: especially the women, maam. She never gave them a chance: she didnt indeed. She never understood that married people should take holidays from one another if they are to keep at all fresh. Not that I ever got tired of her, maam; but my! how I used to get tired of home life sometimes. I used to catch myself envying my brother George: I positively did, maam.

Mrs. Bridgenorth. George was a bachelor then, I suppose?

Collins. Bless you, no, maam. He married a very fine figure of a woman; but she was that changeable and what you might call susceptible, you would not believe. She didnt seem to have any control over herself when she fell in love. She would mope for a couple of days, crying about nothing; and then she would up and say—no matter who was there to hear her— "I must go to him, George"; and away she would go from her home and her husband without with-your-leave or by-your-leave.

Mrs. Bridgenorth. But do you mean that she did this more than once? That she came back?

Collins. Bless you, maam, she done it five times to my own knowledge; and then George gave up telling us about it, he got so used to it.

Mrs. Bridgenorth. But did he always take her back?

Collins. Well, what could he do, maam? Three times out of four the men would bring her back the same evening and no harm done. Other times theyd run away from her. What could any man with a heart do but comfort her when she came back crying at the way they dodged her when she threw herself at their heads, pretending they was too noble to accept the sacrifice she was making. George told her again and again that if she'd only stay at home and hold off a bit theyd be at her feet all day long. She got sensible at last and took his advice. George always liked change of company.

Mrs. Bridgenorth. What an odious woman, Collins! Dont you think so?

Collins [*judicially*]. Well, many ladies with a domestic turn thought so and said so, maam. But I will say for Mrs. George that the variety of experience made her wonderful interesting. Thats where the flighty ones score off the steady ones, maam. Look at my old woman! She's never known any man but me; and she cant properly know me, because she dont know other men to compare me with. Of course she knows her parents in—well, in the way one does know one's parents: not knowing half their lives as you might say, or ever thinking that they was ever young; and she knew her children as children, and never thought of them as independent human beings til they ran away and nigh broke her heart for a week or two. But Mrs. George she came to know a lot about men of all sorts and ages; for the older she got the younger she liked em; and it certainly made her interesting, and gave her a lot of sense. I have often taken her advice on things when my own poor old woman wouldnt have been a bit of use to me.

Mrs. Bridgenorth. I hope you dont tell your wife that you go elsewhere for advice.

Collins. Lord bless you, maam, I'm that fond of my old

Matilda that I never tell her anything at all for fear of hurting her feelings. You see, she's such an out-and-out wife and mother that she's hardly a responsible human being out of her house, except when she's marketing.

Mrs. Bridgenorth. Does she approve of Mrs. George?

Collins. Oh, Mrs. George gets round her. Mrs. George can get round anybody if she wants to. And then Mrs. George is very particular about religion. And she's a clairvoyant.

Mrs. Bridgenorth [*surprised*]. A clairvoyant!

Collins [*calm*]. Oh yes, maam, yes. All you have to do is to mesmerize her a bit; and off she goes into a trance, and says the most wonderful things! not things about herself, but as if it was the whole human race giving you a bit of its mind. Oh, wonderful, maam, I assure you. You couldnt think of a game that Mrs. George isnt up to.

LESBIA GRANTHAM *comes in through the tower. She is a tall, handsome, slender lady in her prime: that is, between thirty-six and fifty-five. She has what is called a well-bred air, dressing very carefully to produce that effect without the least regard for the latest fashions, sure of herself, very terrifying to the young and shy, fastidious to the ends of her long finger-tips, and tolerant and amused rather than sympathetic.*

Lesbia. Good morning, dear big sister.

Mrs. Bridgenorth. Good morning, dear little sister. [*They kiss.*]

Lesbia. Good morning, Collins. How well you are looking! And how young! [*She turns the middle chair away from the table and sits down.*]

Collins. Thats only my professional habit at a wedding, Miss. You should see me at a political dinner. I look nigh seventy. [*Looking at his watch.*] Time's getting along, maam. May I send up word from you to Miss Edith to hurry a bit with her dressing?

Mrs. Bridgenorth. Do, Collins.

COLLINS *goes out through the tower, taking the cake with him.*

Lesbia. Dear old Collins! Has he told you any stories this morning?

Mrs. Bridgenorth. Yes. You were just late for a particularly thrilling invention of his.

Lesbia. About Mrs. George?

Mrs. Bridgenorth. Yes. He says she's a clairvoyant.

Lesbia. I wonder whether he really invented Mrs. George, or stole her out of some book.

Mrs. Bridgenorth. I wonder!

Lesbia. Wheres the Barmecide?

Mrs. Bridgenorth. In the study, working away at his new book. He thinks no more now of having a daughter married than of having an egg for breakfast.

THE GENERAL, *soothed by smoking, comes in from the garden.*

The General [*with resolute bonhomie*]. Ah, Lesbia! How do you do? [*They shake hands; and he takes the chair on her right.*]

MRS. BRIDGENORTH *goes out through the tower.*

Lesbia. How are you, Boxer? You look almost as gorgeous as the wedding cake.

The General. I make a point of appearing in uniform whenever I take part in any ceremony, as a lesson to the subalterns. It is not the custom in England; but it ought to be.

Lesbia. You look very fine, Boxer. What a frightful lot of bravery all these medals must represent!

The General. No, Lesbia. They represent despair and cowardice. I won all the early ones by trying to get killed. You know why.

Lesbia. But you had a charmed life?

The General. Yes, a charmed life. Bayonets bent on my buckles. Bullets passed through me and left no trace: thats the worst of modern bullets: Ive never been hit by a dumdum. When I was only a company officer I had at least the right to expose myself to death in the field. Now I'm a General even that resource is cut off. [*Persuasively drawing his chair nearer to her.*] Listen to me, Lesbia. For the tenth and last time—

Lesbia [*interrupting*]. On Florence's wedding morning, two years ago, you said "For the ninth and last time."

The General. We are two years older, Lesbia. I'm fifty: you are—

Lesbia. Yes, I know. It's no use, Boxer. When will you be old enough to take no for an answer?

The General. Never, Lesbia, never. You have never given me a real reason for refusing me yet. I once thought it was somebody else. There were lots of fellows after you; but now theyve all given it up and married. [*Bending still nearer to her.*] Lesbia: tell me your secret. Why—

Lesbia [*sniffing disgustedly*]. Oh! Youve been smoking. [*She rises and goes to the chair on the hearth.*] Keep away, you wretch.

The General. But for that pipe, I could not have faced you without breaking down. It has soothed me and nerved me.

Lesbia [*sitting down with* The Times *in her hand*]. Well, it has nerved me to tell you why I'm going to be an old maid.

The General [*impulsively approaching her*]. Dont say that, Lesbia. It's not natural: it's not right: it's—

Lesbia [*fanning him off*]. No: no closer, Boxer, please. [*He retreats, discouraged.*] It may not be natural; but it happens all the same. Youll find plenty of women like me, if you care to look for them: women with lots of character and good looks and money and offers, who wont and dont get married. Cant you guess why?

The General. I can understand when there is another.

Lesbia. Yes; but there isnt another. Besides, do you suppose I think, at my time of life, that the difference between one decent sort of man and another is worth bothering about?

The General. The heart has its preferences, Lesbia. One image and one only, gets indelibly—

Lesbia. Yes. Excuse my interrupting you so often; but your sentiments are so correct that I always know what you are going to say before you finish. You see, Boxer, everybody is not like you. You are a sentimental noodle: you dont see women as they really are. You dont see me as I really am. Now I do see men as they really are. I see you as you really are.

The General [*murmuring*]. No: dont say that, Lesbia.

Lesbia. I'm a regular old maid. I'm very particular about my belongings. I like to have my own house, and to have it to myself. I have a very keen sense of beauty and fitness and cleanliness and order. I am proud of my independence and jealous for it. I have a sufficiently well-stocked mind to be very good company for myself if I have plenty of books and music. The one thing I never could stand is a great lout of a man smoking all over my house and going to sleep in his chair after dinner, and untidying everything. Ugh!

The General. But love—

Lesbia. Oh, love! Have you no imagination? Do you think I have never been in love with wonderful men? heroes! archangels! princes! sages! even fascinating rascals! and had the strangest adventures with them? Do you know what it is to look at a mere real man after that? a man with his boots in every corner, and the smell of his tobacco in every curtain?

The General [*somewhat dazed*]. Well but—excuse my mentioning it—dont you want children?

Lesbia. I ought to have children. I should be a good mother to children. I believe it would pay the country very well to pay ME very well to have children. But the country tells me that I cant have a child in my house without a man in it too; so I tell the country that it will have to do without my children. If I am to be a mother, I really cannot have a man bothering me to be a wife at the same time.

The General. My dear Lesbia: you know I dont wish to be impertinent; but these are not correct views for an English lady to express.

Lesbia. That is why I dont express them, except to gentlemen who wont take any other answer. The difficulty, you see, is that I really am an English lady, and am particularly proud of being one.

The General. I'm sure of that, Lesbia: quite sure of it. I never meant—

Lesbia [*rising impatiently*]. Oh, my dear Boxer, do please try to think of something else than whether you have offended me, and whether you are doing the correct thing as an English gentleman. You are faultless, and very dull. [*She shakes her shoulders intolerantly and walks across to the other side of the kitchen.*]

The General [*moodily*]. Ha! thats whats the matter with me. Not clever. A poor silly soldier man.

Lesbia. The whole matter is very simple. As I say, I am an English lady, by which I mean that I have been trained to do without what I cant have on honorable terms, no matter what it is.

The General. I really dont understand you, Lesbia.

Lesbia [*turning on him*]. Then why on earth do you want to marry a woman you dont understand?

The General. I dont know. I suppose I love you.

Lesbia. Well, Boxer, you can love me as much as you like, provided you look happy about it and dont bore me. But you cant marry me; and thats all about it.

The General. It's so frightfully difficult to argue the matter fairly with you without wounding your delicacy by overstepping the bounds of good taste. But surely there are calls of nature—

Lesbia. Dont be ridiculous, Boxer.

The General. Well how am I to express it? Hang it all, Lesbia, dont you want a husband?

Lesbia. No. I want children; and I want to devote myself entirely to my children, and not to their father. The law will not allow me to do that; so I have made up my mind to have neither husband nor children.

The General. But, great Heavens, the natural appetites—

Lesbia. As I said before, an English lady is not the slave of her appetites. That is what an English gentleman seems incapable of understanding. [*She sits down at the end of the table, near the study door.*]

The General [*huffily*]. Oh well, if you refuse, you refuse. I shall not ask you again. I'm sorry I returned to the subject. [*He retires to the hearth and plants himself there, wounded and lofty.*]

Lesbia. Dont be cross, Boxer.

The General. I'm not cross, only wounded, Lesbia. And when you talk like that, I dont feel convinced: I only feel utterly at a loss.

Lesbia. Well, you know our family rule. When at a loss consult the greengrocer. [*Opportunely* COLLINS *comes in through the tower.*] Here he is.

Collins. Sorry to be so much in and out, Miss. I thought Mrs. Bridgenorth was here. The table is ready now for the breakfast, if she would like to see it.

Lesbia. If you are satisfied, Collins, I am sure she will be.

The General. By the way, Collins: I thought theyd made you an alderman.

Collins. So they have, General.

The General. Then wheres your gown?

Collins. I dont wear it in private life, General.

The General. Why? Are you ashamed of it?

Collins. No, General. To tell you the truth, I take a pride in it. I cant help it.

The General. Attention, Collins. Come here. [COLLINS *comes to him.*] Do you see my uniform—all my medals?

Collins. Yes, General. They strike the eye, as it were.

The General. They are meant to. Very well. Now you know, dont you, that your services to the community as a greengrocer are as important and as dignified as mine as a soldier?

Collins. I'm sure it's very honorable of you to say so, General.

The General [*emphatically*]. You know also, dont you, that any man who can see anything ridiculous, or unmanly, or unbecoming in your work or in your civic robes is not a gentleman, but a jumping, bounding, snorting cad?

Collins. Well, strictly between ourselves, that is my opinion, General.

The General. Then why not dignify my niece's wedding by wearing your robes?

Collins. A bargain's a bargain, General. Mrs. Bridgenorth sent for the greengrocer, not for the alderman. It's just as unpleasant to get more than you bargain for as to get less.

The General. I'm sure she will agree with me. I attach importance to this as an affirmation of solidarity in the service of the community. The Bishop's apron, my uniform, your robes: the Church, the Army, and the Municipality.

Collins [*retiring*]. Very well, General. [*He turns dubiously to* LESBIA *on his way to the tower.*] I wonder what my wife will say, Miss?

The General. What! Is your wife ashamed of your robes?

Collins. No, sir, not ashamed of them. But she grudged the money for them; and she will be afraid of my sleeves getting into the gravy.

MRS. BRIDGENORTH, *her placidity quite upset, comes in with a letter; hurries past* COLLINS; *and comes between* LESBIA *and* THE GENERAL.

Mrs. Bridgenorth. Lesbia: Boxer: heres a pretty mess!

COLLINS *goes out discreetly.*

The General. Whats the matter?

Mrs. Bridgenorth. Reginald's in London, and wants to come to the wedding.

The General [*stupended*]. Well, dash my buttons!

Lesbia. Oh, all right, let him come.

The General. Let him come! Why, the decree has not been made absolute yet. Is he to walk in here to Edith's wedding, reeking from the Divorce Court?

Mrs. Bridgenorth [*vexedly sitting down in the middle chair*]. It's too bad. No: I cant forgive him, Lesbia, really. A man of Reginald's age, with a young wife—the best of girls, and as pretty as she can be—to go off with a common woman from the streets! Ugh!

Lesbia. You must make allowances. What can you expect? Reginald was always weak. He was brought up to be weak. The family property was all mortgaged when he inherited it. He had to struggle along in constant money difficulties, hustled by his solicitors, morally bullied by the Barmecide, and physically bullied by Boxer, while they two were fighting their own way and getting well trained. You know very well he couldnt afford to marry until the mortgages were cleared and he was over fifty. And then of course he made a fool of himself marrying a child like Leo.

The General. But to hit her! Absolutely to hit her! He knocked her down—knocked her flat down on a flower bed in the presence of his gardener. He! the head of the family! the man that stands before the Barmecide and myself as Bridgenorth of Bridgenorth! to beat his wife and go off with a low woman and be divorced for it in the face of all England! in the face of my uniform and Alfred's apron! I can never forget what I felt: it was only the King's personal request—virtually a command—that stopped me from resigning my commission. I'd cut Reginald dead if I met him in the street.

Mrs. Bridgenorth. Besides, Leo's coming. Theyd meet. It's impossible, Lesbia.

Lesbia. Oh, I forgot that. That settles it. He mustnt come.

The General. Of course he mustnt. You tell him that if he enters this house, I'll leave it; and so will every decent man and woman in it.

Collins [*returning for a moment to announce*]. Mr. Reginald, maam. [*He withdraws when Reginald enters.*]

The General [*beside himself*]. Well, dash my buttons!!

REGINALD *is just the man* LESBIA *has described. He is hardened and tough physically, and hasty and boyish in his manner and speech, belonging as he does to the large class of English gentlemen of property (solicitor-managed) who have never developed intellectually since their schooldays. He is a muddled, rebellious, hasty, untidy, forgetful, always late sort of man, who very evidently needs the care of a capable woman, and has never been lucky or attractive enough to get it. All the same, a likeable man, from whom nobody apprehends any malice nor expects any achievement. In everything but years he is younger than his brother* THE GENERAL.

Reginald [*coming forward between* THE GENERAL *and* MRS. BRIDGENORTH]. Alice: it's no use. I cant stay away from Edith's wedding. Good morning, Lesbia. How are you, Boxer? [*He offers* THE GENERAL *his hand.*]

The General [*with crushing stiffness*]. I was just telling Alice, sir, that if you entered this house, I should leave it.

Reginald. Well, dont let me detain you, old chap. When you start calling people Sir, youre not particularly good company.

Lesbia. Dont you two begin to quarrel. That wont improve the situation.

Mrs. Bridgenorth. I think you might have waited until you got my answer, Rejjy.

Reginald. It's so jolly easy to say No in a letter. Wont you let me stay?

Mrs. Bridgenorth. How can I? Leo's coming.

Reginald. Well, she wont mind.

The General. Wont mind!!!!!

Lesbia. Dont talk nonsense, Rejjy; and be off with you.

The General [*with biting sarcasm*]. At school you had a theory that women liked being knocked down, I remember.

Reginald. Youre a nice, chivalrous, brotherly sort of swine, you are.

The General. Mr. Bridgenorth: are you going to leave this house or am I?

Reginald. You are, I hope. [*He emphasizes his intention to stay by sitting down.*]

The General. Alice: will you allow me to be driven from Edith's wedding by this—

Lesbia [*warningly*]. Boxer!

The General. —by this Respondent? Is Edith to be given away by him?

Mrs. Bridgenorth. Certainly not. Reginald: you were not asked to come; and I have asked you to go. You know how fond I am of Leo; and you know what she would feel if she came in and found you here.

Collins [*again appearing in the tower*]. Mrs. Reginald, maam.

Lesbia	[*All three*	No, no. Ask her to—
Mrs. Bridgenorth	*clamoring*	Oh how unfortunate!
The General	*together*].	Well, dash my buttons!

It is too late: LEO *is already in the kitchen.* COLLINS *goes out, mutely abandoning a situation which he deplores but has been unable to save.*

LEO *is very pretty, very youthful, very restless, and consequently very charming to people who are touched by youth and beauty, as well as to those who regard young women as more or less appetizing lollipops, and dont regard old women at all. Coldly studied,* LEO's *restlessness is much less lovable than the kittenishness which comes from a rich and fresh vitality. She is a born fusser about herself and everybody else for whom she feels responsible; and her vanity causes her to exaggerate her responsibilities officiously. All her fussing is about little things; but she often calls them by big names, such as Art, the Divine Spark, the world, motherhood, good breeding, the Universe, the Creator, or anything else that happens to strike her imagination as sounding intellectually important. She has more than common imagination and no more than common conception and penetration; so that she is always on the high horse about words and always in the perambulator about things. Considering herself clever, thoughtful, and superior to ordinary weaknesses and prejudices, she recklessly attaches herself to clever men on that understanding, with the result that they are first delighted, then exas-*

perated, and finally bored. When marrying REGINALD *she told her friends that there was a great deal in him which needed bringing out. If she were a middle-aged man she would be the terror of his club. Being a pretty young woman, she is forgiven everything, proving that* Tout comprendre, c'est tout pardonner *is an error, the fact being that the secret of forgiving everything is to understand nothing.*

She runs in fussily, full of her own importance, and swoops on LESBIA, *who is much less disposed to spoil her than* MRS. BRIDGENORTH *is. But* LEO *affects a special intimacy with* LESBIA, *as of two thinkers among the Philistines.*

Leo [*to* LESBIA, *kissing her*]. Good morning. [*Coming to* MRS. BRIDGENORTH.] How do, Alice? [*Passing on towards the hearth.*] Why so gloomy, General? [REGINALD *rises between her and the General.*] Oh, Rejjy! What will the King's Proctor say?

Reginald. Damn the King's Proctor!

Leo. Naughty. Well, I suppose I must kiss you; but dont any of you tell. [*She kisses him. They can hardly believe their eyes.*] Have you kept all your promises?

Reginald. Oh, dont begin bothering about those—

Leo [*insisting*]. Have? You? Kept? Your? Promises? Have you rubbed your head with the lotion every night?

Reginald. Yes, yes. Nearly every night.

Leo. Nearly! I know what that means. Have you worn your liver pad?

The General [*solemnly*]. Leo: forgiveness is one of the most beautiful traits in a woman's nature; but there are things that should not be forgiven to a man. When a man knocks a woman down——[LEO *gives a little shriek of laughter and collapses on a chair next* MRS. BRIDGENORTH, *on her left.*]

Reginald [*sardonically*]. The man that would raise his hand to a woman, save in the way of kindness, is unworthy the name of Bridgenorth. [*He sits down at the end of the table nearest the hearth.*]

The General [*much huffed*]. Oh, well, if Leo does not mind, of course I have no more to say. But I think you might, out of consideration for the family, beat your wife in private and not in the presence of the gardener.

Reginald [*out of patience*]. Whats the good of beating your wife unless theres a witness to prove it afterwards? You dont suppose a man beats his wife for the fun of it, do you? How could she have got her divorce if I hadnt beaten her? Nice state of things, that!

The General [*gasping*]. Do you mean to tell me that you did it in cold blood? simply to get rid of your wife?

Reginald. No, I didnt: I did it to get her rid of me. What would you do if you were fool enough to marry a woman thirty years younger than yourself, and then found that she didnt care for you, and was in love with a young fellow with a face like a mushroom?

Leo. He has not. [*Bursting into tears.*] And you are most unkind to say I didnt care for you. Nobody could have been fonder of you.

Reginald. A nice way of shewing your fondness! I had to go out and dig that flower bed all over with my own hands to soften it. I had to pick all the stones out of it. And then she complained that I hadnt done it properly, because she got a worm down her neck. I had to go to Brighton with a poor creature who took a fancy to me on the way down, and got conscientious scruples about committing perjury after dinner. I had to put her down in the hotel book as Mrs. Reginald Bridgenorth: Leo's name! Do you know what that feels like to a decent man? Do you know what a decent man feels about his wife's name? How would you like to go into a hotel before all the waiters and people with—with that on your arm? Not that it was the poor girl's fault, of course; only she started crying because I couldnt stand her touching me; and now she keeps writing to me. And then I'm held up in the public court for cruelty and adultery, and turned away from Edith's wedding by Alice, and lectured by you! a bachelor, and a precious green one at that. What do you know about it?

The General. Am I to understand that the whole case was one of collusion?

Reginald. Of course it was. Half the cases are collusions: what are people to do? [THE GENERAL, *passing has hand dazedly over his bewildered brow, sinks into the railed chair.*] And what do you take me for, that you should have the cheek to pretend to believe all that rot about my knocking Leo about and leaving her for—for a—a— Ugh! you should have seen her.

The General. This is perfectly astonishing to me. Why did you do it. Why did Leo allow it?

Reginald. Youd better ask her.

Leo [*still in tears*]. I'm sure I never thought it would be so horrid for Rejjy. I offered honorably to do it myself, and let him divorce me; but he wouldnt. And he said himself that it was the only way to do it—that it was the law that he should do it that way. I never saw that hateful creature until that day in Court. If he had only shewn her to me before, I should never have allowed it.

Mrs. Bridgenorth. You did all this for Leo's sake, Rejjy?

Reginald [with an unbearable sense of injury]. I shouldnt mind a bit if it were for Leo's sake. But to have to do it to make room for that mushroom-faced serpent—!

The General [jumping up]. What right had he to be made room for? Are you in your senses? What right?

Reginald. The right of being a young man, suitable to a young woman. I had no right at my age to marry Leo: she knew no more about life than a child.

Leo. I knew a great deal more about it than a great baby like you. I'm sure I don't know how youll get on with no one to take care of you: I often lie awake at night thinking about it. And now youve made me thoroughly miserable.

Reginald. Serve you right! [*She weeps.*] There: dont get into a tantrum, Leo?

Lesbia. May one ask who is the mushroom-faced serpent?

Leo. He isnt.

Reginald. Sinjon Hotchkiss, of course.

Mrs. Bridgenorth. Sinjon Hotchkiss! Why, he's coming to the wedding!

Reginald. What! In that case I'm off. [*He makes for the tower.*]

Leo		[*seizing him*]. No you shant. You promised to be nice to him.
The General	[*all four rushing after him and capturing him on the threshold*].	No, dont go, old chap. Not from Edith's wedding.
Mrs. Bridgenorth		Oh, do stay, Rejjy. I shall really be hurt if you desert us.
Lesbia		Better stay, Reginald. You must meet him sooner or later.

Reginald. A moment ago, when I wanted to stay, you were all shoving me out of the house. Now that I want to go, you wont let me.

Mrs. Bridgenorth. I shall send a note to Mr. Hotchkiss not to come.

Leo [weeping again]. Oh, Alice! [*She comes back to her chair, heartbroken.*]

Reginald [out of patience]. Oh well, let her have her way. Let her have her mushroom. Let him come. Let them all come.

He crosses the kitchen to the oak chest and sits sulkily on it.
MRS. BRIDGENORTH *shrugs her shoulders and sits at the table
in* REGINALD'S *neighborhood listening in placid helplessness.*
LESBIA, *out of patience with* LEO'S *tears, goes into the garden
and sits there near the door, snuffing up the open air in her
relief from the domestic stuffiness of* REGINALD'S *affairs.*

Leo. It's so cruel of you to go on pretending that I dont
care for you, Rejjy.

Reginald [*bitterly*]. She explained to me that it was only
that she had exhausted my conversation.

The General [*coming paternally to* LEO]. My dear girl: all
the conversation in the world has been exhausted long ago.
Heaven knows I have exhausted the conversation of the
British Army these thirty years; but I dont leave it on that
account.

Leo. It's not that Ive exhausted it; but he will keep on
repeating it when I want to read or go to sleep. And Sinjon
amuses me. He's so clever.

The General [*stung*]. Ha! The old complaint. You all want
geniuses to marry. This demand for clever men is ridiculous.
Somebody must marry the plain, honest, stupid fellows. Have
you thought of that?

Leo. But there are such lots of stupid women to marry.
Why do they want to marry us? Besides, Rejjy knows that
I'm quite fond of him. I like him because he wants me; and I
like Sinjon because I want him. I feel that I have a duty to
Rejjy.

The General. Precisely: you have.

Leo. And, of course, Sinjon has the same duty to me.

The General. Tut, tut!

Leo. Oh, how silly the law is! Why cant I marry them both?

The General [*shocked*]. Leo!

Leo. Well, I love them both. I should like to marry a lot
of men. I should like to have Rejjy for every day, and Sinjon
for concerts and theatres and going out in the evenings, and
some great austere saint for about once a year at the end of
the season, and some perfectly blithering idiot of a boy to be
quite wicked with. I so seldom feel wicked; and, when I do,
it's such a pity to waste it merely because it's too silly to
confess to a real grown-up man.

Reginald. This is the kind of thing, you know—[*Helplessly.*] Well, there it is!

The General [*decisively*]. Alice: this is a job for the
Barmecide. He's a Bishop: it's his duty to talk to Leo. I can

stand a good deal; but when it comes to flat polygamy and polyandry, we ought to do something.

Mrs. Bridgenorth [*going to the study door*]. Do come here a moment, Alfred. We're in a difficulty.

The Bishop [*within*]. Ask Collins. I'm busy.

Mrs. Bridgenorth. Collins wont do. It's something very serious. Do come just a moment, dear. [*When she hears him coming she takes a chair at the nearest end of the table.*]

THE BISHOP *comes out of his study. He is still a slim active man, spare of flesh, and younger by temperament than his brothers. He has a delicate skin, fine hands, a salient nose with chin to match, a short beard which accentuates his sharp chin by bristling forward, clever humorous eyes, not without a glint of mischief in them, ready bright speech, and the ways of a successful man who is always interested in himself and generally rather well pleased with himself. When* LESBIA *hears his voice she turns her chair towards him, and presently rises and stands in the doorway listening to the conversation.*

The Bishop [*going to* LEO]. Good morning, my dear. Hullo! Youve brought Reginald with you. Thats very nice of you. Have you reconciled them, Boxer?

The General. Reconciled them! Why, man, the whole divorce was a put-up job. She wants to marry some fellow named Hotchkiss.

Reginald. A fellow with a face like—

Leo. You shant, Rejjy. He has a very fine face.

Mrs. Bridgenorth. And now she says she wants to marry both of them, and a lot of other people as well.

Leo. I didnt say I wanted to marry them: I only said I should like to marry them.

The Bishop. Quite a nice distinction, Leo.

Leo. Just occasionally, you know.

The Bishop [*sitting down cosily beside her*]. Quite so. Sometimes a poet, sometimes a Bishop, sometimes a fairy prince, sometimes somebody quite indescribable, and sometimes nobody at all.

Leo. Yes: thats just it. How did you know?

The Bishop. Oh, I should say most imaginative and cultivated young women feel like that. I wouldnt give a rap for one who didnt. Shakespear pointed out long ago that a woman wanted a Sunday husband as well as a weekday one. But, as usual, he didnt follow up the idea.

The General [*aghast*]. Am I to understand—

The Bishop [*cutting him short*]. Now, Boxer, am I the Bishop or are you?

The General [*sulkily*]. You.

The Bishop. Then dont ask me are you to understand. "Yours not to reason why: yours but to do and die"—

The General. Oh, very well: go on. I'm not clever. Only a silly soldier man. Ha! Go on. [*He throws himself into the railed chair, as one prepared for the worst.*]

Mrs. Bridgenorth. Alfred: dont tease Boxer.

The Bishop. If we are going to discuss ethical questions we must begin by giving the devil fair play. Boxer never does. England never does. We always assume that the devil is guilty: and we wont allow him to prove his innocence, because it would be against public morals if he succeeded. We used to do the same with prisoners accused of high treason. And the consequence is that we overreach ourselves; and the devil gets the better of us after all. Perhaps thats what most of us intend him to do.

The General. Alfred: we asked you here to preach to Leo. You are preaching at me instead. I am not conscious of having said or done anything that calls for that unsolicited attention.

The Bishop. But poor little Leo has only told the simple truth; whilst you, Boxer, are striking moral attitudes.

The General. I suppose thats an epigram. I dont understand epigrams. I'm only a silly soldier man. Ha! But I can put a plain question. Is Leo to be encouraged to be a polygamist?

The Bishop. Remember the British Empire, Boxer. Youre a British General, you know.

The General. What has that to do with polygamy?

The Bishop. Well, the great majority of our fellow-subjects are polygamists. I cant as a British Bishop insult them by speaking disrespectfully of polygamy. It's a very interesting question. Many very interesting men have been polygamists: Solomon, Mahomet, and our friend the Duke of—of—hm! I never can remember his name.

The General. It would become you better, Alfred, to send that silly girl back to her husband and her duty than to talk clever and mock at your religion. "What God hath joined together let not man put asunder." Remember that.

The Bishop. Dont be afraid, Boxer. What God hath joined together no man ever shall put asunder: God will take care of that. [*To* LEO.] By the way, who was it that joined you and Reginald, my dear?

Leo. It was that awful little curate that afterwards drank, and travelled first class with a third-class ticket, and then tried to go on the stage. But they wouldnt have him. He called himself Egerton Fotheringay.

The Bishop. Well, whom Egerton Fotheringay hath joined, let Sir Gorell Barnes put asunder by all means.

The General. I may be a silly soldier man; but I call this blasphemy.

The Bishop [*gravely*]. Better for me to take the name of Mr. Egerton Fotheringay in earnest than for you to take a higher name in vain.

Lesbia. Cant you three brothers ever meet without quarrelling?

The Bishop [*mildly*]. This is not quarrelling, Lesbia: it's only English family life. Good morning.

Leo. You know, Bishop, it's very dear of you to take my part; but I'm not sure that I'm not a little shocked.

The Bishop. Then I think Ive been a little more successful than Boxer in getting you into a proper frame of mind.

The General [*snorting*]. Ha!

Leo. Not a bit; for now I'm going to shock you worse than ever. I think Solomon was an old beast.

The Bishop. Precisely what you ought to think of him, my dear. Dont apologize.

The General [*more shocked*]. Well, but hang it! Solomon was in the Bible. And, after all, Solomon was Solomon.

Leo. And I stick to it: I still want to have a lot of interesting men to know quite intimately—to say everything I think of to them, and have them say everything they think of to me.

The Bishop. So you shall, my dear, if you are lucky. But you know you neednt marry them all. Think of all the buttons you would have to sew on. Besides, nothing is more dreadful than a husband who keeps telling you everything he thinks, and always wants to know what you think.

Leo [*struck by this*]. Well, thats very true of Rejjy: in fact, thats why I had to divorce him.

The Bishop [*condoling*]. Yes: he repeats himself dreadfully, doesnt he?

Reginald. Look here, Alfred. If I have my faults, let her find them out for herself without your help.

The Bishop. She has found them all out already, Reginald.

Leo [*a little huffily*]. After all, there are worse men than Reginald. I daresay he's not so clever as you; but still he's not such a fool as you seem to think him!

The Bishop. Quite right, dear: stand up for your husband. I hope you will always stand up for all your husbands. [*He rises and goes to the hearth, where he stands complacently with his back to the fireplace, beaming at them all as at a roomful of children.*]

Leo. Please dont talk as if I wanted to marry a whole regiment. For me there can never be more than two. I shall never love anybody but Rejjy and Sinjon.

Reginald. A man with a face like a—

Leo. I wont have it, Rejjy. It's disgusting.

The Bishop. You see, my dear, youll exhaust Sinjon's conversation too in a week or so. A man is like a phonograph with half-a-dozen records. You soon get tired of them all; and yet you have to sit at table whilst he reels them off to every new visitor. In the end you have to be content with his common humanity; and when you come down to that, you find out about men what a great English poet of my acquaintance used to say about women: that they all taste alike. Marry whom you please: at the end of a month he'll be Reginald over again. It wasnt worth changing: indeed it wasnt.

Leo. Then it's a mistake to get married.

The Bishop. It is, my dear; but it's a much bigger mistake not to get married.

The General [*rising*]. Ha! You hear that, Lesbia? [*He joins her at the garden door.*]

Lesbia. Thats only an epigram, Boxer.

The General. Sound sense, Lesbia. When a man talks rot, thats epigram: when he talks sense, then I agree with him.

Reginald [*coming off the oak chest and looking at his watch*]. It's getting late. Wheres Edith? Hasnt she got into her veil and orange blossoms yet?

Mrs. Bridgenorth. Do go and hurry her, Lesbia.

Lesbia [*going out through the tower*]. Come with me, Leo.

Leo [*following* LESBIA *out*]. Yes, certainly.

THE BISHOP *goes over to his wife and sits down, taking her hand and kissing it by way of beginning a conversation with her.*

The Bishop. Alice: I've had another letter from the mysterious lady who cant spell. I like that woman's letters. Theres an intensity of passion in them that fascinates me.

Mrs. Bridgenorth. Do you mean Incognita Appassionata?

The Bishop. Yes.

The General [*turning abruptly: he has been looking out into the garden*]. Do you mean to say that women write love-letters to you?

The Bishop. Of course.

The General. They never do to me.

The Bishop. The Army doesnt attract women: the Church does.

Reginald. Do you consider it right to let them? They may be married women, you know.

The Bishop. They always are. This one is. [*To* MRS. BRIDGENORTH.] Dont you think her letters are quite the best love-letters I get? [*To the two men.*] Poor Alice has to read my love-letters aloud to me at breakfast, when theyre worth it.

Mrs. Bridgenorth. There really is something fascinating about Incognita. She never gives her address. Thats a good sign.

The General. Mf! No assignations, you mean?

The Bishop. Oh yes: she began the correspondence by making a very curious but very natural assignation. She wants me to meet her in heaven. I hope I shall.

The General. Well, I must say I hope not, Alfred. I hope not.

Mrs. Bridgenorth. She says she is happily married, and that love is a necessary of life to her, but that she must have, high above all her lovers—

The Bishop. She has several apparently—

Mrs. Bridgenorth. —some great man who will never know her, never touch her, as she is on earth, but whom she can meet in heaven when she has risen above all the everyday vulgarities of earthly love.

The Bishop [*rising*]. Excellent. Very good for her; and no trouble to me. Everybody ought to have one of these idealizations, like Dante's Beatrice. [*He clasps his hands behind him, and strolls to the hearth and back, singing.*]

LESBIA *appears in the tower, rather perturbed.*

Lesbia. Alice: will you come upstairs? Edith is not dressed.

Mrs. Bridgenorth [*rising*]. Not dressed! Does she know what hour it is?

Lesbia. She has locked herself into her room, reading.

THE BISHOP's *song ceases: he stops dead in his stroll.*

The General. Reading!

The Bishop. What is she reading?

Lesbia. Some pamphlet that came by the eleven o'clock post. She wont come out. She wont open the door. And she says she doesnt know whether she's going to be married or not til she's finished the pamphlet. Did you ever hear such a thing? Do come and speak to her.

Mrs. Bridgenorth. Alfred: you had better go.

The Bishop. Try Collins.

Lesbia. Weve tried Collins already. He got all that Ive told you out of her through the keyhole. Come, Alice. [*She vanishes.* MRS. BRIDGENORTH *hurries after her.*]

The Bishop. This means a delay. I shall go back to my work. [*He makes for the study door.*]

Reginald. What are you working at now?

The Bishop [*stopping*]. A chapter in my history of marriage. I'm just at the Roman business, you know.

The General [*coming from the garden door to the chair* MRS. BRIDGENORTH *has just left, and sitting down*]. Not more Ritualism, I hope, Alfred?

The Bishop. Oh no. I mean ancient Rome. [*He seats himself on the edge of the table.*] I've just come to the period when the propertied classes refused to get married and went in for marriage settlements instead. A few of the oldest families stuck to the marriage tradition so as to keep up the supply of vestal virgins, who had to be legitimate; but nobody else dreamt of getting married. It's all very interesting, because we're coming to that here in England; except that as we dont require any vestal virgins, nobody will get married at all, except the poor, perhaps.

The General. You take it devilishly coolly. Reginald: do you think the Barmecide's quite sane?

Reginald. No worse than ever he was.

The General [*to* THE BISHOP]. Do you mean to say you believe such a thing will ever happen in England as that respectable people will give up being married?

The Bishop. In England especially they will. In other countries the introduction of reasonable divorce laws will save the situation; but in England we always let an institution strain itself until it breaks. Ive told our last four Prime Ministers that if they didnt make our marriage laws reasonable there would be a strike against marriage, and that it would begin among the propertied classes, where no Government would dare to interfere with it.

Reginald. What did they say to that?

The Bishop. The usual thing. Quite agreed with me, but were sure that they were the only sensible men in the world and that the least hint of marriage reform would lose them the next election. And then lost it all the same: on cordite, on drink, on Chinese labor in South Africa, on all sorts of trumpery.

Reginald [*lurching across the kitchen towards the hearth with his hands in his pockets*]. It's no use: they wont listen to our sort. [*Turning on them.*] Of course they have to make you a Bishop and Boxer a General, because, after all, their blessed rabble of snobs and cads and half-starved shopkeepers cant do government work; and the bounders and weekenders are too lazy and vulgar. Theyd simply rot without us; but what do they ever do for us? what attention do they ever pay to what we say and what we want? I take it that we Bridgenorths are a pretty typical English family of the sort that has always set things straight and stuck up for the right to think and believe according to our conscience. But nowadays we are expected to dress and eat as the week-end bounders do, and to think and believe as the converted cannibals of Central Africa do, and to lie down and let every snob and every cad and every halfpenny journalist walk over us. Why, theres not a newspaper in England today that represents what I call solid Bridgenorth opinion and tradition. Half of them read as if they were published at the nearest mothers' meeting, and the other half at the nearest motor garage. Do you call these chaps gentlemen? Do you call them Englishmen? I dont. [*He throws himself disgustedly into the nearest chair.*]

The General [*excited by* REGINALD's *eloquence*]. Do you see my uniform? What did Collins say? It strikes the eye. It was meant to. I put it on expressly to give the modern army bounder a smack in the eye. Somebody has to set a right example by beginning. Well, let it be a Bridgenorth. I believe in family blood and tradition, by George.

The Bishop [*musing*]. I wonder who will begin the stand against marriage. It must come some day. I was married myself before I'd thought about it; and even if I had thought about it I was too much in love with Alice to let anything stand in the way. But, you know, Ive seen one of our daughters after another—Ethel, Jane, Fanny, and Christina and Florence—go out at that door in their veils and orange blossoms; and Ive always wondered whether theyd have gone quietly if theyd known what they were doing. Ive a horrible misgiving about that pamphlet. All progress means war with Society. Heaven forbid that Edith should be one of the combatants!

ST. JOHN HOTCHKISS *comes into the tower ushered by* COLLINS. *He is a very smart young gentleman of twenty-nine or thereabouts, correct in dress to the last thread of his collar, but too much preoccupied with his ideas to be embarrassed by any concern as to his appearance. He talks about himself with energetic gaiety. He talks to other people with a sweet forbearance (impling a kindly consideration for their stupidity) which infuriates those whom he does not succeed in amusing.*

They either lose their tempers with him or try in vain to snub him.

Collins [announcing]. Mr. Hotchkiss. *[He withdraws.]*

Hotchkiss [clapping REGINALD *gaily on the shoulder as he passes him].* Tootle loo, Rejjy.

Reginald [curtly, without rising or turning his head]. Morning.

Hotchkiss. Good morning, Bishop.

The Bishop [coming off the table]. What on earth are you doing here, Sinjon? You belong to the bridegroom's party: youve no business here until after the ceremony.

Hotchkiss. Yes, I know: thats just it. May I have a word with you in private? Rejjy or any of the family wont matter; but—*[He glances at* THE GENERAL, *who has risen rather stiffly, as he strongly disapproves of the part played by* HOTCHKISS *in* REGINALD's *domestic affairs.]*

The Bishop. All right, Sinjon. This is our brother, General Bridgenorth. *[He goes to the hearth and posts himself there, with his hands clasped behind him.]*

Hotchkiss. Oh, good! *[He turns to* THE GENERAL, *and takes out a card-case.]* As you are in the service, allow me to introduce myself. Read my card, please. *[He presents his card to the astonished* GENERAL.]

The General [reading]. "Mr. St. John Hotchkiss, the Celebrated Coward, late Lieutenant in the 165th Fusiliers."

Reginald [with a chuckle]. He was sent back from South Africa because he funked an order to attack, and spoiled his commanding officer's plan.

The General [very gravely]. I remember the case now. I had forgotten the name. I'll not refuse your acquaintance, Mr. Hotchkiss; partly because youre my brother's guest, and partly because Ive seen too much active service not to know that every man's nerve plays him false at one time or another, and that some very honorable men should never go into action at all, because theyre not built that way. But if I were you I should not use that visiting card. No doubt it's an honorable trait in your character that you dont wish any man to give you his hand in ignorance of your disgrace; but you had better allow us to forget. We wish to forget. It isnt your disgrace alone: it's a disgrace to the army and to all of us. Pardon my plain speaking.

Hotchkiss [sunnily]. My dear General, I dont know what fear means in the military sense of the word. Ive fought seven duels with the sabre in Italy and Austria, and one with pistols in France, without turning a hair. There was no other way in which I could vindicate my motives in refusing to make that attack at Smutsfontein. I dont pretend to be a brave man. I'm afraid of wasps. I'm afraid of cats. In spite of the voice of reason, I'm afraid of ghosts; and twice Ive fled across Europe from false alarms of cholera. But afraid to fight I am not. [*He turns gaily to* REGINALD *and slaps him on the shoulder.*] Eh, Rejjy? [REGINALD *grunts.*]

The General. Then why did you not do your duty at Smutsfontein?

Hotchkiss. I did my duty—my higher duty. If I had made that attack, my commanding officer's plan would have been successful, and he would have been promoted. Now I happen to think that the British Army should be commanded by gentlemen, and by gentlemen alone. This man was not a gentleman. I sacrified my military career—I faced disgrace and social ostracism—rather than give that man his chance.

The General [*generously indignant*]. Your commanding officer, sir, was my friend Major Billiter.

Hotchkiss. Precisely. What a name!

The General. And pray, sir, on what ground do you dare allege that Major Billiter is not a gentleman?

Hotchkiss. By an infallible sign: one of those trifles that stamp a man. He eats rice pudding with a spoon.

The General [*very angry*]. Confound you, *I* eat rice pudding with a spoon. Now!

Hotchkiss. Oh, so do I, frequently. But there are ways of doing these things. Billiter's way was unmistakable.

The General. Well, *I*'ll tell you something now. When I thought you were only a coward, I pitied you, and would have done what I could to help you back to your place in Society—

Hotchkiss [*interrupting him*]. Thank you: I havnt lost it. My motives have been fully appreciated. I was made an honorary member of two of the smartest clubs in London when the truth came out.

The General. Well, sir, those clubs consist of snobs; and you are a jumping, bounding, prancing, snorting snob yourself.

The Bishop [*amused but hospitably remonstrant*]. My dear Boxer!

Hotchkiss [*delighted*]. How kind of you to say so, General! Youre quite right: I am a snob. Why not? The whole strength of England lies in the fact that the enormous majority of the English people are snobs. They insult poverty. They despise vulgarity. They love nobility. They admire exclusiveness. They will not obey a man risen from the ranks. They never trust one of their own class. I agree with them. I share their instincts. In my undergraduate days I was a Republican—a Socialist. I tried hard to feel toward a comman man as I do towards a duke. I couldnt. Neither can you. Well, why should we be ashamed of this aspiration towards what is above us? Why dont I say that an honest man's the noblest work of God? Because I dont think so. If he's not a gentleman, I dont care whether he's honest or not: I shouldnt let his son marry my daughter. And thats the test, mind. Thats the test. You feel as I do. You are a snob in fact: I am a snob, not only in fact, but on principle. I shall go down in history, not as the first snob, but as the first avowed champion of English snobbery, and its first martyr in the army. The navy boasts two such martyrs in Captains Kirby and Wade, who were shot for refusing to fight under Admiral Benbow, a promoted cabin boy. I have always envied them their glory.

The General. As a British General, sir, I have to inform you that if any office under my command violated the sacred equality of our profession by putting a single jot of his duty or his risk on the shoulders of the humblest drummer boy, I'd shoot him with my own hand.

Hotchkiss. That sentiment is not your equality, General, but your superiority. Ask the Bishop. [*He seats himself on the edge of the table.*]

The Bishop. I cant support you, Sinjon. My profession also compels me to turn my back on snobbery. You see, I have to do such a terribly democratic thing to every child that is brought to me. Without distinction of class I have to confer on it a rank so high and awful that all the grades in Debrett and Burke seem like the medals they give children in Infant Schools in comparison. I'm not allowed to make any class distinction. They are all soldiers and servants, not officers and masters.

Hotchkiss. Ah, youre quoting the Baptism service. Thats not a bit real, you know. If I may say so, you would both feel so much more at peace with yourselves if you would acknowledge and confess your real convictions. You know you dont really think a Bishop the equal of a curate, or a lieutenant in a line regiment the equal of a general.

The Bishop. Of course I do. I was a curate myself.

The General. And I was a lieutenant in a line regiment.

Reginald. And I was nothing. But we're all our own and one-another's equals, arnt we? So perhaps when youve quite done talking about yourselves, we shall get to whatever business Sinjon came about.

Hotchkiss [*coming off the table hastily*]. Oh! true, my dear fellow. I beg a thousand pardons. It's about the wedding!

The General. What about the wedding?

Hotchkiss. Well, we cant get our man up to the scratch. Cecil has locked himself in his room and wont see or speak to anyone. I went up to his room and banged at the door. I told him I should look through the keyhole if he didn't answer. I looked through the keyhole. He was sitting on his bed, reading a book. [REGINALD *rises in consternation.* THE GENERAL *recoils.*] I told him not to be an ass, and so forth. He said he was not going to budge until he had finished the book. I asked him did he know what time it was, and whether he happened to recollect that he had a rather important appointment to marry Edith. He said the sooner I stopped interrupting him, the sooner he'd be ready. Then he stuffed his fingers in his ears; turned over on his elbows; and buried himself in his beastly book. I couldnt get another word out of him; so I thought I'd better come here and warn you.

Reginald. This looks to me like a practical joke. Theyve arranged it between them.

The Bishop. No. Edith has no sense of humor. And Ive never seen a man in a jocular mood on his wedding morning.

COLLINS *appears in the tower, ushering in the bridegroom, a young gentleman with good looks of the serious kind, somewhat careworn by an exacting conscience, and just now distracted by insoluble problems of conduct.*

Collins [*announcing*]. Mr. Cecil Sykes. [*He retires.*]

Hotchkiss. Look here, Cecil: this is all wrong. Youve no business here until after the wedding. Hang it, man! youre the bridegroom.

Sykes [*coming to* THE BISHOP, *and addressing him with dogged desperation*]. Ive come here to say this. When I proposed to Edith I was in utter ignorance of what I was letting myself in for legally. Having given my word, I will stand to it. You have me at your mercy: marry me if you insist. But take notice that I protest. [*He sits down distractedly in the railed chair.*]

The General	[*both highly incensed*].	What the devil do you mean by this? What the—
Reginald		Confound your impertinence, what do you—
Hotchkiss.		Easy, Rejjy. Easy, old man. Steady, steady, steady. [REGINALD *subsides into his chair.* HOTCHKISS *sits on his right, appeasing him.*]
The Bishop.		No, please, Rej. Control yourself, Boxer, I beg you.

The General. I tell you I cant control myself. Ive been controlling myself for the last half-hour until I feel like bursting. [*He sits down furiously at the end of the table next the study.*]

Sykes [*pointing to the simmering* REGINALD *and the boiling* GENERAL]. Thats just it, Bishop. Edith is her uncles' niece. She cant control herself any more than they can. And she's a Bishop's daughter. That means that she's engaged in social work of all sorts: organizing shop assistants and sweated work girls and all that. When her blood boils about it (and it boils at least once a week) she doesnt care what she says.

Reginald. Well: you knew that when you proposed to her.

Sykes. Yes; but I didnt know that when we were married I should be legally responsible if she libelled anybody, though all her property is protected against me as if I were the lowest thief and cadger. This morning somebody sent me Belfort Bax's essays on Men's Wrongs; and they have been a perfect eye-opener to me. Bishop: I'm not thinking of myself: I would face anything for Edith. But my mother and sisters are wholly dependent on my property. I'd rather have to cut off an inch from my right arm than a hundred a year from my mother's income. I owe everything to her care of me.

EDITH, *in dressing-jacket and petticoat, comes in through the tower, swiftly and determinedly, pamphlet in hand, principles up in arms, more of a bishop than her father, yet as much a gentlewoman as her mother. She is the typical spoilt child of a clerical household: almost as terrible a product as the typical spoilt child of a Bohemian household: that is, all her childish affectations of conscientious scruple and religious impulse have been applauded and deferred to until she has become an ethical snob of the first water. Her father's sense of humor and her mother's placid balance have done something to save her humanity; but her impetuous temper and energetic will, unrestrained by any touch of humor or scepticism, carry everything before them. Imperious and dogmatic, she takes command of the party at once.*

Edith [*standing behind* CECIL's *chair*]. Cecil: I heard your voice. I must speak to you very particularly. Papa: go away. Go away everybody.

The Bishop [*crossing to the study door*]. I think there can be no doubt that Edith wishes us to retire. Come. [*He stands in the doorway, waiting for them to follow.*]

Sykes. Thats it, you see. It's just this outspokenness that makes my position hard, much as I admire her for it.

Edith. Do you want me to flatter and be untruthful?

Sykes. No, not exactly that.

Edith. Does anybody want me to flatter and be untruthful?

Hotchkiss. Well, since you ask me, I do. Surely it's the very first qualification for tolerable social intercourse.

The General [*markedly*]. I hope you will always tell me the truth, my darling, at all events.

Edith [*complacently coming to the fireplace*]. You can depend on me for that, Uncle Boxer.

Hotchkiss. Are you sure you have any adequate idea of what the truth about a military man really is?

Reginald [*aggressively*]. Whats the truth about you, I wonder?

Hotchkiss. Oh, quite unfit for publication in its entirety. If Miss Bridgenorth begins telling it, I shall have to leave the room.

Reginald. I'm not at all surprised to hear it. [*Rising.*] But whats it got to do with our business here today? Is it you thats going to be married or is it Edith?

Hotchkiss. I'm so sorry. I get so interested in myself that I thrust myself into the front of every discussion in the most insufferable way. [REGINALD, *with an exclamation of disgust, crosses the kitchen towards the study door.*] But, my dear Rejjy, are you quite sure that Miss Bridgenorth is going to to be married? Are you, Miss Bridgenorth?

Before EDITH *has time to answer her mother returns with* LEO *and* LESBIA.

Leo. Yes, here she is, of course. I told you I heard her dash downstairs. [*She comes to the end of the table next the fireplace.*]

Mrs. Bridgenorth [*transfixed in the middle of the kitchen*]. And Cecil!!

Lesbia. And Sinjon!

The Bishop. Edith wishes to speak to Cecil. [MRS. BRIDGE-NORTH *comes to him.* LESBIA *goes into the garden, as before.*] Let us go into my study.

Leo. But she must come and dress. Look at the hour!

Mrs. Bridgenorth. Come, Leo dear. [LEO *follows her reluctantly. They are about to go into the study with* THE BISHOP.]

Hotchkiss. Do you know, Miss Bridgenorth, I should most awfully like to hear what you have to say to poor Cecil.

Reginald [*scandalized*]. Well!

Edith. Who is poor Cecil, pray?

Hotchkiss. One always calls a man that on his wedding morning: I dont know why. I'm his best man, you know. Dont you think it gives me a certain right to be present in Cecil's interest?

The General [*gravely*]. There is such a thing as delicacy, Mr. Hotchkiss.

Hotchkiss. There is such a thing as curiosity, General.

The General [*furious*]. Delicacy is thrown away here, Alfred. Edith: you had better take Sykes into the study.

The group at the study door breaks up. THE GENERAL *flings himself into the last chair on the long side of the table, near the garden door.* LEO *sits at the end, next him, and* MRS. BRIDGENORTH *next* LEO. REGINALD *returns to the oak chest, to be near* LEO; *and* THE BISHOP *goes to his wife and stands by her.*

Hotchkiss [*to* EDITH]. Of course I'll go if you wish me to. But Cecil's objection to go through with it was so entirely on public grounds—

Edith [*with quick suspicion*]. His objection?

Sykes. Sinjon: you have no right to say that. I expressly said that I'm ready to go through with it.

Edith. Cecil: do you mean to say that you have been raising difficulties about our marriage?

Sykes. I raise no difficulty. But I do beg you to be careful what you say about people. You must remember, my dear, that when we are married I shall be responsible for everything you say. Only last week you said on a public platform that Slattox and Chinnery were scoundrels. They could have got a thousand pounds damages apiece from me for that if we'd been married at the time.

Edith [*austerely*]. I never said anything of the sort. I never stoop to mere vituperation: what would my girls say of me if I did? I chose my words most carefully. I said they were tyrants, liars, and thieves; and so they are. Slattox is even worse.

Hotchkiss. I'm afraid that would be at least five thousand pounds.

Sykes. If it were only myself, I shouldnt care. But my mother and sisters! I've no right to sacrifice them.

Edith. You neednt be alarmed. I'm not going to be married.

All the Rest. Not!

Sykes [*in consternation*]. Edith! Are you throwing me over?

Edith. How can I? You have been beforehand with me.

Sykes. On my honor, no. All I said was that I didnt know the law when I asked you to be my wife.

Edith. And you wouldnt have asked me if you had. Is that it?

Sykes. No. I should have asked you for my sake to be a little more careful—not to ruin me uselessly.

Edith. You think the truth useless?

Hotchkiss. Much worse than useless, I assure you. Frequently most mischievous.

Edith. Sinjon: hold your tongue. You are a chatterbox and a fool!

Mrs. *Bridgenorth* ⎱ [*shocked*]. ⎰Edith!
The *Bishop*   ⎰   ⎱My love!

Hotchkiss [*mildly*]. I shall not take an action, Cecil.

Edith [*to* HOTCHKISS]. Sorry; but you are old enough to know better. [*To the others.*] And now since there is to be no wedding, we had better get back to our work. Mamma: will you tell Collins to cut up the wedding cake into thirty-three pieces for the club girls. My not being married is no reason why they should be disappointed. [*She turns to go.*]

Hotchkiss [*gallantly*]. If youll allow me to take Cecil's place, Miss Bridgenorth—

Leo. Sinjon!

Hotchkiss. Oh, I forgot. I beg your pardon. [*To* EDITH, *apologetically.*] A prior engagement.

Edith. What! You and Leo! I thought so. Well, hadnt you two better get married at once? I dont approve of long engagements. The breakfast's ready: the cake's ready: everything's ready. I'll lend Leo my veil and things.

The Bishop. I'm afraid they must wait until the decree is made absolute, my dear. And the license is not transferable.

Edith. Oh well, it cant be helped. Is there anything else before I go off to the Club?

Sykes. You dont seem much disappointed, Edith. I cant help saying that much.

Edith. And you cant help looking enormously relieved, Cecil. We shant be any worse friends, shall we?

Sykes [*distractedly*]. Of course not. Still—I'm perfectly ready—at least—if it were not for my mother—Oh, I dont know what to do. Ive been so fond of you; and when the worry of the wedding was over I should have been so fond of you again—

Edith [*petting him*]. Come, come! dont make a scene, dear. Youre quite right. I dont think a woman doing public work ought to get married unless her husband feels about it as she does. I dont blame you at all for throwing me over.

Reginald [*bouncing off the chest, and passing behind* THE GENERAL *to the other end of the table.*] No: dash it! I'm not going to stand this. Why is the man always to be put in the wrong? Be honest, Edith. Why werent you dressed? Were you going to throw him over? If you were, take your fair share of the blame; and dont put it all on him.

Hotchkiss [*sweetly*]. Would it not be better—

Reginald [*violently*]. Now look here, Hotchkiss. Who asked you to cut in? Is your name Edith? Am I your uncle?

Hotchkiss. I wish you were: I should like to have an uncle Reginald.

Reginald. Yah! Sykes: are you ready to marry Edith or are you not?

Sykes. Ive already said that I'm quite ready. A promise is a promise.

Reginald. We dont want to know whether a promise is a promise or not. Cant you answer yes or no without spoiling it and setting Hotchkiss here grinning like a Cheshire cat? If she puts on her veil and goes to Church, will you marry her?

Sykes. Certainly. Yes.

Reginald. Thats all right. Now, Edie, put on your veil and off with you to Church. The bridegroom's waiting. [*He sits down at the table.*]

Edith. Is it understood that Slattox and Chinnery are liars and thieves, and that I hope by next Wednesday to have in my hands conclusive evidence that Slattox is something much worse?

Sykes. I made no conditions as to that when I proposed to you; and now I cant go back. I hope Providence will spare my poor mother. I say again I'm ready to marry you.

Edith. Then I think you shew great weakness of character; and instead of taking advantage of it I shall set you a better example. I want to know is this true. [*She produces a pamphlet and takes it to* THE BISHOP; *then sits down between* HOTCHKISS *and her mother.*]

The Bishop [*reading the title*]. DO YOU KNOW WHAT YOU ARE GOING TO DO? BY A WOMAN WHO HAS DONE IT. May I ask, my dear, what she did?

Edith. She got married. When she had three children—the eldest only four years old—her husband committed a murder, and then attempted to commit suicide, but only succeeded in disfiguring himself. Instead of hanging him, they sent him to penal servitude for life, for the sake, they said, of his wife and infant children. And she could not get a divorce from that horrible murderer. They would not even keep him imprisoned for life. For twenty years she had to live singly, bringing up her children by her own work, and knowing that just when they were grown up and beginning life, this dreadful creature would be let out to disgrace them all, and prevent the two girls getting decently married, and drive the son out of the country perhaps. Is that really the law? Am I to understand that if Cecil commits a murder, or forges, or steals, or becomes an atheist, I cant get divorced from him?

The Bishop. Yes, my dear. That is so. You must take him for better for worse.

Edith. Then I most certainly refuse to enter into any such wicked contract. What sort of servants? what sort of friends? what sort of Prime Ministers should we have if we took them for better for worse for all their lives? We should simply encourage them in every sort of wickedness. Surely my husband's conduct is of more importance to me than Mr. Balfour's or Mr. Asquith's. If I had known the law I would never have consented. I dont believe any woman would if she realized what she was doing.

Sykes. But I'm not going to commit murder.

Edith. How do you know? Ive sometimes wanted to murder Slattox. Have you never wanted to murder somebody, Uncle Rejjy?

Reginald [*at* HOTCHKISS, *with intense expression*]. Yes.

Leo. Rejjy!

Reginald. I said yes; and I mean yes. There was one night, Hotchkiss, when I jolly nearly shot you and Leo and finished up with myself; and thats the truth.

Leo [*suddenly whimpering*]. Oh Rejjy. [*She runs to him and kisses him.*]

Reginald [*wrathfully*]. Be off. [*She returns weeping to her seat.*]

Mrs. Bridgenorth [*petting* LEO, *but speaking to the company at large*]. But isnt all this great nonsense? What likelihood is there of any of us committing a crime?

Hotchkiss. Oh yes, I assure you. I went into the matter once very carefully; and I found that things I have actually done—things that everybody does, I imagine—would expose me, if I were found out and prosecuted, to ten years penal servitude, two years hard labor, and the loss of all civil rights. Not counting that I'm a private trustee, and, like all private trustees, a fraudulent one. Otherwise, the widow for whom I am trustee would starve occasionally, and the children get no education. And I'm probably as honest a man as any here.

The General [*outraged*]. Do you imply that I have been guilty of conduct that would expose me to penal servitude?

Hotchkiss. I should think it quite likely. But of course I dont know.

Mrs. Bridgenorth. But bless me! marriage is not a question of law, is it? Have you children no affection for one-another? Surely thats enough?

Hotchkiss. If it's enough, why get married?

Mrs. Bridgenorth. Stuff, Sinjon! Of course people must get married. [*Uneasily.*] Alfred: why dont you say something? Surely youre not going to let this go on?

The General. Ive been waiting for the last twenty minutes, Alfred, in amazement! in stupefaction! to hear you put a stop to all this. We look to you: it's your place, your office, your duty. Exert your authority at once.

The Bishop. You must give the devil fair play, Boxer. Until you have heard and weighed his case you have no right to condemn him. I'm sorry you have been kept waiting twenty minutes; but I myself have waited twenty years for this to happen. Ive often wrestled with the temptation to pray that it might not happen in my own household. Perhaps it was a presentiment that it might become a part of our old Bridgenorth burden that made me warn our Governments so earnestly that unless the law of marriage were first made human, it could never become divine.

Mrs. Bridgenorth. Oh, do be sensible about this. People must get married. What would you have said if Cecil's parents had not been married?

The Bishop. They were not, my dear.

Hotchkiss.	Hallo!
Reginald.	What d'ye mean?
The General.	Eh?
Leo.	Not married!
Mrs. Bridgenorth.	What!

Sykes [*rising in amazement*]. What on earth do you mean, Bishop? My parents were married.

Hotchkiss. You cant remember, Cecil.

Sykes. Well, I never asked my mother to shew me her marriage lines, if thats what you mean. What man ever has? I never suspected—I never knew—Are you joking? Or have we all gone mad?

The Bishop. Dont be alarmed, Cecil. Let me explain. Your parents were not Anglicans. You were not, I think, Anglican yourself, until your second year at Oxford. They were Positivists. They went through the Positivist ceremony at Newton Hall in Fetter Lane after entering into the civil contract before the Registrar of the West Strand District. I ask you, as an Anglican Catholic, was that a marriage?

Sykes [*overwhelmed*]. Great Heavens, no! a thousand times, no. I never thought of that. I'm a child of sin. [*He collapses into the railed chair.*]

The Bishop. Oh, come, come! You are no more a child of sin than any Jew, or Mahometan, or Nonconformist, or anyone else born outside the Church. But you see how it affects my view of the situation. To me there is only one marriage that is holy: the Church's sacrament of marriage. Outside that, I can recognize no distinction between one civil contract and another. There was a time when all marriages were made in Heaven. But because the Church was unwise and would not make its ordinances reasonable, its power over men and women was taken away from it; and marriages gave place to contracts at a registry office. And now that our Governments refuse to make these contracts reasonable, those whom we in our blindness drove out of the Church will be driven out of the registry office; and we shall have the history of Ancient Rome repeated. We shall be joined by our solicitors for seven, fourteen, or twenty-one years—or perhaps months. Deeds of partnership will replace the old vows.

The General. Would you, a Bishop, approve of such partnerships?

The Bishop. Do you think that I, a Bishop, approve of the Deceased Wife's Sister Act? That did not prevent its becoming law.

The General. But when the Government sounded you as to whether youd marry a man to his deceased wife's sister you very naturally and properly told them youd see them damned first.

The Bishop [*horrified*]. No, no, really, Boxer! You must not—

The General [*impatiently*]. Oh, of course I dont mean that you used those words. But that was the meaning and the spirit of it.

The Bishop. Not the spirit, Boxer, I protest. But never mind that. The point is that State marriage is already divorced from Church marriage. The relations between Leo and Rejjy and Sinjon are perfectly legal; but do you expect me, as a Bishop, to approve of them?

The General. I dont defend Reginald. He should have kicked you out of the house, Mr. Hotchkiss.

Reginald [*rising*]. How could I kick him out of the house? He's stronger than me: he could have kicked me out if it came to that. He did kick me out: what else was it but kicking out, to take my wife's affections from me and establish himself in my place? [*He comes to the hearth.*]

Hotchkiss. I protest, Reginald, I said all that a man could to prevent the smash.

Reginald. Oh, I know you did: I dont blame you: people dont do these things to one another: they happen and they cant be helped. What was I to do? I was old: she was young. I was dull: he was brilliant. I had a face like a walnut: he had a face like a mushroom. I was as glad to have him in the house as she was: he amused me. And we were a couple of fools: he gave us good advice—told us what to do when we didnt know. She found out that I wasnt any use to her and he was; so she nabbed him and gave me the chuck.

Leo. If you dont stop talking in that disgraceful way about our married life, I'll leave the room and never speak to you again.

Reginald. Youre not going to speak to me again, anyhow, are you? Do you suppose I'm going to visit you when you marry him?

Hotchkiss. I hope so. Surely youre not going to be vindictive, Rejjy. Besides, youll have all the advantages I formerly enjoyed. Youll be the visitor, the relief, the new face, the fresh news, the hopeless attachment: *I* shall only be the husband.

Reginald [*savagely*]. Will you tell me this, any of you? how is it that we always get talking about Hotchkiss when our business is about Edith? [*He fumes up the kitchen to the tower and back to his chair.*]

Mrs. Bridgenorth. Will somebody tell me how the world is to get on if nobody is to get married?

Sykes. Will somebody tell me what an honorable man and a sincere Anglican is to propose to a woman whom he loves and who loves him and wont marry him?

Leo. Will somebody tell me how I'm to arrange to take care of Rejjy when I'm married to Sinjon. Rejjy must not be allowed to marry anyone else, especially that odious nasty creature that told all those wicked lies about him in Court.

Hotchkiss. Let us draw up the first English partnership deed.

Leo. For shame, Sinjon!

The Bishop. Somebody must begin, my dear. I've a very strong suspicion that when it is drawn up it will be so much worse than the existing law that you will all prefer getting married. We shall therefore be doing the greatest possible service to morality by just trying how the new system would work.

Lesbia [*suddenly reminding them of her forgotten presence as she stands thoughtfully in the garden doorway*]. Ive been thinking.

The Bishop [*to* HOTCHKISS]. Nothing like making people think: is there, Sinjon?

Lesbia [*coming to the table, on* THE GENERAL'*s left*]. A woman has no right to refuse motherhood. That is clear, after the statistics given in *The Times* by Mr. Sidney Webb.

The General. Mr. Webb has nothing to do with it. It is the Voice of Nature.

Lesbia. But if she is an English lady it is her right and her duty to stand out for honorable conditions. If we can agree on the conditions, I am willing to enter into an alliance with Boxer.

THE GENERAL *staggers to his feet, momentarily stupent and speechless.*

Edith [*rising*]. And I with Cecil.

Leo [*rising*]. And I with Rejjy and St. John.

The General [*aghast*]. An alliance! Do you mean a—a—a—

Reginald. She only means bigamy, as I understand her.

The General. Alfred: how long more are you going to stand there and countenance this lunacy? Is it a horrible dream or am I awake? In the name of common sense and sanity, let us get back to real life—

COLLINS *comes in through the tower, in alderman's robes. The ladies who are standing sit down hastily, and look as unconcerned as possible.*

Collins. Sorry to hurry you, my lord; but the Church has been full this hour past; and the organist has played all the wedding music in Lohengrin three times over.

The General. The very man we want. Alfred: I'm not equal to this crisis. You are not equal to it. The Army has failed. The Church has failed. I shall put aside all idle social distinctions and appeal to the Municipality.

Mrs. Bridgenorth. Do, Boxer. He is sure to get us out of this difficulty.

COLLINS, *a little puzzled, comes forward affably to* HOTCHKISS'*s left.*

Hotchkiss [*rising, impressed by the aldermanic gown*]. Ive not had the pleasure. Will you introduce me?

Collins [*confidentially*]. All right, sir. Only the greengrocer, sir, in charge of the wedding breakfast. Mr. Alderman Collins, sir, when I'm in my gown.

Hotchkiss [*staggered*]. Very pleased indeed [*He sits down again.*]

The Bishop. Personally I value the counsel of my old friend, Mr. Alderman Collins, very highly. If Edith and Cecil will allow him—

Edith. Collins has known me from my childhood: I'm sure he will agree with me.

Collins. Yes, miss: you may depend on me for that. Might I ask what the difficulty is?

Edith. Simply this. Do you expect me to get married in the existing state of the law?

Sykes [*rising and coming to* COLLINS'S *left elbow*]. I put it to you as a sensible man: is it any worse for her than for me?

Reginald [*leaving his place and thrusting himself between* COLLINS *and* SYKES, *who returns to his chair*]. Thats not the point. Let this be understood, Mr. Collins. It's not the man who is backing out: it's the woman. [*He posts himself on the hearth.*]

Lesbia. We do not admit that, Collins. The women are perfectly ready to make a reasonable arrangement.

Leo. With both men.

The General. The case is now before you, Mr. Collins. And I put it to you as one man to another: did you ever hear such crazy nonsense?

Mrs. Bridgenorth. The world must go on, mustnt it, Collins?

Collins [*snatching at this, the first intelligible proposition he has heard*]. Oh, the world will go on, maam: dont you be afraid of that. It aint so easy to stop it as the earnest kind of people think.

Edith. I knew you would agree with me, Collins. Thank you.

Hotchkiss. Have you the least idea of what they are talking about, Mr. Alderman?

Collins. Oh, thats all right, sir. The particulars dont matter. I never read the report of a Committee: after all, what can they say that you dont know? You pick it up as they go on talking. [*He goes to the corner of the table and speaks across it to the company.*] Well, my Lord and Miss Edith and Madam and Gentlemen, it's like this. Marriage is tolerable enough in its way if youre easygoing and dont expect too much from it. But it doesnt bear thinking about. The great thing is to get the young people tied up before they know what theyre letting themselves in for. Theres Miss Lesbia now. She waited till she started thinking about it; and then it was all over. If you once start arguing, Miss Edith and

Mr. Sykes, youll never get married. Go and get married first: youll have plenty of arguing afterwards, miss, believe me.

Hotchkiss. Your warning comes too late. Theyve started arguing already.

The General. But you dont take in the full—well, I dont wish to exaggerate; but the only word I can find is the full horror of the situation. These ladies not only refuse our honorable offers, but as I understand it—and I'm sure I beg your pardon most heartily, Lesbia, if I'm wrong, as I hope I am—they actually call on us to enter into—I'm sorry to use the expression; but what can I say?—into ALLIANCES with them under contracts to be drawn up by our confounded solicitors.

Collins. Dear me, General: thats something new when the parties belong to the same class.

The Bishop. Not new, Collins. The Romans did it.

Collins. Yes: they would, them Romans. When youre in Rome do as the Romans do, is an old saying. But we're not in Rome at present, my lord.

The Bishop. We have got into many of their ways. What do you think of the contract system, Collins?

Collins. Well, my lord, when theres a question of a contract, I always say, shew it to me on paper. If it's to be talk, let it be talk; but if it's to be a contract, down with it in black and white; and then we shall know what we're about.

Hotchkiss. Quite right, Mr. Alderman. Let us draft it at once. May I go into the study for writing materials, Bishop?

The Bishop. Do, Sinjon.

HOTCHKISS *goes into the library.*

Collins. If I might point out a difficulty, my lord—

The Bishop. Certainly. [*He goes to the fourth chair from* THE GENERAL'S *left, but before sitting down, courteously points to the chair at the end of the table next the hearth*]. Wont you sit down, Mr. Alderman? [COLLINS, *very appreciative of* THE BISHOP'S *distinguished consideration, sits down.* THE BISHOP *then takes his seat.*]

Collins. We are at present six men to four ladies. Thats not fair.

Reginald. Not fair to the men, you mean.

Leo. Oh! Rejjy has said something clever! Can I be mistaken in him?

HOTCHKISS *comes back with a blotter and some paper. He takes the vacant place in the middle of the table between* LESBIA *and* THE BISHOP.

Collins. I tell you the truth, my lord and ladies and gentle-men: I dont trust my judgment on this subject. Theres a certain lady that I always consult on delicate points like this. She has a very exceptional experience, and a wonderful temperament and instinct in affairs of the heart.

Hotchkiss. Excuse me, Mr. Alderman: I'm a snob, and I warn you that theres no use consulting anyone who will not advise us frankly on class lines. Marriage is good enough for the lower classes: they have facilities for desertion that are denied to us. What is the social position of this lady?

Collins. The highest in the borough, sir. She is the Mayoress. But you need not stand in awe of her, sir. She is my sister-in-law. [*To* THE BISHOP.] Ive often spoken of her to your lady, my lord. [*To* MRS. BRIDGENORTH.] Mrs. George, maam.

Mrs. Bridgenorth [*startled*]. Do you mean to say, Collins, that Mrs. George is a real person?

Collins [*equally startled*]. Didnt you believe in her, maam?

Mrs. Bridgenorth. Never for a moment.

The Bishop. We always thought that Mrs. George was too good to be true. I still dont believe in her, Collins. You must produce her if you are to convince me.

Collins [*overwhelmed*]. Well, I'm so taken aback by this that—Well I never!!! Why! she's at the church at this moment, waiting to see the wedding.

The Bishop. Then produce her. [COLLINS *shakes his head.*] Come, Collins! confess. Theres no such person.

Collins. There is, my lord: there is, I assure you. You ask George. It's true *I* cant produce her; but you can, my lord.

The Bishop. I!

Collins. Yes, my lord, you. For some reason that I never could make out, she has forbidden me to talk about you, or to let her meet you. Ive asked her to come here of a wedding morning to help with the flowers or the like; and she has always refused. But if you order her to come as her Bishop, she'll come. She has some very strange fancies, has Mrs. George. Send your ring to her, my lord—the official ring—send it by some very stylish gentleman—perhaps Mr. Hotchkiss here would be good enough to take it—and she'll come.

The Bishop [*taking off his ring and handing it to* HOTCH-KISS]. Oblige me by undertaking the mission.

Hotchkiss. But how am I to know the lady?

Collins. She has gone to the church in state, sir, and will be attended by a Beadle with a mace. He will point her out to you; and he will take the front seat of the carriage on the way back.

Hotchkiss. No, by heavens! Forgive me, Bishop; but you are asking too much. I ran away from the Boers because I was a snob. I run away from the Beadle for the same reason. I absolutely decline the mission.

The General [*rising impressively*]. Be good enough to give me that ring, Mr. Hotchkiss.

Hotchkiss. With pleasure. [*He hands it to him.*]

The General. I shall have great pleasure, Mr. Alderman, in waiting on the Mayoress with the Bishop's orders; and I shall be proud to return with municipal honors. [*He stalks out gallantly,* COLLINS *rising for a moment to bow to him with marked dignity.*]

Reginald. Boxer is rather a fine old josser in his way.

Hotchkiss. His uniform gives him an unfair advantage. He will take all the attention off the Beadle.

Collins. I think it would be as well, my lord, to go on with the contract while we're waiting. The truth is, we shall none of us have much of a look-in when Mrs. George comes; so we had better finish the writing part of the business before she arrives.

Hotchkiss. I think I have the preliminaries down all right. [*Reading.*] 'Memorandum of Agreement made this day of blank blank between blank blank of blank blank in the County of blank, Esquire, hereinafter called the Gentleman, of the one part, and blank blank of blank in the County of blank, hereinafter called the Lady, of the other part, whereby it is declared and agreed as follows.'

Leo [*rising*]. You might remember your manners, Sinjon. The lady comes first. [*She goes behind him and stoops to look at the draft over his shoulder.*]

Hotchkiss. To be sure. I beg your pardon. [*He alters the draft.*]

Leo. And you have got only one lady and one gentleman. There ought to be two gentlemen.

Collins. Oh, thats a mere matter of form, maam. Any number of ladies or gentlemen can be put in.

Leo. Not any number of ladies. Only one lady. Besides, that creature wasnt a lady.

Reginald. You shut your head, Leo. This is a general sort of contract for everybody: it's not your contract.

Leo. Then what use is it to me?

Hotchkiss. You will get some hints from it for your own contract.

Edith. I hope there will be no hinting. Let us have the plain straightforward truth and nothing but the truth.

Collins. Yes, yes, miss: it will be all right. Theres nothing underhand, I assure you. It's a model agreement, as it were.

Edith [*unconvinced*]. I hope so.

Hotchkiss. What is the first clause in an agreement, usually? You know, Mr. Alderman?

Collins [*at a loss*]. Well, sir, the Town Clerk always sees to that. Ive got out of the habit of thinking for myself in these little matters. Perhaps his lordship knows.

The Bishop. I'm sorry to say I dont. But Soames will know. Alice: where is Soames?

Hotchkiss. He's in there. [*Pointing to the study.*]

The Bishop [*to his wife*]. Coax him to join us, my love. [MRS. BRIDGENORTH *goes into the study.*] Soames is my chaplain, Mr. Collins. The great difficulty about Bishops in the Church of England today is that the affairs of the diocese make it necessary that a Bishop should be before everything a man of business, capable of sticking to his desk for sixteen hours a day. But the result of having Bishops of this sort is that the spiritual interests of the Church, and its influence on the souls and imaginations of the people, very soon begin to go rapidly to the devil—

Edith [*shocked*]. Papa!

The Bishop. I am speaking technically, not in Boxer's manner. Indeed the Bishops themselves went so far in that direction that they gained a reputation for being spiritually the stupidest men in the country and commercially the sharpest. I found a way out of this difficulty. Soames was my solicitor. I found that Soames, though a very capable man of business, had a romantic secret history. His father was an eminent Nonconformist divine who habitually spoke of the Church of England as The Scarlet Woman. Soames became secretly converted to Anglicanism at the age of fifteen. He longed to take holy orders, but didn't dare to, because his father had a weak heart and habitually threatened to drop dead if anybody hurt his feelings. You may have noticed that people with weak hearts are the tyrants of English family life. So poor Soames had to become a solicitor. When his father died—by a curious stroke of poetic justice he died of scarlet fever, and was found to have had a perfectly sound heart—I ordained Soames and made him my chaplain. He is now quite happy. He is a celibate; fasts strictly on Fridays and throughout Lent; wears a cassock and biretta; and has more legal business to do than ever he had in his old office in Ely Place. And he sets me free for the spiritual and scholarly pursuits proper to a Bishop.

Mrs. Bridgenorth [*coming back from the study with a*

knitting basket]. Here he is. [*She resumes her seat, and knits.*]

SOAMES *comes in in cassock and biretta. He salutes the company by blessing them with two fingers.*

Hotchkiss. Take my place, Mr. Soames. [*He gives up his chair to him, and retires to the oak chest, on which he seats himself.*]

The Bishop. No longer Mr. Soames, Sinjon. Father Anthony.

Soames [*taking his seat*]. I was christened Oliver Cromwell Soames. My father had no right to do it. I have taken the name of Anthony. When you become parents, young gentlemen, be very careful not to label a helpless child with views which it may come to hold in abhorrence.

The Bishop. Has Alice explained to you the nature of the document we are drafting?

Soames. She has indeed.

Lesbia. That sounds as if you disapproved.

Soames. It is not for me to approve or disapprove. I do the work that comes to my hand from my ecclesiastical superior.

The Bishop. Dont be uncharitable, Anthony. You must give us your best advice.

Soames. My advice to you all is to do your duty by taking the Christian vows of celibacy and poverty. The Church was founded to put an end to marriage and to put an end to property.

Mrs. Bridgenorth. But how could the world go on, Anthony?

Soames. Do your duty and see. Doing your duty is your business: keeping the world going is in higher hands.

Lesbia. Anthony: youre impossible.

Soames [*taking up his pen*]. You wont take my advice. I didnt expect you would. Well, I await your instructions.

Reginald. We got stuck on the first clause. What should we begin with?

Soames. It is usual to begin with the term of the contract.

Edith. What does that mean?

Soames. The term of years for which it is to hold good.

Leo. But this is a marriage contract.

Soames. Is the marriage to be for a year, a week, or a day?

Reginald. Come, I say, Anthony! Youre worse than any of us. A day!

Soames. Off the path is off the path. An inch or a mile: what does it matter?

Leo. If the marriage is not to be for ever, I'll have nothing to do with it. I call it immoral to have a marriage for a term of years. If the people dont like it they can get divorced.

Reginald. It ought to be for just as long as the two people like. Thats what I say.

Collins. They may not agree on the point, sir. It's often fast with one and loose with the other.

Lesbia. I should say for as long as the man behaves himself.

The Bishop. Suppose the woman doesnt behave herself?

Mrs. Bridgenorth. The woman may have lost all her chances of a good marriage with anybody else. She should not be cast adrift.

Reginald. So may the man! What about his home?

Leo. The wife ought to keep an eye on him, and see that he is comfortable and takes care of himself properly. The other man wont want her all the time.

Lesbia. There may not be another man.

Leo. Then why on earth should she leave him?

Lesbia. Because she wants to.

Leo. Oh, if people are going to be let do what they want to, then I call it simple immorality. [*She goes indignantly to the oak chest, and perches herself on it close beside* HOTCHKISS.]

Reginald [*watching them sourly*]. You do it yourself, dont you?

Leo. Oh, thats quite different. Dont make foolish witticisms, Rejjy.

The Bishop. We dont seem to be getting on. What do you say, Mr. Alderman?

Collins. Well my lord, you see people do persist in talking as if marriages was all of one sort. But theres almost as many different sorts of marriages as theres different sorts of people. Theres the young things that marry for love, not knowing what theyre doing, and the old things that marry for money and comfort and companionship. Theres the people that marry for children. Theres the people that dont intend to have children and that arnt fit to have them. Theres the people that marry because theyre so much run after by the other sex that they have to put a stop to it somehow. Theres the people that want to try a new experience, and the people that want to have done with experiences. How are you to please them all? Why, youll want half a dozen different sorts of contract.

The Bishop. Well, if so, let us draw them all up. Let us face it.

Reginald. Why should we be held together whether we

like it or not? Thats the question thats at the bottom of it all.

Mrs. Bridgenorth. Because of the children, Rejjy.

Collins. But even then, maam, why should we be held together when thats all over—when the girls are married and the boys out in the world and in business for themselves? When thats done with, the real work of the marriage is done with. If the two like to stay together, let them stay together. But if not, let them part, as old people in the workhouses do. Theyve had enough of one another. Theyve found one another out. Why should they be tied together to sit there grudging and hating and spiting one another like so many do? Put it twenty years from the birth of the youngest child.

Soames. How if there be no children?

Collins. Let em take one another on liking.

Mrs. Bridgenorth. Collins!

Leo. You wicked old man!

The Bishop [*remonstrating*]. My dear, my dear!

Lesbia. And what is a woman to live on, pray, when she is no longer liked, as you call it?

Soames [*with sardonic formality*]. It is proposed that the term of the agreement be twenty years from the birth of the youngest child when there are children. Any amendment?

Leo. I protest. It must be for life. It would not be a marriage at all if it were not for life.

Soames. Mrs. Reginald Bridgenorth proposes life. Any seconder?

Leo. Dont be soulless, Anthony.

Lesbia. I have a very important amendment. If there are any children, the man must be cleared completely out of the house for two years on each occasion. At such times he is superfluous, importunate, and ridiculous.

Collins. But where is he to go, miss?

Lesbia. He can go where he likes as long as he does not bother the mother.

Reginald. And is she to be left lonely—

Lesbia. Lonely! With her child. The poor woman would be only too glad to have a moment to herself. Dont be absurd, Rejjy.

Reginald. The father is to be a wandering wretched outcast, living at his club, and seeing nobody but his friends' wives!

Lesbia [*ironically*]. Poor fellow!

Hotchkiss. The friends' wives are perhaps the solution of the problem. You see, their husbands will also be outcasts; and the poor ladies will occasionally pine for male society.

Lesbia. There is no reason why a mother should not have male society. What she clearly should not have is a husband.

Soames. Anything else, Miss Grantham?

Lesbia. Yes: I must have my own separate house, or my own separate part of a house. Boxer smokes: I cant endure tobacco. Boxer believes that an open window means death from cold and exposure to the night air: I must have fresh air always. We can be friends; but we cant live together; and that must be put in the agreement.

Edith. Ive no objection to smoking; and as to opening the windows, Cecil will of course have to do what is best for his health.

The Bishop. Who is to be the judge of that, my dear? You or he?

Edith. Neither of us. We must do what the doctor orders.

Reginald. Doctor be—!

Leo [*admonitorily*]. Rejjy!

Reginald [*to* SOAMES]. You take my tip, Anthony. Put a clause into that agreement that the doctor is to have no say in the job. It's bad enough for the two people to be married to one another without their both being married to the doctor as well.

Lesbia. That reminds me of something very important. Boxer believes in vaccination: I do not. There must be a clause that I am to decide on such questions as I think best.

Leo [*to* THE BISHOP]. Baptism is nearly as important as vaccination: isnt it?

The Bishop. It used to be considered so, my dear.

Leo. Well, Sinjon scoffs at it: he says that godfathers are ridiculous. I must be allowed to decide.

Reginald. Theyll be his children as well as yours, you know.

Leo. Dont be indelicate, Rejjy.

Edith. You are forgetting the very important matter of money.

Collins. Ah! Money! Now we're coming to it!

Edith. When I'm married I shall have practically no money except what I shall earn.

The Bishop. I'm sorry, Cecil. A Bishop's daughter is a poor man's daughter.

Sykes. But surely you dont imagine that I'm going to let Edith work when we're married. I'm not a rich man; but Ive enough to spare her that; and when my mother dies—

Edith. What nonsense! Of course I shall work when I'm married. I shall keep your house.

Sykes. Oh, that!

Reginald. You call that work?

Edith. Dont you? Leo used to do it for nothing; so no doubt you thought it wasnt work at all. Does your present housekeeper do it for nothing?

Reginald. But it will be part of your duty as a wife.

Edith. Not under this contract. I'll not have it so. If I'm to keep the house, I shall expect Cecil to pay me at least as well as he would pay a hired housekeeper. I'll not go begging to him every time I want a new dress or a cab fare, as so many women have to do.

Sykes. You know very well I would grudge you nothing, Edie.

Edith. Then dont grudge me my self-respect and independence. I insist on it in fairness to you, Cecil, because in this way there will be a fund belonging solely to me; and if Slattox takes an action against you for anything I say, you can pay the damages and stop the interest out of my salary.

Soames. You forget that under this contract he will not be liable, because you will not be his wife in law.

Edith. Nonsense! Of course I shall be his wife.

Collins [*his curiosity roused*]. Is Slattox taking an action against you, miss? Slattox is on the Council with me. Could I settle it?

Edith. He has not taken an action; but Cecil says he will.

Collins. What for, miss, if I may ask?

Edith. Slattox is a liar and a thief; and it is my duty to expose him.

Collins. You surprise me, miss. Of course Slattox is in a manner of speaking a liar. If I may say so without offence, we're all liars, if it was only to spare one another's feelings. But I shouldn't call Slattox a thief. He's not all that he should be, perhaps; but he pays his way.

Edith. If that is only your nice way of saying that Slattox is entirely unfit to have two hundred girls in his power as absolute slaves, then I shall say that too about him at the very next public meeting I address. He steals their wages under pretence of fining them. He steals their food under pretence of buying it for them. He lies when he denies having done it. And he does other things, as you evidently know, Collins. Therefore I give you notice that I shall expose him before all England without the least regard to the consequences to myself.

Sykes. Or to me?

Edith. I take equal risks. Suppose you felt it to be your duty to shoot Slattox, what would become of me and the children? I'm sure I dont want anybody to be shot: not even Slattox; but if the public never will take any notice of even the most crying evil until somebody is shot, what are people to do but shoot somebody?

Soames [*inexorably*]. I'm waiting for my instructions as to the term of the agreement.

Reginald [*impatiently, leaving the hearth and going behind* Soames]. It's no good talking all over the shop like this. We shall be here all day. I propose that the agreement holds good until the parties are divorced.

Soames. They cant be divorced. They will not be married.

Reginald. But if they cant be divorced, then this will be worse than marriage.

Mrs. Bridgenorth. Of course it will. Do stop this nonsense. Why, who are the children to belong to?

Lesbia. We have already settled that they are to belong to the mother.

Reginald. No: I'm dashed if you have. I'll fight for the ownership of my own children tooth and nail; and so will a good many other fellows, I can tell you.

Edith. It seems to me that they should be divided between the parents. If Cecil wishes any of the children to be his exclusively, he should pay me a certain sum for the risk and trouble of bringing them into the world: say a thousand pounds apiece. The interest on this could go towards the support of the child as long as we live together. But the principal would be my property. In that way, if Cecil took the child away from me, I should at least be paid for what it had cost me.

Mrs. Bridgenorth [*putting down her knitting in amazement*]. Edith! Who ever heard of such a thing!!

Edith. Well, how else do you propose to settle it?

The Bishop. There is such a thing as a favorite child. What about the youngest child—the Benjamin—the child of its parents' matured strength and charity, always better treated and better loved than the unfortunate eldest children of their youthful ignorance and wilfulness? Which parent is to own the youngest child, payment or no payment?

Collins. Theres a third party, my lord. Theres the child itself. My wife is so fond of her children that they cant call their lives their own. They all run away from home to escape from her. A child hasnt a grown-up person's appetite for affection. A little of it goes a long way with them; and they like a good imitation of it better than the real thing, as every nurse knows.

Soames. Are you sure that any of us, young or old, like the real thing as well as we like an artistic imitation of it? Is not the real thing accursed? Are not the best beloved always the good actors rather than the true sufferers? Is not love always falsified in novels and plays to make it endurable? I have noticed in myself a great delight in pictures of the Saints and of Our Lady; but when I fall under the most terrible curse of the priest's lot, the curse of Joseph pursued by the wife of Potiphar, I am invariably repelled and terrified.

Hotchkiss. Are you now speaking as a saint, Father Anthony, or as a solicitor?

Soames. There is no difference. There is not one Christian rule for solicitors and another for saints. Their hearts are alike; and their way of salvation is along the same road.

The Bishop. But "few there be that find it." Can you find it for us, Anthony?

Soames. It lies broad before you. It is the way to destruction that is narrow and tortuous. Marriage is an abomination which the Church was founded to cast out and replace by the communion of saints. I learnt that from every marriage settlement I drew up as a solicitor no less than from inspired revelation. You have set yourselves here to put your sin before you in black and white; and you cant agree upon or endure one article of it.

Sykes. It's certainly rather odd that the whole thing seems to fall to pieces the moment you touch it.

The Bishop. You see, when you give the devil fair play he loses his case. He has not been able to produce even the first clause of a working agreement; so I'm afraid we cant wait for him any longer.

Lesbia. Then the community will have to do without my children.

Edith. And Cecil will have to do without me.

Leo [*getting off the chest*]. And I positively will not marry Sinjon if he is not clever enough to make some provision for my looking after Rejjy. [*She leaves* HOTCHKISS, *and goes back to her chair at the end of the table behind* MRS. BRIDGE-NORTH.

Mrs. Bridgenorth. And the world will come to an end with this generation, I suppose.

Collins. Cant nothing be done, my lord?

The Bishop. You can make divorce reasonable and decent: that is all.

Lesbia. Thank you for nothing. If you will only make marriage reasonable and decent, you can do as you like about divorce. I have not stated my deepest objection to marriage; and I dont intend to. There are certain rights I will not give any person over me.

Reginald. Well, I think it jolly hard that a man should support his wife for years, and lose the chance of getting a really good wife, and then have her refuse to be a wife to him.

Lesbia. I'm not going to discuss it with you, Rejjy. If your sense of personal honor doesnt make you understand, nothing will.

Soames [*implacably*]. I'm still awaiting my instructions.

They look at one another, each waiting for one of the others to suggest something. Silence.

Reginald [*blankly*]. I suppose, after all, marriage is better than—well, than the usual alternative.

Soames [*turning fiercely on him*]. What right have you to say so? You know that the sins that are wasting and maddening this unhappy nation are those committed in wedlock.

Collins. Well, the single ones cant afford to indulge their affections the same as married people.

Soames. Away with it all, I say. You have your Master's commandments. Obey them.

Hotchkiss [*rising and leaning on the back of the chair left vacant by* THE GENERAL]. I really must point out to you, Father Anthony, that the early Christian rules of life were not made to last, because the early Christians did not believe that the world itself was going to last. Now we know that we shall have to go through with it. We have found that there are millions of years behind us; and we know that there are millions before us. Mrs. Bridgenorth's question remains unanswered. How is the world to go on? You say that that is not our business—that it is the business of Providence. But the modern Christian view is that we are here to do the business of Providence and nothing else. The question is, how? Am I not to use my reason to find out why? Isnt that what my reason is for? Well, all my reason tells me at present is that you are an impracticable lunatic.

Soames. Does that help?

Hotchkiss. No.

Soames. Then pray for light.

Hotchkiss. No: I am a snob, not a beggar. [*He sits down in* THE GENERAL'*s chair.*]

Collins. We dont seem to be getting on, do we? Miss Edith: you and Mr. Sykes had better go off to church and settle the right and wrong of it afterwards. Itll ease your minds, believe me: I speak from experience. You will burn your boats, as one might say.

Soames. We should never burn our boats. It is death in life.

Collins. Well, Father, I will say for you that you have views of your own and are not afraid to out with them. But some of us are of a more cheerful disposition. On the Borough Council now, you would be in a minority of one. You must take human nature as it is.

Soames. Upon what compulsion must I? I'll take divine nature as it is. I'll not hold a candle to the devil.

The Bishop. Thats a very unchristian way of treating the devil.

Reginald. Well, we dont seem to be getting any further, do we?

The Bishop. Will you give it up and get married, Edith?

Edith. No. What I propose seems to me quite reasonable.

The Bishop. And you, Lesbia?

Lesbia. Never.

Mrs. Bridgenorth. Never is a long word, Lesbia. Dont say it.

Lesbia [with a flash of temper]. Dont pity me, Alice, please. As I said before, I am an English lady, quite prepared to do without anything I cant have on honorable conditions.

Soames [after a silence expressive of utter deadlock]. I am still awaiting my instructions.

Reginald. Well, we dont seem to be getting along, do we?

Leo [out of patience]. You said that before, Rejjy. Do not repeat yourself.

Reginald. Oh, bother! [He goes to the garden door and looks out gloomily.]

Soames [rising with the paper in his hands]. Psha! [He tears it in pieces.] So much for your contract!

The Voice of the Beadle. By your leave there, gentlemen. Make way for the Mayoress. Way for the worshipful the Mayoress, my lords and gentlemen. [He comes in through the tower, in cocked hat and gold-braided overcoat, bearing the borough mace, and posts himself at the entrance.] By your leave, gentlemen, way for the worshipful Mayoress.

Collins [moving back towards the wall]. Mrs. George, my lord.

MRS. GEORGE *is every inch a Mayoress in point of stylish dressing; and she does it very well indeed. There is nothing quiet about* MRS. GEORGE: *she is not afraid of colors, and knows how to make the most of them. Not at all a lady in* LESBIA'S *use of the term as a class label, she proclaims herself to the first glance as the triumphant, pampered, wilful, intensely alive woman who has always been rich among poor people. In a historical museum she would explain Edward the Fourth's taste for shopkeepers' wives. Her age, which is certainly 40, and might be 50, is carried off by her vitality, her resilient figure, and her confident carriage. So far, a remark-*

*ably well-preserved woman. But her beauty is wrecked, like
an ageless landscape ravaged by long and fierce war. Her
eyes are alive, arresting, and haunting; and there is still a
turn of delicate beauty and pride in her indomitable chin;
but her cheeks are wasted and lined, her mouth writhen and
piteous. The whole face is a battle-field of the passions, quite
deplorable until she speaks, when an alert sense of fun re-
juvenates her in a moment, and makes her company ir-
resistible.*

All rise except SOAMES, *who sits down.* LEO *joins* REGINALD
at the garden door. MRS. BRIDGENORTH *hurries to the tower
to receive her guest, and gets as far as* SOAMES's *chair when*
MRS. GEORGE *appears.* HOTCHKISS, *apparently recognizing
her, recoils in consternation to the study door at the furthest
corner of the room from her.*

Mrs. George [*coming straight to* THE BISHOP *with the
ring in her hand*]. Here is your ring, my lord; and here am
I. It's your doing, remember: not mine.

The Bishop. Good of you to come.

Mrs Bridgenorth. How do you do, Mrs. Collins?

Mrs. George [*going to her past* THE BISHOP, *and gazing
intently at her*]. Are you his wife?

Mrs. Bridgenorth. The Bishop's wife? Yes.

Mrs. George. What a destiny! And you look like any other
woman!

Mrs. Bridgenorth [*introducing* LESBIA]. My sister, Miss
Grantham.

Mrs. George. So strangely mixed up with the story of the
General's life?

The Bishop. You know the story of his life, then.

Mrs. George. Not all. We reached the house before he
brought it up to the present day. But enough to know the
part played in it by Miss Grantham.

Mrs. Bridgenorth [*introducing* LEO]. Mrs. Reginald Bridgenorth.

Reginald. The late Mrs. Reginald Bridgenorth.

Leo. Hold your tongue, Rejjy. At least have the decency to
wait until the decree is made absolute.

Mrs. George [*to* LEO]. Well, youve more time to get married again than he has, havnt you?

Mrs. Bridgenorth [*introducing* HOTCHKISS]. Mr. St. John
Hotchkiss.

HOTCHKISS, *still far aloof by the study door, bows.*

Mrs. George. What! That! [*She makes a half tour of the*

kitchen and ends right in front of him.] Young man: do you remember coming into my shop and telling me that my husband's coals were out of place in your cellar, as Nature evidently intended them for the roof?

Hotchkiss. I remember that deplorable impertinence with shame and confusion. You were kind enough to answer that Mr. Collins was looking out for a clever young man to write advertisements, and that I could take the job if I liked.

Mrs. George. It's still open. [*She turns to* EDITH.]

Mrs. Bridgenorth. My daughter Edith. [*She comes towards the study door to make the introduction.*]

Mrs. George. The bride! [*Looking at* EDITH'S *dressing-jacket.*] Youre not going to get married like that, are you?

The Bishop [*coming round the table to* EDITH'S *left*]. Thats just what we are discussing. Will you be so good as to join us and allow us the benefit of your wisdom and experience?

Mrs. George. Do you want the Beadle as well? He's a married man.

They all turn involuntarily and contemplate THE BEADLE, *who sustains their gaze with dignity.*

The Bishop. We think there are already too many men to be quite fair to the women.

Mrs. George. Right, my lord. [*She goes back to the tower and addresses* THE BEADLE.] Take away that bauble, Joseph. Wait for me wherever you find yourself most comfortable in the neighborhood. [THE BEADLE *withdraws. She notices* COLLINS *for the first time.*] Hullo, Bill: youve got em all on too. Go and hunt up a drink for Joseph: theres a dear. [COLLINS *goes out. She looks at* SOAMES'S *cassock and biretta.*] What! Another uniform! Are you the sexton? [*He rises.*]

The Bishop. My chaplain, Father Anthony.

Mrs. George. Oh Lord! [*To* SOAMES, *coaxingly.*] You dont mind, do you?

Soames. I mind nothing but my duties.

The Bishop. You know everybody now, I think.

Mrs. George [*turning to the railed chair*]. Who's this?

The Bishop. Oh, I beg your pardon, Cecil. Mr. Sykes. The bridegroom.

Mrs. George [*to* SYKES]. Adorned for the sacrifice, arnt you?

Sykes. It seems doubtful whether there is going to be any sacrifice.

Mrs. George. Well, I want to talk to the women first. Shall we go upstairs and look at the presents and dresses?

Mrs. Bridgenorth. If you wish, certainly.

Reginald. But the men want to hear what you have to say too.

Mrs. George. I'll talk to them afterwards: one by one.

Hotchkiss [*to himself*]. Great heavens!

Mrs. Brigenorth. This way, Mrs. Collins. [*She leads the way out through the tower, followed by* MRS. GEORGE, LESBIA, LEO, *and* EDITH.]

The Bishop. Shall we try to get through the last batch of letters whilst they are away, Soames?

Soames. Yes, certainly. [*To* HOTCHKISS, *who is in his way.*] Excuse me.

THE BISHOP *and* SOAMES *go into the study, disturbing* HOTCHKISS, *who, plunged in a strange reverie, has forgotten where he is. Awakened by* SOAMES, *he stares distractedly; then, with sudden resolution, goes swiftly to the middle of the kitchen.*

Hotchkiss. Cecil. Rejjy. [*Startled by his urgency, they hurry to him.*] I'm frightfully sorry to desert on this day; but I must bolt. This time it really is pure cowardice. I cant help it.

Reginald. What are you afraid of?

Hotchkiss. I dont know. Listen to me. I was a young fool living by myself in London. I ordered my first ton of coals from that woman's husband. At that time I did not know that it is not true economy to buy the lowest priced article: I thought all coals were alike, and tried the thirteen shilling kind because it seemed cheap. It proved unexpectedly inferior to the family Silkstone; and in the irritation into which the first scuttle threw me, I called at the shop and made an idiot of myself as she described.

Sykes. Well, suppose you did! Laugh at it, man.

Hotchkiss. At that, yes. But there was something worse. Judge of my horror when, calling on the coal merchant to make a trifling complaint at finding my grate acting as a battery of quick-firing guns, and being confronted by his vulgar wife, I felt in her presence an extraordinary sensation of unrest, of emotion, of unsatisfied need. I'll not disgust you with details of the madness and folly that followed that meeting. But it went as far as this: that I actually found myself prowling past the shop at night under a sort of desperate necessity to be near some place where she had been. A hideous temptation to kiss the doorstep because her foot had pressed it made me realize how mad I was. I tore myself away from London by a supreme effort; but I was on the point of returning like

a needle to the lodestone when the outbreak of the war saved
me. On the field of battle the infatuation wore off. The Billiter
affair made a new man of me: I felt that I had left the follies
and puerilities of the old days behind me for ever. But half-
an-hour ago—when the Bishop sent off that ring—a sudden
grip at the base of my heart filled me with a nameless terror
—me, the fearless! I recognized its cause when she walked
into the room. Cecil: this woman is a harpy, a siren, a mermaid, a vampire. There is only one chance for me: flight,
instant precipitate flight. Make my excuses. Forget me. Fare-
well. [*He makes for the door and is confronted by* MRS.
GEORGE *entering.*] Too late: I'm lost. [*He turns back and
throws himself desperately into the chair nearest the study
door: that being the furthest away from her.*]

Mrs. George [*coming to the hearth and addressing* REGI-
NALD]. Mr. Bridgenorth: will you oblige me by leaving me
with this young man. I want to talk to him like a mother, on
your business.

Reginald. Do, maam. He needs it badly. Come along, Sykes.
[*He goes into the study.*]

Sykes [*looks irresolutely at* HOTCHKISS].—?

Hotchkiss. Too late: you cant save me now, Cecil. Go.

SYKES *goes into the study.* MRS. GEORGE *strolls across to*
HOTCHKISS *and contemplates him curiously.*

Hotchkiss. Useless to prolong this agony. [*Rising.*] Fatal
woman—if woman you are indeed and not a fiend in human
form—

Mrs. George. Is this out of a book? Or is it your usual
society small talk?

Hotchkiss [*recklessly*]. Jibes are useless: the force that is
sweeping me away will not spare you. I must know the worst
at once. What was your father?

Mrs. George. A licensed victualler who married his bar-
maid. You would call him a publican, most likely.

Hotchkiss. Then you are a woman totally beneath me. Do
you deny it? Do you set up any sort of pretence to be my
equal in rank, in age, or in culture?

Mrs. George. Have you eaten anything that has disagreed
with you?

Hotchkiss [*witheringly*]. Inferior!

Mrs. George. Thank you. Anything else?

Hotchkiss. This. I love you. My intentions are not honorable. [*She shews no dismay.*] Scream. Ring the bell. Have
me turned out of the house.

Mrs. George [*with sudden depth of feeling*]. Oh, if you

could restore to this wasted exhausted heart one ray of the passion that once welled up at the glance—at the touch of a lover! It's you who would scream then, young man. Do you see this face, once fresh and rosy like your own, now scarred and riven by a hundred burnt-out fires?

Hotchkiss [*wildly*]. Slate fires. Thirteen shillings a ton. Fires that shoot out destructive meteors, blinding and burning, sending men into the streets to make fools of themselves.

Mrs. George. You seem to have got it pretty bad, Sinjon.

Hotchkiss. Dont dare call me Sinjon.

Mrs. George. My name is Zenobia Alexandrina. You may call me Polly for short.

Hotchkiss. Your name is Ashtoreth—Durga—there is no name yet invented malign enough for you.

Mrs. George [*sitting down comfortably*]. Come! Do you really think youre better suited to that young saucebox than her husband? You enjoyed her company when you were only the friend of the family—when there was the husband there to shew off against and to take all the responsibility. Are you sure youll enjoy it as much when you are the husband? She isnt clever, you know. She's only silly-clever.

Hotchkiss [*uneasily leaning against the table and holding on to it to control his nervous movements*]. Need you tell me? fiend that you are!

Mrs. George. You amused the husband, didnt you?

Hotchkiss. He has more real sense of humor than she. He's better bred. That was not my fault.

Mrs. George. My husband has a sense of humor too.

Hotchkiss. The coal merchant?—I mean the slate merchant.

Mrs. George [*appreciatively*]. He would just love to hear you talk. He's been dull lately for want of a change of company and a bit of fresh fun.

Hotchkiss [*flinging a chair opposite her and sitting down with an overdone attempt at studied insolence*]. And pray what is your wretched husband's vulgar conviviality to me?

Mrs. George. You love me?

Hotchkiss. I loathe you.

Mrs. George. It's the same thing.

Hotchkiss. Then I'm lost.

Mrs. George. You may come and see me if you promise to amuse George.

Hotchkiss. I'll insult him, sneer at him, wipe my boots on him.

Mrs. George. No you wont, dear boy. Youll be a perfect gentleman.

Hotchkiss [*beaten; appealing to her mercy*]. Zenobia—

Mrs. George. Polly, please.

Hotchkiss. Mrs. Collins—

Mrs. George. Sir?

Hotchkiss. Something stronger than my reason and common sense is holding my hands and tearing me along. I make no attempt to deny that it can drag me where you please and make me do what you like. But at least let me know your soul as you seem to know mine. Do you love this absurd coal merchant.

Mrs. George. Call him George.

Hotchkiss. Do you love your Jorjy Porjy?

Mrs. George. Oh, I dont know that I love him. He's my husband, you know. But if I got anxious about George's health, and I thought it would nourish him, I would fry you with onions for his breakfast and think nothing of it. George and I are good friends. George belongs to me. Other men may come and go; but George goes on for ever.

Hotchkiss. Yes: a husband soon becomes nothing but a habit. Listen: I suppose this detestable fascination you have for me is love.

Mrs. George. Any sort of feeling for a woman is called love nowadays.

Hotchkiss. Do you love me?

Mrs. George [*promptly*]. My love is not quite so cheap an article as that, my lad. I wouldnt cross the street to have another look at you—not yet. *I'*m not starving for love like the robins in winter, as the good ladies youre accustomed to are. Youll have to be very clever, and very good, and very real, if you are to interest me. If George takes a fancy to you, and you amuse him enough, I'll just tolerate you coming in and out occasionally for—well, say a month. If you can make a friend of me in that time so much the better for you. If you can touch my poor dying heart even for an instant, I'll bless you, and never forget you. You may try—if George takes to you.

Hotchkiss. I'm to come on liking for the month?

Mrs. George. On condition that you drop Mrs. Reginald.

Hotchkiss. But she wont drop me. Do you suppose I ever wanted to marry her? I was a homeless bachelor; and I felt quite happy at their house as their friend. Leo was an amusing little devil; but I liked Reginald much more than I liked her. She didnt understand. One day she came to me and told me that the inevitable had happened. I had tact enough not to ask her what the inevitable was; and I gathered presently that she had told Reginald that their marriage was a mistake and that she loved me and could no longer see me breaking my heart for her in suffering silence. What could I say? What could I do? What can I say now? What can I do now?

Mrs. George. Tell her that the habit of falling in love with other men's wives is growing on you; and that I'm your latest.

Hotchkiss. What! Throw her over when she has thrown Reginald over for me!

Mrs. George [*rising*]. You wont then? Very well. Sorry we shant meet again: I should have liked to see more of you for George's sake. Goodbye. [*She moves away from him towards the hearth.*]

Hotchkiss [*appealing*]. Zenobia—

Mrs. George. I thought I had made a difficult conquest. Now I see you are only one of those poor petticoat-hunting creatures that any woman can pick up. Not for me, thank you. [*Inexorable, she turns towards the tower to go.*]

Hotchkiss [*following*]. Dont be an ass, Polly.

Mrs. George [*stopping*]. Thats better.

Hotchkiss. Cant you see that I maynt throw Leo over just because I should be only too glad to. It would be dishonorable.

Mrs. George. Will you be happy if you marry her?

Hotchkiss. No, great heavens, NO!

Mrs. George. Will she be happy when she finds you out?

Hotchkiss. She's incapable of happiness. But she's not incapable of the pleasure of holding a man against his will.

Mrs. George. Right, young man. You will tell her, please, that you love me: before everybody, mind, the very next time you see her.

Hotchkiss. But—

Mrs. George. Those are my orders, Sinjon. I cant have you marry another woman until George is tired of you.

Hotchkiss. Oh, if only I didnt selfishly want to obey you!

THE GENERAL *comes in from the garden.* MRS. GEORGE *goes half way to the garden door to speak to him.* HOTCHKISS *posts himself on the hearth.*

Mrs. George. Where have you been all this time?

The General. I'm afraid my nerves were a little upset by our conversation. I just went into the garden and had a smoke. I'm all right now. [*He strolls down to the study door and presently takes a chair at that end of the big table.*]

Mrs. George. A smoke! Why, you said she couldnt bear it.

The General. Good heavens! I forgot! It's such a natural thing to do, somehow.

LESBIA *comes in through the tower.*

Mrs. George. He's been smoking again.

Lesbia. So my nose tells me. [*She goes to the end of the table nearest the hearth, and sits down.*]

The General. Lesbia: I'm very sorry. But if I gave it up, I should become so melancholy and irritable that you would be the first to implore me to take to it again.

Mrs. George. Thats true. Women drive their husbands into all sorts of wickedness to keep them in good humor. Sinjon: be off with you: this doesnt concern you.

Lesbia. Please dont disturb yourself, Sinjon. Boxer's broken heart has been worn on his sleeve too long for any pretence of privacy.

The General. You are cruel, Lesbia: devilishly cruel. [*He sits down, wounded.*]

Lesbia. You are vulgar, Boxer.

Hotchkiss. In what way? I ask, as an expert in vulgarity.

Lesbia. In two ways. First, he talks as if the only thing of any importance in life was which particular woman he shall marry. Second, he has no self-control.

The General. Women are not all the same to me, Lesbia.

Mrs. George. Why should they be, pray? Women are all different: it's the men who are all the same. Besides, what does Miss Grantham know about either men or women? She's got too much self-control.

Lesbia [*widening her eyes and lifting her chin haughtily*]. And pray how does that prevent me from knowing as much about men and women as people who have no self-control?

Mrs. George. Because it frightens people into behaving themselves before you; and then how can you tell what they really are? Look at me! I was a spoilt child. My brothers and sisters were well brought up, like all children of respectable publicans. So should I have been if I hadnt been the youngest: ten years younger than my youngest brother. My parents were tired of doing their duty by their children by that time; and they spoilt me for all they were worth. I never knew what it was to want money or anything that money could buy. When I wanted my own way, I had nothing to do but scream for it til I got it. When I was annoyed *I* didnt control myself: I scratched and called names. Did you ever, after you were grown up, pull a grown-up woman's hair? Did you ever bite a grown-up man? Did you ever call both of them every name you could lay your tongue to?

Lesbia [*shivering with disgust*]. No.

Mrs. George. Well, I did. I know what a woman is like when her hair's pulled. I know what a man is like when he's bit. I know what theyre both like when you tell them what you really feel about them. And thats how I know more of the world than you.

Lesbia. The Chinese know what a man is like when he is cut into a thousand pieces, or boiled in oil. That sort of knowledge is of no use to me. I'm afraid we shall never get on with one another, Mrs. George. I live like a fencer, always on guard. I like to be confronted with people who are always on guard. I hate sloppy people, slovenly people, people who cant sit up straight, sentimental people!

Mrs. George. Oh, sentimental your grandmother! You dont learn to hold your own in the world by standing on guard, but by attacking, and getting well hammered yourself.

Lesbia. I'm not a prize-fighter, Mrs. Collins. If I cant get a thing without the indignity of fighting for it, I do without it.

Mrs. George. Do you? Does it strike you that if we were all as clever as you at doing without, there wouldnt be much to live for, would there?

The General. I'm afraid, Lesbia, the things you do without are the things you dont want.

Lesbia [*surprised at his wit*]. Thats not bad for the silly soldier man. Yes, Boxer: the truth is, I dont want you enough to make the very unreasonable sacrifices required by marriage. And yet that is exactly why I ought to be married. Just because I have the qualities my country wants most I shall go barren to my grave; whilst the women who have neither the strength to resist marriage nor the intelligence to understand its infinite dishonor will make the England of the future. [*She rises and walks towards the study.*]

The General [*as she is about to pass him*]. Well, I shall not ask you again, Lesbia.

Lesbia. Thank you, Boxer. [*She passes on to the study door.*]

Mrs. George. Youre quite done with him, are you?

Lesbia. As far as marriage is concerned, yes. The field is clear for you, Mrs. George. [*She goes into the study.*]

THE GENERAL *buries his face in his hands.* MRS. GEORGE *comes round the table to him.*

Mrs. George [*sympathetically*]. She's a nice woman, that. And a sort of beauty about her too, different from anyone else.

The General [*overwhelmed*]. Oh Mrs. Collins, thank you, thank you a thousand times. [*He rises effusively.*] You have

thawed the long-frozen springs [*He kisses her hand.*], forgive
me; and thank you: bless you—[*He again takes refuge in the
garden, choked with emotion.*]

Mrs. George [*looking after him triumphantly*]. Just caught
the dear old warrior on the bounce, eh?

Hotchkiss. Unfaithful to me already!

Mrs. George. I'm not your property, young man: dont you
think it. [*She goes over to him and faces him.*] You understand that? [*He suddenly snatches her into his arms and
kisses her.*] Oh! You dare do that again, you young blackguard; and I'll jab one of these chairs in your face. [*She
seizes one and holds it in readiness.*] Now you shall not see
me for another month.

Hotchkiss [*deliberately*]. I shall pay my first visit to your
husband this afternoon.

Mrs. George. Youll see what he'll say to you when I tell him
what youve just done.

Hotchkiss. What can he say? What dare he say?

Mrs. George. Suppose he kicks you out of the house?

Hotchkiss. How can he? Ive fought seven duels with sabres.
Ive muscles of iron. Nothing hurts me: not even broken bones.
Fighting is absolutely uninteresting to me because it doesnt
frighten me or amuse me; and I always win. Your husband is
in all these respects an average man, probably. He will be
horribly afraid of me; and if under the stimulus of your presence, and for your sake, and because it is the right thing to
do among vulgar people, he were to attack me, I should simply
defeat him and humiliate him. [*He gradually gets his hands on
the chair and takes it from her, as his words go home phrase
by phrase.*] Sooner than expose him to that, you would suffer a
thousand stolen kisses, wouldnt you?

Mrs. George [*in utter consternation*]. You young viper!

Hotchkiss. Ha ha! You are in my power. That is one of the
oversights of your code of honor for husbands: the man who
can bully them can insult their wives with impunity. Tell him
if you dare. If I choose to take ten kisses, how will you prevent me?

Mrs. George. You come within reach of me and I'll not
leave a hair on your head.

Hotchkiss [*catching her wrists dexterously*]. Ive got your
hands.

Mrs. George. Youve not got my teeth. Let go; or I'll bite.
I will, I tell you. Let go.

Hotchkiss. Bite away: I shall taste quite as nice as George.

Mrs. George. You beast. Let me go. Do you call yourself
a gentleman, to use your brute strength against a woman?

Hotchkiss. You are stronger than me in every way but this. Do you think I will give up my one advantage? Promise youll receive me when I call this afternoon.

Mrs. George. After what youve just done? Not if it was to save my life.

Hotchkiss. I'll amuse George.

Mrs. George. He wont be in.

Hotchkiss [*taken aback*]. Do you mean that we should be alone?

Mrs. George [*snatching away her hands triumphantly as his grasp relaxes*]. Aha! Thats cooled you, has it?

Hotchkiss [*anxiously*]. When will George be at home?

Mrs. George. It wont matter to you whether he's at home or not. The door will be slammed in your face whenever you call.

Hotchkiss. No servant in London is strong enough to close a door that I mean to keep open. You cant escape me. If you persist, I'll go into the coal trade; make George's acquaintance on the coal exchange; and coax him to take me home with him to make your acquaintance.

Mrs. George. We have no use for you, young man: neither George nor I. [*She sails away from him and sits down at the end of the table near the study door.*]

Hotchkiss [*following her and taking the next chair round the corner of the table*]. Yes you have. George cant fight for you: I can.

Mrs. George [*turning to face him*]. You bully. You low bully.

Hotchkiss. You have courage and fascination: I have courage and a pair of fists. We're both bullies, Polly.

Mrs. George. You have a mischievous tongue. Thats enough to keep you out of my house.

Hotchkiss. It must be rather a house of cards. A word from me to George—just the right word, said in the right way— and down comes your house.

Mrs. George. Thats why I'll die sooner than let you into it.

Hotchkiss. Then as surely as you live, I enter the coal trade tomorrow. George's taste for amusing company will deliver him into my hands. Before a month passes your home will be at my mercy.

Mrs. George [*rising, at bay*]. Do you think I'll let myself be driven into a trap like this?

Hotchkiss. You are in it already. Marriage is a trap. You are married. Any man who has the power to spoil your marriage has the power to spoil your life. I have that power over you.

Mrs. George [*desperate*]. You mean it?

Hotchkiss. I do.

Mrs. George [*resolutely*]. Well, spoil my marriage and be—

Hotchkiss [*springing up*]. Polly!

Mrs. George. Sooner than be your slave I'd face any unhappiness.

Hotchkiss. What! Even for George?

Mrs. George. There must be honor between me and George, happiness or no happiness. Do your worst.

Hotchkiss [*admiring her*]. Are you really game, Polly? Dare you defy me?

Mrs. George. If you ask me another question I shant be able to keep my hands off you. [*She dashes distractedly past him to the other end of the table, her fingers crisping.*]

Hotchkiss. That settles it. Polly: I adore you: we were born for one another. As I happen to be a gentleman, I'll never do anything to annoy or injure you except that I reserve the right to give you a black eye if you bite me; but youll never get rid of me now to the end of your life.

Mrs. George. I shall get rid of you if the Beadle has to brain you with the mace for it. [*She makes for the tower.*]

Hotchkiss [*running between the table and the oak chest and across to the tower to cut her off*]. You shant.

Mrs. George [*panting*]. Shant I though?

Hotchkiss. No you shant. I have one card left to play that youve forgotten. Why were you so unlike yourself when you spoke to the Bishop?

Mrs. George [*agitated beyond measure*]. Stop. Not that. You shall respect that if you respect nothing else. I forbid you. [*He kneels at her feet.*] What are you doing? Get up: dont be a fool.

Hotchkiss. Polly: I ask you on my knees to let me make George's acquaintance in his home this afternoon; and I shall remain on my knees til the Bishop comes in and sees us. What will he think of you then?

Mrs. George [*beside herself*]. Wheres the poker?

She rushes to the fireplace; seizes the poker; and makes for HOTCHKISS, *who flies to the study door.* THE BISHOP *enters just then and finds himself between them, narrowly escaping a blow from the poker.*

The Bishop. Dont hit him, Mrs. Collins. He is my guest.

MRS. GEORGE *throws down the poker; collapses into the nearest chair; and bursts into tears.* THE BISHOP *goes to her and pats her consolingly on the shoulder. She shudders all through at his touch.*

The Bishop. Come! you are in the house of your friends. Can we help you?

Mrs. George [*to* HOTCHKISS, *pointing to the study*]. Go in there, you. Youre not wanted here.

Hotchkiss. You understand, Bishop, that Mrs. Collins is not to blame for this scene. I'm afraid Ive been rather irritating.

The Bishop. I can quite believe it, Sinjon.

HOTCHKISS *goes into the study*

The Bishop [*turning to* MRS. GEORGE *with great kindness of manner*]. I'm sorry you have been worried. [*He sits down on her left.*] Never mind him. A little pluck, a little gaiety of heart, a little prayer; and youll be laughing at him.

Mrs. George. Never fear. I have all that. It was as much my fault as his; and I should have put him in his place with a clip of that poker on the side of his head if you hadnt come in.

The Bishop. You might have put him in his coffin that way, Mrs. Collins. And I should have been very sorry; because we are all fond of Sinjon.

Mrs. George. Yes: it's your duty to rebuke me. But do you think I dont know?

The Bishop. I dont rebuke you. Who am I that I should rebuke you? Besides, I know there are discussions in which the poker is the only possible argument.

Mrs. George. My lord: be earnest with me. I'm a very funny woman, I daresay; but I come from the same workshop as you. I heard you say that yourself years ago.

The Bishop. Quite so; but then I'm a very funny Bishop. Since we are both funny people, let us not forget that humor is a divine attribute.

Mrs. George. I know nothing about divine attributes or whatever you call them; but I can feel when I am being belittled. It was from you that I learnt first to respect myself. It was through you that I came to be able to walk safely through many wild and wilful paths. Dont go back on your own teaching.

The Bishop. I'm not a teacher: only a fellow-traveller of whom you asked the way. I pointed ahead—ahead of myself as well as of you.

Mrs. George [*rising and standing over him almost threateningly*]. As I'm a living woman this day, if I find you out to be a fraud, I'll kill myself.

The Bishop. What! Kill yourself for finding out something!

For becoming a wiser and therefore a better woman! What a bad reason!

Mrs. George. I have sometimes thought of killing you, and then killing myself.

The Bishop. Why on earth should you kill yourself—not to mention me?

Mrs. George. So that we might keep our assignation in Heaven.

The Bishop [*rising and facing her, breathless*]. Mrs. Collins! You are Incognita Appassionata!

Mrs. George. You read my letters, then? [*With a sigh of grateful relief, she sits down quietly, and says.*] Thank you.

The Bishop [*remorsefully*]. And I have broken the spell by making you come here. [*Sitting down again.*] Can you ever forgive me?

Mrs. George. You couldnt know that it was only the coal merchant's wife, could you?

The Bishop. Why do you say only the coal merchant's wife?

Mrs. George. Many people would laugh at it.

The Bishop. Poor people! It's so hard to know the right place to laugh, isnt it?

Mrs. George. I didnt mean to make you think the letters were from a fine lady. I wrote on cheap paper; and I never could spell.

The Bishop. Neither could I. So that told me nothing.

Mrs. George. One thing I should like you to know.

The Bishop. Yes?

Mrs. George. We didnt cheat your friend. They were as good as we could do at thirteen shillings a ton.

The Bishop. Thats important. Thank you for telling me.

Mrs. George. I have something else to say; but will you please ask somebody to come and stay here while we talk? [*He rises and turns to the study door.*] Not a woman, if you dont mind. [*He nods understandingly and passes on.*] Not a man either.

The Bishop [*stopping*]. Not a man and not a woman! We have no children left, Mrs. Collins. They are all grown up and married.

Mrs. George. That other clergyman would do.

The Bishop. What! The sexton?

Mrs. George. Yes. He didnt mind my calling him that, did he? It was only my ignorance.

The Bishop. Not at all. [*He opens the study door and calls.*] Soames! Anthony! [*To* Mrs. George.] Call him Father: he likes it. [Soames *appears at the study door.*] Mrs. Collins wishes you to join us, Anthony.

SOAMES *looks puzzled.*

Mrs. George. You dont mind, Dad, do you? [*As this greeting visibly gives him a shock that hardly bears out* THE BISHOP's *advice, she says anxiously.*] That was what you told me to call him, wasn't it?

Soames. I am called Father Anthony, Mrs. Collins. But it does not matter what you call me. [*He comes in, and walks past her to the hearth.*]

The Bishop. Mrs. Collins has something to say to me that she wants you to hear.

Soames. I am listening.

The Bishop [*going back to his seat next her*]. Now.

Mrs. George. My lord: you should never have married.

Soames. This woman is inspired. Listen to her, my lord.

The Bishop [*taken aback by the directness of the attack*]. I married because I was so much in love with Alice that all the difficulties and doubts and dangers of marriage seemed to me the merest moonshine.

Mrs. George. Yes: it's mean to let poor young things in for so much while theyre in that state. Would you marry now that you know better if you were a widower?

The Bishop. I'm old now. It wouldnt matter.

Mrs. George. But would you if it did matter?

The Bishop. I think I should marry again lest anyone should imagine I had found marriage unhappy with Alice.

Soames [*sternly*]. Are you fonder of your wife than of your salvation?

The Bishop. Oh, very much. When you meet a man who is very particular about his salvation, look out for a woman who is very particular about her character; and marry them to one another: theyll make a perfect pair. I advise you to fall in love, Anthony.

Soames [*with horror*]. I!!

The Bishop. Yes, you! think of what it would do for you. For her sake you would come to care unselfishly and diligently for money instead of being selfishly and lazily indifferent to it. For her sake you would come to care in the same way for preferment. For her sake you would come to care for your health, your appearance, the good opinion of your fellow creatures, and all the really important things that make men work and strive instead of mooning and nursing their salvation.

Soames. In one word, for the sake of one deadly sin I should come to care for all the others.

The Bishop. Saint Anthony! Tempt him, Mrs. Collins: tempt him.

Mrs. George [*rising and looking strangely before her*]. Take care, my lord: you still have the power to make me obey your commands. And do you, Mr. Sexton, beware of an empty heart.

The Bishop. Yes. Nature abhors a vacuum, Anthony. I would not dare go about with an empty heart: why, the first girl I met would fly into it by mere atmospheric pressure. Alice keeps them out now. Mrs. Collins knows.

Mrs. George [*a faint convulsion passing like a wave over her*]. I know more than either of you. One of you has not yet exhausted his first love: the other has not yet reached it. But I—I—[*She reels and is again convulsed.*]

The Bishop [*saving her from falling*]. Whats the matter? Are you ill, Mrs. Collins? [*He gets her back into her chair.*] Soames: theres a glass of water in the study—quick. [SOAMES *hurries to the study door.*]

Mrs. George. No. [SOAMES *stops.*] Dont call. Dont bring anyone. Cant you hear anything?

The Bishop. Nothing unusual. [*He sits by her, watching her with intense surprise and interest.*]

Mrs. George. No music?

Soames. No. [*He steals to the end of the table and sits on her right, equally interested.*]

Mrs. George. Do you see nothing—not a great light?

The Bishop. We are still walking in darkness.

Mrs. George. Put your hand on my forehead: the hand with the ring. [*He does so. Her eyes close.*]

Soames [*inspired to prophesy*]. There was a certain woman, the wife of a coal merchant, which had been a great sinner—

THE BISHOP, *startled, takes his hand away.* MRS. GEORGE'S *eyes open vividly as she interrupts* SOAMES.

Mrs. George. You prophesy falsely, Anthony: never in all my life have I done anything that was not ordained for me. [*More quietly.*] Ive been myself. Ive not been afraid of myself. And at last I have escaped from myself, and am become a voice for them that are afraid to speak, and a cry for the hearts that break in silence.

Soames [*whispering*]. Is she inspired?

The Bishop. Marvellous. Hush.

Mrs. George. I have earned the right to speak. I have dared: I have gone through: I have not fallen withered in the fire: I have come at last out beyond, to the back of God-speed.

The Bishop. And what do you see there, at the back of Godspeed?

Soames [*hungrily*]. Give us your message.

Mrs. George [*with intensely sad reproach*]. When you loved me I gave you the whole sun and stars to play with. I gave you eternity in a single moment, strength of the mountains in one clasp of your arms, and the volume of all the seas in one impulse of your souls. A moment only; but was it not enough? Were you not paid then for all the rest of your struggle on earth? Must I mend your clothes and sweep your floors as well? Was it not enough? I paid the price without bargaining: I bore the children without flinching: was that a reason for heaping fresh burdens on me? I carried the child in my arms: must I carry the father too? When I opened the gates of paradise, were you blind? was it nothing to you? When all the stars sang in your ears and all the winds swept you into the heart of heaven, were you deaf? were you dull? was I no more to you than a bone to a dog? Was it not enough? We spent eternity together; and you ask me for a little lifetime more. We possessed all the universe together; and you ask me to give you my scanty wages as well. I have given you the greatest of all things; and you ask me to give you little things. I gave you your own soul: you ask me for my body as a plaything. Was it not enough? Was it not enough?

Soames. Do you understand this, my lord?

The Bishop. I have that advantage over you, Anthony, thanks to Alice. [*He takes* MRS. GEORGE's *hand.*] Your hand is very cold. Can you come down to earth? Do you remember who I am, and who you are?

Mrs. George. It was enough for me. I did not ask to meet you—to touch you—[THE BISHOP *quickly releases her hand.*] When you spoke to my soul years ago from your pulpit, you opened the doors of my salvation to me; and now they stand open for ever. It was enough. I have asked you for nothing since: I ask you for nothing now. I have lived: it is enough. I have had my wages; and I am ready for my work. I thank you and bless you and leave you. You are happier in that than I am; for when I do for men what you did for me, I have no thanks, and no blessing: I am their prey; and there is no rest from their loving and no mercy from their loathing.

The Bishop. You must take us as we are, Mrs. Collins.

Soames. No. Take us as we are capable of becoming.

Mrs. George. Take me as I am: I ask no more. [*She turns her head to the study door and cries.*] Yes: come in, come in.

HOTCHKISS *comes softly in from the study.*

Hotchkiss. Will you be so kind as to tell me whether I am dreaming? In there I have heard Mrs. Collins saying the strangest things, and not a syllable from you two.

Soames. My lord: is this possession by the devil?

The Bishop. Or the ecstasy of a saint?

Hotchkiss. Or the convulsion of the pythoness on the tripod?

The Bishop. May not the three be one?

Mrs. George [*troubled*]. You are paining and tiring me with idle questions. You are dragging me back to myself. You are tormenting me with your evil dreams of saints and devils and —what was it?—[*Striving to fathom it.*] the pythoness—the pythoness—[*Giving it up.*] I dont understand. I am a woman: a human creature like yourselves. Will you not take me as I am?

Soames. Yes; but shall we take you and burn you?

The Bishop. Or take you and canonize you?

Hotchkiss [*gaily*]. Or take you as a matter of course? [*Swiftly to* THE BISHOP.] We must get her out of this: it's dangerous. [*Aloud to her.*] May I suggest that you shall be Anthony's devil and the Bishop's saint and my adored Polly? [*Slipping behind her, he picks up her hand from her lap and kisses it over her shoulder.*]

Mrs. George [*waking*]. What was that? Who kissed my hand? [*To* THE BISHOP, *eagerly.*] Was it you? [*He shakes his head. She is mortified.*] I beg your pardon.

The Bishop. Not at all. I'm not repudiating that honor. Allow me. [*He kisses her hand.*]

Mrs. George. Thank you for that. It was not the sexton, was it?

Soames. I!

Hotchkiss. It was I, Polly, your ever faithful.

Mrs. George [*turning and seeing him*]. Let me catch you doing it again: thats all. How do you come there? I sent you away. [*With great energy, becoming quite herself again.*] What the goodness gracious has been happening?

Hotchkiss. As far as I can make out, you have been having a very charming and eloquent sort of fit.

Mrs. George [*delighted*]. What! My second sight! [*To* THE BISHOP.] Oh, how I have prayed that it might come to me if ever I met you! And now it has come. How stunning! You may believe every word I said: I cant remember it now; but it was something that was just bursting to be said; and so it laid hold of me and said itself. Thats how it is, you see.

EDITH *and* CECIL SYKES *come in through the tower. She has her hat on.* LEO *follows. They have evidently been out together.* SYKES, *with an unnatural air, half foolish, half rakish, as if he had lost all his self-respect and were determined not to let it prey on his spirits, throws himself into a chair at the end of the table near the hearth and thrusts his hands into his pockets, like Hogarth's Rake, without waiting for* EDITH *to sit down. She sits in the railed chair.* LEO *takes the chair nearest the tower on the long side of the table, brooding, with closed lips.*

The Bishop. Have you been out, my dear?

Edith. Yes.

The Bishop. With Cecil?

Edith. Yes.

The Bishop. Have you come to an understanding?

No reply. Blank silence.

Sykes. You had better tell them, Edie.

Edith. Tell them yourself.

THE GENERAL *comes in from the garden.*

The General [*coming forward to the table*]. Can anybody oblige me with some tobacco? Ive finished mine; and my nerves are still far from settled.

The Bishop. Wait a moment, Boxer. Cecil has something important to tell us.

Sykes. Weve done it. Thats all.

Hotchkiss. Done what, Cecil?

Sykes. Well, what do you suppose?

Edith. Got married, of course.

The General. Married! Who gave you away?

Sykes [*jerking his head towards the tower*]. This gentleman did. [*Seeing that they do not understand, he looks round and sees that there is no one there.*] Oh! I thought he came in with us. He's gone downstairs, I suppose. The Beadle.

The General. The Beadle! What the devil did he do that for?

Sykes. Oh, I dont know: I didnt make any bargain with him. [*To* MRS. GEORGE.] How much ought I to give him, Mrs. Collins?

Mrs. George. Five shillings. [*To* THE BISHOP.] I want to rest for a moment: there! in your study. I saw it here [*She touches her forehead.*]

The Bishop [*opening the study door for her*]. By all means.

Turn my brother out if he disturbs you. Soames: bring the letters out here.

Sykes. He wont be offended at my offering it, will he?

Mrs. George. Not he! He touches children with the mace to cure them of ringworm for fourpence apiece. [*She goes into the study.* SOAMES *follows her.*]

The General. Well, Edith, I'm a little disappointed, I must say. However, I'm glad it was done by somebody in a public uniform.

MRS. BRIDGENORTH *and* LESBIA *come in through the tower.* MRS. BRIDGENORTH *makes for* THE BISHOP. *He goes to her, and they meet near the oak chest.* LESBIA *comes between* SYKES *and* EDITH.

The Bishop. Alice, my love, theyre married.

Mrs. Bridgenorth [*placidly*]. Oh, well, thats all right. Better tell Collins.

SOAMES *comes back from the study with his writing materials. He seats himself at the nearest end of the table and goes on with his work.* HOTCHKISS *sits down in the next chair round the table corner, with his back to him.*

Lesbia. You have both given in, have you?

Edith. Not at all. We have provided for everything.

Soames. How?

Edith. Before going to the church, we went to the office of that insurance company—whats its name, Cecil?

Sykes. The British Family Insurance Corporation. It insures you against poor relations and all sorts of family contingencies.

Edith. It has consented to insure Cecil against libel actions brought against him on my account. It will give us specially low terms because I am a Bishop's daughter.

Sykes. And I have given Edie my solemn word that if I ever commit a crime I'll knock her down before a witness and go off to Brighton with another lady.

Lesbia. Thats what you call providing for everything! [*She goes to the middle of the table on the garden side and sits down.*]

Leo. Do make him see that there are no worms before he knocks you down, Edith. Wheres Rejjy?

Reginald [*coming in from the study*]. Here. Whats the matter?

Leo [*springing up and flouncing round to him*]. Whats the matter! You may well ask. While Edie and Cecil were at the insurance office I took a taxi and went off to your lodgings; and a nice mess I found everything in. Your clothes are in a disgraceful state. Your liver-pad has been made into a kettle-holder. Youre no more fit to be left to yourself than a one-year-old baby.

Reginald. Oh, I cant be bothered looking after things like that. I'm all right.

Leo. Youre not: youre a disgrace. You never consider that youre a disgrace to me: you think only of yourself. You must come home with me and be taken proper care of: my conscience will not allow me to let you live like a pig. [*She arranges his necktie.*] You must stay with me until I marry Sinjon; and then we can adopt you or something.

Reginald [*breaking loose from her and stumping off past* HOTCHKISS *towards the hearth*]. No, I'm dashed if I'll be adopted by Sinjon. You can adopt him if you like.

Hotchkiss [*rising*]. I suggest that that would really be the better plan, Leo. Ive a confession to make to you. I'm not the man you took me for. Your objection to Rejjy was that he had low tastes.

Reginald [*turning*]. Was it? by George!

Leo. I said slovenly habits. I never thought he had really low tastes until I saw that woman in court. How he could have chosen such a creature and let her write to him after—

Reginald. Is this fair? I never—

Hotchkiss. Of course you didnt, Rejjy. Dont be silly, Leo. It's I who really have low tastes.

Leo. You!

Hotchkiss. Ive fallen in love with a coal merchant's wife. I adore her. I would rather have one of her boot-laces than a lock of your hair. [*He folds his arms and stands like a rock.*]

Reginald. You damned scoundrel, how dare you throw my wife over like that before my face? [*He seems on the point of assaulting* HOTCHKISS *when* LEO *gets between them and draws* REGINALD *away towards the study door.*]

Leo. Dont take any notice of him, Rejjy. Go at once and get that odious decree demolished or annulled or whatever it is. Tell Sir Gorell Barnes that I have changed my mind. [*To* HOTCHKISS.] I might have known that you were too clever to be really a gentleman. [*She takes* REGINALD *away to the oak chest and seats him there. He chuckles.* HOTCHKISS *resumes his seat, brooding.*]

The Bishop. All the problems appear to be solving themselves.

Lesbia. Except mine.

The General. But, my dear Lesbia, you see what has happened here today. [*Coming a little nearer and bending his face towards hers.*] Now I put it to you, does it not shew you the folly of not marrying?

Lesbia. No: I cant say it does. And [*Rising.*] you have been smoking again.

The General. You drive me to it, Lesbia. I cant help it.

Lesbia [*standing behind her chair with her hands on the back of it and looking radiant*]. Well, I wont scold you today. I feel in particularly good humor just now.

The General. May I ask why, Lesbia?

Lesbia [*drawing a large breath*]. To think that after all the dangers of the morning I am still unmarried! still independent! still my own mistress! still a glorious strong-minded old maid of old England!

SOAMES *silently springs up and makes a long stretch from his end of the table to shake her hand across it.*

The General. Do you find any real happiness in being your own mistress? Would it not be more generous—would you not be happier as someone else's mistress—

Lesbia. Boxer!

The General [*rising, horrified*]. No, no, you must know, my dear Lesbia, that I was not using the word in its improper sense. I am sometimes unfortunate in my choice of expressions; but you know what I mean. I feel sure you would be happier as my wife.

Lesbia. I daresay I should, in a frowsty sort of way. But I prefer my dignity and my independence. I'm afraid I think this rage for happiness rather vulgar.

The General. Oh, very well, Lesbia. I shall not ask you again. [*He sits down huffily.*]

Lesbia. You will, Boxer; but it will be no use. [*She also sits down again and puts her hand almost affectionately on his.*] Some day I hope to make a friend of you; and then we shall get on very nicely.

The General [*starting up again*]. Ha! I think you are hard, Lesbia. I shall make a fool of myself if I remain here. Alice: I shall go into the garden for a while.

Collins [*appearing in the tower*]. I think everything is in order now, maam.

The General [*going to him*]. Oh, by the way, could you oblige me—[*The rest of the sentence is lost in a whisper.*]

Collins. Certainly, General. [*He takes out a tobacco pouch and hands it to* THE GENERAL, *who takes it and goes into the garden.*]

Lesbia. I dont believe theres a man in England who really and truly loves his wife as much as he loves his pipe.

The Bishop. By the way, what has happened to the wedding party?

Sykes. I dont know. There wasnt a soul in the church when we were married except the pew opener and the curate who did the job.

Edith. They had all gone home.

Mrs. Bridgenorth. But the bridesmaids?

Collins. Me and the Beadle have been all over the place in a couple of taxies, maam; and weve collected them all. They were a good deal disappointed on account of their dresses, and thought it all rather irregular; but theyve agreed to come to the breakfast. The truth is, theyre wild with curiosity to know how it all happened. The organist held on until the organ was nigh worn out, and himself worse than the organ. He asked me particularly to tell you, my lord, that he held back Mendelssohn til the very last; but when that was gone he thought he might as well go too. So he played God Save The King and cleared out the church. He's coming to the breakfast to explain.

Leo. Please remember, Collins, that there is no truth whatever in the rumor that I am separated from my husband, or that there is, or ever has been, anything between me and Mr. Hotchkiss.

Collins. Bless you, maam! one could always see that. [*To* MRS. BRIDGENORTH.] Will you receive here or in the hall, maam?

Mrs. Bridgenorth. In the hall. Alfred: you and Boxer must go there and be ready to keep the first arrivals talking til we come. We have to dress Edith. Come, Lesbia: come, Leo: we must all help. Now, Edith. [LESBIA, LEO, *and* EDITH *go out through the tower.*] Collins: we shall want you when Miss Edith's dressed to look over her veil and things and see that theyre all right.

Collins. Yes, maam. Anything you would like mentioned about Miss Lesbia, maam?

Mrs. Bridgenorth. No. She wont have the General. I think you may take that as final.

Collins. What a pity, maam! A fine lady wasted, maam. [*They shake their heads sadly; and* MRS. BRIDGENORTH *goes out through the tower.*]

The Bishop. I'm going to the hall, Collins, to receive. Rejjy: go and tell Boxer; and come both of you to help with the small talk. Come, Cecil. [*He goes out through the tower, followed by* SYKES.]

Reginald [*to* HOTCHKISS]. Youve always talked a precious lot about behaving like a gentleman. Well, if you think youve behaved like a gentleman to Leo, youre mistaken. And I shall have to take her part, remember that.

Hotchkiss. I understand. Your doors are closed to me.

Reginald [*quickly*]. Oh no. Dont be hasty. I think I should like you to drop in after a while, you know. She gets so cross and upset when theres nobody to liven up the house a bit.

Hotchkiss. I'll do my best.

Reginald [*relieved*]. Righto. You dont mind, old chap, do you?

Hotchkiss. It's Fate. Ive touched coal; and my hands are black; but theyre clean. So long, Rejjy. [*They shake hands; and* REGINALD *goes into the garden to collect Boxer.*]

Collins. Excuse me, sir; but do you stay to breakfast? Your name is on one of the covers; and I should like to change it if youre not remaining.

Hotchkiss. How do I know? Is my destiny any longer in my own hands? Go: ask SHE WHO MUST BE OBEYED.

Collins [*awestruck*]. Has Mrs. George taken a fancy to you, sir?

Hotchkiss. Would she had! Worse, man, worse: Ive taken a fancy to Mrs. George.

Collins. Dont despair, sir: if George likes your conversation youll find their house a very pleasant one: livelier than Mr. Reginald's was, I daresay.

Hotchkiss [*calling*]. Polly.

Collins [*promptly*]. Oh, if it's come to Polly already, sir, I should say you were all right.

MRS. GEORGE *appears at the door of the study.*

Hotchkiss. Your brother-in-law wishes to know whether I'm to stay for the wedding breakfast. Tell him.

Mrs. George. He stays, Bill, if he chooses to behave himself.

Hotchkiss [*to* COLLINS]. May I, as a friend of the family, have the privilege of calling you Bill?

Collins. With pleasure, sir, I'm sure, sir.

Hotchkiss. My own pet name in the bosom of my family is Sonny.

Mrs. George. Why didnt you tell me that before? Sonny is just the name I wanted for you. [*She pats his cheek familiarly: he rises abruptly and goes to the hearth, where he throws himself moodily into the railed chair.*] Bill: I'm not going into the hall until there are enough people there to make a proper little court for me. Send the Beadle for me when you think it looks good enough.

Collins. Right, maam. [*He goes out through the tower.*]

MRS. GEORGE, *left alone with* HOTCHKISS *and* SOAMES, *suddenly puts her hands on* SOAMES'S *shoulders and bends over him.*

Mrs. George. The Bishop said I was to tempt you, Anthony.

Soames [*without looking round*]. Woman: go away.

Mrs. George. Anthony:

> "When other lips and other hearts
> Their tale of love shall tell

Hotchkiss [*sardonically*].

> In language whose excess imparts
> The power they feel so well.

Mrs. George.

> Though hollow hearts may wear a mask
> Twould break your own to see,
> In such a moment I but ask
> That youll remember me."

And you will, Anthony. I shall put my spell on you.

Soames. Do you think that a man who has sung the Magnificat and adored the Queen of Heaven has any ears for such trash as that or any eyes for such trash as you—saving your poor little soul's presence. Go home to your duties, woman.

Mrs. George [*highly approving his fortitude*]. Anthony: I adopt you as my father. Thats the talk! Give me a man whose whole life doesnt hang on some scrubby woman in the next street; and I'll never let him go. [*She slaps him heartily on the back.*]

Soames. Thats enough. You have another man to talk to. I'm busy.

Mrs. George [*leaving* SOAMES *and going a step or two nearer* HOTCHKISS]. Why arnt you like him, Sonny? Why do you hang on to a scrubby woman in the next street?

Hotchkiss [*thoughtfully*]. I must apologize to Billiter.

Mrs. George. Who is Billiter?

Hotchkiss. A man who eats rice pudding with a spoon. Ive been eating rice pudding with a spoon ever since I saw you first. [*He rises.*] We all eat our rice pudding with a spoon, dont we, Soames?

Soames. We are members of one another. There is no need

to refer to me. In the first place, I'm busy: in the second, youll find it all in the Church Catechism, which contains most of the new discoveries with which the age is bursting. Of course you should apologize to Billiter. He is your equal. He will go to the same heaven if he behaves himself and to the same hell if he doesnt.

Mrs. George [*sitting down*]. And so will my husband the coal merchant.

Hotchkiss. If I were your husband's superior here I should be his superior in heaven or hell: equality lies deeper than that. The coal merchant and I are in love with the same woman. That settles the question for me for ever. [*He prowls across the kitchen to the garden door, deep in thought.*]

Soames. Psha!

Mrs. George. You dont believe in women, do you, Anthony? He might as well say that he and George both like fried fish.

Hotchkiss. I do not like fried fish. Dont be low, Polly.

Soames. Woman: do not presume to accuse me of unbelief. And do you, Hotchkiss, not despise this woman's soul because she speaks of fried fish. Some of the victims of the Miraculous Draught of Fishes were fried. And I eat fried fish every Friday and like it. You are as ingrained a snob as ever.

Hotchkiss [*impatiently*]. My dear Anthony: I find you merely ridiculous as a preacher, because you keep referring me to places and documents and alleged occurrences in which, as a matter of fact, I dont believe. I dont believe in anything but my own will and my own pride and honor. Your fishes and your catechisms and all the rest of it make a charming poem which you call your faith. It fits you to perfection; but it doesnt fit me. I happen, like Napoleon, to prefer Mahometanism. [MRS. GEORGE, *associating Mahometanism with polygamy, looks at him with quick suspicion.*] I believe the whole British Empire will adopt a reformed Mahometanism before the end of the century. The character of Mahomet is congenial to me. I admire him, and share his views of life to a considerable extent. That beats you, you see, Soames. Religion is a great force: the only real motive force in the world; but what you fellows dont understand is that you must get at a man through his own religion and not through yours. Instead of facing that fact, you persist in trying to convert all men to your own little sect, so that you can use it against them afterwards. You are all missionaries and proselytizers trying to uproot the native religion from your neighbor's flowerbeds and plant your own in its place. You would rather let a child perish in ignorance than have it taught by a rival sectary. You talk to me of the quintessential equality of coal merchants and British officers; and yet you cant see the quintessential equality of all the religions. Who are you, anyhow, that you should know better than Mahomet or Confucius or any of the other Johnnies who have been on this job since the world existed?

Mrs. George [*admiring his eloquence*]. George will like you, Sonny. You should hear him talking about the Church.

Soames. Very well, then: go to your doom, both of you. There is only one religion for me: that which my soul knows to be true; but even irreligion has one tenet; and that is the sacredness of marriage. You two are on the verge of deadly sin. Do you deny that?

Hotchkiss. You forget, Anthony: the marriage itself is the deadly sin according to you.

Soames. The question is not now what I believe, but what you believe. Take the vows with me; and give up that woman if you have the strength and the light. But if you are still in the grip of this world, at least respect its institutions. Do you believe in marriage or do you not?

Hotchkiss. My soul is utterly free from any such superstition. I solemnly declare that between this woman, as you impolitely call her, and me, I see no barrier that my conscience bids me respect. I loathe the whole marriage morality of the middle classes with all my instincts. If I were an eighteenth century marquis I could not feel more free with regard to a Parisian citizen's wife than I do with regard to Polly. I despise all this domestic purity business as the lowest depth of narrow, selfish, sensual, wife-grabbing vulgarity.

Mrs. George [*rising promptly*]. Oh, indeed. Then youre not coming home with me, young man. I'm sorry; for it's refreshing to have met once in my life a man who wasnt frightened by my wedding ring; but I'm looking out for a friend and not for a French marquis; so youre not coming home with me.

Hotchkiss [*inexorably*]. Yes, I am.

Mrs. George. No.

Hotchkiss. Yes. Think again. You know your set pretty well, I suppose, your petty tradesmen's set. You know all its scandals and hypocrisies, its jealousies and squabbles, its hundreds of divorce cases that never come into court, as well as its tens that do.

Mrs. George. We're not angels. I know a few scandals; but most of us are too dull to be anything but good.

Hotchkiss. Then you must have noticed that just as all murderers, judging by their edifying remarks on the scaffold, seem to be devout Christians, so all libertines, both male and female, are invariably people overflowing with domestic sentimentality and professions of respect for the conventions they violate in secret.

Mrs. George. Well, you dont expect them to give themselves away, do you?

Hotchkiss. They are people of sentiment, not of honor. Now, I'm not a man of sentiment, but a man of honor. I know well what will happen to me when once I cross the threshold of your husband's house and break bread with him. This marriage bond which I despise will bind me as it never seems to bind the people who believe in it, and whose chief amusement it is to go the theatres where it is laughed at. Soames: youre a Communist, arnt you?

Soames. I am a Christian. That obliges me to be a Communist.

Hotchkiss. And you believe that many of our landed estates were stolen from the Church by Henry the eighth?

Soames. I do not merely believe that: I know it as a lawyer.

Hotchkiss. Would you steal a turnip from one of the landlords of those stolen lands?

Soames [*fencing with the question*]. They have no right to their lands.

Hotchkiss. Thats not what I ask you. Would you steal a turnip from one of the fields they have no right to?

Soames. I do not like turnips.

Hotchkiss. As you are a lawyer, answer me.

Soames. I admit that I should probably not do so. I should perhaps be wrong not to steal the turnip: I cant defend my reluctance to do so; but I think I should not do so. I know I should not do so.

Hotchkiss. Neither shall I be able to steal George's wife. I have stretched out my hand for that forbidden fruit before; and I know that my hand will always come back empty. To disbelieve in marriage is easy: to love a married woman is easy; but to betray a comrade, to be disloyal to a host, to break the covenant of bread and salt, is impossible. You may take me home with you, Polly: you have nothing to fear.

Mrs. George. And nothing to hope?

Hotchkiss. Since you put it in that more kind way, Polly, absolutely nothing.

Mrs. George. Hm! Like most men, you think you know everything a woman wants, dont you? But the thing one wants most has nothing to do with marriage at all. Perhaps Anthony here has a glimmering of it. Eh, Anthony?

Soames. Christian fellowship.

Mrs. George. You call it that, do you?

Soames. What do you call it?

Collins [appearing in the tower with THE BEADLE*].* Now, Polly, the hall's full; and theyre waiting for you.

The Beadle. Make way there, gentlemen, please. Way for the worshipful the Mayoress. If you please, my lords and gentlemen. By your leave, ladies and gentleman: way for the Mayoress.

MRS. GEORGE *takes* HOTCHKISS's *arm, and goes out, preceded by* THE BEADLE.

SOAMES *resumes his writing tranquilly.*

MID–CHANNEL

by

ARTHUR WING PINERO

CHARACTERS

THEODORE BLUNDELL
THE HONBLE. PETER MOTTRAM
LEONARD FERRIS
WARREN, *servant at Lancaster Gate*
COLE, *servant at the flat in Cavendish Square*
RIDEOUT, *Mr. Ferris' servant*
UPHOLSTERERS

ZOE BLUNDELL
MRS. PIERPOINT
ETHEL PIERPOINT
MRS. ANNERLY
LENA

The scene is laid in London. The events of the first act take place on an afternoon in January. The rest of the action occurs on a day in the following June.

MID–CHANNEL

ACT ONE

A drawing room, decorated and furnished in the French style. In the wall opposite the spectator there is a door, the upper part of which is glazed. A silk curtain hangs across the glazed panels, but above the curtain there is a view of the corridor beyond. The fireplace, where a bright fire is burning, is in the wall on the right. There is a door on the farther side of the fireplace, another on the nearer side. Both these doors are supposed to lead to a second drawing room.

On either side of the fireplace there is an armchair, and on the farther side, standing out in the room, is a settee. Some illustrated papers of the popular sort are lying upon the armchair next to the settee. Behind the settee are an oblong table and a chair. In the middle of the room, on the left of the settee and facing the fire, is another armchair; and on the left of the armchair on the nearer side of the fireplace there is a fauteuil stool. A writing table, with a chair before it, stands on the left-hand side of the room, and among the objects on the writing table are a hand mirror and some photographs in frames. Other pieces of furniture, of a more formal kind than those already specified, fill spaces against the walls. One of these, on the left of the glazed door, is a second settee.

The room is lighted only by the blaze of the fire, and the corridor also is in semidarkness.

(Note: Throughout, "right" and "left" are the spectators' right and left, not the actor's.)

The corridor is suddenly lighted up. Then WARREN *enters at the glazed door and switches on the light in the room. He is followed by* MRS. PIERPOINT, *a pleasant-looking, middle-aged lady, and by* ETHEL, *a pretty girl of five and twenty.*

MRS. PIERPOINT [*to the servant*]. You are sure Mrs. Blundell will be in soon?

Warren. She said half past four, ma'am.

Mrs. Pierpoint. It's that now, isn't it?

Warren. Just upon, ma'am. [WARREN *withdraws, closing the door.*]

Ethel. What beautiful rooms these are!

Mrs. Pierpoint. Money!

223

Ethel. I always feel I'm in Paris when I'm here, in some smart house in the Champs Elysées—not at Lancaster Gate. What *is* Mr. Blundell, Mother?

Mrs. Pierpoint. A stockbroker.

Ethel. Stockbroker?

Mrs. Pierpoint. Blundell—something-or-other—and Mottram. He goes to the city every morning.

Ethel. I know that. But I've never heard him, or Zoe, mention the Stock Exchange.

Mrs. Pierpoint [*sitting on the settee by the fireplace*]. Prosperous stockbrokers and their wives—those who move in a decent set—*don't* mention the Stock Exchange.

Ethel. Then that nice person, Mr. Mottram, is a stockbroker, too?

Mrs. Pierpoint. Of course, dear. He's the "Mottram" of the firm.

Ethel. And *he's* the son of a peer.

Mrs. Pierpoint. Peers' sons are common enough in the city nowadays—and peers, for that matter.

Ethel [*moving to the fireplace and warming her hands*]. Zoe is a doctor's daughter.

Mrs. Pierpoint. Has she given you leave to call her Zoe?

Ethel. Yes, last week—asked me to. I'm so glad; I've taken such a liking to her.

Mrs. Pierpoint. She was a Miss Tucker. Her father practiced in New Cavendish Street. He was a great gout man.

Ethel. You *are* full of information, Mother.

Mrs. Pierpoint. Emma Lawton was giving me the whole history of the Blundells at lunch today. She has money, of her own.

Ethel. Zoe?

Mrs. Pierpoint. Doctor Tucker left sixty or seventy thousand pounds, and she came in for it all. But they'd got on before then.

Ethel. H'm! There are stockbrokers and stockbrokers, I suppose.

Mrs. Pierpoint. Straight and crooked, as in every other business or profession.

Ethel. I do think, though, that a girl in Zoe's position might have chosen somebody slightly more refined than Mr. Blundell.

Mrs. Pierpoint. What's wrong with him? He's extremely amiable and inoffensive.

Ethel. Amiable!

Mrs. Pierpoint. He strikes me as being so.

Ethel. I don't call it particularly amiable or inoffensive in a husband to be as snappy with his wife as he is with Zoe.

Mrs. Pierpoint. Snappy?

Ethel. Irritable—impatient.

Mrs. Pierpoint. Oh, I dare say there's an excellent understanding between them. They've been married a good many years.

Ethel. Thirteen, she's told me.

Mrs. Pierpoint. Married people are allowed to be out of humor with each other occasionally.

Ethel. A considerable allowance must be made for Mr. Blundell, I'm afraid.

Mrs. Pierpoint. You're prejudiced, Ethel. I've seen her just as snappy, as you term it, with him.

Ethel. You can't blame her, if she's provoked.

Mrs. Pierpoint. Nor him, if he's provoked. The argument cuts both ways . . .

Ethel [*listening*]. Sssh!

ZOE, *a charming, animated, bright-eyed woman, wearing her hat and some costly furs, enters quickly at the glazed door.*

Zoe. Delightful!

Mrs. Pierpoint [*rising*]. Your servant insisted on our coming up.

Zoe [*shaking hands with* MRS. PIERPOINT]. If he hadn't, I'd have wrung his neck. [*Kissing* ETHEL.] How are you, dear? [*Stripping off her gloves.*] The weather! Isn't it filthy! Do you remember what the sun's like? I had the blinds drawn all over the house at eleven o'clock this morning. What's the good of trying to make believe it's day? [*Taking off her coat.*] Do sit down. Ugh! Why is it that more people commit suicide in summer than in winter?

Mrs. Pierpoint [*resuming her seat on the settee by the fire*]. Do they?

Ethel [*sitting upon the fauteuil stool*]. Why, yes, Mother; what do you call them?—statistics—prove it.

Zoe [*throwing her coat and gloves upon the settee at the back and unpinning her hat*]. You'll see, when I put an end to myself, it will be in the wintertime.

Mrs. Pierpoint. My dear!

Ethel. Zoe!

Mrs. Pierpoint. If you are in this frame of mind, why don't you pack your trunks and fly?

Zoe. Fly?

Ethel. Mother means cut it.

Mrs. Pierpoint. Ethel!

Zoe [*tossing her hat on to the settee and taking up the hand mirror from the writing table and adjusting her hair*]. Don't scold her; she picks up her slang from me.

Ethel. Evil communications!

Mrs. Pierpoint. I mean, go abroad for a couple of months —Egypt—

Ethel. Mother, how horrid of you! I should miss her terribly.

Mrs. Pierpoint. Cairo—Aswan——

Zoe [*looking into the hand glass steadily*]. That's funny, I have been thinking lately of "cutting it."

Mrs. Pierpoint. But I suppose it would have to be without your busy husband.

Zoe [*replacing the mirror*]. Yes, it would be without Theo. [*Turning to* Mrs. Pierpoint *and* Ethel *and rattling on again.*] Well! How have you been amusing yourselves? You wretches, you haven't been near me since Monday, either of you. Done anything—seen anything?

Ethel. Nothing.

Mrs. Pierpoint [*to* Zoe]. If *you're* under the weather, there's some excuse for me.

Zoe [*walking about restlessly*]. Oh, but I will keep moving, though the heavens fall. I've been to the theatre every night this week, and supped out afterward. They've opened such a ripping restaurant in Jermyn Street. [*Pausing.*] You haven't seen the new play at the St. Martin's, then?

Mrs. Pierpoint. No.

Ethel. I want to, badly.

Zoe. I'll take you. We'll make up a party. [*Scribbling a memorandum at the writing table.*] I'll tell Lenny Ferris to get seats.

Ethel. Good business!

Mrs. Pierpoint. Ethel!

Zoe. It's all about children—kiddies. There are the sweetest little tots in it. Two especially—a tiny, round-eyed boy and a mite of a girl with straw-colored hair—you feel you must clamber on to the stage and hug them. You feel you *must!*

Mrs. Pierpoint. Aren't there any grownups?

Zoe [*dropping into the armchair facing the fire*]. Oh, yes; they bore me.

Ethel. I was reading the story to you, Mother . . .

Zoe. The story's no account—it's the kiddies. The man who wrote the thing must be awfully fond of children. I wonder whether he has any little 'uns. If he hasn't, it's of no consequence to him; he can imagine them. What a jolly gift! Fancy! To have the power of imagining children—bringing them to life! Just by shutting the door, and sitting down at your writing table, and saying to your brain, "Now, then! I'm ready for them . . . !" [*Breaking off.*] Ring the bell, Ethel. [ETHEL *rises, and, going to the fireplace, rings the bell.*] Let's have tea.

Mrs. Pierpoint. I'm afraid we can't stay for tea. I've promised to be at old Miss Fremantle's at five o'clock. Ethel . . .

Ethel. Yes, Mother?

Mrs. Pierpoint. Go downstairs for a few minutes. I want a little private conversation with Mrs. Blundell.

Ethel [*surprised*]. Private conversation!

Mrs. Pierpoint. If she won't think me too troublesome.

Zoe [*rising and opening the nearer door on the right—to* ETHEL]. Come in here. There's a lovely fire. [*Disappearing.*] I'll switch the light on.

Ethel [*following* ZOE—*at the door*]. What is it about, Mother?

Mrs. Pierpoint [*rising*]. Now, don't be inquisitive, Ethel.

Zoe [*from the adjoining room*]. Come along!

ETHEL *goes into the next room.* WARREN *enters at the glazed door.*

Mrs. Pierpoint [*to* WARREN]. Mrs. Blundell rang for tea.

Warren. Very good, ma'am. [WARREN *withdraws as* ZOE *returns.*]

Mrs. Pierpoint. We shan't be heard?

Zoe [*closing the door*]. No.

Mrs. Pierpoint. It's really most improper of me to bother you in this way.

Zoe [*advancing to* MRS. PIERPOINT]. Can I be of any use to you?

Mrs. Pierpoint. Well, yes, you can. You can give me— what shall I call it?—a hint . . .

Zoe [*sitting on the fauteuil stool*]. A hint?

Mrs. Pierpoint. On a subject that concerns Ethel. [*Sitting in the chair facing the fire.*] We're quite new friends of yours, dear Mrs. Blundell—is it six weeks since we dined at the Darrells'?

Zoe. There or thereabout.

Mrs. Pierpoint. A fortnight or so before Christmas, wasn't it? But my girl has formed a great attachment to you, and I fancy you are inclined to be interested in her.

Zoe. Rather! She and I are going to be tremendous pals.

Mrs. Pierpoint. That's splendid. Now, don't laugh at me for my extreme cautiousness, if you can help it.

Zoe. Cautiousness?

Mrs. Pierpoint. Tell me—as one woman to another—do you consider it advisable for Ethel to see much of Mr. Ferris?

Zoe. Advisable?

Mrs. Pierpoint. Oh, I've no doubt he's a highly respectable young man, as young men go—I'm not implying anything to the contrary. . . .

Zoe. Is she seeing much of Mr. Ferris?

Mrs. Pierpoint. She meets him here.

Zoe. Ah, yes.

Mrs. Pierpoint. And he has suddenly taken to dropping in to tea with us pretty regularly; and twice this week—twice—he has sent her some magnificent flowers—magnificent.

Zoe. Dear old Lenny!

Mrs. Pierpoint. There's something in his manner, too—one can't describe it . . .

Zoe [*a little ruefully*]. Ha! Ha, ha, ha!

Mrs. Pierpoint. I *am* amusing you.

Zoe. No, no. I beg your pardon. [*Rising and going to the fire.*] Somehow I've never pictured Lenny with a wife.

Mrs. Pierpoint. It may be only an excess of politeness on his part; there mayn't be the least foundation for my suspicions.

Zoe. I suppose every married woman believes that her bachelor chums will remain bachelors.

Mrs. Pierpoint. And pray, dear Mrs. Blundell, don't take me for a matchmaking mother. I've no desire to lose my girl yet awhile, I assure you. But I want to know, naturally—it's my duty to know—exactly who and what are the men who come into my drawing room.

Zoe. Why, naturally.

Mrs. Pierpoint. And it occurred to me that, as we made Mr. Ferris' acquaintance in your house, you wouldn't object to giving me, as I put it, the merest hint . . .

Zoe. Ethel—what about her? Does she like him?

Mrs. Pierpoint. It's evident she doesn't dislike him. But she's not a girl who would be in a hurry to confide in anybody over a love affair, not even in her mother. True, there may be nothing to confide, in the present case. I repeat, I may be altogether mistaken. At the same time . . .

Zoe. You wish me to advise you as to whether Lenny Ferris should be encouraged.

Mrs. Pierpoint. Whether he should be cold-shouldered—I prefer that expression.

Zoe. Very well; I'll furnish you with his character, dear Mrs. Pierpoint, with pleasure.

LEONARD FERRIS, *a fresh, boyish young man, enters at the glazed door, with the air of one who is at home.*

Leonard. Hello!

Zoe [*just as carelessly*]. Hello, Len!

Leonard [*shaking hands with* MRS. PIERPOINT]. How d'ye do? How's Miss Ethel?

Mrs. Pierpoint [*inclining her head*]. Thank you. . . .

Leonard [*rubbing his hands together*]. Here's a day!

Zoe [*taking his hand*]. Your hands are frozen.

Leonard [*going to the fire*]. I drove my car up here.

Zoe. You're crazy. [*Sitting on the settee by the fire.*] You never rang me up this morning, to ask if I was tired.

Leonard. Wire was engaged. First-rate night, last night.

Zoe [*languidly*]. The summit. Lenny . . .

Leonard. Eh?

Zoe. Mrs. Pierpoint and I are talking secrets. Go into the next room for a second.

Leonard [*genially*]. Shan't, if there isn't a fire.

Zoe. Of course there's a fire. Things ain't so bad in the city as all that.

Leonard [*at the nearer door on the right*]. Any tea?

Zoe. By and by. You'll find somebody in there you know.

Leonard [*going into the room*]. Who?

Zoe [*calling out*]. Shut the door. [*The door is closed.*] Talk of the . . . !

Mrs. Pierpoint. Bless me, I hope not!

Zoe. No, I shouldn't turn him in there at this moment if he wasn't what he is—the dearest boy in the world—should I?

Mrs. Pierpoint. Boy?

Zoe. He's thirty-two. A man of two-and-thirty *is* a boy to a woman of—to an old married woman. He's the simplest, wholesomest, best-natured fellow living. If you had him for a son-in-law, you'd be lucky.

Mrs. Pierpoint. It's a relief to me, at any rate . . .

Zoe. And I should lose one of my tame robins.

Mrs. Pierpoint. Tame robins?

Zoe [*rising and going over to the writing table and taking up two of the photographs*]. I always have his photo on my table—his and Peter Mottram's. Peter Mottram is my husband's partner—you've met him here. I call them my tame

robins. They come and eat crumbs off my windowsill. I've
no end of tame robins—men chums—but these two are my
specials. [*Replacing the photographs.*] Well! If Lenny ever
goes, I shall have to promote Harry Estridge or Jim Mallandain or Cossy Rawlings.

Mrs. Pierpoint [*who has risen and followed* ZOE *to the
writing table*]. But why should Mr. Ferris ever "go" completely?

Zoe [*smiling*]. Oh, when a robin marries, Jenny doesn't
share him with another wren. Not much!

WARREN *enters at the glazed door with a female servant.
They carry in the tea and lay it upon the table behind the
settee by the fire.*

Zoe [*after glancing at the servants—dropping her voice*].
I'd better finish drawing up the prospectus, while I'm at it.

Mrs. Pierpoint. Prospectus?

Zoe. He's got two thousand a year. Both his people are
dead. There's an aunt in the country who may leave him a
bit extra; but she's a cantankerous old cat and, in my opinion,
charity'll have every sou. Still, two thousand a year . . .

Mrs. Pierpoint. I oughtn't to hear any more. But you understand, don't you?

Zoe. Perfectly. And he lives in a comfy little flat behind
the Albert Hall and is mad on motorcars. He's invented a
wonderful wheel which is to give the knock to pneumatics.
If anything will bring him to ruin, that will. [*Walking away
toward the tea table laughingly.*] There!

Warren. Tea is served, ma'am.

Mrs. Pierpoint [*to* ZOE, *who returns to her*]. I'm exceedingly obliged to you. You won't breathe a word to Ethel?

Zoe. Not a syllable. It would break my heart, but I hope
it'll come off, for her sake.

Mrs. Pierpoint. She's a sweet, sensible child.

Zoe. And as for him, I'll tell you this for your comfort—
I'm honestly certain that Lenny Ferris would be the sort of
husband that lasts.

Mrs. Pierpoint. That lasts? What do you mean?

Zoe. Oh—never mind. [*Gaily.*] Tea! [*The servants have
withdrawn. She runs across to the farther door at the right,
opens it, and calls.*] Tea! [*Seating herself at the tea table.*]
Are you firm about going on?

Mrs. Pierpoint. It's Lizzie Fremantle's birthday. She's
Ethel's godmother. [*To* ETHEL, *who enters with* LEONARD.]
Are you ready, Ethel?

Ethel [*to* MRS. PIERPOINT]. Must we?

Mrs. Pierpoint. Now, my dear . . . !

Zoe [*to* LEONARD]. Lenny, you've got to get tickets for the St. Martin's and take the whole crowd of us.

Leonard [*with a wry face*]. That kids' play again!

Zoe. Very well; Peter will do it.

Leonard. No, no; right you are.

Zoe. I stand.

Leonard. Rot!

Zoe. Then Peter has the job. [*To the ladies.*] We'll ask Peter Mottram to be one of us anyhow.

Leonard. The supper's mine, then.

Zoe. Anything for peace. [*Shaking hands with* MRS. PIERPOINT, *who comes to her.*] Monday night?

Mrs. Pierpoint. You're a great deal too good.

LEONARD *has opened the glazed door and is now in the corridor.* MRS. PIERPOINT *joins him.*

Leonard [*to* MRS PIERPOINT, *as they disappear*]. Got a vehicle?

Mrs. Pierpoint. My venerable four-wheeler—the oldest friend I have in London.

Ethel [*to* ZOE, *who rises*]. What did Mother have to say to you so mysteriously?

Zoe. Er—she wants me to consult Theo about something.

Ethel. Her railway shares?

Zoe [*nodding*]. H'm.

Ethel [*satisfied*]. Oh? Good-by.

Zoe. When are we to have a nice long jaw together—just you and I?

Ethel. Mother won't let me out alone in these fogs.

Zoe. Fog or no fog, try and shunt her tomorrow.

Ethel. I'll do my best.

Zoe. I'll be in all the morning. [*They turn their heads toward the door, listening.*] Lenny's whistling for you.

Ethel. Mother . . . !

They kiss affectionately and ETHEL *hurries away.* ZOE *resumes her seat at the table and pours out tea. Presently* LEONARD *returns and, after closing the door, comes to her.*

Leonard [*cheerfully*]. It's beginning to sleet now. 'Pon my soul . . . ! [*She hands him a cup of tea in silence. He looks at her inquiringly.*] Anything wrong, Zoe?

Zoe [*with an air of indifference*]. No.

Leonard. Positive?

Zoe [*in the same tone, offering him a plate of bread and butter*]. Quite.

Leonard [*taking a slice*]. Thought there'd been another row, perhaps.

Zoe [*putting the plate of bread and butter aside and taking up her cup and saucer*]. Hell of a row last night.

Leonard. Last night?

Zoe. This morning, rather.

Leonard. When you came home?

Zoe [*sipping her tea*]. After you and Peter brought me home.

Leonard. What over?

Zoe. Nothing.

Leonard [*drinking*]. Must have been over something.

Zoe. Oh, some trifle—as usual.

Leonard. Too bad of Theo—damned sight too bad.

Zoe. I dare say it was as much my fault as his.

Leonard [*hotly*]. It's a cursed shame!

Zoe. Drop it, Len. [*Handing him a dish of cakes.*] Cake?

Leonard [*putting his empty cup down before her and taking a cake*]. Tea.

Zoe [*pouring out another cup of tea for him*]. First time you've drunk tea with me this week. Honored!

Leonard. Sorry.

Zoe. M'yes—[*Giving him his tea.*]—sorry that Mrs. Pierpoint and Ethel can't receive you this afternoon.

Leonard [*after a pause, uncomfortably*]. Mrs. Pierpoint been telling you anything about me?

Zoe. Mentioned that you frequently turn up in Sloane Street at teatime.

Leonard. There's a man down that way who's frightfully gone on my wheel.

Zoe [*drinking*]. Indeed?

Leonard. My great difficulty, you know, is to get it onto the market.

Zoe. India-rubber people opposing you, I expect.

Leonard. Tooth and nail.

Zoe [*nibbling a cake*]. And the man who lives Sloane Street way . . . ?

Leonard. Very influential chap.

Zoe. Capitalist?

Leonard. Millionaire.

Zoe. H'm! And when you're down Sloane Street way, do you take your flowers to Miss Pierpoint, or does your florist send them?

Again there is silence. He lays his cup down, leaves her side,
and produces his cigarette case. Sticking a cigarette between
his lips; he is about to close the case when she rises and
takes a cigarette from it. She moves to the fireplace, lighting
her cigarette with a match from a box attached to a gold
chatelaine hanging from her waist. He seats himself in the
chair facing the fire and lights his own cigarette.

Leonard [*moodily*]. I don't want to marry, Zoe.

Zoe. There's no reason why you shouldn't, if you feel
disposed to; but you needn't be a sneak about it.

Leonard. The aunt's pitching into me again like billy-oh.
High time I settled down—high time I became a reputable
member of society! I ask you, what the deuce have I ever
done that's particularly disreputable? Then come two verses
of Scripture . . .

Zoe [*advancing to him*]. She hasn't ordered you to be
underhanded with your best friends, I assume?

Leonard. I'm not underhanded.

Zoe. Why this concealment, then?

Leonard. There's no concealment; there's nothing to conceal; I give you my word there isn't. I—I haven't made
up my mind one way or the other.

Zoe [*witheringly*]. You're weighing the question!

Leonard. Very well; I'm weighing it, if you like. [*Flinging
the end of his match into the fireplace and jumping up.*] Confound it all! Mayn't a man send a basket or two of rotten
flowers to a girl without having his special license bought for
him by meddling people?

Zoe. Thank you.

Leonard. I don't mean you, Zoe. You know I don't mean
you. [*Pacing the room.*] Ethel—Miss Pierpoint—is a charming girl, but I'm no more in love with her than I am with my
old hat.

Zoe. Then you oughtn't to pay her marked attention.

Leonard. I'm not paying her marked attention. [ZOE *shrugs
her shoulders.*] If Mrs. Pierpoint says I've been making love
to her daughter . . .

Zoe. She has said nothing of the kind.

Leonard [*sitting in the chair before the writing table, in a
huff*]. That's all right. Pity she can't hold her tongue over
trifles.

There is another pause. Then, partly kneeling upon the chair
in the middle of the room, and resting her elbow on the back
of it, ZOE *softens.*

Zoe [*making rings with her cigarette smoke*]. Don't be wild, Len. I was only vexed with you for not consulting me. It would hurt my feelings dreadfully if you got engaged to anybody on the sly. Len—[*He turns to her, but with his head down.*] she *is* a charming girl. I'm not surprised at your being spoons on her. If I were a man, she's just the sort of girl *I'd* marry, if I were on the lookout for a wife.

Leonard [*in a low voice*]. Perhaps I *have* made myself a bit of an ass over her, Zoe. [*She laughs lightly. He raises his eyes.*] Zoe . . .

Zoe. Well?

Leonard [*gazing at* ZOE]. Do you know that she reminds me very often of you?

Zoe. She! I'm old enough to be her grandmother.

Leonard. Oh, hang that! She's got hold of a lot of your odd little tricks—a lot of 'em.

Zoe. She's been with me a goodish deal lately.

Leonard. That's it; and she has the most enormous admiration for you—enormous.

Zoe. She's a dear.

Leonard [*gently hitting his knee with his fist*]. I've thought of all that when I've been worrying it out in my mind.

Zoe. Thought of all what?

Leonard. That you'd always be pals, you two—close pals.

Zoe. If she became Mrs. Lenny?

Leonard [*nodding*]. And so, if I did screw myself up to—to speaking to her, it wouldn't make the least difference to our friendship—yours and mine.

Zoe. No difference!

Leonard. I should still be your tame robin.

Zoe. Ah, no; don't make that mistake, Len.

Leonard. Mistake?

Zoe [*shaking her head*]. It never works. I've seen similar cases over and over again. There's any amount of gush at the start, between the young wife and the husband's women pals; but the end is always the same.

Leonard. The end?

Zoe. Gradually the wife draws the husband away. She manages it somehow. We have a gift for it. I did it myself when I married Theo.

Leonard [*rising and walking about*]. If I believed what you say, Zoe, I'd never size up a girl with a view to marrying as long as I live.

Zoe [*teasingly*]. You're a vain creature. I've plenty of other boys, Len, to fill your place.

Leonard [*not heeding her*]. If things were smoother with you and Theo, one mightn't hesitate half as much.

Zoe. There's Peter Mottram, Gus Hedmont, Harry Estridge, Claud Lowenstein . . .

Leonard. As it is—Great Scott!—I'm a brute even to think of taking the risk.

Zoe. Cossy Rawlings, Jim Mallandain, Robby Relf . . .

Leonard [*stopping in his walk*]. Yes, but my friendship's more to you than the friendship of most of those other fellows, I should hope.

Zoe [*making a grimace at him*]. Not a scrap.

Leonard [*his brow darkening*]. You told me once I was your favorite.

Zoe. My chaff; I've no favorite.

Leonard [*laying the remains of his cigarette upon a little bronze tray on the writing table*]. Peter's a trump, and Harry Estridge and Rawlings are sound enough; but I often feel I'd like to knock young Lowenstein's teeth down his fat throat.

Zoe [*blowing her smoke in his direction as he comes to her and stands before her*]. You get married and mind your own concerns.

Leonard. Zoe, I hate to see men of that class buzzing around you.

Zoe [*mockingly*]. Do you!

Leonard. Look here! Whatever happens between you and Theo in the future, you'll never let anything or anybody drive you off the rails, will you?

Zoe [*frowning*]. Len!

Leonard. I couldn't stand it. [*Putting his hands upon her shoulders.*] I tell you straight, it 'ud break me. [*Passionately, his grip tightening.*] Zoe . . . !

She shakes herself free and backs away from him, confronting him with a flushed face.

Zoe [*quietly*]. Don't be silly. [*Brushing her hair from her forehead.*] If ever you do that again, Len, I'll box your ears.

The HONBLE. PETER MOTTRAM, *a spruce, well-preserved man of fifty, enters at the glazed door.*

Peter [*cheerily*]. Good mornin'—or whatever it is.

Zoe [*dropping the end of her cigarette into the grate*]. That you, Peter?

Leonard [*surlily*]. I'm just off.

Peter. Don't apologize.

Leonard [*at the glazed door, to* PETER]. See you later. [*He goes out.*]

Peter [*to* ZOE]. What's the matter with the youth?

Zoe [*with a shrug*]. Got the hump over something. [*Facing him.*] Tea?

Peter. No, thanks. [*Sitting in the chair in the middle of the room.*] And how are you today, my dear lady? [*She makes a wry mouth, sighs, and throws herself disconsolately upon the settee by the fire. He nods intelligently.*] Yes, sorry to hear you and old Theo have had another bad fall-out.

Zoe [*arranging a pillow for her head*]. I guessed he'd carry it all to you.

Peter. Shockin'ly grieved, I am.

Zoe. He began this one.

Peter. By blowin' you up for goin' on the frisk every night.

Zoe. And I answered him back. I was dog-weary. It was nearly one o'clock. He needn't have jumped upon me almost before I'd taken the key out of the lock.

Peter [*demurely*]. I also have been reproved, for aidin' and abettin'.

Zoe. Serves you jolly well right. Why didn't you and Lenny come in with me, you cowards? That might have saved a squabble. I begged you to have a whisky.

Peter [*after a brief pause*]. Zoe . . .

Zoe [*in a muffled voice, her head in the pillow*]. Oh, be kind to me, Peter.

Peter. Why *do* you sally forth night after night?

Zoe. Because I must.

Peter. Must?

Zoe. I've got the fidgets.

Peter. I get the fidgets at times, in bed. D'ye know how I cure 'em?

Zoe. Of course I don't.

Peter. I lie perfectly stiff and still; I *make* myself lie perfectly still. I *won't* stir. I say to myself, "Peter, you *shan't* twist or turn." And I win.

Zoe. How easy it is to talk! I defy you to control yourself if you're shut up with a person who goads you to desperation.

Peter. Theo?

Zoe [*beating her pillow*]. How *can* I stay at home and eat a long dinner, and spend an entire evening, alone with Theo? We're not entertaining just now; he says he's fed up with having people here.

Peter. Take him out with you.

Zoe. Then we quarrel before others. That's too degrading. Oh, it's tiff, tiff, wrangle, jangle, outdoors *and* indoors with us!

Peter. You say things to Theo when you're angry, Zoe, that wound him to the quick.

Zoe. [*satirically*]. Really!

Peter. Really. You mayn't be aware of it; you scratch the poor old chap till he bleeds.

Zoe. Do you imagine he never says things to me that wound me to the quick?

Peter. He doesn't mean half of 'em.

Zoe. Neither do I.

Peter [*rising and going to the fire*]. No; there's the crass foolishness of it all. [*In a tone of expostulation.*] My dear lady . . .

Zoe [*suddenly sitting upright*]. We're on each other's nerves, Peter. That's the plain truth, we're on each other's nerves.

Peter. Worryin' each other.

Zoe. Sick to death of each other! We shall have been married fourteen years on the thirtieth of next June. Isn't it appaling! He's getting so stodgy and pompous and flat-footed. He drives me mad with his elderly ways.

Peter [*soothingly*]. Oh . . . !

Zoe. He's sick and tired of *me*, at any rate. My little jokes and pranks, that used to amuse him so—they annoy him now, scandalize him. He's continually finding fault with me—bullying me. That's all the notice he takes of me. As for my gowns or my hats—anything I put on—I might dress in sackcloth; he'd never observe it. [*Tearfully.*] Ah . . . ! [*She searches for her handkerchief and fails to find it.* PETER *produces a folded handkerchief from his breast pocket, shakes it out, and gives it to her. She wipes her eyes as she proceeds.*] Sometimes, I own, I'm aggravating; but he forgets how useful I was to him in the old days, when we were climbing. Yes, *those* were the days—the first six or seven years of our marriage, when we were up north, in Fitzjohn's Avenue! [*Tossing* PETER'S *handkerchief to him and getting to her feet.*] Oh! Oh, we were happy then, Peter! You didn't know us then, when we were up north!

Peter [*wagging his head*]. My dear lady, we were all happier when we were up north.

Zoe [*giving him a look of surprise as she paces the room on the left*]. You!

Peter. I mean, in a previous stage of our careers.

Zoe. Ah, yes, yes.

Peter. That's the lesson of life, Mrs. Zoe. We've all had our Fitzjohn's Avenue, in a sense. In other words, we've all been young and keen as mustard; with everythin' before us, instead of havin' most things behind us.

Zoe [*leaning on the back of the chair before the writing table*]. Oh, don't!

Peter [*thoughtfully*]. D'ye know, I often wonder whether there's anythin' more depressin' than to see the row of trophies standin' on the sideboard?

Zoe [*sitting at the writing table and digging her fingers into her hair*]. Be quiet, Peter!

Peter. That silver gilt vase there! The old horse that gained it for you is lyin' in the paddock with a stone a'top of him, and you're usin' his hoof as an inkpot. Those goblets you won on the river, and the cup you helped yourself to on the links at Biarritz or St. Moritz—there's a little pile of ashes at the bottom of every one of 'em! So it is with life generally. You scoop in the prizes—and there are the pots on the sideboard to remind you that it ain't the *prizes* that count, but the pushin' and the strugglin' and the cheerin'. Ah, they preach to us on Sundays about cherubim and seraphim! It's my firm hope and conviction that when we die and go to heaven we shall all find ourselves up north again—in Fitzjohn's Avenue! [*Coming to the chair in the middle of the room.*] Meanwhile, it's no good repinin'. [*Turning the chair toward her and sitting.*] The trophies *are* on the sideboard, dear lady, and they've got to be kep' clean and shiny. [*Gravely.*] Now, Zoe—[*She whimpers.*] Zoe, Zoe—[*She turns to him.*] Zoe, one ugly word passed between you and Theo last night . . .

Zoe. One . . . ?

Peter. One ugly word that must never be repeated.

Zoe. What word?

The glazed door opens and WARREN *appears carrying a teapot on a tray. He comes to the table and exchanges the teapot he is carrying for the one that is already there.*

Zoe [*to the man*]. Mr. Mottram won't have any tea, Warren.

Warren [*removing the cups and saucers which have been*

used and putting them on to his tray]. No, ma'am; but Mr. Blundell's just come in, ma'am.

WARREN *withdraws, closing the door.* ZOE *rises stiffly, and gathers up her hat, coat, and gloves. Then she returns to* PETER, *who remains seated.*

Zoe. What word was it?
Peter. Separation.

THEODORE BLUNDELL, *a big, burly, but good-looking man, enters at the glazed door. He halts on entering and glances furtively at* ZOE, *as if expecting her to speak; but, without meeting his eyes, she passes him and leaves the room.*

Theodore [*with a shrug*]. Ha! [PETER, *looking over his shoulder, sees that he and* THEODORE *are alone.* THEODORE *seats himself at the tea table and pours out his tea grimly.*] Lots o' good you seem to have done, Peter.

Peter. Haven't done much, I admit. Pity you came home quite so soon.

Theodore. You left the office at half past two.

Peter. She wasn't in when I first got here.

Theodore [*taking a slice of bread and butter*]. Anyhow, kind of you to offer to have a talk to her. [*Munching.*] Plenty of abuse of me, h'm?

Peter. She says you're on each other's nerves, Theo.

Theodore. I'm afraid there's something in that.

Peter. And that you are growin' a bit heavy in hand, old man.

Theodore [*dryly*]. Exceedingly sorry.

Peter [*after a pause*]. Theo . . .

Theodore. Hello?

Peter. Shall I tell you what's at the bottom of it all?

Theodore. Well?

Peter. She's got a feelin' that you're tired of her.

Theodore [*gulping his tea*]. If you knew how constantly I have that served up to me . . . !

Peter. Will you allow me to speak out?

Theodore. Don't be so polite.

Peter. My belief is that, if you could avoid conveyin' that impression to Zoe, matters would improve considerably in this establishment.

Theodore. Oh?

Peter. It's as easy as brushin' your hat. A little pettin'—a little sweetheartin' . . .

Theodore. Yes?

Peter [*discouraged*]. Well, those are my views, for what they're worth.

Theodore [*pouring out another cup of tea*]. My dear fellow, if you'd get married, and have thirteen or fourteen years of it, as I've had, your views would be worth more than they are.

Peter. Oh, that won't wash. [*Rising.*] When a man's sufferin' from gout in the toe, he doesn't stipulate that his M.D. shall be writhin' from the same ailment. No, very frequently, the outsider . . .

Theodore. Good gracious, you're not going to remark that lookers-on see most of the game!

Peter. Words to that effect.

Theodore. Ho! Why is it that, the moment a man's matrimonial affairs are in a tangle, every platitude in the language is chewed out at him? [*Leaning his head on his hands.*] If you've nothing fresher to say on the subject . . . !

Peter [*oracularly*]. My dear chap, it's tryin' to say somethin' fresh on the subject of marriage that's responsible for a large share of the domestic unhappiness and discontent existin' at the present day. There's too much of this tryin' to say somethin' fresh on *every* subject, in my opinion.

Theodore. Nobody can accuse *you*, Peter . . .

Peter. You take it from me, there are two institootions in this world that are never goin' to alter—men and women and the shape of chickens' eggs. Chickens' eggs are never goin' to be laid square; and men and women will continue to be mere men and women till the last contango.* [THEODORE *finishes his tea, rises, and comes to the fire.*] I'm referrin', of course, to real men and women. I don't inclood persons in petticoats with flat chests and no hips; or individuals wearin' beards and trousers who dine on a basin of farinaceous food and a drink o' water out o' the filter. They belong to a distinct species. No; I mean the genuine article, like you and me and your missus—men and women with blood in their veins, and one and a half per cent of good, humanizin' alcohol in *that*.

Theodore [*throwing a log on the fire*]. What's the moral of your eloquent, but rather vague, discourse?

Peter [*at the chair in the middle of the room*]. The moral? Oh, the moral is that men and women of the ordinary, regula-

* "Contango-day"—a Stock Exchange expression: the second day before settling day, i.e., the last day on which continuation of an account may be arranged.

tion pattern must put up with the defects of each other's qualities. [*Turning the chair so that it faces* THEODORE *and again sitting in it.*] She complains that you don't admire her frocks and frills, Theo.

Theodore [*groaning*]. Oh!

Peter. Now, come! Where's the trouble? There's my old mother—seventy-five in April! Whenever I'm at Stillwood, I make a reg'lar practice of complimentin' her on her rig-out. "By Jove, Mater," I say, "you *are* a buck this mornin'!" Or evenin', as the case may be. I couldn't tell you what she's wearin', to save my life; but there's no harm done.

Theodore. Yes, *you* do it; but your father doesn't do it, I'll be bound. [PETER *looks glum and is silent.*] It's too trivial! [*Producing his cigar case.*] A husband can't be ever-lastingly praising his wife's clothes. [*Offering a cigar to* PETER, *which he declines.*] The absence of comment on my part is a sign that I'm satisfied with Zoe's appearance, surely.

Peter. She's one of the smartest women in London.

Theodore [*irritably*]. I know she is. I've told her so till I'm sick. [*Cutting and lighting a cigar.*] I've always been intensely proud of Zoe, as a matter of fact—intensely proud of her.

Peter. No more than her due.

Theodore [*with increasing indignation*]. Good God, how often, at a dinner party, have I caught myself looking along the table and thinking she's the handsomest woman in the room! Tsk! It's a ridiculous thing to say . . .

Peter. What?

Theodore. I suppose no man has ever been "in love" with his wife for longer than I've been with mine.

Peter [*significantly*]. Been.

Theodore. And I have a very great affection for her still—or should have, if her behavior didn't check it.

Peter. If you showed your affection more plainly, wouldn't that check her behavior?

Theodore [*leaving the fireplace and moving about the room*]. Oh, my dear fellow, haven't you brains enough to see! We're middle-aged people, Zoe and I. I *am* middle-aged, and she's not far off it, poor girl. There must come a time on a journey when your pair of horses stops prancing and settles down to a trot.

Peter. How's that for a platitude!

Theodore. I thought that worm-eaten illustration might appeal to you.

Peter. She keeps wonderfully young, Theo.

Theodore. Isn't that a little to my credit? But Zoe's within three years of forty. You can't put the clock back.

Peter. A woman's as old as she looks . . .

Theodore. And a man's as old as he feels! Another ancient wheeze!

Peter. And a *married* woman's as old as her husband *makes* her feel.

Theodore. My dear Peter, I don't want Zoe to feel older than her years by a single hour. But I confess I do ask her occasionally to feel as old *as* her years, and not to make herself damnably absurd.

Peter. Absurd?

Theodore. This infernal fooling about with the boys, for instance—the cause of last night's flare-up—her "tame robins" —you're one! [PETER *rises hastily and goes to the fire.*] Yes, you ought to be ashamed of yourself, for encouraging her.

Peter. Who's in fault? Because a man's wife has ceased to be attractive to him, it doesn't follow that she ain't attractive to others.

Theodore [*contemptuously*]. Attractive? The vanity of "attracting" a parcel of empty-headed young men! You're the patriarch of the group! [*Throwing himself into the chair just vacated by* PETER.] The whole thing's undignified— raffish.

Peter [*extending a forefinger*]. *You* contrive to be a trifle more sprightly at home, Theo . . .

Theodore [*moving his head from side to side*]. Oh, you will hammer away at that! I'm forty-six. My sprightly days are over.

Peter [*emphatically*]. Humbug, old chap.

Theodore. What's humbug?

Peter. Men are the biggest humbugs goin'—especially to themselves. And a man of your age or mine—and I'm four years your senior—is never a bigger humbug than when he's deloodin' himself with the notion that he's scrap iron.

Theodore. You're a gay old spark . . .

Peter. No, it's when the sun's workin' round to the west— it's when men are where we are now, that they're most liable to get into mischief.

Theodore. Mischief? What are you driving at?

Peter. Nothin'. I'm simply layin' down a general principle.

Theodore [*angrily*]. Confound your general principles! Don't be an ass.

Peter [*coming to* THEODORE]. That stoopid nonsense talked last night—early this mornin'—about livin' apart—who started it?

Theodore. Zoe. I fancy it was Zoe—last night.

Peter. Oh, it wasn't the first time?

Theodore [*smoking with fierce puffs*]. We had an awful scene—disgraceful. I felt inclined to rush out of the house then and there.

Peter. Why didn't you? You could have let yourself in again when she'd gone to bye-bye.

Theodore [*sullenly*]. No, that's not my style. If ever I do bang the front door, it'll be once and for all, my friend.

Peter [*shaking him*]. Oh! Oh!

Theodore. She's independent; she has her own income—you know—and I've told her I'd supplement it, if necessary. I've settled this house on her as it is; she'd be welcome to it, and every stick in it, worst come to the worst.

Peter. Theo!

Theodore. And I'd go and live in a garret, in peace.

Peter. You're not considerin' such a step seriously?

Theodore [*turning upon him roughly*]. No, I'm not—not when I'm sitting here chatting quietly with you. Nor when she's rational and—and—and amenable, as she can be when she chooses. [*Clenching his hands.*] But when she's irritating me till I'm half beside myself, I—I . . .

Peter. You . . . ?

Theodore [*looking up at* PETER]. My God, Peter, you're a wise man, never to have taken it on!

Peter. Marriage?

Theodore [*throwing his head back*]. Oh, my dear fellow!

The glazed door opens and ZOE *enters meekly. Her eyes are red, and a handkerchief is crumpled up in her hand. She glances at the tea table and comes to* THEODORE. PETER *retreats to the fireplace.*

Zoe [*to* THEODORE, *in a piteous voice*]. Have you—had your tea?

Theodore [*frigidly*]. I poured it out myself.

After a moment's hesitation, she bends over him and gives him a kiss. Then she turns away and, seating herself at the writing table, proceeds to write a note. There is an awkward silence.

Theodore [*breaking the silence, gruffly*]. Er—Zoe . . .
Zoe [*with a sniff, writing*]. Yes?

Theodore. What are you doing tonight?

Zoe. Jim Mallandain was going to take me to the Palace. I'm putting him off.

Theodore. I'll dine you out and take you somewhere.

Zoe. No, I'd rather have a quiet evening at home, Theo— just you and me. [*Blowing her nose.*] I've ordered Mrs. Killick to send up an extra-nice dinner.

Theodore. Perhaps Peter . . .

Zoe [*stamping her foot*]. No, I won't have him.

Peter. Besides, I'm booked.

Zoe [*petulantly*]. I don't care whether you are or not. I want to dine alone with my husband. [*There is another pause, during which* ZOE *scratches away with her pen.*]

Peter [*clearing his throat*]. Well, I'll be gettin' along. [THEODORE *rises.*] I say . . .

Theodore. H'm?

Peter. Why don't you and Zoe have a week or a fortnight in Paris? It 'ud do you both a heap of good.

Theodore. Impossible. How can I?

Peter. Cert'nly you can. If anythin' important crops up, Tom Slade or I will run over to you; or you could come back. [*Again there is a pause.* ZOE *stops writing.*] Do, old chap. [*Another pause.*] Won't you?

Theodore [*without enthusiasm*]. All right.

Peter. A fortnight? Nothin'll happen.

Theodore [*nodding*]. A fortnight.

Uttering a little chirp of delight, ZOE *resumes writing.* PETER *goes to her as* THEODORE *moves away to the fireplace.*

Peter [*to* ZOE]. Good-by, ma'am. [*She gives him her left hand over her shoulder. He squeezes it and makes for the glazed door. There he appears to be struck by an idea. After a silence, he turns slowly, contemplates the pair for a moment with a puckered brow, and advances a step or two.*] Theo . . .

Theodore [*who has picked up one of the illustrated papers and has seated himself upon the settee*]. H'm?

Peter [*his hands in his pockets, rattling his keys*]. About halfway between Dover and Calais—no, it's between Folkestone and Boulogne, ain't it?

Theodore [*examining the pictures*]. What?

Peter. Of course! About halfway between Folkestone and Boulogne—mid-Channel—there's a shoal.

Theodore [*turning a page of his paper*]. What of it?

Peter. Le Colbart, the French sailormen call it—Le Colbart.

We call it the Ridge. [*Coming forward.*] If you go by Folkestone and Boulogne, you'll pass over it.

Theodore [*glancing at him suspiciously*]. Thanks for the
valuable information.

Peter. D'ye know, I've never encountered that blessed
shoal without experiencin' a most unpleasant time?

Zoe [*addressing an envelope*]. Oh, my dear Peter!

Peter. I've crossed on some of the finest days o' the year.
The sun's been shinin', and outside the harbor the water's been
as smooth as it's been *in*side. Everythin's looked as enticin'
as could be; but as we've neared the Ridge—mid-Channel—
I've begun to feel fidgety, restless, out o' sorts—hatin' myself and hatin' the man who's been sharin' my cabin with me.
But the sensation hasn't lasted long.

Zoe [*sealing her letter*]. Glad to hear it.

Peter. No; gradually the beastly motion has died down, and
in a quarter of an hour or so I've found myself pacin' the
deck again, arm in arm with the travelin' companion I've
been positively loathin' a few minutes earlier.

Theodore [*gaping demonstratively*]. Very interesting.

Peter. My dear pals, I remember the idea once occurrin'
to me—I mentioned it to Charlie Westbrook at the time—
there's a resemblance between *that* and marriage.

Theodore [*shortly*]. Ha! Thought that was coming.

ZOE *turns in her chair, to listen to* PETER.

Peter. Yes, and marriage, mark you, at its best and bright-
est. The happiest and luckiest of married couples have got
to cross that wretched Ridge. However successful the first
half of their journey may be, there's the rough-and-tumble
of mid-Channel to negotiate. Some arrive there quicker than
others, some later; it depends on wind and tide. But they
get there; and a bad time it is, and must be—a time when
travelin' companions see nothin' but the spots on each other's
yellow faces, and when innoomerable kind words and innoomerable kind acts are clean forgotten. [ZOE, *her letter
in her hand, rises impulsively and comes to* PETER.] But, as
I tell you, it's soon over—*well* over, if only Mr. Jack and
Mrs. Jill will understand the situation; if only they'll say to
themselves, "We're on the Ridge; we're in mid-Channel; in
another quarter of an hour the boat'll be steady again—as
steady as when we stepped onto the gangway." [*To* THEO-
DORE.] Not offended, old man?

Theodore [*uncomfortably*]. Ha, ha, ha!

Zoe [*gently, giving her letter to* PETER]. Tell Warren to give that to a messenger boy. [*To* THEODORE.] Theo! [*She puts her hands upon* PETER's *shoulders and kisses him.*]

Peter [*chuckling*]. Ha, ha! [*To* THEODORE.] Division of profits. [*At the glazed door.*] When'll you be off?

Theodore. Oh—one day next week.

Peter [*nodding*]. Tomorrow mornin', then. [*He goes out, closing the door.*]

Zoe. Dear old Peter!

Theodore [*deep in his paper*]. Peter's getting a bit of a bore, though.

Zoe [*mimicking* PETER, *as she wipes her eyes*]. He's amusin'. [*Going to* THEODORE *and seating herself beside him.*] Theo . . .

Theodore. H'm?

Zoe [*edging up to him*]. Let's go by Folkestone and Boulogne—shall we?

Theodore. *I* don't mind.

Zoe [*wistfully*]. Let's go by Folkestone and Boulogne—and have done with it. [*Slipping her arm through his.*] Theo—last night—sorry. [*He nods and looks at another picture.*] I take it all back—the things I said. I didn't mean them.

Theodore. That's all right.

Zoe. And *you* didn't mean . . . ?

Theodore [*impatiently*]. Of course I didn't.

Zoe [*giving herself a shake*]. Ah! [*After a brief pause.*] Theo . . .

Theodore. H'm?

Zoe [*taking the paper from him playfully*]. Don't look at those improper young ladies. [*Coaxingly.*] Couldn't you manage to get away on Sunday?

Theodore. Oh—I might.

Zoe. It's your treat to me, isn't it—and the beginning of better times? The *sooner* we begin . . .

Theodore [*nodding*]. You shall have it all your own way.

Zoe [*gleefully*]. Sunday!

Theodore. H'm.

Zoe. I'm dreadfully shabby. I've no new clothes. You don't object?

Theodore [*distinctly*]. Now, my dear Zoe—my darling—understand this from me clearly. You are *never* shabby; you *couldn't* be shabby. As far as I am a judge, you are always dressed beautifully and—and—and in perfect taste.

Zoe. Beautifully!

Theodore. If you were *not* well-dressed, I should venture to call your attention to it.

Zoe. Silence is approval?

Theodore. Absolutely. So don't expect me—a busy man—to be eternally praising your gowns and what not; because I cannot and will not do it.

Zoe. I won't—I won't. I know I'm inconsiderate—[*Stamping her foot.*] beastly inconsiderate. [*Excitedly.*] Write out a telegram now . . .

Theodore. Telegram?

Zoe. To the hotel.

Theodore. Yes, that 'ud be wise. [*He rises and goes over to the writing table where, taking a sheet of notepaper, he sits and writes.*] We couldn't get an answer to a letter.

Zoe [*jumping up and walking about*]. Jolly nice rooms, Theo!

Theodore [*assentingly*]. H'm, h'm.

Zoe [*humming*]. Tra, la! ra, la! la, ra, la . . . !

Theodore [*in the throes of composition*]. Sssh, sssh!

Zoe [*opening the illustrated paper*]. Beg pardon.

Theodore [*writing*]. ". . . deux bonnes chambres à coucher —salle de bain—et salon . . ."

Zoe. There's Lena. Don't forget the maid.

Theodore. Oh, they shove her anywhere.

Zoe [*imperatively*]. No, no; I must have her handy. [*He writes.*] What hotel are we going to, Theo?

Theodore [*writing*]. ". . . aussi chambre pour servante même étage . . ."

Zoe. The Ritz?

Theodore. Oh, blow the Ritz!

Zoe. We've always *been* comfortable at the Ritz.

Theodore [*putting the finishing touches to his telegram*]. Twenty francs a minute.

Zoe [*disappointed*]. Where then? The Elysée Palace is too far out this weather. The Régina?

Theodore [*reading*]. "Pouvez-vous réserver pour Monsieur et Madame Blundell pour dimanche et nuits suivantes appartement composé deux bonnes chambres à coucher, salle de bain, et salon, aussi chambre pour servante même étage? Réponse télégraphique. Theodorus, London."

Zoe [*advancing*]. Oh, Theo! Shall we try the new Meurice? The Langdales had a suite there that made them feel like royalties.

Theodore [*half turning to her*]. Gerald Duckfield was telling me of a capital little hotel where he and Bessie stayed— the Vendôme . . .

Zoe. Where's that?

Theodore. In the Place Vendôme.

Zoe. The Ritz—the Bristol—the Rhin—they're the only hotels in the Place.

Theodore. Oh, but this is in the part of the Place that runs down to the top of the Rue Castiglione.

Zoe. The *narrow* part!

Theodore. Well, it isn't the broad part, certainly.

Zoe. The traffic of the Rue St. Honoré to help to send you to sleep!

Theodore. No, no; there are double windows, Gerald says, to the best bedrooms. [*Turning to the writing table.*] It 'ud be an experiment.

Zoe [*sitting in the chair in the middle of the room, with her back to him*]. Yes, it would be an experiment.

Theodore. Shall we risk it?

Zoe [*coldly*]. By all means.

Theodore [*writing*]. "Directeur—Hôtel Vendôme."

Zoe [*tapping her feet upon the floor*]. Ha!

Theodore. H'm? ". . . Place Vendôme . . ."

Zoe [*holding up the illustrated paper so that he may see, over her head, a risqué picture*]. If you were taking this sort of woman with you, nothing 'ud be good enough for her.

Theodore [*glancing at the picture, angrily*]. Oh, don't be so coarse! [*There is a pause. He leans back in his chair, biting his pen. Suddenly she flings the illustrated paper away from her into the air. Throwing down his pen, he rises and paces the room.*] This promises well for an enjoyable fortnight in Paris!

Zoe [*rising and moving to the left*]. Look here, old man! This trip was going to be *your* treat. Very well, that's off! I'll take *you* to Paris; *I'll* pay the expenses; and I won't stuff you up in a frowsy rabbit hutch.

Theodore [*coming forward on the right*]. Don't insult me!

Zoe [*facing him*]. Anyway, your treat or mine, I stay at no hotel in Paris that isn't top-hole.

Theodore [*furiously*]. Oh, stop your damned slang, for God's sake!

Zoe [*her eyes blazing*]. What!

Theodore [*sitting on the fauteuil stool and rocking himself to and fro*]. Oh! Oh!

Zoe. Stop my damned slang!

Theodore [*his head in his hands*]. Hold your tongue!

Zoe [*coming to him*]. And how did I learn my damned slang, pray? [*He waves her from him.*] I learned it from the crew you surrounded me with when I condescended to marry you and went out of my world into yours.

Theodore [*starting up*]. Oh . . . ! [*He goes to the bell and rings it continuously.*]

Zoe [*following him*]. Yes, you were hugely tickled by it *then!* And so were *they*—the men you thought might be serviceable to you; and who *were* serviceable to you, often through *me!*

Theodore. Oh!

Zoe. Ha! And now that my tongue's furred with it, and it isn't necessary to attract the vulgar brutes any more, you round on me and rag me! [*Pacing the room on the left.*] Oh! Oh! If only my dear old dad were alive! He'd fuss over me and protect me. My father was a gentleman. He warned me I was chucking myself away!

Theodore. Oh!

Zoe [*wildly*]. Why do you keep on ringing that bell?

Theodore [*in a loud voice*]. I suppose I can ring the bell if I like!

Zoe. You—you can go to the devil if you like! [*She goes out at the glazed door. As she disappears*, WARREN *passes her and enters.*]

Theodore [*crossing to the writing table*] Warren . . .

Warren. Yessir?

Theodore [*picking up the sheet of paper on which he has written the message to the hotel*]. Pack me a bag.

Warren. Bag, Sir?

Theodore [*tearing the paper into small pieces*]. Yes; I'm not sleeping at home tonight.

Warren [*coming to the table and preparing to remove the tea things*]. Very good, Sir.

ACT TWO

The same, but the disposition of some of the furniture is changed. The settee on the right is now placed with its back to the fireplace. At the farther end of the settee are the oblong table and chair, and on the left of the table, facing the settee, is the chair which in the preceding act stood in the middle of the room. An armchair is at the nearer end of

*the settee; and another armchair and the fauteuil stool stand
together, not far from the glazed door.*

*On the oblong table are a box of cigarettes, matches, and an
ashtray.*

*The fireplace is banked with flowers, there are flowers in
vases upon the tables, and the room is full of sunlight.*

Two men—an UPHOLSTERER *and his* ASSISTANT—*are engaged
in putting covers of gay chintz upon the chairs and settees.
The* UPHOLSTERER *is on his knees at the settee on the right,
the* ASSISTANT *is at the chair by the writing table.* LENA,
ZOE'*s maid—a bright, buxom woman—is arranging the furniture in the middle of the room. Presently the* ASSISTANT *proceeds to collect the brown paper and cord which litter the
floor.*

UPHOLSTERER [*rising from his knees—to* LENA]. That's all
right.

Lena [*coming to him*]. And when are we to have the
pleasure of seeing *you* again?

Upholsterer. Tomorrow.

Lena. What about next year, or the year after! [*Producing
her purse and giving him a tip.*] In case I shouldn't live so
long.

Upholsterer. Thank you very much. [*Moving away—
quietly.*] William——

The ASSISTANT, *laden with brown paper, advances, and* LENA
tips him.

Assistant. Thank you, miss. Good morning, miss.

Lena. Good morning.

Upholsterer [*at the glazed door*]. Good morning.

Lena [*tidying the furniture on the right*]. Good morning.

*The men depart. Almost immediately, the glazed door is re-
opened and* WARREN *appears showing in* LEONARD. LEONARD
*is gloved and is carrying a straw hat and a walking cane. He
has lost his fresh, boyish appearance and is sallow and lined.*

Leonard [*to* LENA]. Good morning.

Lena [*familiarly*]. Oh, good morning. [*To* WARREN.] I'll
let Mrs. Blundell know. [*To* LEONARD, *as* WARREN *withdraws.*] She'll be down soon. Will you have a paper?

Leonard. Thanks; seen 'em. How is she, Lena?

Lena. Middling. She's a little feverish, the doctor says. She
must have caught a chill coming over. [LEONARD *nods.*] She

would sit on deck, talking to Mr. Mallandain. We met him by accident on the platform as we were leaving Paris.

Leonard [*nodding again*]. She's told me.

Lena. She's to remain indoors again today and keep out o' drafts. [*Looking at a watch which she wears on her wrist and at the clock on the mantelpiece.*] What do you say the right time is?

Leonard [*looking at his watch*]. Quarter to twelve.

Lena [*going to the mantelpiece*]. I'm to give her her med'cine an hour before meals. [*Moving the hands of the clock.*] Ha! They've all been playing tricks here while we've been away, clockwinder included.

Leonard [*absently*]. Indeed?

Lena. Servants, tradespeople, everybody! [*Unbuckling her bracelet.*] Because Mrs. Blundell is now on her own, I s'pose they fancy they can take advantage of her. [*Returning to* LEONARD.] I'll teach 'em! [*Timing her watch.*] Think we're getting fairly straight?

Leonard [*glancing idly at the room as he sits in the arm-chair near the glazed door*]. Wonderfully.

Lena. Not bad, is it, considering we've been home only two days?

Leonard [*placing his hat and cane upon the fauteuil stool*]. Capital.

Lena [*refastening her bracelet*]. Ouf! The relief, after some of those foreign hotels!

Leonard [*drawing off his gloves*]. Tired of traveling, eh?

Lena. Don't ask me! I was saying to Mrs. Killick at break-fast—I've had enough of Italy to last me my life. Over four months of it, and without a courier! [*Going toward the glazed door.*] That's a bit too stiff.

Leonard. It is rather.

Lena [*halting by him and dropping her voice slightly*]. Not that we wanted a courier when *you* came out to us. A splendid courier you were; I couldn't wish for a better.

Leonard [*uncomfortably*]. Ha, ha!

Lena [*laughing*]. Do you remember our losing her hatbox at that wretched old Siena?

Leonard. Yes—yes.

Lena. You woke 'em up there in grand style. Ha, ha! Your friend, the Italian policeman—the image in the feathers . . . !

Leonard. Ha, ha!

Lena. You did give him a dressing! [*Sobering herself.*] Yes, those three or four weeks you were with us were the pleasantest o' the lot, to my idea. [*Going.*] Well, good-day.

[*Stopping again.*] Oh, but I must show you this. [*Taking a ring from her finger.*] A present from her—last Saturday— one of the best shops in the Roo Royarl. [*Handing it to him.*] She went out and bought it herself.

Leonard. Turquoise . . .

Lena. And diamonds.

Leonard [*returning the ring*]. Beautiful.

Lena. Wasn't it kind of her! I'm as vain as a peacock. [*Replacing the ring on her finger.*] But there, you've both been extremely good to me.

Leonard. Not at all.

Lena. You have; you've spoiled me completely. [*At the door, speaking louder.*] Treacherous weather for June, isn't it?

Leonard. Very.

Lena [*in the corridor*]. Oh, here you are! Here's Mr. Ferris —I was just coming up to tell you . . .

LEONARD *rises as* ZOE *appears in the corridor. She is dressed in an elegant robe of rich, soft material and carries a little bag in which are a few opened letters, her handkerchief, etc. She also is changed. Her face is wan and there are dark circles around her eyes.*

Zoe. Ah? [*To* LEONARD, *formally, as she enters the room.*] Good morning.

Leonard. Good morning.

Zoe. Lena, how charming the old chintz looks!

Lena [*who is lingering*]. It's English!

Zoe [*laying her bag upon the oblong table*]. If we could all be freshened up by the same process!

Lena [*her hand on the door handle*]. Don't forget you're to take your med'cine in three quarters of an hour.

Zoe. Oh, bring me the filthy stuff when you like.

Lena [*in the corridor, closing the door*]. Now, don't be naughty.

As the woman disappears, LEONARD *walks over to* ZOE. *She puts out her hand to check him, and they stand for a moment or two watching the door and listening. Then she drops her hand and turns her face to him perfunctorily, and he kisses her as a matter of course.*

Zoe. Your motor isn't outside?

Leonard. No; I walked across the park.

Zoe. That yellow car of yours is so conspicuous. [*Arranging a pillow on the settee.*] Sorry I wasn't visible yesterday.

Leonard. You're better?

Zoe [*evasively*]. Oh, more or less decrepit. [*Sitting.*] What have you been doing with yourself?

Leonard. Nothing much. [*Sitting in the armchair opposite to her.*] Except . . .

Zoe [*taking her bag from the table*]. By-the-bye, I've had a note this morning from an old friend of yours.

Leonard. Who?

Zoe [*producing a letter from the bag*]. Ethel Pierpoint.

Leonard [*inexpressively*]. Oh? [*She extracts the letter from its envelope and tosses it across to him. He reads it silently, with a frown. She takes a cigarette from the box on the table.*] I thought you'd dropped her.

Zoe. I did, in a fashion. I stopped her letters by ceasing to answer them. [*Striking a match.*] I hated calling myself hers affectionately, knowing I'd been the cause of your slacking away from her.

Leonard [*under his breath*]. Pish!

Zoe [*lighting her cigarette*]. *What* does she say?

Leonard [*reading aloud*]. "Dearest Zoe. Quite by chance I hear you are back at Lancaster Gate. Why do you still make no sign? I never wanted your friendship more than now— or the friendship of somebody who will give me good advice, or a sound shaking for being a fool. Please take pity on your troubled but ever devoted, Ethel Drayson Pierpoint." [*To* ZOE.] What does she mean by never wanting your friendship more than now? [ZOE *shakes her head. He continues to ponder over the letter.*] ". . . or the friendship of somebody who will give me good advice, or a sound shaking for being a fool."

Zoe [*smoking, thoughtfully*]. When did you see the Pierpoints last?

Leonard. About a month after you left London—just before I followed you. [*Returning the letter to her.*] I cooled off them gradually.

Zoe [*after a pause*]. She's a nice girl—Ethel.

Leonard. Ye—es, she was nice enough.

There is a further pause. Then ZOE *jumps up, as if to dismiss disagreeable reflections, and crosses to the writing table. There she empties her bag of the letters it contains.*

Leonard [*gloomily*]. Am I in the way?

Zoe [*fretfully*]. Of course not. [*She sits at the writing table and busies herself with rereading her letters and destroying some of them.* LEONARD *rises and takes a cigarette from the box.*] Poor Robby Relf has got neuritis.

Leonard [*lighting his cigarette*]. Zo . . .

Zoe. Eh?

Leonard. I was going to tell you—I dined at the Carlton last night.

Zoe [*indifferently*]. Oh?

Leonard. With Cossy Rawlings. Guess who was there.

Zoe [*becoming attentive*]. Dun'no.

Leonard. He didn't see me—he was at a table the other side of the room . . .

Zoe [*holding her breath*]. Theodore?

Leonard. Yes.

She throws the pieces of a letter into the wastepaper basket and leans back in her chair.

Zoe. How—how did he look?

Leonard [*curling his lip*]. I didn't study his appearance.

Zoe. He—he wasn't—by himself?

Leonard. Hardly!

Zoe. That—that woman?

Leonard [*nodding*]. Same lady.

Zoe. Simply the two?

Leonard [*sitting upon the settee on the right*]. The two turtledoves.

After a brief silence, she pushes her letters from her, rises, and moves about the room quietly but agitatedly.

Zoe. Who is this creature?

Leonard [*impatiently*]. I've told you—and Jim told you on Sunday.

Zoe. Hatherly—Annerly . . . ?

Leonard. Her husband was a Major Annerly—Frank Annerly. He divorced her over a man of the name of Bettison.

Zoe. Where's *he?*

Leonard. He's dead. She's been through a good many hands since.

Zoe. Ho!

Leonard. Fred Wishart was one—and Tod Arnold . . .

Zoe. She's quite young, isn't she?

Leonard. Looks a baby.

Zoe. Ha!

Leonard. I should put her at thirty.

Zoe. Pretty? They all are!

Leonard. Passable.

Zoe [*behind the chair on the left of the oblong table*]. Do you think she's—with him?

Leonard. Not regularly. She's still living in Egerton Crescent, according to Cossy.

Zoe [*gripping the back of the chair*]. She'll ruin him; she'll ruin him, Len.

Leonard. Oh, I dare say there'll be a bit left, when she's done with him.

Zoe. There are other ways of dragging a man down besides through his pocket. Jim Mallandain says she's a vampire.

Leonard. Why should you worry yourself . . . ?

Zoe. I don't want him to come to grief. Why should I?

Leonard. If he does, you've nothing to reproach yourself with.

Zoe [*giving him a swift look*]. *What!*

Leonard [*sullenly*]. Oh, you know what I mean—nothing that occurred before he took himself off.

Zoe [*moving to the oblong table, with a longdrawn sigh*]. Ah-h-h! [*Sitting, her elbows on the table, leaning her head on her hand.*] It will always be on my conscience that I drove him away.

Leonard. You didn't drive him away.

Zoe. I did.

Leonard. You were quite justified in doing it, anyhow. He made your life a burden to you.

Zoe. I might have been more patient with him; I might have waited.

Leonard. Waited?

Zoe. Waited til we'd got through the middle period of our lives. [*Raising her head.*] Peter warned us, the very day we parted . . .

Leonard [*sneeringly*]. Peter!

Zoe. Mid-Channel! We should soon have reached the other side.

Leonard. There's a limit to human endurance; you'd passed it.

Zoe [*staring before her*]. It seems to me now, there wasn't so very much for me to put up with—not so very much. [*Rising and walking to the back of the settee on which* LEONARD *is sitting.*] There was a lot of good in him, really. After all, he only needed managing, humoring . . .

Leonard [*starting up and turning to her*]. Upon my soul, Zoe! Ha! You're discovering no end of fine qualities in him suddenly!

Zoe [*bitterly*]. Am I?

Leonard. You hadn't a decent word for him when we were in Italy! Now he's perfect!

Zoe [*facing him*]. No, he's not.

Leonard [*satirically*]. Sounds like it.

Zoe [*flaring up*]. Neither he nor you! You can be just as unkind to me as he ever was.

Leonard [*angrily*]. I!

Zoe. Yes! And, with all his faults, he did try to take care of me—to keep me from harm! [*Her eyes ablaze.*] My God, what have *you* done!

They remain confronting one another for a moment without speaking. Then he turns away abruptly and picks up his hat and cane. She runs after him and clings to him.

Zoe. No, no; don't be hasty. I didn't mean it—I didn't mean it . . .

Leonard [*endeavoring to free himself*]. Let me go . . .

Zoe. Ah, no! I'm not well today . . .

Leonard. I'll come back when you're better-tempered.

Zoe. I *am* better-tempered. Look! it's all over. [*Coaxing him to give up his hat and cane.*] Lenny—Lenny, dear—Lenny [*Placing the hat and can upon the writing table, she takes her handkerchief from her bag and dries her eyes. He sits in the armchair near the glazed door sulkily.*] Ha, ha! Now you're beginning to see what sort of a time poor Theo had with me.

Leonard. Oh, can't you leave off talking about him for a single second!

Zoe [*coming to him meekly*]. I beg your pardon, dear.

Leonard. You've got that fellow on the brain.

Zoe [*standing behind him*]. You started it, by telling me of last night.

Leonard. Why the deuce *shouldn't* I tell you of last night! Do sit down. [*She sits near him, upon the fauteuil stool.*] I can't make you out, Zo. This woman's only what we've been waiting for. I've said all along he'd soon give you an opportunity of divorcing him. She completes your case for you.

Zoe [*dully*]. Yes.

Leonard [*grumbling*]. You ought to be tremendously obliged to Jim for being the first to open your eyes—my eyes too—to what's going on. Instead of which, you're upset by it. And now, because *I've* seen Blundell and the lady together, I'm favored by hearing Mr. B. described as a model husband . . .

Zoe [*to silence him*]. Ah!

Leonard [*changing his tone*]. When do you interview your lawyers?

Zoe. I—I haven't written to them yet.

Leonard. You were to do it after I left you on Monday.

Zoe. I—I've been feeling so cheap, Len.

Leonard [*with a short laugh*]. We shall be gray-haired before we're married, at this rate. [*She lays her hand on his appeasingly. He retains her hand.*] I believe you'll have to go through the form of trying to compel Blundell to return to you. Of course, he'll refuse. Meanwhile we must have the lady's house watched—or Blundell's flat. I shouldn't be surprised if he'd arrange that part of the business with you, to save trouble and expense. Drop a line to Maxwells today, will you?

Zoe [*obediently*]. Yes.

Leonard. Or ring them up. You'll be able to get out tomorrow—or one of them would wait on you.

Zoe. Yes.

Leonard. That's right, old girlie. Kiss me. [*They kiss, quickly and cautiously, without ardor.*] Sorry.

Zoe [*turning to him and lowering her voice almost to a whisper*]. Lenny . . .

Leonard. What?

Zoe. Don't forget—Perugia.

Leonard [*in an outburst*]. Oh, yes—curse the place!—let's foget Perugia. I was off my head there. I behaved like a blackguard. You needn't be continually throwing it in my teeth.

Zoe. No, no; I'm not scolding you again. [*Gently.*] What I mean is—your breaking your word to me at Perugia—staying in the same hotel . . .

Leonard. Well?

Zoe. If Theodore's solicitors got hold of that . . .

Leonard [*rising and walking away*]. Yes, but they won't get hold of it.

Zoe [*twisting herself around toward him*]. You remember our meeting Claud Lowenstein at the railway station at Arezzo?

Leonard. I explained to him that my being in the train with you was pure chance. I made that square.

Zoe. He was going on to Perugia—to the Brufani. [*Rising.*] He may have been suspicious—he may have inquired . . .

Leonard. Even that little swine wouldn't tell tales.

Zoe [*coming to him*]. Then there's Lena—they might pump Lena . . .

Leonard. My dear girl, all this would be very terrible if Blundell wasn't as anxious to get rid of you as we are to get rid of him. No, you take my word for it—he won't defend. His game is to be free at any price.

Zoe. To marry again perhaps!

Leonard. Probably.

Zoe [*clenching her hands*]. Ah, no!

Leonard [*his brow darkening again*]. Doesn't *that* please you? There's no satisfying you, Zoe. [*She leaves him and paces the room distractedly.*] A minute ago you were frightened lest he should be ruined by Mrs. Annerly!

Zoe [*on the left*]. I—I couldn't bear the idea of another woman being a better wife to him than I was! I couldn't bear it, Lenny!

Leonard. Why, what concern would it be of yours . . . !

Zoe [*with a gesture, as the glazed door opens*]. Sssh!

WARREN *appears.*

Warren [*to* ZOE]. I beg your pardon, ma'am—Mr. Mottram.

Zoe [*uttering a little, eager cry*]. Ah!

Warren. He'll call again, ma'am, if you're engaged.

Zoe. Did you say I—I'd anybody with me?

Warren. No, ma'am.

Zoe [*after a slight pause—indicating the adjoining room*]. Is that room still covered up?

Warren. Yes, ma'am.

Zoe. Well—show him in there for the moment.

Warren. Yes, ma'am. [*He withdraws, closing the door.*]

Zoe [*to* LEONARD, *in a low voice*]. He'd better not find you here so early.

Leonard [*also dropping his voice, testily*]. Why need you bother yourself with old Peter this morning?

Zoe [*bringing* LEONARD *his hat and cane*]. I haven't seen him since January. Don't look so cross. [*Caressing his cheek.*] Are you engaged to lunch anywhere?

Leonard. No.

Zoe. Will you eat your lunch with me?

He nods. She takes a powder puff from her bag and, looking into the hand mirror, hurriedly removes the traces of her tears. While she is thus occupied, LEONARD *listens at the nearer door on the right.*

Leonard [*leaving the door—in a whisper*]. He's there.

WARREN *reappears.*

Warren [*to* ZOE]. Mr. Mottram is in the next room, ma'am.

Zoe. Thank you.

Zoe [*to* LEONARD, *in a whisper, accompanying him to the glazed door*]. Go into the park and sit under the trees. Blow a kiss for me to all the kiddies. [*She watches him disappear down the corridor. Then, having closed the glazed door, she opens the farther door on the right.*] Peter!

Peter [*out of sight*]. My dear lady!

Zoe [*going into the next room*]. Why on earth have they put you into this dismal room! Come into the light. [*Returning with him, her arm tucked through his.*] Oh, my dear Peter—my dear Peter . . . !

Peter. Ah, yes, yes, yes! A nice way to serve a pal!

Zoe [*closing the door*]. How did you . . . ?

Peter. Jim Mallandain dropped in at the office this morning. [*They leave the door.*] He traveled with you from Paris on Sunday.

Zoe. I collided with him at the Gare du Nord.

Peter. And this is Wednesday!

Zoe [*withdrawing her arm*]. I funked sending for you; that's a fact.

Peter. Funked it?

Zoe [*with the air of a child in disgrace*]. Your letters to me have been awfully sweet, but I know you despise me for making a muck of things.

Peter [*protestingly*]. Ah, Mrs. Zoe!

Zoe. And I'm rather a sick rabbit, Peter. [*Turning away.*] A sick rabbit has only one desire—to hide in its burrow. [*Facing him.*] My heart bounded when you were announced, though.

Peter [*following her*]. You don't look very fit. Seen a doctor?

Zoe. I've let Lena call in Rashleigh, to humor her. [*Sitting on the settee on the right.*] And I've promised to swallow his pig wash.

Peter. What's he say?

Zoe. Chill; but—[*Raising her eyes to his.*]—between ourselves?

Peter. Honor.

Zoe [*with quivering lips*]. Life, dear old chum!

Peter [*tenderly*]. Ain't much in it?

Zoe. Damn little. [*Putting her hair back from her brow.*] Phew! Can't sleep, Peter.

Peter. Oh, lor'!

Zoe. I tumble into bed at twelve—one—two. I get an hour's stupor, from sheer fatigue, and then I'm wide awake—

thinking! Then, dressing gown and slippers and the cigarettes; and then it's to and fro, up and down—smoke—smoke— smoke—often till the servants start brushing the stairs. No game, eh?

Peter. How long has this . . . ?

Zoe. It began at—[*Checking herself.*]—oh, a devil of a while. [*With a shiver.*] But I'm worse now I've set foot again in this house.

Peter [*eying her keenly*]. Ghosts? [*Avoiding his gaze, she stretches out her hand toward the cigarette box. He pushes the box beyond her reach. She makes a grimace. There is a pause.*] Zoe . . .

Zoe. Well?

Peter [*deliberately*]. Why shouldn't you pick up the pieces?

Zoe. Pick up—the pieces?

Peter. You and Theodore.

Zoe. Oh—don't be—funny, Peter.

Peter. I'm not funny; I'm as serious as the clown at the circus. [*Another pause.*] Write to him—or give me a message to take to him. *See* him.

She gets to her feet and attempts to pass PETER. *He detains her and she sinks back among her pillows.*

Zoe. Ha, ha! You ridiculous man! [*Faintly.*] Pick up the pieces! As if that were possible!

Peter. Oh, the valuable family china is in a good many fragments, I admit. But there *are* the fragments, lyin' on the carpet. They can be collected, fitted together.

Zoe [*with a sudden gesture of entreaty*]. Ah, for God's sake, Peter . . . !

Peter. Why, I'm suggestin' nothin' unusual.

Zoe [*repeating her gesture*]. Sssh!

Peter. Go into the homes of three fifths of the married people you know—*I* know—and you'll find some imposin' specimens of porcelain that won't bear inspectin' very narrowly.

Zoe [*waving the subject away*]. Sssh, sssh!

Peter. Only yesterday afternoon I was callin' at a house in —never mind the district. I was wanderin' 'round the drawin' room, lookin' at the bric-a-brac, and there, on a Louis Quatorze console table, were as handsome a pair of old Chinese jars—genuine Mings—as ever I've met with. Such a sooperb glaze they've got, such depth o' color! They appear to be priceless, perfect, till you examine 'em closely; and then . . . ! My dear Zoe, they're cracked; they've both had

a nasty knock at some time or another; they're scarred
shockin'ly with rivets and cement. And while I was sheddin'
tears over 'em, in sailed Madam, smilin' and holdin' out her
hand to me—she'd been upstairs, rubbin' carmine on her
lips . . .

Zoe [*in a murmur*]. You horror!

Peter. How kind of me to call—and how wild Tom 'ud be
at missin' me! To the casual observer, she's the happiest
woman goin'; and Tom, who strolled in just as I was leavin',
might be the most domesticated of husbands. You follow me?
You grasp the poetic allegory? Those faulty old Mings are
emblematic of the establishment they adorn. Mr. and Mrs.
Tom fell out years ago; they turned against each other one
fine day—in mid-Channel—and hadn't the sense to kiss and
be friends on landin'; their lives are as damaged as those
wounded crocks of theirs on the console table. [*Persuasively.*]
Well, but ain't it wiser to repair the broken china, rather
than chuck the bits into the dustbin? It's still showy and
effective at a distance; and there are cases—rare, but they
exist—where the mendin's been done so neatly that the flaws
are almost imperceptible. [*Seating himself opposite* ZOE.]
Zoe . . .

Zoe [*almost inaudibly*]. Yes, Peter?

Peter [*leaning forward*]. I believe yours is one of the
cases—yours and Theodore's—where the mendin' would be
exceptionally successful.

Zoe. What do you—what do you mean?

Peter. My dear, old Theo is as miserable over this affair as
you are.

Zoe. [*attempting a disdainful smile*]. N-nonsense!

Peter. Oh, no, it ain't nonsense.

Zoe. W-what makes you think that?

Peter. Between ourselves?

Zoe [*a note of eagerness in her voice*]. Honor.

Peter. He shows it in all manner o' ways. Neglects his business—ain't much good at it when he doesn't—is losin' his
grip—looks confoundedly ill—*is* ill. Altogether he's a different
man from the man he was, even when matters were at boilin'
point here.

Zoe [*locking and unlocking her fingers*]. Does he ever—
speak of me?

Peter. Oh, lor', yes.

Zoe. N-not kindly?

Peter. Very. Very kindly.

Zoe [*after a silence, as if in pain*]. Oh . . . ! [*She rises,*

passes him, and goes to the other side of the room where she moves from one piece of furniture to another aimlessly.]
W-what's he say about me?

Peter [*not turning*]. Frets about you—wonders how you're gettin' along—wonders as to the state of your finances—can't bear the idea of your bein' in the least pinched—wants to help you.

Zoe. He's extremely generous!

Peter. Theo? Never was anythin' else.

Zoe [*her eyes flashing*]. His own expenses must be pretty considerable just now, too!

Peter [*pricking up his ears*]. Must they? [*With great artlessness.*] Why?

Zoe. Oh, do you imagine I live wtih wool in my ears?

Peter [*over his shoulder*]. Wool . . . ?

Zoe. This woman he's continually with! [PETER'S *face is still averted from* ZOE. *At this juncture his eyes open widely and his mouth shapes to a whistle.*] This—Mrs—Mrs.—what's her name—Annerly! [*Pacing the room.*] A notorious woman —a woman without a shred of character—an any-man's woman . . . !

Peter [*settling his features and turning his chair toward* ZOE—*in a tone of expostulation*]. Oh!

Zoe. A baby-faced thing—seven years younger than I am! Precisely the class of goods a man of Theo's age flies at!

Peter. Oh—oh!

Zoes. They're rather costly articles, aren't they?

Peter. My dear Mrs. Zoe . . .

Zoe. Oh, don't you pretend to be so innocent, Peter! You know jolly well he's all over the place with her. They were at Hurlingham together Saturday week.

Peter [*coolly*]. I dessay.

Zoe. And they dine tête-à-tête at the Savoy, Ritz's, the Carlton . . .

Peter. Who supplies the information?

Zoe. They were at the Carlton last night.

Peter. Who's told you *that?*

Zoe. L . . . [*She pulls herself up.*]

Peter [*curiously*]. Who?

Zoe [*moistening her lips*]. Oh, I—I first heard of it all from Jim Mallandain. He was full of it on board the boat on Sunday.

Peter. Was he! [*Rising lazily.*] A busy gentleman—Jim.

Zoe. It was Jim who met them at Hurlingham—had tea with 'em.

Peter [*curiously again*]. But it can't be Jim who's blabbed about last night.

Zoe. Why?

Peter [*shrugging his shoulders*]. He happened to mention this mornin' that he was with a party at Jules'.

Zoe [*confused*]. N-no, it isn't from Jim I've got that. I . . . [*Throwing herself into the armchair near the glazed door.*] Oh, but really, it's a matter of supreme indifference to me, Peter, my dear boy, whom Theodore entertains at the Carlton, or whom he entertains at his flat . . .

Peter [*coming to her*]. My dear Zoe . . .

Zoe [*laughing heartily*]. Ha, ha, ha! His flat! I hear it's quite sumptuous. After his pathetic yearnings for peace and quiet in a garret, he sets up, within a month of our separating, in an enormous flat in Cavendish Square! I received that bit of news when I was in Florence. I—I was intensely amused. Oh, let him wallow in his precious flat!

Peter [*argumentatively*]. My dear lady . . .

Zoe [*her hand to her brow, exhausted*]. Ah, drop it, Peter; drop it!

Peter. I ask you—a liberal-minded person—what 'ud become of friendship as an institootion if men and women couldn't be pals without havin' the—the—what-d'ye-call-it—the tongue of scandal wagged at 'em? The world 'ud be intolerable. It ain't all marmalade as it is; but if a fellow can't take the fresh air in the company of a female at Hurlingham, or give her a bite o' food at a restaurant . . .

Zoe [*her head against the back of her chair, her eyes closed*]. Ah, la, la, la!

Peter. As for this—er—this Mrs. Annerly . . . [*He again purses his mouth and is evidently in a difficulty.*]

Zoe [*her eyes still shut*]. Well?

Peter. It's true she chucked Annerly for another chap. I don't condone an act of that description—except that I knew Annerly, and if ever there was a dull dog . . .

Zoe. Was he duller than Theo?

Peter. Oh, go on with yer! And since then she's been a trifle—flighty—perhaps, now and again [*With a gulp.*] but today she might be your maiden aunt.

Zoe [*dreamily*]. You humbug, Peter!

Peter [*sitting beside her, upon the fauteuil stool*]. Oh, I'm not maintainin' that we men always select our women pals from the right basket. I'm not sayin' that we don't make asses of ourselves occasionally, sometimes from sentiment, sometimes from vanity, sometimes from—various causes. But the same remark applies to you women over your men pals. [*Laying a hand on her arm.*] For instance—[*She opens her eyes.*] —for instance, here you are, throwin' stones at old Theo with regard to Alice Annerly. [*Significantly.*] My dear, there are a few panes o' glass in the house *you* live in, bear in mind.

> *She sits upright, looking at him.*

Zoe. In the house—I . . . ?

Peter [*gravely*]. Mrs. Zoe, what you did when you were under your husband's protection is one thing; what you do now is another bag o' nuts entirely. And a woman situated as you are ought to be careful of retainin' a cub among her intimates.

Zoe. A cub?

Peter. Cub.

Zoe [*apprehensively*]. To whom—are you alluding?

Peter. Lenny Ferris.

Zoe. L—enny?

Peter. It ain't an agreeable job, pitchin' into a fellow you've been on good terms with; but the fact remains—to put it mildly—that Master Lenny's a stoopid, blunderin' cub.

Zoe [*haughtily but palpitatingly*]. He's nothing of the kind. What has he done that you should abuse him?

Peter. It's he who's told you that Theodore was at the Carlton last night, ain't it? [*She drops her eyes.*] Been here this mornin'?

Zoe [*raising her eyes, boldly*]. Yes.

Peter. H'm! The sick rabbit doesn't hide in her burrow from everybody.

Zoe. H-how . . . ?

Peter. I saw your lips make an "L" just now, before you could put the stopper on.

Zoe. Ha, ha! You ought to have been a professional detective.

Peter [*scowling*]. Ferris has kept out of my way lately, or I . . .

Zoe. If he *has* run in here for a moment—to ask whether I'm back—is there anything particularly cubbish in that?

Peter. It wasn't *that* I was referrin' to.

Zoe. N-no?

Peter. I was referrin' to his havin' the damned presumption to dance attendance on you in Italy.

Zoe [*aghast*]. I—Italy?

Peter. He was at Perugia while you were there.

Zoe. Oh—Perugia . . .

Peter [*with a shrug*]. And other places, I assoom.

Zoe [*after a pause, pulling herself together*]. H—ho! [*Mimicking* PETER.] And who supplies the information? [PETER *waves the question from him.*] Lowenstein, by any chance—Claud Lowenstein? [PETER, *looking down his nose, is silent. She rises and walks away from him.*] The hound—the little hound!

Peter. Lowenstein came across you both at some railway station. He arrived at Perugia the day you left.

Zoe [*pacing the room on the right*]. The contemptible little hound!

Peter. He put up at the Brufani too.

Zoe [*stopping in her walk—under her breath*]. Ah!

Peter. Master Lenny might at least have had the common decency to quarter himself at another hotel.

Zoe. The—the Brufani is the most comfortable—the . . . [*A pause.*] I—I suppose it *was* thoughtless of Lenny.

Peter [*quietly*]. Cub!

Zoe [*approaching* PETER]. Does—Theodore—know?

Peter [*nodding*]. Lowenstein went to him with it.

Zoe. Ha, ha! A busy gentleman—Claudy Lowenstein! [*Falteringly.*] It—it was all my fault, Peter. If—if anybody's to blame, I am. I—I wrote to the boy from Florence—complaining of feeling lonely. . . .

Peter. That doesn't excuse him.

Zoe [*touching* PETER's *shoulder with the tips of her fingers*]. What—what does Theodore . . . ?

Peter. He's savage.

Zoe. Savage?

Peter [*rising*]. He'd like to punch Ferris' head—as I should.

Zoe [*in a low voice*]. Savage! [*Slowly.*] He—he's jealous, then? [*A shrug from* PETER. *Her eyes light up.*] Jealous! [*A pause.*] Peter—no man's jealous over a woman—unless he—unless he cares for her! [*Plucking at his sleeve.*] Peter!

Peter. You've heard me say old Theo's miserable—desperately wretched.

Zoe. He—he's grown fond of me again—fond of me!

Peter. My dear, you and he have never left off bein' fond o' one another, actually. As I warned you, you've only been tossin' about, both of you, on a bit o' troubled water.

She stares at him for a moment with an expressionless face and then, as if stupefied, seats herself in the chair on the left of the oblong table.

Peter [*standing before her*]. Well, at any rate, you'll let this Italian business be a lesson to you not to rush at con-

clusions respectin' other people. So, come now; won't you try
to patch it up? I'll bet my noo hat, Theodore'll meet you
half-way. [*Urgently.*] Zoe!

Zoe [*locking and unlocking her fingers again*]. Peter . . .

Peter. Eh?

Zoe. Your Mr. and Mrs. Tom—the world perhaps never
heard of *their* fall-out.

Peter. What o' that?

Zoe. Everybody is aware of the split between me and Theo.

Peter. Everybody! A handful! Besides, nothin' is even a
nine-days' wonder in these times. [*A pause.*] Will you do it?

Zoe [*suddenly, starting up and walking away to the left*].
Oh, no, no, no! I can't—I can't!

Peter [*following her*]. Can't?

Zoe [*helplessly*]. I can't, Peter!

Peter [*taking her by the arms*]. Oh!

Zoe. I—I mean I—I'm sure it wouldn't answer—I'm
sure. . . .

Peter. My dear girl . . .

Zoe [*piteously*]. Ah, don't—don't! [*Escaping from him and
crossing to the right.*] Oh, leave me alone!

WARREN *enters at the glazed door.*

Warren [*to* ZOE]. Miss Pierpoint is downstairs, ma'am.

Zoe [*seizing upon the interruption*]. Ah, yes!

Warren. I'm to give you her love, ma'am, and if it isn't
convenient for you to see her . . .

Zoe. It is—it *is*—quite convenient—quite. [WARREN *withdraws, closing the door.*] I'm awfully sorry, my dear Peter,
but this child wants to consult me about something—something important. [*Giving him her hands.*] I must kick you out.
You don't feel hurt, do you?

Peter [*ruefully*]. Confound Miss Pierpoint! Zoe . . .

Zoe. What?

Peter. You'll think it over?

Zoe [*putting her hand to his lips*]. Ah!

Peter [*holding her hand*]. No, no. Think it over. Ask me
to dine with you one night next week.

Zoe. Monday—Tuesday . . . ?

Peter. Monday.

Zoe [*artfully*]. Ah, but I shall lay in a chaperon for the
occasion.

Peter. Rats! How can I talk to you before a chaperon?

Zoe. Ha, ha, ha, ha! [*She runs to the glazed door, opens it,
and, going into the corridor, calls loudly and excitedly.*]

Ethel—Ethel—Ethel! [ETHEL *appears in the corridor and* ZOE *embraces her with an excess of warmth.*] My dear Ethel! My dear child! [*They kiss.*] What ages since we've seen each other! [*Bringing* ETHEL *into the room.*] You know Mr. Mottram?

Ethel [*going to* PETER]. Oh, yes.

Peter [*shaking hands with her*]. How d'ye do, Miss Pierpoint—and *au revoir*.

Ethel [*as he moves toward the glazed door*]. I'm not driving you away?

Peter. I forgive you. [*He rejoins* ZOE, *who is near the door.* ETHEL *lays her sunshade upon the writing table.*]

Zoe [*to* PETER]. Monday night?

Peter. Monday night.

Zoe. Half-past eight.

Peter [*at the door, dropping his voice*]. A chaperon?

Zoe [*mockingly*]. The proprieties!

Peter. You cat! [*He goes.*]

Zoe [*closing the door*]. Ha, ha! [*She leans wearily against the door for a moment and again puts back her hair from her brow. Her manner now becomes strained, artificial, distrait. She advances to* ETHEL.] Now, then! [ETHEL *turns to her.*] Let me have a good squint at you. How's your dear mother?

Ethel [*who is pale and sad-looking*]. Mother's flourishing. [*Leaving the writing table.*] You're not angry with me for rushing you at this hour?

Zoe. Isn't this our old hour for a chat?

Ethel. We were at Madame Levine's yesterday—Mother and I—ordering frocks, and Camille, the skirt-maker, told us you were back. Zoe, how unkind you've been!

Zoe. Am I in your bad books?

Ethel. Why have you treated us so horridly?

Zoe. Well, my dear child, the fact is—the fact is it suddenly dawned on me that perhaps your mother mightn't consider me any longer a suitable pal for her daughter.

Ethel [*protestingly*]. Oh!

Zoe. Heaps of folks, you know, haven't much use for single married women.

Ethel. But we both showed you that our sympathies were on your side!

Zoe. Yes, we often sympathize with people we wouldn't touch with the end of a wet umbrella.

Ethel [*coming close to* ZOE]. So that's the reason you left off answering my letters!

Zoe. C-certainly.

Ethel. And why we hear of your return through fat old Camille! [*Fingering a jewel at* ZOE'S *neck.*] You've had a pleasant time abroad?

Zoe [*taking* ETHEL'S *face between her hands, abruptly.*] How thin your face is, Ethel!

Ethel [*gazing at* ZOE]. Your cheeks are not as round as they were.

Zoe [*leading* ETHEL *to the settee on the right*]. I caught a rotten chill on board the boat and have been beastly seedy. [*Putting* ETHEL *on the settee.*] What's wrong with you? That's a dreary note I've had from you this morning.

Ethel [*tracing a pattern on the floor with the point of her shoe*]. Now I'm with you, I—I can't. . . .

Zoe [*looking down upon her*]. You want advice, you say.

Ethel [*tremulously*]. Yes.

Zoe. Or a good shaking.

Ethel. I—I suppose I ought to be ashamed of myself for being so, but I—I'm very unhappy, Zoe.

Zoe. Unhappy?

Ethel. It's no use my attempting to talk to Mother. Mother's a person who prides herself on her levelheadedness. Anybody with a fixed income and a poor circulation can be levelheaded! It only means you're fishlike. But you—you're warm-blooded and human. . . .

Zoe. Well?

Ethel. Z-Zoe . . .

Zoe. Yes?

Ethel [*her eyes on the ground*]. Did you ever suspect that there was anything between Mr. Ferris and me?

Zoe [*calmly, steadying herself*]. Mr. Ferris—and you?

Ethel. An attachment.

Zoe [*with affected astonishment*]. My dear child!

Ethel [*looking up*]. Oh, don't keep on calling me "child"! I'm nearly six-and-twenty. [*Taking* ZOE'S *hands.*] Didn't you ever guess?

Zoe. He—he always seemed delighted to meet you here.

Ethel. He's one of your "boys"—hasn't he ever talked to you about me?

Zoe. Of course, frequently.

Ethel. Never as if he were—in love with me?

Zoe [*withdrawing her hands*]. I—I can't say that it—struck me. . . .

Ethel [*dejectedly*]. You didn't know, perhaps, that at the beginning of the year—before you went away—he was a great deal in Sloane Street?

Zoe. Why, yes, he used to have tea with you and your mother sometimes, didn't he? [*Turning from* ETHEL.] How did I hear that?

Ethel [*hanging her head*]. Very often he came early in the afternoon—by arrangement with me—while Mother was resting.

Zoe [*with a hard laugh*]. Ha, ha! Ethel!

Ethel. Yes, worthy of a vulgar shopgirl, wasn't it?

Zoe [*sitting in the chair opposite* ETHEL]. He—he came early in the afternoon . . . ?

Ethel. And we sat together, in the firelight. I'm sure he loved me, Zoe—then.

Zoe [*breathing heavily*]. And—and *you* . . . ?

Ethel [*her elbows on her knees, hiding her face in her hands*]. Oh, I'm a fool—an awful fool!

Zoe [*after a silence*]. Did he ever—hint—at marriage? [ETHEL *nods, without uncovering her face.*] He did!

Ethel [*raising her head*]. Well, we got as far as agreeing that a small house in the country, near his aunt, would be an ideal state of existence. [*Mirthlessly.*] Ha, ha, ha! And there matters broke off.

Zoe. What—what?

Ethel. All of a sudden there was a change—a change in his manner toward me. He still called on us, but not so regularly; and by degrees his visits—ceased altogether. [*She passes her hand across her eyes angrily and, stamping her foot, rises and moves to the other side of the room.*] The last time I spoke to him was one morning in the Row. Mother and I were walking and we came face to face with him. That was at the end of February. He was out of sorts, he said, and was going into Devonshire. I presume he went. [*Turning to* ZOE *who, with parted lips, is staring guiltily at the carpet.*] He's in London now, though. I saw him about a fortnight ago, at the opera. I was with the Ormerods, in their box; he was in the stalls. [*Touching* ZOE's *shoulder.*] Zoe . . .

Zoe. Yes?

Ethel. He's so altered.

Zoe. Altered?

Ethel. In his appearance. You recollect how boyish and fresh-looking he was?

Zoe. Y-Yes.

Ethel. All that's gone. He's become—oh, but I dare say you've seen him since you've been home?

Zoe. J-just for a minute or two.

Ethel. You must have noticed . . . ?

Zoe. N-now you mention it. . . .

Ethel. I watched him through the opera glass several times during the evening. [*Simply.*] He looks like a lost soul.

Zoe. I—I've never—ha, ha!—I never made the acquaintance of a lost—ha, ha! . . . .

Ethel [*after a pause*]. Zoe, do you think anything has happened to Lenny Ferris?

Zoe. H-happened?

Ethel. Anything bad.

Zoe. Bad?

Ethel. Men's lives are constantly being wrecked by racing, or cards, or. . . . [*Half turning from* ZOE.] Oh, I oughtn't to know about such things, but one doesn't live in the dark— he may have got mixed up with some woman of the wrong sort, mayn't he?

Zoe [*rising quickly and walking away to the left*]. I—I really can't discuss topics of that kind with you, Ethel.

Ethel [*wistfully*]. No; but if he *is* in any scrape—any entanglement—and one could help him . . .

Zoe [*at the writing table, taking up a bottle of salts— faintly*]. Help him?

Ethel. Save him!

Zoe [*sniffing the salts*]. How—how romantic you are!

Ethel. Am I! [*Her elbows on the back of the armchair by the oblong table, timidly.*] Zoe, would it be possible—in your opinion—would it be possible for me to—to see him?

Zoe [*sitting in the chair at the writing table*]. See Mr. Ferris?

Ethel [*plucking at the cover of the chair on which she is leaning*]. Here—in your house—or elsewhere—see him and offer him my friendship—a sister's friendship? *You* could manage it.

Zoe. My—my dear!

Ethel. Oh, yes, I'm lacking in dignity, aren't I—and self-respect! [*Coming forward.*] I've told myself that a thousand times. [*Warmly.*] But there are quite enough dignified people in the world without me; and if I could influence Lenny, any one might have my dignity for twopence.

Zoe. Influence him?

Ethel. For his good. Oh, I don't want to boast, but I'm a straight, clean girl; and it may be that, at this particular moment of his life, the more he sees of women like you and me the better. However, if you tell me the idea's improper, I'll accept it from you. [*Approaching* ZOE.] I'll take anything from you. [*Appealingly.*] But don't tell me that, if you can avoid it. Give me the opportunity, if you can, of showing him that I'm different from most girls—that I'm above petty, resentful feelings. [*Bending over* ZOE.] Zoe . . .

LENA *enters at the further door on the right, carrying a silver salver on which are a dose of medicine in a medicine glass and a dish of sweetmeats.*

Lena. Your med'cine! [*Closing the door.*] Good morning, Miss Pierpoint.

Ethel. Ah, Lena!

Zoe [*to* ETHEL, *rising hastily*]. Excuse me. . . .

LENA *advances and* ZOE *goes to her and, with a shaking hand, drinks the medicine.*

Lena [*to* ZOE]. Good gracious, how queer you look! [*To* ETHEL.] She's doing too much today, Miss Pierpoint. [*Going to* ETHEL.] Doctor Rashleigh says she's frightfully below par.

Ethel [*picking up her sunshade*]. What a shame of me! [*Running to* ZOE.] I won't stay another minute.

Zoe [*sitting on the settee on the right*]. I *am* a little fatigued.

Ethel. I ought to have seen it.

Zoe. I—I'll write to you. [*They kiss.*] My love to your mother.

Ethel. And when you are well enough . . . ?

Zoe. I'll call upon her.

Ethel [*to* LENA, *who precedes her into the corridor*]. No, no; stop with Mrs. Blundell. I'm so sorry, Lena. . . .

LENA *and* ETHEL *talk together for a little while in undertones; then the girl disappears.* LENA *returns.*

Lena [*shutting the door*]. Silly chatterbox! [*Finding* ZOE *lying at full length upon the settee, her head buried in a pillow.*] Why do you tire yourself like this? Shall I fetch you some brandy?

Zoe. No.

Lena [*lowering her voice*]. He's in the house again.

Zoe. Who?

Lena. Mr. Ferris.

Zoe [*raising herself*]. Mr. Ferris!

Lena [*with a jerk of her head in the direction of the next room*]. In there. [ZOE *sits upright.*] Warren's making himself beautiful and Clara answered the door. She thought you were by yourself and let him come up. [ZOE *gets to her feet.*] I was just bringing you your med'cine and met him. [ZOE *goes to the writing table, takes up the hand mirror, and puts her hair in order.*] Lucky I'd heard that Miss Pierpoint was here; he didn't want to see her! Another second . . . !

Zoe. That'll do. [*Calmly.*] Take care I'm not interrupted again.

Lena. Ah, now! Mayn't I get rid of him?

Zoe. No. [*Turning.*] Run away, please.

Lena. Oh, very good. [*Picking up the salver which she has placed upon a piece of furniture near the glazed door.*] You'll do exactly as you choose. [*In the corridor.*] I declare I'd rather look after a pack of unruly children any day in the week. . . .

She closes the door. ZOE *glances over her shoulder, to assure herself that the woman has left the room, and then, with a fierce light in her eyes, goes to the nearest door on the right and throws it open.*

Zoe [*in a hard voice, speaking into the adjoining room*]. I'm alone. [*She moves from the door as* LEONARD, *still carrying his hat and cane, enters.*]

Leonard. By George, that was a narrow squeak! [*Closing the door.*] Whatever possessed you to be at home to the Pierpoint girl this morning?

Zoe [*coldly*]. I didn't expect you back before lunch.

Leonard [*putting his hat and cane on the chair at the nearer end of the settee on the right*]. I was talking to a man at Victoria Gate and I saw Peter driving away in a taxi. [*Facing her.*] I got sick of the park. [*Seeing that something is amiss.*] Hello! [*A pause.*] Any one been running me down?

She advances to him and, drawing herself to her full height, regards him scornfully.

Zoe [*making a motion with her hands as if she would strike him.*] You—you . . . ! [*Dropping her hands to her side.*] Oh, cruel—cruel—[*Walking away from him.*]—cruel!

Leonard. What's cruel? Who's cruel?

Zoe [*at the further end of the room, on the right*]. Ah—ah . . . !

Leonard [*moving to the left*]. Oh, come! Let's have it out; let's have it out.

Zoe. Sssh! Don't raise your voice here.

Leonard. Somebody's been talking against me. Ethel Pierpoint?

Zoe [*coming to the oblong table*]. You've behaved abominably to this girl.

Leonard. Ho, it *is* Miss Pierpoint!

Zoe. No, she hasn't spoken a word against you. But she's opened her heart to me.

Leonard [*going to* ZOE]. You've known all about me and Ethel.

Zoe. It's a lie. How much have I known? I knew that you were sizing her up, as you expressed it; but I never surmised that you'd as good as proposed marriage to her.

Leonard. I told you months ago—admitted it—that I'd made myself a bit of an idiot over Ethel. I fancied you tumbled to the state o' things.

Zoe. Did you! Why, do you think—maniac as I was when you came through to me to Florence!—do you think I'd have allowed you to remain near for five minutes if I'd known as much as I do now!

Leonard. Look here, Zoe . . .

Zoe. Oh, you're a cruel fellow! You've been cruel to her and cruel to me. I believe you're capable of being cruel to any woman who comes your way. Still, *she's* the fortunate one. Her scratches'll heal; but I [*Sitting at the oblong table and hitting it with her fist.*] I loathe myself more than ever —more than ever!

Leonard [*after a pause*]. Zoe, I wish you'd try to be a little fair to me.

Zoe [*ironically*]. Fair!

Leonard. Perhaps I did go rather further with Ethel Pierpoint than I led you to understand.

Zoe. Oh!

Leonard. I own up. Yes, but what prospect was there, when I was thick with her, of your being free of Blundell? None. And what was I to you? Merely a pal of yours—one of your "tame robins"—one of a dozen; and I'd come to a loose end in my life. It was simply the fact that there *was* no prospect for me with you that drove me to consider whether I hadn't better settle down to a humdrum with a decent girl of the Ethel breed. Otherwise, do you imagine I'd have crossed the street to speak to another woman? [*Leaving* ZOE.] Oh, you might do me common justice! [*Hotly.*] If circumstances *have* made a cad of me, am I *all* black? Can't you find *any* good in me? [*Turning to her.*] What did I tell you at Perugia?

Zoe [*rising*]. Ah, don't . . . !

Leonard. That I'd been in love with you from the day I first met you—from the very moment Mrs. Hope-Cornish introduced me to you at Sandown! Well! Isn't there anything to my credit on that score? Didn't I keep my secret? For four years I kept it; though, with matters as they often were be-

tween you and Blundell, many a man might have thought
you ripe grapes. [*Walking across to the right.*] Only once I
was off my guard with you—when I laid hold of you and
begged you, whatever happened, never to—never to . . .

Zoe [*leaning against the table, her back to him*]. Ha, ha,
ha!

Leonard. Yes, and I meant it; as God hears me, I meant it.
If anybody had told me that afternoon that it was I who—oh,
hang! [*Sitting upon the settee.*] But what I want to impress
upon you is that, if I were quite the low scoundrel you make
me out to be, I shouldn't have gone through what I *have*
gone through these past four years and more. Great Scot, it's
been nothing but hell—hot hell—all the time! Four whole
years of pretending I was just an ordinary friend of yours
—hell! Four years of reasoning with myself—preaching to
myself—hell! That awful month after Blundell left you—
when you'd gone to Italy and I was in London—worse than
hell! My chase after you—our little tour together—my struggle even then to play the correct game—and I *did* struggle—
hell! And since then—hell! [*His elbows on his knees, digging
his knuckles into his forehead.*] Hell all the time! Hell all the
time!

*There is a silence, and then, with a look of settled determina-
tion, she comes to him slowly and lays her hands upon his
head.*

Zoe. Poor boy! I'm sorry I blackguarded you. [*Sitting in
the chair opposite to him and speaking in a steady, level
voice.*] Len . . .

Leonard. Eh?

Zoe. Let's part.

Leonard [*raising his head*]. Part?

Zoe. Say good-by to each other. [*Meeting his eyes.*] Go
back to that girl.

Leonard. To Ethel!

Zoe. Take up with her again.

Leonard. Oh, stop it, Zo.

Zoe. She's devoted to you; and she's sound right through,
if ever a girl was. She's one of the best, Len.

Leonard. Suppose she *is* . . .

Zoe. Be careful that she doesn't guess I've given her away.
[*He rises impatiently. She rises with him and holds him by
the lapels of his jacket.*] Tell her—she's sure to ask you—tell
her that you haven't seen me since last Monday, nor had a
line from me. Fake up some tale to account for your break-

ing off with her—you were in doubt whether you'd coin enough to marry on . . .

Leonard [*who has become thoughtful*]. Zoe . . .

Zoe. Yes?

Leonard [*looking her full in the face*]. Are you giving me the boot?

Zoe [*releasing him and returning his gaze firmly*]. Yes; I am.

Leonard [*after a pause*]. Oh? [*Another pause.*] What's your motive?

Zoe. Motive?

Leonard. What's behind all this?

Zoe [*simply.*] I want you to be happy, Len—really and truly happy. I believe you'd stand a jolly good chance of being so with Ethel Pierpoint; never with me.

Leonard. And *you?*

Zoe. I?

Leonard. What's to become of *you?* What are your plans for yourself?

Zoe [*avoiding his eyes*]. Oh, don't you—don't you worry about me.

Leonard. Rot!

Zoe [*nervously*]. Perhaps some day—when Theodore's tired of Mrs. Annerly—ha, ha!—stranger things have happened. . . .

Leonard. Rot, I say. [*She retreats a little.*] Do you think you can drum me out like this! [*Following her.*] Have you got some other . . . ? [*He checks himself.*]

Zoe [*confronting him*]. Some other . . . ?

Leonard. Oh, never mind.

Zoe. Out with it!

Leonard. Some other fancy man in tow?

Zoe. Ah! You brute! [*Hitting him in the chest.*] You brute! [*Throwing herself into the armchair near the glazed door.*] You coward! You coward!

There is a pause and then he slouches up to her.

Leonard. I—I beg your pardon. I beg your pardon. [*He sits beside her, upon the fauteuil stool.*] Knock my damned head off. Go on. Knock my damned head off.

Zoe [*panting*]. Well—we won't part—on top of a row. [*Dashing a tear away.*] After all, why *should* you think better of me than that?

Leonard [*penitently*]. Zoe . . .

Zoe. Sssh! Listen. Putting Ethel Pierpoint out of the ques-

tion, do you ever picture to yourself what our married life
would be?

Leonard. What it 'ud be?

Zoe. The marriage of a woman of seven—nearly eight—
and thirty to a man of thirty-two! *I* do. I walk my bedroom
half the night and act it all over to myself. And you've had
the best of me, too; I'm not even a novelty to you. Why, of
course you've realized what you've let yourself in for.

Leonard. I take my oath . . .

Zoe. Sssh! When you're in front of your glass in the morning, what do you see there?

Leonard. See?

Zoe. This girl has noticed the alteration in your looks. She
took stock of you at the opera the other night.

Leonard [*passing his hands over his face consciously*]. Men
can't go to hell, Zo, without getting a bit scorched.

Zoe [*imitating his action*]. No, nor women either. [*Turning
to him.*] But it's only quite lately that you've lost your bloom,
Len.

Leonard. Oh, naturally I've been horribly bothered about
you—about both of us—since . . .

Zoe. Since your trip to Italy? [*He nods.*] Yes, and naturally
you've told yourself, over and over again, the truth—since
your trip to Italy.

Leonard. Truth?

Zoe. The simple truth—that you've got into a mess with a
married woman. . . .

Leonard. I—I . . .

Zoe. And that you must go through with it, at all costs.

Leonard. I swear to you, Zoe . . .

Zoe [*touching his hand*]. Oh, my dear boy, you haven't
perhaps *said* these things to yourself, in so many words, but
they're at the back of your brain just the same. [*She rises
and crosses to the fireplace and rings three times.*]

Leonard [*rising*]. What—what are you doing?

Zoe. Ringing for Lena, to tell her I'm not lunching downstairs.

Leonard. By God, Zoe . . . !

Zoe [*imperiously*]. Be quiet!

Leonard [*shaking his fist at her*]. You dare treat me in this
way! You dare!

Zoe [*advancing*]. Ah, I'm only hurting your pride a little;
I'm only mortifying your vanity. You'll get over that in
twenty-four hours.

Leonard. Do you know what you *are;* do you know what
you make yourself by this!

Zoe. Yes, what you made of me at Perugia, and at Siena, and at . . . ! [*Suddenly, clinging to him.*] Lenny—Lenny— kiss me . . . !

Leonard [*pushing her from him*]. Not I.

Zoe. Ah, yes. Don't let's part enemies. It's good-by. Lenny!

Leonard. No.

Zoe [*struggling with him entreatingly*]. Quick! It's for the last time. You'll never be alone with me again. [*Her arms tightly around him.*] It's for the last time. [*Kissing him passionately.*] Good luck to you! Good luck to you! Good luck to you! [*She leaves him and sits at the writing table where she makes a pretense of busying herself with her papers.*]

Leonard [*glancing expectantly at the glazed door—between his teeth*]. You—you . . . !

Presently he goes to the chair on the right and snatches up his hat and cane. LENA *enters at the glazed door.*

Lena [*to* ZOE]. Is it me you've rung for?

Zoe. Yes. [*Sharply.*] Wait.

There is a pause. Struck by ZOE'S *tone, and the attitude of the pair,* LENA *looks inquisitively at* LEONARD *and* ZOE *out of the corners of her eyes, as if she guesses there has been a quarrel.* LEONARD *moves toward the door.*

Leonard [*to* ZOE]. Good morning.

Zoe. Good morning.

Leonard [*to* LENA, *as he passes her*]. Good morning.

Lena. Good morning.

He departs and LENA *quietly closes the door.*

Zoe [*rising*]. Lena . . .

Lena. Yes?

Zoe [*walking across to the settee on the right*]. I'm not coming down to the dining room. [*Sitting, feebly.*] Let me have a snack upstairs.

Lena. Very well.

Zoe. That's all.

LENA *withdraws, almost on tiptoe, and* ZOE *instantly produces her handkerchief and cries into it softly. Then she gets to her feet and searches for the cigarette box. Still shaken by little sobs, she puts a cigarette between her lips and, as she does so, the expression of her face changes and her body stiffens.*

Zoe [*under her breath*]. Oh! [*After a moment's resolu-*

tion, she hurriedly dries her eyes and, going to the glazed door, opens it, and calls.] Lena—Lena!

Lena [*in the distance*]. Yes?

ZOE *returns to the oblong table and is lighting her cigarette when* LENA *reappears.*

Zoe. Lena . . .

Lena. Well?

Zoe. I'll dress directly after lunch.

Lena [*coming to her, surprised*]. Dress?

Zoe. Yes; I'm going out this afternoon.

Lena. Going out! Why, you must be crazy . . . !

ACT THREE

A fine, spacious room, richly furnished and decorated. In the center of the wall at the back is the fireplace, and on the left of the fireplace is a door which when open reveals part of a dining room. In the right-hand wall there is a bay window hung with lace and other curtains. Facing the window, in the wall on the left, is a double door opening into the room from a corridor.

On either side of the fireplace there is an armchair, and between the fireplace and the dining-room door stands a small table on which are a decanter of whisky, a syphon of soda water, and two or three tumblers. A grand piano and a music stool are in the right-hand corner of the room, and on the left of the piano is a settee. Some photographs are on the top of the piano. On the other side of the room there is a second settee with a table at the nearer end of it. An armchair stands by this table, another at the farther end of the settee. In the bay window there is a writing table with a writing chair before it, and on the writing table is a telephone instrument. Other articles of furniture, some pieces of sculpture, and some handsome lamps on pedestal, fill spaces not provided for in this description.

A scarf of mousseline de soie *and a pair of white gloves lie on the chair on the right of the fireplace.*

The fireless grate is hidden by a screen and, through the lace curtains, which are drawn over the window, a fierce sunlight is seen.

The door at the back is slightly ajar.

The telephone bell rings and presently THEODORE BLUNDELL *enters at the door at the back, and goes to the writing table. His step has become heavier, his shoulders are somewhat bent, and he looks a "bad color."*

THEODORE [*at the telephone*]. Halloo! . . . Yes? . . . I *am* Mr. Blundell. . . . Oh, is that you, Peter? . . . What? . . . Want to see me? . . . Anything wrong? . . . Where are you? . . . Where? . . . Café Royal? . . . Come along to me now, then? . . . Oh, I say! . . . Are you there? . . . [*Dropping his voice.*] I say! Mrs. A. is lunching with me. . . . Mrs. A. —Alice. . . . No, but I thought I'd tell you. . . . Good-by.

He is about to return to the dining room when MRS. AN-NERLY *appears in the doorway at the back. She is a pretty, charmingly dressed creature with classical, immobile features and a simple, virginal air.*

Mrs. Annerly [*advancing*]. I've told Cole we'll have coffee in this room. [*He nods and sits moodily upon the settee on the right. Resting her elbows on the back of the armchair at the further end of the settee on the left, she surveys her face in a tiny mirror which she carries, with some other trinkets, attached to a chain.*] Who's that you were talking to on the phone, boy, dear?

Theodore [*who is smoking a big cigar*]. Mottram.

Mrs Annerly. What's *he* want?

Theodore. Wants to see me about something.

Mrs. Annerly. Business?

Theodore. Dun'no.

Mrs. Annerly [*sweetly*]. He doesn't like poor little me.

Theodore [*indifferently*]. Doesn't he?

Mrs. Annerly. You know he doesn't. [*Arranging a curl.*] That's why you gave him the tip that I'm lunching here.

Theodore. Ho! Listeners—et cetera.

Mrs. Annerly. I couldn't help hearing you; positively I couldn't. [*Examining her teeth in the mirror.*] He's one of your wife's tame cats, isn't he?

Theodore. He's a friend of hers—yes.

Mrs. Annerly. *Just* a friend, and nothing else.

Theodore [*angrily*]. Now, look here, Alice!

COLE, *a manservant, enters from the dining room with the coffee and liqueurs.* MRS. ANNERLY *takes a cup of coffee.*

Cole [*to* MRS. ANNERLY]. Brandy—Kümmel, ma'am?

Mrs. Annerly. No, thanks.

Theodore [*to* COLE, *who comes to him with the tray—irritably*]. Leave it. [*Cole places the tray on the top of the piano and is returning to the dining room.*] Cole . . .

Cole. Yessir?

Theodore. I'm expecting Mr. Mottram.

Cole. Very good, sir.

The man withdraws, closing the door. THEODORE *rises and pours some brandy into a large liqueur glass.*]

Mrs. Annerly [*who has seated herself upon the settee on the left*]. What's the matter with you today, boy, dear? You're as cross as two sticks.

Theodore. Liver.

Mrs. Annerly [*sipping her coffee*]. I don't wonder.

Theodore. Why?

Mrs. Annerly. You're getting rather too fond of—[*Pointing to the brandy.*]—h'm, h'm.

Theodore [*bluntly*]. It's false.

Mrs. Annerly [*with undisturbed complacency*]. I've seen so much of that sort o' thing in my time. [*He makes a movement, as if to put down his glass without drinking.*] Still, I must say you've every excuse.

Theodore. Alice . . .

Mrs. Annerly. What?

He gulps his brandy, puts the empty glass on the tray, and comes to her.]

Theodore [*standing before her*]. Alice, will you oblige me by refraining from making any allusion to my wife, direct or indirect, in the future? It annoys me.

Mrs. Annerly. Everything annoys you this afternoon.

Theodore. You were at it last night, at the Carlton. And today, during lunch . . .

Mrs. Annerly [*in an injured tone*]. It was you who told me that that little Jew chap had met her careering about Italy with young what's-his-name. [*He sits in the armchair at the farther end of the settee and leans his head on his hand.*] Ah, but that was in your loving days—when you used to confide in me.

Theodore. I was in a rage and said a great deal more than I thought.

Mrs. Annerly. If you did, you needn't jump on me for trying to feel interested in you and your affairs.

Theodore [*facing her*]. At any rate, understand me clearly,

Alice—and then drop the subject. [*Shortly.*] Mrs. Blundell and I are separated; she's gone one way, I another. There were faults on both sides, as usual, but I was mainly to blame. There's the thing in a nutshell.

Mrs. Annerly. This isn't in the least your old story.

Theodore. Never mind my old story. [*Extending a forefinger.*] *You* forget the old story, my girl, if you wish our acquaintance to continue—d'ye hear?

Mrs. Annerly [*shaking herself*]. You're a nasty savage.

Theodore. As for that interfering cad, Lowenstein, it unfortunately happens that one of Mrs. Blundell's characteristics is a habit of disregarding *les convenances*—a habit which I didn't go the right way to check. It's probable that, before she's done, she won't leave herself with as much reputation as 'ud cover a sixpence. She's impulsive, reckless, a fool—but she's no worse. [*Eying the stump of his cigar fiercely.*] My wife's no worse. So, hands off, if you please, in my presence. Whatever reports are circulated to her discredit, the man who speaks against her in my hearing is kicked for his pains; and the woman who does so, if she's under my roof, gets taken by the shoulders and shown the mat. [*Looking at her.*] *Comprenez?*

Mrs. Annerly [*pouting*]. I should be a juggins if I didn't. *Parfaitement*—in my very best French.

Theodore [*rising and walking about*]. That's settled, then.

Mrs. Annerly [*after a pause, rising and depositing her cup upon the table on the left—thoughtfully*]. Boy, dear . . .

Theodore [*at the back*]. Hey?

Mrs. Annerly. It was regular cat-and-dog between you two at the end, wasn't it?

Theodore [*breaking out again*]. It's no concern of yours whether it was or was not. I've asked you . . .

Mrs. Annerly [*crossing to the right, with a shrug*]. Oh!

Theodore. Yes, it *was*. [*Half sitting upon the back of the settee on the left.*] I—I tired of her.

Mrs. Annerly [*philosophically*]. Ah, men *do* tire.

Theodore. And she of me. We'd been married close upon fourteen years.

Mrs. Annerly. Oh, well, come; that's a long while.

Theodore [*as much to himself as to her*]. Our wedding day's on the thirtieth of this month. [*Hitting the back of the settee softly with his fist.*] We'd reached a time in our lives when—when we were in mid-Channel . . .

Mrs. Annerly. Mid-Channel?

Theodore [*rising*]. Oh, you don't know anything about that.

*There is a further silence. She sits upon the settee on the
right, watching him as he moves about the room again.*

Mrs. Annerly. Here! [*Beckoning him with a motion of her
head.*] Here! [*He goes to her. She looks up into his face.*]
Why don't you marry *me*, Theo?

Theodore [*staring at her*]. Marry—you?

Mrs. Annerly. You'd find me awfully easy to get on with.

Theodore [*turning from her, quietly*]. Oh!

Mrs. Annerly. Wait; you might listen, anyhow. [*He turns
to her.*] I *am*—awfully easy to get on with. And I'd be as
strict as—as strict as a nun. Honest Injun! I treated Annerly
pretty badly, but that's ancient history. I was only seventeen
when I married Frank—too inexperienced for words. I've
learned a lot since.

Theodore [*bitterly*]. Ha!

Mrs. Annerly. Now, don't be satirical. [*Inviting him to sit
by her side.*] Theo . . . [*He sits beside her.*] I say—bar
chaff—I wish you *would*.

Theodore [*absently*]. What?

Mrs. Annerly. Marry me. Really I do. [*A note of wistfulness in her voice.*] I really do want to re-establish myself.
My life, these past few years, has been frightfully unsatis-
factory.

Theodore [*touching her dress, sympathetically*]. Ah!

Mrs. Annerly. And I'm a lady, remember—giddy as I may
have been. Put me in any society and I'm presentable, as far
as manners go. I'd soon right myself, with your assistance.
[*Slipping her arm through his.*] I suppose, under the circumstances, you couldn't divorce *her*, could you?

Theodore. What d'ye mean?

Mrs. Annerly. Your wife—over that Italian business.

Theodore [*jumping up*]. Damn!

Mrs. Annerly. Oh, I beg your pardon; it slipped out. [*He
walks away to the table at the back and begins to mix himself a whisky and soda.*] I'm dreadfully grieved; gospel, I
am. [*Rising.*] Don't—don't, boy, dear. Do leave that stuff
alone. [*He puts down the decanter and comes to the settee
on the left.*] I can't do more than apologize.

Theodore [*sitting*]. Tsch! Hold your tongue.

Mrs. Annerly [*sitting beside him*]. No, but you could let
her go for *you*, though; *that* could be fixed up. I'd even consent to be dragged into the case myself, if it would help matters forward; and goodness knows I've no ambition to appear
in the divorce court again—I hate the hole. [*Coaxingly.*] You
will consider it, won't you?

Theodore. Consider *what*?

Mrs. Annerly. Marrying me. Just say you'll consider it and I won't tease you any more today. You do owe me something, you know.

Theodore. Owe you . . . ?

Mrs. Annerly. Well, you *have* compromised me by being seen about with me at different places lately; now, haven't you? [THEODORE *throws his head back and laughs boisterously*.] There's nothing to laugh at. Perhaps I haven't a shred of character left, in your estimation!

Theodore. Ho, ho!

Mrs. Annerly [*rising, piqued*]. I presume you think I'm a person who'll accept a dinner at a restaurant from any man who holds up a finger to me!

Theodore. Why, my dear girl, you were always bothering me to take you to the cook shops.

Mrs. Annerly. Bothering! [*Going to the chair on the right of the fireplace and gathering up her scarf*.] Oh, you're too rude!

Theodore. I was perfectly content with our quiet little means here or in Egerton Crescent.

Mrs. Annerly. Yes, and to bore me to tears!

Theodore. Bore . . . ?

Mrs. Annerly [*winding her scarf around her shoulders*.] Bore, bore, bore!

Theodore [*scowling*]. Oh, I—I bored you, did I?

Mrs. Annerly. Talking to me, as you used to, like a sentimental young fellow of five-and-twenty! Ridiculous! [*Picking up her gloves*.] I want a taxicab.

Theodore [*rising*]. Stop—stop . . .

Mrs. Annerly. I've had quite sufficient of you for today.

Theodore [*with a set jaw*]. I'm glad you've brought matters to a head, Ally. I've something to propose to you.

Mrs. Annerly [*pulling on a glove*]. I've no desire to hear it.

Theodore. Something that's been on my mind for—oh, a month or more.

Mrs. Annerly. You can keep it to yourself. I'm not accustomed to being jeered at.

Theodore [*slowly walking over to the right*]. I'm sorry if I've hurt your feelings . . .

Mrs. Annerly. It's the first time I've ever made advances to a man, and I assure you it'll be the last.

Theodore. Ally . . .

Mrs. Annerly [*moving toward the double door*]. Cole will get me a taxi.

Theodore [*authoritatively*]. Come here; come here; come here.

Mrs. Annerly [*halting behind the settee on the left, with a twist of her body*]. I shall not.

Theodore [*snapping his finger and thumb*]. Ally—[*She approaches him with assumed reluctance.*]—Ally—[*Deliberately.*] What'll you take?

Mrs. Annerly [*elevating her brows*]. Take?

Theodore. To put an end to this.

Mrs. Annerly. An end!

Theodore. To end your boredom—and mine; terminate our —friendship.

Mrs. Annerly [*uncomfortably*]. Oh, you—you needn't cut up as rough as all this.

Theodore. Ah, no, no, no; I'm not angry. I'm in earnest, though. Come! What'll satisfy you? [*She curls her lip fretfully.*] A man of my years deserves to pay heavily at this game. What'll make you easy and comfortable for a bit? I'll be liberal with you, my dear, and—[*Offering his hand.*]— shake hands—[*She turns her shoulder to him.*]—shake hands —[*She gives him her hand sulkily.*]—and I—I'll ask you to forgive me . . .

Mrs. Annerly [*withdrawing her hand*]. Oh, for goodness' sake, don't let's have any more of *that*. [*Contemptuously.*] You elderlies always wind up in the same way.

He seats himself at the writing table and, unlocking a drawer, produces his checkbook.

Theodore. Would a couple of thousand be of any service to you?

Mrs. Annerly [*opening her eyes widely*]. A couple of . . . !

Theodore [*preparing to write*]. I mean it.

Mrs. Annerly [*breathlessly*]. You don't! [*He writes.*] Why, of course it would. [*Melting completely.*] Oh, but it's too much; it is positively. *I couldn't.* And I've had such a lot out of you already. You *are* generous. [*Behind his chair.*] Fancy my being huffy with you just now! [*Bending over him and arresting his pen.*] Boy, dear . . .

Theodore. Hey?

Mrs. Annerly [*in a whisper*]. Make it—three—will you? [*He looks at her over his shoulder with a cynical smile. She retreats.*] Oh, well! One isn't young and attractive forever, you know.

He finishes writing the check and, having locked up his checkbook methodically, rises and comes to her.

Theodore [*giving her the check*]. There you are.

Mrs. Annerly [*examining it*]. You—you've split the difference! You *are* kind. I didn't expect it in the least. [*Folding the check neatly and finding a place for it in her bosom.*] I *am* ashamed of myself for hinting so broadly. Thanks, a hundred times. [*Blinking at him.*] Shan't I miss you!

COLE *enters at the double door followed by* PETER.

Cole. Mr. Mottram.

Theodore [*greeting* PETER *at the fireplace as* COLE *retires*]. Hello!

Peter. Hello! [*Bowing to* MRS. ANNERLY.] How d'ye do?

Mrs. Annerly [*who has moved over to the right—distantly*]. How do you do?

Theodore [*to* MRS. ANNERLY]. By-the-bye, did you say you want a taxicab?

Mrs. Annerly. If I'm not troubling you.

THEODORE *goes out at the double door, closing it upon* PETER *and* MRS. ANNERLY. *There is a pause,* MRS. ANNERLY, *pulling on her second glove, looks out of the window;* PETER *whistles silently.*

Peter [*after a while*]. Fine afternoon.

Mrs. Annerly. Delightful. [*After another pause, turning to him.*] Er—h'm—how do you think he's looking?

Peter. Blundell? Seen him looking better.

Mrs. Annerly [*with a sigh*]. Ah! [*In a mincing voice, approaching* PETER.] Mr. Mottram, will you excuse me for offering a suggestion?

Peter [*politely*]. Fire away.

Mrs. Annerly [*sweetly*]. Why don't you use your endeavors to bring Blundell and his wife together again?

Peter [*staring at her*]. Eh?

Mrs. Annerly. It would be *such* a good thing, wouldn't it?

Peter. I agree with you; it would indeed.

Mrs. Annerly. I've done all *I* can to persuade him. [PETER's *eyes open wider and wider. She busies herself daintily with her glove.*] And now, as he and I are breaking off with one another . . .

Peter [*quickly*]. I beg pardon?

Mrs. Annerly. Perhaps *you'll* take on the job—see what *you* can do.

Peter. Breaking off . . . ?

Mrs. Annerly [*loftily*]. Yes; I can't stand the annoyance any longer.

Peter. Annoyance?

Mrs. Annerly. People are so spiteful. It's shocking—the ill-natured construction they put upon the most harmless little friendly acts! I admit I'm rather a careless woman—haven't I suffered from it!

Peter [*delicately*]. Then, do I happen—may I ask—to be assistin' at the grand finale?

Mrs. Annerly. Certainly . . . [*With sudden mistrust.*] Don't you try to pull my leg, Mr. Mottram, please.

She draws her skirt aside and passes him haughtily as THEODORE *returns. Then she goes out, followed by* THEODORE, *who closes the door; whereupon* PETER *skips to the piano, seats himself at it, and strikes up a lively air. Presently* THEODORE *reappears, shuts the door again, and resumes mixing his whisky and soda.*

Theodore. Ouf! [PETER *takes his hands from the keyboard.*] That's over.

Peter [*innocently*]. Over?

Theodore. You've seen the last of that lady, as far as I'm concerned. [*He comes forward, carrying his tumbler, as* PETER *rises.*] What d'ye think? [*Grinning.*] She's been at me to marry her.

Peter [*startled*]. Not really!

Theodore. To get rid of—present ties, and marry her.

Peter. When—when did she . . . ?

Theodore. Just now—five minutes ago. [*Struck by an odd expression on* PETER'S *face.*] Why, has she been saying anything . . . ?

Peter [*soberly*]. No, no; not a word.

Theodore. Poor little devil! [*He sits upon the settee on the left and drinks.*] Poor—silly—little devil!

Peter [*coming to him*]. And so you took the opportunity of—er . . . ? [THEODORE *nods.*] Just so.

Theodore. Ha! I expect I shall hear from her from time to time.

Peter. Till the end o' your life. [*Another nod from* THEODORE.] Or hers. And the nearer the end the oftener you'll hear.

Theodore. Well, she shall have a trifle whenever she wants it. [*Looking at* PETER.] That's the least we can do, ol' man.

Peter. Decidedly. That's the least we can do.

Theodore [*emptying his tumbler and jumping up*]. Ugh! [*Placing the glass upon the table at the end of the settee.*] I'll burn some pastilles here later on. [*Confronting* PETER.] Yes, you can have your crow; you're entitled to it.

Peter. Crow?

Theodore. Your crow over me. Everything's turned out as you predicted.

Peter [*demurely*]. Did *I* . . . ?

Theodore. You know you did. "It's when the sun's working round to the west"—I often recall your damned words . . .

Peter. Ah, that day . . .

Theodore. The day I left Lancaster Gate. "It's when men are where we are now"—you remember?—"It's when men are where we are now that they're most liable to fall into mischief." [*Walking away.*] God! the idiot I've made of myself! [*He goes to the fireplace and leans upon the mantelpiece.*]

Peter [*quietly*]. Theo . . .

Theodore. H'm?

Peter [*moving to the settee on the left*]. Talkin' of Lancaster Gate—I've got a bit o' noos for you. [*Sitting upon the settee.*] She's home. [*There is no response from* THEODORE.] Zoe I'm speakin' of. She's home.

Theodore [*leaving the fireplace*]. Thank'ee; I know.

Peter. You know?

Theodore. I was there on Monday.

Peter [*surprised*]. There?

Theodore. Passing the house.

Peter. Signs o' life in the winders?

Theodore [*nodding*]. H'm. [*Coming forward.*] You've seen her?

Peter. This mornin'.

Theodore [*simply*]. *I* was there again this morning.

Peter. Passin' the house?

Theodore [*nodding*]. H'm.

Peter. You seem to take a great deal of exercise in that locality.

Theodore [*forcing a laugh*]. Ha, ha! [*Drearily.*] Well, one had good times there as well as bad; and when one views it all from a distance . . .

Peter. The good times stand out?

Without replying, THEODORE *turns from* PETER *and sits upon the settee on the right.*

Theodore [*after a pause*]. How—how did you find her?

Peter. She ain't up to much.

Theodore. What's . . . ?

Peter. Chill.

Theodore. Doctor? [PETER *nods.*] Rashleigh?

Peter. That's the feller. Oh, it's nothin' serious.

Theodore. Chill? Ha! I'll be bound she caught it through

doing something foolish. [*Fidgeting with his hands.*] She has nobody to look after her—nobody to look after her.

Peter. Her maid . . .

Theodore. Lena? Is Lena still with her? [*A nod from* PETER.] I'm glad Lena's still with her. Lena's fond of her. [*Starting up and pacing the room.*] Not that Lena can control her; a maid hasn't any authority. [*Stopping before* PETER.] She isn't *very* poorly?

Peter. No, no. A little pulled down; that's all. And as charmin' as ever. [THEODORE *walks away and, with his hands in his pockets, gazes out of the window.*] She ain't sleepin'; that's the real bother.

Theodore. Not sleeping?

Peter. Walks her room half the night and consooms too many cigarettes.

Theodore. Why?

Peter. I can only give you my impression . . .

Theodore [*impatiently*]. Well?

Peter. My dear chap, d'ye think that *she* don't recollect the happy times as well as the bad 'uns? Ain't *she* viewin' it all from a distance, as you are; [*Rising.*] and don't the good times stand out in *her* mind as they do in yours? [*Approaching* THEODORE.] Theo . . .

Theodore. H'm?

Peter. I had a long confab with her this mornin'.

Theodore. What about?

Peter. The possibility of a—a reconciliation.

There is a pause and then THEODORE *turns to* PETER.

Theodore [*in a husky voice*]. Ho! So that's what you're after, is it?

Peter. Yes; and I'm bent on carryin' it through.

Theodore. You—you meddlesome old buffer!

Peter [*chuckling*]. Ha, ha!

Theodore. How—how did she take it?

Peter. In a way that convinced me you've only to assure her that your old feelin's for her have returned, and in spite of everythin' . . .

Theodore. Everything! Wait till she hears of sweet Alice.

Peter. Wait!

Theodore [*looking at* PETER]. Why, d'ye mean . . . ?

Peter. Oh, yes; it's got to her.

Theodore [*dully*]. Already?

Peter. Jim Mallandain traveled with her from Paris on Sunday.

Theodore. Did *he* . . . ?

MID-CHANNEL 289

Peter. I suppose he thought it 'ud amuse her.

Theodore. The skunk!

Peter. If it hadn't been Jim, it 'ud have been somebody else.

Theodore [*thickly*]. You're right; somebody had to be first.

Peter. However, I did my best for yer.

Theodore. Denied it?

Peter. Warmly. I defended you and the young lady with all the eloquence I could command.

Theodore. Zoe didn't believe you? [*A pause.*] She didn't believe you? [PETER *shrugs his shoulders.*] Of course she didn't. [*Passing* PETER *and walking about the room.*] What did she say? Hey? Oh, I can guess; you needn't tell me. What's everybody saying? Peter, I'd give half as much as I'm worth to wipe the Annerly incident off my slate. I would, on the nail. Just fancy! To reach my age—and to be of decent repute—and then to have your name linked with a brainless, mercenary little trull like Alice Annerly! Ha, ha! Glorious fun for 'em in the city, and at the club! *You* hear it all. Confound you, can't you open your mouth! Ho! *Of course* Zoe sums it all up; she's cute enough when she chooses. [*Sitting upon the settee on the left and mopping his face and throat with his handkerchief.*] How did it end?

Peter. End?

Theodore. Your chat with my missus.

Peter. It ended in my urgin' her to consider the matter— think it over. [*Coming to him.*] I'm dinin' with her next week. [*Sitting in the chair at the further end of the settee.*] If you'll authorize me to open negotiations with her on your behalf . . .

Theodore. I—I approach her!

Peter. Cert'nly.

Theodore [*twisting his handkerchief into a rope*]. No— no . . .

Peter. Why not?

Theodore. A couple o' months back I could have done it. Even as late as a fortnight ago—before I'd given myself away by showing myself in public with Alice—it might have been feasible. [*Between his teeth.*] But now—when I—when I've lost any remnant of claim I may have had—on her respect!

Peter [*in his judicial manner*]. My dear chap, here is a case . . .

Theodore. Hell with you and your case! [*Jumping up and walking away to the right.*] I couldn't screw myself up to it; I—I couldn't humble myself to that extent. [*Moving about.*]

Ho! How she'd grin! She's got a cruel sense o' humor, Peter—or had once. You see, I always posed to her as being a *strong*, rather cold-blooded man . . .

Peter. A favorite pose, that, of husbands.

Theodore. It was more than a pose—I thought I *was* a strong man. And then—to crawl back to her—all over mud! [*He halts in the middle of the room and, with a shaky hand, produces his cigar case from his pocket and takes out a cigar.*]

Peter. I was about to remark, when you chipped in with your usual politeness—I was about to remark that this is a case where *two* persons have behaved more or less stoopidly.

Theodore. Two . . . ?

Peter. You more, she less.

Theodore [*his brow darkening*]. You—you're referring to . . . ?

Peter. Er—Mrs. Zoe . . .

Theodore [*cutting his cigar viciously*]. With—Ferris.

Peter. Yes; and I think that the friend of both parties— the individual on whose shoulders the task of adjustin' matters would fall—[*Rising.*]—I think that that friend might manage to impose a condition which 'ud be greatly to your advantage.

Theodore. Condition?

Peter. No imputations to be made on either side.

Theodore [*broodingly*]. No—imputations . . . ?

Peter. Each party acceptin' the statement of the other party, and promisin' not to rake up anythin' that's occurred durin' the past four months.

Theodore. I—I understand.

Peter. It 'ud help to save your face for the moment, and the healin' hand of time might be trusted to do the rest.

Theodore [*quietly*]. Peter . . .

Peter. Hello!

Theodore. When I was at the house on Monday—my wife's house—half-past eleven in the morning . . .

Peter. Well?

Theodore. There was a yellow car at the door.

Peter. Yaller car?

Theodore. I couldn't get near, but—that fellow has a yellow car.

Peter. Has he?

Theodore [*grimly*]. Why, he's driven you in it.

Peter [*carelessly*]. I'd forgotten.

Theodore [*looking at* PETER]. He's still hanging on to her skirts, hey?

Peter. He's an ill-bred tactless cub. But he's got a nice 'ead of 'air and smells o' soap; and that's the sort women love to have danglin' about after 'em.

Theodore [*with an effort*]. There—there's nothing in it, Peter, beyond that?

Peter [*waving his hand disdainfully*]. Good God!

Theodore. Oh, I know there isn't; I know there isn't. With all her faults, I know she's as straight as a die. [*Looking at* PETER *again.*] Did you touch on the subject with her?

Peter [*nodding*]. I rubbed it in. I told her her conduct had been indiscreet to a degree. I thought it policy to rub it in.

Theodore. Did she—offer any explanation?

Peter [*nodding*]. Pure thoughtlessness.

Theodore. And you felt that she was—speaking the truth?

Peter [*testily*]. My dear Theodore . . .

Theodore. You swear that? [*Suddenly, grasping the lapel of* PETER'S *coat.*] Damn it, man, *you* began talking about the thing!

COLE *enters at the double door carrying a note in the shape of a cocked hat.*

Theodore [*angrily*]. What d'ye want?

Cole. I beg your pardon, sir.

Theodore [*going to him*]. Hey? [*He snatches the note from the man and, as he glances at the writing on it, his jaw drops.*]

Cole [*in a low voice*]. An answer, sir?

Theodore [*trying to unfold the note*]. Messenger?

Cole. The lady herself, I think, sir.

There is a pause, and then THEODORE *slowly gets the note open and reads it.*

Theodore [*to* COLE]. Where . . . ?

Cole. In the smoking room, sir.

Theodore. Er—wait.

Cole. Yessir. [COLE *withdraws.*]

Theodore [*to* PETER, *who has wandered away*]. Peter. . . .

PETER *comes to him and* THEODORE *hands him the note.* PETER'S *eyes bolt as he recognizes the handwriting.*

Peter [*reading the note*]. "Will you see me?" Short— [*Examining both sides of the paper and then returning the note to* THEODORE.]—Sweet.

Theodore [*chewing his unlighted cigar*]. This is your doing.

Peter [*beaming*]. I flatter myself it must be. [*Laying a hand on* THEODORE's *shoulder.*] My dear Theo, this puts a noo aspect on the affair—clears the air.

Theodore. New aspect . . . ?

Peter. She makes the first advances, dear kind soul as she is. [*A pause.*] Shall I—fetch her in?

Theodore. Hold hard, hold hard; don't be in such a devil of a hurry. [*He leaves* PETER *and seats himself in a heap in the chair on the right of the fireplace.* PETER *moves softly to the double door.*]

Peter [*his hand on the door handle—to* THEODORE]. *May* I?

THEODORE *raises his head and nods.* PETER *goes out. As the door closes,* THEODORE *gets to his feet and flings his cigar into the grate. Then, hastily, he proceeds to put the room in order, closing the piano and beating out and rearranging the pillows on the settees. Finally, he comes upon* MRS. AN-NERLY's *empty coffee cup, picks it up, and vanishes with it into the dining room. After a little while, the double door opens and* PETER *returns. He glances around the room, looks surprised at not finding* THEODORE *and, with a motion of the head, invites* ZOE *to enter. Presently she appears, beautifully dressed. She also looks around; and, passing* PETER, *she moves tremblingly to the fireplace. He closes the door and joins her.*

Peter [*to* ZOE]. You're a brick to do this.

Zoe [*almost inaudibly*]. Am I?

Peter. You'll never regret it.

Zoe [*clutching* PETER's *arm*]. He will be—kind to me?

Peter. As kind as you are to him.

Zoe [*drawing a deep breath*]. Ah! [*She sits upon the settee on the right and her eyes roam about the room.*] What a ripping flat!

Peter [*disparagingly*]. Oh, I dun'no.

Zoe [*with a wry mouth, plaintively*]. He *has* been doing himself jolly well, in all conscience.

The dining-room door opens and THEODORE *appears. He shuts the door and edges toward* PETER, *who leads him to* ZOE.

Peter. My dear old pals. . . .

ZOE *gets to her feet and* THEODORE *awkwardly holds out his hand to her.*

Theodore. How are you, Zoe?

Zoe. Fairly—thanks. . . .

She hurriedly produces her handkerchief from a gold bag

hanging from her wrist and moves away to the left. There she sits upon the settee, struggling to command herself. PETER *gives* THEODORE's *arm a friendly grip and makes for the double door. As he passes behind the settee on which* ZOE *is seated, he stops to pat her shoulder.*

Zoe [*in a whisper, seizing his hand*]. Don't go, Peter; don't go.

He releases his hand, giving hers a reassuring squeeze, and goes to the door.

Peter [*at the door, to* THEODORE]. I shall be in the city till six.

He departs. After a silence, THEODORE *approaches* ZOE. *They carefully avoid meeting each other's eyes.*

Theodore. It—it's very good of you, Zo, to—to hunt me up.
Zoe. I—I went first to Copthall Court. [*Wiping a tear from her cheek.*] I—I thought I should find you there.
Theodore. I—I haven't been at all regular at the office lately. [*A pause. They look about the room in opposite directions.*] Er—Peter tells me he had a little talk with you this morning.
Zoe. Y-yes.
Theodore. About our—being reconciled.
Zoe. Yes.
Theodore. W-well? [*She puts her handkerchief away and takes from her bag a torn envelope with some enclosures. She gives it to him timidly and he extracts from the envelope a letter and a key.*] The—the damned cruel letter I left behind me—that evening—with my latchkey. [*She inclines her head.*] May I—destroy it?

She nods assent, and he tears up the envelope and letter and crams the pieces into his trouser pocket.

Theodore [*looking at the key*]. The—the key . . . ?
Zoe. It—it's yours again—if you like.
Theodore. You—you're willing . . . ? [*Again she inclines her head, and he puts the key into a pocket in his waistcoat and seats himself humbly in the chair at the farther end of the settee.*] Thank'ee. [*After a pause.*] Zo . . .
Zoe. Yes?
Theodore [*turning to her but not lifting his eyes*]. Look here. I'm not going to—try to deceive you. I—I want you to understand exactly what you're offering to take back.
Zoe. Exactly . . . ?

Theodore. I gather from Peter that you came over from Paris on Sunday in the company of Mr. Jim Mallandain.

Zoe. I picked him up by chance at the Gare du Nord.

Theodore. And Mr. Jim whiled away the journey by—by gossiping to you about me and—a woman of the name of Annerly?

Zoe. On the boat.

Theodore. Quite so. [*A pause.*] When you mentioned the matter to Peter, he produced the whitewash bucket, didn't he?

Zoe. Slapped it on thick.

Theodore [*looking at her from under his brows*]. But you didn't . . . ? [*She shakes her head.*] You're right; Peter's a liar. It's a true bill. I wish it wasn't; but it is.

Zoe [*after a pause, steadily*]. Well?

Theodore [*looking at her again*]. Are you prepared to forgive me that too, then? [*She nods, but with compressed lips. He bows his head.*] Anyhow, I'm easier for making a clean breast of it.

Zoe. How—how did you—come to . . . ?

Theodore. Lower myself with this hussy? [*Looking up.*] Isn't it all of a piece? Isn't it the natural finish of the mistakes of the last year or so—the errors we've committed since we began kicking each other's shins? [*Quickly.*] Oh, I'm not reproaching you now for your share o' the transaction. It was my job—the husband's job—to be patient with you; to smooth you down gently, and to wait. But instead of doing that, I let my mind dwell on my own grievances; with the result that latterly the one being in the world I envied was the fellow who'd kept his liberty, or who'd had the pluck to knock off the shackles. [*Rising and walking about, gathering his thoughts as he proceeds.*] Well, I got my freedom at last, didn't I! And a nice mess I made of it. I started by taking a furnished lodging in St. James's Street—ski-high, quiet, *peaceful!* Ha! Hardly a fortnight was out before I had blue-devils and was groaning to myself at the very state of things I'd been longing for. Why should I be condemned, I said to myself—why should I be condemned to an infernal dull life while others around me were enjoying themselves like fighting cocks! And just then this flat was offered to me as it stands; and in less than a month after I'd slammed the front door at Lancaster Gate I was giving a dinner party here—a house-warming—[*Halting at the window, his back to* Zoe.]—a dinner party to four-and-twenty people, and not all of' em men.

Zoe [*in a low voice*]. I heard of your setting up here while I was—in Florence—[*Clenching her hands.*]—in Florence.

Theodore [*resuming his walk*]. However, so far it was nothing but folly on my part—egregious folly. And so it continued till I—till I had the honor of being introduced to Mrs. Annerly at a supper at Jack Poncerot's. [*Eying* ZOE *askance.*] I won't give you the details of the pretty story; your imagination'll supply those—the heading o' the chapters, at any rate. Chapter One, Conceit—I had the besotted vanity to fancy she—she liked me and was genuinely sympathetic toward me; [*At the mantelpiece, looking down into the grate.*] and so on to Chapter the Last—the chapter with the inevitable title— Disgust—Loathing!

Zoe [*thoughtfully*]. You—you're sure you've reached the— the final chapter?

Theodore [*turning to her*]. Heavens, yes! [*Shaking himself.*] It's all over. I've paid her off—today, as it happens. I've been itching to do it; and I've done it. [*Sitting upon the settee on the right.*] Another month of her society, and I believe I'd have gone to the dogs completely [*His elbows on his knees, holding his head.*] Zo . . .

Zoe. Eh?

Theodore. Peter says you're walking your room half the night and smoking your nerves raw.

Zoe. Does he? He needn't have repeated . . .

Theodore. Zo, I've been walking this horrible flat in the same way. *I* can't get to bed till I hear the rattle of the milk carts. And *I'm* smoking too much—and—not only that . . .

Zoe [*looking at him for the first time*]. Not only *what?*

Theodore. Well, a man doesn't smoke till four or five o'clock in the morning on cocoa, does he?

There is a moment's silence, and then she rises and goes to him.

Zoe. Oh—Theo!

Theodore [*looking up at her*]. So your liberty hasn't made you over happy, either, has it, old girl?

Zoe [*faintly*]. No.

Theodore. You've been thinking, too, of the good times we've had together, hey?

Zoe. Y-yes. [*He rises and places his hands upon her shoulders yearningly as if about to draw her to him. She shrinks from him with a startled look.*] Theo . . .

Theodore [*dropping his hands*]. What?

Zoe [*nervously*]. There—there's one thing I—I want to say to you—before we—before we go further . . .

Theodore [*feeling the rebuff*]. H'm?

Zoe. As I've told you, I'm willing that you should return to Lancaster Gate. You may return as soon as you please; but . . .

Theodore. But?

Zoe. It must be—simply as a companion, Theo; a friend.

Theodore [*stiffly*]. A friend?

Zoe [*with a slight shrug*]. Not that we've been much else to each other these last few years—except enemies. Still. . . .

Theodore [*frowning*]. You wish to make it perfectly clear.

Zoe. Yes.

Theodore [*after a pause, icily*]. I beg your pardon. I was forgetting myself just now. Thanks for the reminder. [*Walking away from her.*] Oh, I know you can feel only the most utter contempt for me—wholesale contempt.

Zoe [*entreatingly*]. Ah, no; don't take that tone.

Theodore. Stand the naughty boy in the corner; he's earned any amount of humiliation you choose to inflict.

Zoe. You shall never be humiliated by me, Theo.

Theodore [*throwing himself upon the settee on the left*]. Evidently!

Zoe [*turning away*]. Oh, for God's sake, don't let's begin fighting again. [*Sitting on the settee on the right.*] Don't let's do that.

Theodore. Ha, ha! No, no; we won't squabble. Right you are; I accept the terms—*any* terms. [*Lying at full length upon his back on the settee.*] As you say, we've been little more than friends of late years—good friends or bad. [*Throwing one leg over the other.*] It's your laying down the law so emphatically that riled me. Sorry I growled. [*There is silence between them. She watches him guiltily. Suddenly he changes the position of his legs.*] Zoe . . .

Zoe. Yes?

Theodore [*gazing at the ceiling*]. At the same time, I'm blessed if I wouldn't rather you wanted to tear my eyes out than that you should treat me in this lofty, condescending style—scratch my face and tear my eyes out.

Zoe. Well, I—I don't, you see.

Theodore [*smiling unpleasantly*]. Alice Annerly's an extremely handsome creature, my dear, whatever else she may be.

Zoe. I'm—I'm sure of it.

Theodore. Her photo's on the top of the piano.

Zoe [*restraining an impulse to glance over her shoulder*]. I—I'm not curious.

Theodore. Ho! You mayn't be aware of the fact, but I've

paid you the compliment of resenting the deep devotion your pet poodle—Master Lenny Ferris—has been paying you recently. You might do me a similar honor. [*Meditatively.*] Master—blooming—Lenny! [*Again there is a pause; and then, slowly, he turns upon his side so that he may face her.*] I say, that was a pretty disgraceful business—your traipsing about Italy with that fellow. [*Another pause.*] Hey?

Zoe [*holding her breath*]. It *was*—unwise of me, I own.

Theodore. Unwise! Peter and I were discussing it when your note was brought in.

Zoe [*moistening her lips*]. Were you?

Theodore [*harshly*]. Yes, we were. [*Another pause.*] My God, I think it's *I* who ought to dictate what our domestic arrangements are to be in the future—not you! [*A pause. With a motion of the head, he invites her to come to him.*] Zoe . . . [*A pause.*] Don't you hear me!

She hesitates; then she nerves herself and rises and, with a light step, crosses the room.

Zoe [*resting her arms on the back of the chair at the farther end of the settee on which he is lying*]. Still the same dear old bully, I notice.

Theodore. Sit down.

Zoe. Your gentle voice is quite audible where I am.

Theodore [*putting his feet to the ground*]. You sit down a minute.

Zoe. Puh! [*She sits haughtily.*]

Theodore. Now, you look here, my lady; I should like an account of that Italian affair from the word go.

Zoe. I'm not in the mood to furnish it.

Theodore. Perhaps not; but I'm in the mood to receive it. [*A pause.*] When did he join you?

Zoe. He—he didn't join me; that's not the way to put it.

Theodore. Put it any way you like. When was it?

Zoe. At the—end of February, I think.

Theodore. You think! [*A pause.*] What made him go out to you?

Zoe. He knew I was awfully in the dumps . . .

Theodore. Did he? How did he know that?

Zoe. He—guessed I must be.

Theodore. Guessed!

Zoe. Well, I'd seen him before I went away. I *was* dreadfully depressed, Theo—dreadfully désolée. I never thought you'd bang out of the house as you did. I never meant, for a single moment . . .

Theodore. Where were you when he turned up?

Zoe. I—I'd got to Florence. I'd been to Genoa and Pisa—
I was drifting about . . .

Theodore. Did he dream you were in Florence?

Zoe. Dream?

Theodore. He *must* have dreamt it.

Zoe. Oh, I see what you're driving at. He—he'd had a
post card from me . . .

Theodore. A post card!

Zoe [*feebly*]. I—I don't mean *one*—you—you silly! I—I
sent him a picture from each town—so I did to Peter . . .

Theodore. Why don't you admit that you and Ferris were
corresponding?

Zoe. I—I am admitting it. It's nothing to admit.

Theodore. Isn't it? [*A pause.*] Well, he arrives in Florence . . .

Zoe. Don't worry me this afternoon, Theo . . .

Theodore. How long was he with you in Florence?

Zoe. I'm seedy; I had quite a temperature yesterday. Lena
called in Rashleigh . . .

Theodore. How long was he with you in Florence?

Zoe. He wasn't "with" me.

Theodore. How long?

Zoe. A week—eight days . . .

Theodore. Same hotel?

Zoe. No, no, no!

Theodore. And afterward . . . ?

Zoe. I wanted to do a little tour of the quiet old places—
Perugia—Siena . . .

Theodore. So did *he*, hey?

Zoe. He tacked on. I saw no harm in it at the time.

Theodore. At the time!

Zoe. Nor do I now.

Theodore. It was coming from Perugia you fell up against
Lowenstein.

Zoe. If you were a man you'd thrash that beast.

Theodore. Lowenstein had the room at the hotel there—the
Brufani—that Ferris had had.

Zoe [*protestingly*]. Ah!

Theodore. In the same corridor as yours was.

Zoe. It was stupid—stupid—stupid of Lenny to let them
carry his bag up to the Brufani. It was all done before—before it dawned on him . . .

Theodore. Where were you moving on to when Lowenstein
met you at Arezzo? [*A pause.*] Hey?

Zoe [*passing her hand across her brow, weakly*]. Let me off today, Theo; my head's going like a clock. [*Getting to her feet.*] Take it up again another time. [*She goes to the settee on the right and picks up her bag which she has left there. He rises and follows her, so that when she turns they come face to face. She steadies herself.*] Well, you turn it over in your mind about coming back to me. I don't want to put pressure on you; only I—I understood from Peter you were feeling kindly toward me again.

Theodore [*quickly*]. When did you see Ferris last?

Zoe. Oh, drop Ferris.

Theodore. When?

Zoe. Oh—over two months ago—at the end of the little jaunt.

Theodore. Not since? [*She looks at him vacantly and shakes her head.*] That's a lie. He was with you on Monday morning at half-past eleven. D'ye deny it?

Zoe. You—you're so jealous, one—one's afraid . . .

Theodore [*with sudden, fierce earnestness*]. Zoe . . .

Zoe [*helplessly*]. I'm not going to remain here to be . . .

Theodore. Give me your word nothing wrong's occurred between you and Ferris. [*A pause.*] I don't ask for your oath; I'll be satisfied with your word. [*A pause.*] Give me your word.

She sits upon the settee, her hands lying in her lap.

Zoe [*staring at him*]. Theo—I've forgiven you; forgive me.

There is a silence and then, dumfounded, he moves to the chair at the further end of the settee on the left and sits there.

Theodore [*after a while*]. Florence?

Zoe. No. Perugia—Siena . . . [*Brokenly.*] It was in Florence I first lost my senses. I'd been pitying you, hating myself for the way I'd served you, and had been trying to concoct a letter to you. And then one arrived from *him*, telling me you'd taken this big flat and were having a splendid time. It made me furious; and when he came through to me, I was half beside myself. And then he planned out the little tour, and I said yes to it. [*Wringing her hands.*] Why! Why did I fall in with it! I shall never know why—except that I was mad—blind mad! [*Leaning back, her eyes closed.*] Get me a drop o' water.

He rouses himself and goes to the table on the left of the fireplace and half fills a tumbler with soda water. Then he brings her the tumbler and holds it out to her.

Theodore. Here. . . .

Zoe [*opening her eyes and looking up at him beseechingly*]. Be—merciful to me.

Theodore [*peremptorily*]. Take it.

Zoe [*barely touching the glass*]. Don't—don't be hard on me, old man.

He thrusts the tumbler into her hand and she drinks.

Theodore [*heavily*]. I—I must have some advice about this—some advice.

Zoe. Advice? [*He goes to the writing table, sits there, and places the telephone receiver to his ear.*] You—you won't do anything to disgrace me publicly, will you, Theo? [*He taps the arm of the instrument impatiently.*] You won't do anything spiteful? [*He rings again.*] You and I are both sinners, Theo; we've both gone amuck.

Theodore [*speaking into the telephone*]. London Wall, one, three, double five, eight.

Zoe. That's Peter. *He* won't advise you to do anything spiteful? [*She rises painfully, puts the tumbler on the top of the piano, and walks about the room.*] What *can* you do? You can do nothing to hurt me; nor I you. We're both sinners.

Theodore [*into the telephone*]. Hello! . . . Are you Blundell, Slade, and Mottram? . . . Is that Mr. Ewart? . . . Mr. Blundell. . . . Mr. Mottram not back yet, I suppose? . . .

Zoe [*in a murmur*]. Both—both gone amuck.

Theodore [*into the telephone*]. . . . When he comes in, tell him I want to see him at once. . . . Cavendish Square . . . at once. . . . [*Replacing the receiver.*] Good-by.

Zoe [*on the left*]. Peter—Peter won't let you—be too rough on me.

Theodore [*leaning his head on his hands*]. Ho, ho! An eye opener for Peter! But he's been a first-rate prophet all the same. [*In a muffled voice.*] Yes, Peter's been right all along the line, with his precious mid-Channel!

Zoe [*looking at him and speaking in low, measured tones*]. Theo. . . . [*He makes no response.*] Theo. . . . [*Coming to him slowly.*] I—I was thinking it over—beating it all out—driving into the city and back again. *Our* marriage was doomed long, long before we reached mid-Channel.

Theodore [*absently, not stirring*]. Oh?

Zoe. It was doomed nearly fourteen years ago.

Theodore [*as before*]. Oh?

Zoe. From the very beginning.

Theodore [*raising his head*]. What d'ye . . . ?

Zoe. It was doomed from the moment we agreed that we'd never be encumbered in our career with any—brats of children. [*He partly turns in his chair, to listen to her.*] I want you to remember that bargain, in judging me; and I want you to tell Peter of it.

Theodore. Yes, it suits you to rake that up now. . . .

Zoe [*pressing her fingers to her temples*]. If there had been "brats of children" at home, it would have made a different woman of me, Theo; such a different woman of me—and a different man of you. But, no; everything in the earlier years of our marriage was sacrificed to coining money—to shoving our way through the crowd—to "getting on"; everything was sacrificed to that.

Theodore [*angrily*]. Oh!

Zoe. And then, when we had succeeded—when we had *got* on—we had commenced to draw apart from each other; and there was the great, showy, empty house at Lancaster Gate for me to fret and pine in. [*He waves his arm scornfully.*] Oh, yes, we were happy in those climbing days—greedily, feverishly happy; but we didn't look to the time when we should need another interest in life to bind us together—the time when we'd got on in years as well as in position. [THEO-DORE *starts up.*] Ah, Theo, I believe we should have crossed that Ridge safely enough [*Laying her hands upon his breast.*] but for our cursed, cursed selfishness!

Theodore [*shaking himself free*]. Well, there's not the slightest use in talking about what might, or might not, have been. [*Passing her and pacing the room.*] One thing is absolutely certain—it's impossible for us ever to live under the same roof again under *any* conditions. That's out o' the question; I couldn't stoop to that.

Zoe [*leaning against the chair at the writing table*]. No, you draw the line at stooping to Mrs. Annerly.

Theodore. Oh, don't keep on harping on that string. The cases are as far apart as the poles.

Zoe [*faintly*]. Ha, ha!

Theodore [*halting in the middle of the room and drumming upon his brow with his fingers*]. Of course, we can make our separation a legal one; but that wouldn't give us release. And as long as we're tied to one another—[*Abruptly, looking at her.*] Zoe . . .

Zoe [*meekly*]. Eh?

Theodore. If I allowed you to divorce me—made it easy for you—would Ferris—would that scoundrel marry you?

Zoe [*turning to him, blankly*]. M-marry me?

Theodore. Because—if it 'ud save you from going utterly to the bad . . .

Zoe [*advancing a step or two*]. No, no; I wouldn't—I wouldn't marry Lenny.

Theodore [*after a moment's pause, sharply*]. You wouldn't?

Zoe. No—no . . .

Theodore [*coming close to her*]. Why not? [*She shrugs her shoulders confusedly.*] Why not?

She wavers, then grasps his arm. Again he shakes her off.

Zoe [*appealingly*]. Oh, Theo, stick to me. Don't throw me over. Wait—wait for Peter. Theo, I've never ceased to be fond of you . . .

Theodore. Faugh!

Zoe. Not at the bottom of my heart. No, nor you of me; there's the tragedy of it. Peter says the same. [*Seizing his hand.*] Take time; don't decide today . . .

Theodore [*freeing his hand and looking at her piercingly*]. When did you see him last?

Zoe. H-him?

Theodore. Ferris.

Zoe. This—this morning.

Theodore. This morning!

Zoe. I—I confess—this morning. I—I sent him away.

Theodore. Sent him—away?

Zoe [*noddingly*]. Yes—yes. . . .

Theodore [*slowly*]. And so you rush off to me—straight from the young gentleman . . .

Zoe. W-well?

Theodore [*suddenly*]. Why, damn you, you've quarreled!

Zoe. No . . .

Theodore. He's chucked you!

Zoe. No . . .

Theodore. Had enough of you!

Zoe [*her eyes blazing*]. That's not true!

Theodore. Ho, ho! You bring me his cast-off trash, do you!

Zoe. It's a lie!

Theodore. Mr. Lenny Ferris' leavings!

Zoe. It's a lie! He'd give his soul to make me his wife.

Theodore. Will he tell *me* that?

Zoe. Tell *you!*

Theodore [*between his teeth*]. If he doesn't, I'll break every bone in his carcass.

Zoe [*throwing her head up defiantly*]. Of course he'd tell you.

Theodore [*walking away to the fireplace*]. He shall have a chance of doing it.

Zoe [*making for the door, wildly*]. The sooner the better!

Theodore [*looking at his watch*]. If Peter were here. . . .

Zoe [*behind the settee on the left, turning to* THEODORE]. Mind! I've your bond! If Lenny promises to marry me, you'll let me free myself from you?

Theodore. I've said so.

Zoe [*missing her bag, which is again lying upon the settee on the left, and pointing to it*]. Please. . . .

He picks up the bag, and is about to take it to her, when he remembers that he has the latchkey in his pocket. He produces the key and drops it into the bag.

Theodore [*as he does so*]. You'll want this for your *new* husband.

Zoe. Thank God, I've done with the old one! [*He tosses the bag to her in a fury and she catches it.*] Ha, ha! [*At the door.*] Ta, ta! [*She disappears.*]

Theodore [*flourishing his hands*]. Oh. . . . [*Going to the piano, he takes the decanter of brandy and a glass from the tray and fills the glass to the brim.*]

ACT FOUR

A pretty, irregularly shaped room, simply but tastefully furnished. At the back, facing the spectator, are two double windows opening to the floor. These windows give on to a balcony which appears to continue its course outside the adjoining rooms both on the right and left. Beyond the balcony there is an open space and, in the distance, a view of the upper part of the Albert Hall and of other lofty buildings. On the left is the fireplace—its grate empty, save for a few pots of flowers—and, nearer the spectator, there is a door opening from a corridor. Opposite this door is a door of like dimensions, admitting to a bedroom.

On either side of the fireplace and of the left-hand window there is an armchair; facing the fireplace there is a settee; and at the back of the settee are a small writing table and writing chair. A leather tub for wastepaper stands beside the writing table. On the right of the room is a round table upon which tea is laid for three persons. Two chairs—one on the left, another at the farther side—and a settee on the right are drawn up close to this table. Elsewhere are a bookcase, a smoking cabinet, and some odds and ends of furniture—the whole being characteristic of a room in a small flat occupied by a well-to-do, but not weathy, young man.

Both the windows are open, and the glare of the afternoon sun is on the balcony and the opposite buildings.

MRS. PIERPOINT, ETHEL, *and* LEONARD—*the ladies in their hats and gaily dressed—are seated at the round table.*

LEONARD [*in the chair on the left of the table—handing a dish of cakes to* MRS. PIERPOINT]. Do try one of these little cakes.

   Mrs. Pierpoint [*in the chair at the farther side of the table*]. I couldn't.

   Leonard. I bought them and carried 'em home myself.

   Mrs. Pierpoint. You really must excuse me.

   Leonard [*pushing the dish toward* ETHEL, *who is on the settee facing him*]. Buck up, Ethel.

   Ethel. Good-by to my dinner, then. [*Taking a cake and biting it as she speaks.*] May I, Mother?

   Mrs. Pierpoint [*cheerfully*]. Now, isn't that the modern young lady exactly! "May I, Mother!" And the cake is half-eaten before the poor mother can even nod her head.

   Ethel [*laughing*]. Ha, ha!

   Mrs. Pierpoint. "May I go out for a walk, Mother?" and the front door bangs on the very words!! "May I do this?" "May I do that?" And a nice life the mother leads if she dares to say "No."

   Ethel. This sounds suspiciously like a sermon. [*To* LEONARD.] Lenny, sit up straight and be preached to. [*Pushing her cup to* MRS. PIERPOINT *who has the tea tray before her.*] Another cup of tea, your reverence.

   Mrs. Pierpoint. Ethel! How—how irreligious! [*Pouring out tea.*] Ah, but it's true, every syllable of it. And in nothing is this spirit of—what shall I describe it as?

   Ethel. Go-as-you-pleasèdness.

   Mrs. Pierpoint [*giving* ETHEL *her tea*]. In nothing is this willful, thoughtless spirit more plainly shown than in the way love affairs are conducted at the present day.

   Ethel [*whistling slyly*]. Phew!

   Mrs. Pierpoint [*to* LEONARD]. More tea, Leonard?

   Leonard. No, thanks.

Mrs. Pierpoint [*resignedly*]. I *suppose* I must call you Leonard now?

Ethel [*into her teacup*]. What's the matter with "Lenny"?

Mrs. Pierpoint. I may be wrong, but I don't *think* that it was the fashion in my youth for a young lady suddenly to appear before her mother and to say, without a note of warning, "Mr. So-and-so is in the drawing room and we wish to be engaged." Take the case of Ethel's papa—*there's* a case in point . . .

Leonard. I certainly intended to speak to you first, Mrs. Pierpoint.

Ethel [*to* LEONARD]. You fibber!

Mrs. Pierpoint. Ethel!

Leonard. Well, I—what I mean is . . .

Ethel. If you *had* done so, I'd never have looked at you again. Surely, if there is one thing which is a girl's own particular business, it is settling preliminaries with her best young man.

Mrs. Pierpoint. My dear!

Ethel [*jumping up*]. Anyhow, Mother, if you wanted to play the dragon, you shouldn't have been upstairs, sleeping off the effects of an exceedingly heavy lunch, when Lenny arrived this afternoon.

Mrs. Pierpoint. Fiddle, heavy lunch! A morsel of minced chicken!

Ethel. Ha, ha! [*Bending over* MRS. PIERPOINT.] And you don't mind, do you—not actually—[*Kissing* MRS. PIERPOINT.] —as long as . . . ?

Mrs. Pierpoint. As long as what?

Ethel. As long as—Lenny's contented?

Mrs. Pierpoint [*shaking herself*]. Oh, go away.

Laughingly, ETHEL *wanders about inspecting the various objects in the room.*

Leonard [*to* MRS. PIERPOINT, *producing his cigarette case*]. Do you object?

Mrs. Pierpoint. Not in the least. Ethel's papa used to indulge, in moderation.

Leonard [*to* ETHEL, *over his shoulder*]. Cigarette, Ethel?

Mrs. Pierpoint. Ethel, I forbid it.

Ethel [*putting on her gloves*]. I would, but it makes me swimmy.

Mrs. Pierpoint [*to* ETHEL]. How do *you* know?

Ethel. I've smoked with Zoe Blundell.

Mrs. Pierpoint. This is news to *me*.

Ethel. Zoe smokes like a chimney.

Mrs. Pierpoint [*to* LEONARD]. By-the-bye, she's in London again.

Leonard [*uncomfortably*]. Yes—yes.

Mrs. Pierpoint. Ethel called on her this morning at Lancaster Gate.

Leonard. Did she?

Ethel [*to* LEONARD]. I told you, Len.

Leonard. Ah, yes.

Mrs. Pierpoint [*to* LEONARD]. Have *you* seen her? I presume not.

Leonard. Er—for a few minutes. I was in the neighborhood on—on Monday, and I noticed the blinds were up, and I—I just rang the bell to—to inquire.

Mrs. Pierpoint [*elevating her eyebrows.*] She received you?

Leonard. She—she happened to be in the hall.

Mrs. Pierpoint. I was going to *say*—a woman in her peculiar position ought hardly . . .

Leonard. No, of course.

Mrs. Pierpoint. Looks ill, I understand?

Ethel. Frightfully.

Leonard. Does she?

Mrs. Pierpoint. I am afraid—I am very much afraid—that dear Mrs. Blundell was not *entirely* free from blame in her treatment of that big, rough husband of hers.

Ethel [*at the left-hand window*]. Rubbish, Mother!

Mrs. Pierpoint. Ethel, you are *too* disrespectful.

Ethel. Sorry.

Mrs. Pierpoint. At the same time, she is an exceedingly attractive person—a trifle vulgar, poor soul, occasionally . . .

Ethel [*hotly*]. Mother!

Mrs. Pierpoint [*to* LEONARD]. But good-natured people frequently *are* vulgar—aren't they?

Ethel [*going on to the balcony*]. Oh!

Mrs. Pierpoint [*to* LEONARD]. You were quite a friend of hers before the sad split, weren't you—quite a friend?

Leonard. Yes, I—I always found her a very decent sort.

Ethel [*her hands upon the rail of the balustrade, calling*]. Mother, do come and look at the tiny men and women.

Mrs. Pierpoint. Men and women . . . ? [MRS. PIERPOINT *rises and goes to the window, whereupon* LEONARD *jumps up as if relieved by the interruption.*] You're soiling your gloves, Ethel.

Ethel. Look down there. What tots!

Mrs. Pierpoint [*drawing back from the window*]. Oh, my dear, I can't. . . .

Ethel. Do, Mother.

Mrs. Pierpoint. You know I don't care for heights.

Ethel. I'll steady you. [MRS. PIERPOINT *timidly ventures on to the balcony.* ETHEL *takes her arm.*] There's been a concert—or a meeting. [*Calling.*] Lenny. . . .

LEONARD *has walked away to the writing table gloomily. He is about to join the ladies on the balcony when the door on the left opens and* RIDEOUT, *his servant, appears.*

Leonard [*to* RIDEOUT]. Eh?

After glancing discreetly in the direction of the ladies on the balcony, RIDEOUT *produces a visiting card from behind his back.* LEONARD *goes to him and takes the card, and looks at it in astonishment.*

Rideout [*quietly*]. There's some writing on it, sir.

Leonard. I see. [*In a low voice.*] Where is she?

Rideout. In my room, sir. I said you were engaged.

Leonard [*uneasily*]. You didn't tell her who's here.

Rideout. No, sir; merely some friends to tea.

Leonard. All right. I shan't be very long. [RIDEOUT *is going.*] Tss——!

Rideout [*stopping*]. Yessir?

Leonard. Keep your door shut.

Rideout. Yessir.

RIDEOUT *withdraws.* LEONARD *crams the card into his waistcoat pocket and is again about to join the ladies when* MRS. PIERPOINT *comes back into the room.*

Mrs. Pierpoint [*to* LEONARD]. Thank you for showing us your charming little nest. Quite—quite delightful!

Leonard [*standing by the round table*]. Oh, for bachelor quarters. . . .

Mrs. Pierpoint [*in the middle of the room*]. There! I declare I often wonder what there is to tempt a bachelor to marry in these days.

Leonard. You're not a bachelor, Mrs. Pierpoint.

Mrs. Pierpoint. No; that's true. That's perfectly true. But I've a distinct remembrance of the rooms Ethel's papa lived in when *he* was a bachelor. [ETHEL *returns and goes to the fireplace.*] They were in Keppel Street, and vastly different from these. [*Turning to* ETHEL.] Have I ever told you that poor papa lived in Keppel Street?

Ethel [*demurely*]. Yes, Mother.

Mrs. Pierpoint [*to* ETHEL]. And now, my dear, as we have

to dine at half-past seven—[*To* LEONARD.] what time does *Louise* begin?

Leonard. Oh, if we get there at nine. . . .

Mrs. Pierpoint. So kind of you to take us—and as Ethel must lie down on her bed for an hour if we want her to look her best—[*Pointing to the tea table.*]—may I trouble you—my fan?——

LEONARD *searches for* MRS. PIERPOINT'S *fan among the tea things.*

Ethel [*kneeling upon the settee on the left, her elbows on the back of it, gazing into space*]. Mother . . .

Mrs. Pierpoint. Eh? [*Receiving her fan from* LEONARD.] Thank you.

Ethel [*slowly*]. Mother—this is going to be an awfully happy night.

Mrs. Pierpoint. I'm sure I hope so, my darling. It won't be my fault if it isn't—[*Tapping* LEONARD'S *shoulder with her fan.*]—nor Leonard's.

Ethel. Ah, no; I mean *the* night of one's life perhaps.

Mrs. Pierpoint. Oh, I trust we shall have many, many . . .

Leonard. Rather!

Ethel [*raising herself and gripping the back of the settee*]. No, no; you don't understand, you gabbies. In everybody's life there's one especial moment . . .

Mrs. Pierpoint. Moment?

Ethel. Hour—day—night; when all the world seems *yours* —as if it had been made for *you,* and when you can't help pitying other people—they seem so ordinary and insignificant. Well, I believe this is to be *my* evening.

Mrs. Pierpoint. One would imagine *I* had never given you *any* pleasure, to hear you talk.

Ethel [*rising*]. I say, Mother, don't make me lie down and lose consciousness when I get home. [*Going to* MRS. PIER-POINT *with extended arms.*] Ah ha! You duck!

In advancing to MRS. PIERPOINT, ETHEL *knocks over the wastepaper tub with her skirt and its contents are scattered on the floor.*

Ethel [*going down on her knees and replacing the litter*]. Sorry.

Mrs. Pierpoint [*to* ETHEL]. You'll crease your skirt, Ethel.

Leonard [*going to* ETHEL]. Never mind that.

Ethel. Oh, but if I do anything clumsy at home . . . ! [*Coming upon some fragments of a photograph.*] Oh! [*Trying to fit the pieces together.*] Zoe!

Leonard. Yes, I—I. . . .

Mrs. Pierpoint [*who has moved to the fireplace*]. Pray get off the floor, child.

Ethel [*finding more pieces*]. Why, you've been tearing up Zoe's photos.

Leonard. They're old things.

Ethel. *That* they're not. *This* one isn't, at all events. [*Examining one of the scraps closely.*] ". . . Firenze."

Mrs. Pierpoint. Ethel, we *must* be going.

Leonard [*almost roughly*]. Leave them alone, Ethel.

A little startled by his tone, she drops the pieces into the basket and he assists her to rise.

Mrs. Pierpoint [*opening the door on the left*]. Come along at once, I insist.

MRS. PIERPOINT *goes out.* ETHEL *is following her mother when she turns to* LEONARD *who is behind her.*

Ethel [*to* LEONARD, *with a smile*]. Sorry I contradicted you.

They kiss hurriedly and ETHEL *runs after her mother.* LEONARD *follows and closes the door. After a little while, the door is reopened, and* RIDEOUT *enters with* ZOE. ZOE *is dressed as when last seen.*

Rideout [*to* ZOE, *as she passes him*]. Mr. Ferris has gone to the lift, ma'am. He won't be a minute.

Zoe [*going to the left-hand window, languidly*]. All right.

Rideout [*at the round table, putting the tea things together upon the tray*]. Shall I make you some tea, ma'am?

Zoe [*looking out of the window, speaking in a dull voice*]. No; I've had tea, in a tea shop. [*Turning.*] Rideout . . .

Rideout. Yes, ma'am?

Zoe. I should like to tidy myself, if I may; I've been walking about.

Rideout [*going to the door on the right and opening it*]. Cert'nly, ma'am. [*As* ZOE *approaches.*] The hot water flows cold for a few seconds, ma'am.

Zoe. Is there any scent?

Rideout. There's some Eau de Cologne on the dressing table, ma'am.

She disappears and RIDEOUT *closes the door and continues his preparations for removing the tea things.* LEONARD *returns.*

Rideout [*answering a look of inquiry from* LEONARD]. Mrs. Blundell's tidying herself, sir.

Leonard. Oh, yes. [*Moving about the room, irritably.*] Won't she have some tea?

Rideout. I did ask her, sir. She's had it.

Leonard [*halting*]. Did Mrs. Blundell—say anything, Rideout?

Rideout [*folding the tablecloth*]. Only that she wanted to see you just for ten minutes, sir, and that she thought she'd wait. And then she wrote on her card and told me to slip it into your hand if I got the opportunity.

Leonard [*resuming his walk*]. Yes, yes.

Rideout [*after a pause*]. What time'll you dress, sir?

Leonard. Quarter to seven. I have to dine at half-past.

Rideout. Which suit'll you wear, sir?

Leonard [*considering*]. Er—pink lining.

Rideout. Theatre, sir?

Leonard. Opera. Two pairs o' gloves. [RIDEOUT *goes toward the door on the left, carrying the tea tray.*] Tss——!

Rideout. Yessir?

Leonard. There's no necessity to put out my clothes yet a while.

Rideout [*placing the tray upon a piece of furniture so that he can open the door*]. No, sir.

Leonard. I'll ring when you can come through.

Rideout [*opening the door*]. Yessir.

Leonard. And I'm not at home to anybody else.

Rideout [*taking up the tray*]. No, sir. [*As the man is leaving the room,* LEONARD *comes to the door to close it.*] Thank you very much, sir.

RIDEOUT *goes out and* LEONARD *shuts the door. As he turns from the door, his eyes fall upon the wastepaper tub. He snatches it up angrily.*

Leonard [*reopening the door and calling*]. Rideout . . .

Rideout [*out of sight*]. Yessir? [RIDEOUT *presents himself at the door without the tray.*]

Leonard [*shaking up the contents of the tub and then giving it to* RIDEOUT]. Burn this wastepaper.

Rideout. Yessir.

RIDEOUT *closes the door and* LEONARD *is again walking about the room when* ZOE, *carrying her hat, gloves, and bag, appears on the balcony outside the right-hand window. She enters and they look at one another for a moment without speaking.*

Leonard. Hello, Zo!

Zoe. Hello, Len!

Leonard. This *is* a surprise.

Zoe [*putting her hat, gloves, and bag upon the round table —nervously*]. Is it?

Leonard. I thought you'd dropped my acquaintance for good and all.

Zoe. N-no, Len. Why should you think that?

Leonard. Ha! Well, I bear the marks of the point of your shoe somewhere about me.

Zoe. Oh, you—you mustn't take me too seriously when I'm in one of my vile tempers. [*A pause.*] I—I'm not—keeping you . . . ?

Leonard. No, no.

Zoe [*turning the chair on the left of the round table so that it faces the writing table*]. May I sit down?

Leonard. Do.

Zoe. I was here three quarters of an hour ago, but the porter said you were out; so I went and got some tea. [*Sitting.*] You've been entertaining, according to Rideout.

Leonard [*turning the chair at the writing table and sitting facing her*]. A couple o' people turned up—old friends. . . .

Zoe. You *are* a gay dog. [*Suddenly, staring at the writing table.*] Why—where—where am *I*?

Leonard. You?

Zoe. You always have a photograph of me, standing on your writing table.

Leonard. Oh—oh, it's . . .

Zoe [*remembering*]. And there isn't one now—[*Glancing at the door on the right.*]—in your . . . !

Leonard. The frames had got beastly shabby. Rideout's taken 'em to be done up.

Zoe [*flutteringly*]. Honor? [*A pause.*] Honor?

Leonard. If—if I say so. . . .

Zoe. I beg your pardon. No, you wouldn't *out* my photos because of a—because of a little tiff, would you?

Leonard. L-likely!

Zoe [*rising and going to him*]. I'm sure you wouldn't, dear boy; I'm sure you wouldn't. [*Again there is a pause, during which she passes her hand over his shoulder caressingly.*] Len . . .

Leonard. Eh?

Zoe [*standing behind him*]. After that—stupid fall-out of ours this morning—what d'ye think I did?

Leonard. Did?

Zoe. Ha, ha! I—I took it into my head to—to pay Theodore a visit.

Leonard. Pay him a visit!

Zoe. It—it was one of my silly impulses—I was so upset at having offended you. . . .

Leonard. Did you see him?

Zoe. Y-yes.

Leonard. And what had *he* to say for himself?

Zoe. Oh, I—I made such a mash of it, Len.

Leonard. Mash . . . ?

Zoe. Yes, I—I let him worm it out of me.

Leonard. Worm it out of you?

Zoe. Worm it—all out. . . .

Leonard. Worm *what* out of you?

Zoe [*faintly*]. P-Perugia. . . .

There is a silence, and then LEONARD *rises with an angry look.*

Zoe [*holding the lapels of his coat*]. Don't be savage with me, Len. It wasn't altogether my fault. He *had* heard of it from Claud Lowenstein. And it's of no consequence; none whatever. It's just as you said this morning—he *is* ready to make matters smooth for us.

Leonard [*blankly*]. Smooth—for us!

Zoe. Yes, to let *me* divorce *him*. He's promised—he's promised to do so, if you'll—only . . .

Leonard [*his jaw dropping*]. If *I* . . . ?

Zoe. If you'll give him your word that you'll do the right thing by me.

Leonard. The right thing!

Zoe. Marry me. [*A pause.*] I—I suppose he—I suppose he'll demand to see you. Or perhaps he'll make Peter Mottram a go-between.

Again there is a silence, and then he walks away from her. She follows him with her eyes.

Leonard [*thickly*]. But you—you wished me good-by this morning—finished with me.

Zoe [*clenching her hands*]. I know—I know! [*Coming to him.*] But he—he insulted me, Len—stung me. He flung it in my face that you—that you'd chucked me; that I was your castoff, your leavings. I couldn't bear it from him; and I—I told him that you were all eagerness to make me your wife. [*A pause.*] Well! And so you were—this morning!

He sits in the chair on the left of the round table, his elbows on his knees, holding his head.

Leonard. Zoe . . .

Zoe. W-what?

Leonard. These people I've had to tea this afternoon—ladies—two ladies . . .

Zoe. Yes?

Leonard. Mrs. Pierpoint was one of them—and—and . . .

Zoe. Mrs. Pierpoint . . . ?

Leonard [raising his head and looking at her]. The other was—Ethel.

Zoe. Eth-el!

Leonard [in a low voice]. You—you made me do it.

Zoe [dazed]. I—I made you! *[Drawing a deep breath.]* Oh-h-h! *[She turns from him slowly and seats herself in the chair at the writing table.]* I—I'd forgotten Ethel.

Leonard. Yes, you persuaded me to do it. *[A pause.]* Zo, you egged me on to do it.

Zoe [quietly]. You—you didn't lose much time, did you?

Leonard. I—I was furious when I left you—furious.

Zoe [with an attempt at a smile]. Why, you—you must have bolted straight off to her.

Leonard. I—I went to the club and had some food; and then I came back here and changed—and . . .

Zoe. Got rid of those photos!

Leonard. I was furious—furious.

Zoe. And then you—you bustled off to Sloane Street! *[She rises and paces the room. After a while she pulls herself together.]* Oh, well, it—it can't be helped, old boy.

Leonard [agitatedly]. It *must* be helped; it *must* be helped. I must get out of it; I must get out of it. Somehow or other, I must get out of it.

Zoe. Get out of it?

Leonard. The—Pierpoints!

Zoe. Oh, don't talk such utter rubbish; I'd kill myself sooner. *[She throws herself into the chair on the right of the left-hand window.]* No, I'm a rotter, Len, but I'm not as low as that. Oh, no, I'm not as low as all that. *[She rises and goes slowly to the round table and, in a listless way, pulls the pins out of her hat.]* I—I'll be toddling home now. *[Tracing a pattern on the crown of her hat with the hatpins.]* Home! *[Knitting her brows.]* I shall clear out of that—big—flashy—empty . . . ! *[Putting on her hat.]* Ha, ha! I *have* made a mash of it, haven't I? My father always said I was a heedless, irresponsible little puss. *[With a puzzled look, her arms hanging at her side.]* There was a lot o' good in me, too—any amount o' good! *[She is drawing on a glove when she turns in*

the direction of the door on the left. At the same moment,
LEONARD, *also looking at the door, gets to his feet.*]

   Zoe [*listening*]. What's that, dear?

*He tiptoes to the door, opens it an inch or two, and puts his
ear to the opening.*

   Leonard [*carefully closing the door and turning to her*].
Blundell.

   Zoe [*under her breath*]. Oh!

   Leonard [*in a whisper*]. Don't worry. I've told Rideout.
. . . [*There is a pause. They stand looking at each other in
silence, waiting. Suddenly* LEONARD *returns to the door and,
without opening it, listens again.*] Curse the brute, he won't
go!

*He faces her irresolutely and, in a panic, she picks up her
bag and her other glove and runs out at the door on the right.*
LEONARD *is in the middle of the room when the door on the
left is thrown open and* THEODORE *and* PETER *enter followed
by* RIDEOUT. THEODORE *and* PETER *have their hats on.*

   Rideout [*to* LEONARD]. I—I beg your pardon, sir . . .
   Leonard [*to* RIDEOUT]. All right.
   Theodore [*to* PETER, *with a horse laugh*]. You give the man
half a sovereign, Peter; that'll soothe his feelings.
   Peter [*to* THEODORE, *sharply*]. Sssh, sssh! Theo!

RIDEOUT *withdraws.*

   Theodore [*advancing to* LEONARD]. Ho! Not at home, hey?
   Leonard [*facing him*]. No, I'm not; not to *you.*
   Peter. You be quiet, Ferris.
   Leonard [*to* THEODORE]. What the devil do you mean by
forcing your way into my place?
   Theodore [*raising a walking cane which he carries*].
You . . . !

PETER *quickly puts himself between the two men as* LEONARD
seizes the chair on the left of the round table.

   Peter [*to* THEODORE, *endeavoring to get the walking cane
from him*]. Give me that. [*To* LEONARD.] You keep a civil
tongue in your head. [*To* THEODORE.] Give it me. [*Holding
the cane.*] You know what you promised. Give it up. [THEO-
DORE *resigns the cane to* PETER *and walks away to the fireplace where he stands with his back to the others.* PETER *lays
the cane upon the writing table and then turns to* LEONARD.]

You ought to be ashamed o' yourself. [*Lowering his voice.*]
You see the man's laborin' under great excitement.

Leonard [*sullenly*]. I dare say a good many people in
London are laboring under excitement. That's no reason
why they should have the run of my flat.

Peter [*coolly*]. Will you oblige me by sittin' down and
listenin' to me for a moment?

Leonard. Any man who treats me courteously'll be treated
courteously in return. [*Sitting in the chair on the left of the
round table.*] I can do with *you*, Peter.

Peter. Can you? Then you'll be so kind as to drop addressin'
me by my Christian name. [*Sitting in the chair at the writing
table.*] Ferris . . .

Leonard [*curling his lip*]. Yes, Mister Mottram?

Peter. Mrs. Blundell called upon her husband today—this
afternoon, about three o'clock. . . .

Leonard [*with an assumption of ease*]. Oh? Did she?

Peter. And made a communication to him—a communication of a very painful, very shockin' character. [*A pause.*] I
presoom you don't require me—or Blundell—to enter into
particklers?

Leonard [*in a low voice*]. Oh, for heaven's sake, no.

Peter. We may take it, without goin' further, that what
Mrs. Blundell has stated is absolutely the truth?

Leonard. Absolutely. [*A pause.* THEODORE *moves from the
fireplace to the left-hand window and stands there staring at
the prospect.*] One thing, though, she mayn't have stated as
clearly as she might . . .

Peter. What's that?

Leonard. That she—that she's an injured woman—badly
dealt with by her husband, and worse by your humble
servant; and . . .

Peter. And . . . ?

Leonard. And that both Blundell and I damn well deserve
to be hanged.

THEODORE *turns to* LEONARD *fiercely.*

Peter [*to* THEODORE]. Well! Have you any objection to
that?

THEODORE *draws himself up, as if to retort; then his body
relaxes and he drops into the chair on the left of the window.*

Peter [*to* LEONARD]. Now, then! Attend to me.

Leonard. Yes?

Peter. Obviously it's impossible, after what's transpired, that Mr. and Mrs. Blundell should ever live together again.

Leonard [*slightly surprised*]. She didn't . . . ?

Peter. I believe there *was* an idea that her husband should go back to Lancaster Gate. [*With a wave of the hand.*] But we needn't discuss *that*. We'd better come at once to the object of this meetin'.

Leonard. Object . . . ?

Peter. The best method of providin' for the safety—and happiness, we hope—of the unfortunate lady who's gone and made a bit of a munge of her affairs.

Leonard [*steadily*]. Yes?

Peter [*deliberately*]. Ferris, Mrs. Blundell has given her husband to understand that, if existin' obstacles were re-moved—if she were a free woman, in point o' fact—you'd be willin' to marry her.

Leonard. She's correct.

Peter. That you're keen on it.

Leonard [*with a nod*]. Keen on it.

Peter. Good. [*Droping his voice.*] We're all tiled here. Are you prepared to give Blundell your word of—of . . . ?

Leonard. Honor? Can't you say it? [*Hotly.*] D'ye think that because a fellow's done a scoundrelly act once in his life . . . !

Peter. That'll do—your word of honor. That bein' so, Blundell undertakes, on his part, not to oppose Mrs. Blun-dell's action for divorce. On the contrary . . . [*Turning to* THEODORE.] Theo . . . ?

Theodore. H'm?

Peter. Your word of honor?

Theodore [*in a muffled voice*]. My—word of honor.

Peter [*to* THEODORE *and* LEONARD, *shortly*]. Thank'ee. And both of you empower me to—to go to Mrs. Zoe . . . ? [*A pause.* PETER *turns to* THEODORE.] Eh?

Theodore. Yes.

Peter [*to* LEONARD]. And you? [LEONARD *is silent.*] What's the matter?

Leonard [*after a further pause, slowly*]. Look here. I don't want either of you two men to suspect me of—of play-ing double . . .

Peter. Playing double!

Leonard. I tell you honestly—Mrs. Blundell—Mrs. Blun-dell declines . . .

Peter. Declines . . . ?

Leonard. Yes; she—she refuses . . .

THEODORE *rises.*

Peter [*also rising—to* THEODORE]. Sssh! You keep out of it. [*To* LEONARD.] Ah, but you haven't seen Mrs. Blundell since . . . ?

Theodore [*to* PETER, *prompting him*]. Since she left me today. . . .

Peter [*to* LEONARD]. Since she left her husband this afternoon—[*A pause.*]—have you?

Leonard. Y-yes; I have.

Theodore [*to* PETER]. Where?

Peter [*to* LEONARD]. Where?

There is a further silence.

Theodore [*under his breath*]. What's this game, Peter? [*Loudly.*] What's this game?

Peter [*restraining him*]. Don't you interfere. [*To* LEONARD.] Ferris . . .

Leonard [*rising*]. Mottram—Mrs. Blundell called on me—about a quarter of an hour ago. We—we were talking the matter over in this room when we heard Blundell kicking up a riot in the passage. [*Glancing at the door on the right.*] She—she's here. [*There is a movement from* THEODORE.] Mottram, I depend on you. . . .

PETER *looks at* THEODORE *who, in obedience to the look, goes back to the fireplace.* LEONARD *moves to the door on the right and then turns.*

Leonard [*speaking across the room to* THEODORE]. Blundell, I—I've given you my word of honor—and—and I abide by Mrs. Blundell's decision. [*To* PETER, *pointing to* THEODORE.] Mottram, I—I depend on you . . . [*He opens the door and calls softly.*] Mrs. Blundell—— [*There is no response.*] Mrs. Blundell. . . .

Theodore [*looking down into the grate*]. Call her Zoe. [*Laughing again hoarsely.*] Why the devil don't you call her Zoe?

Leonard [*calling*]. Zoe. . . .

Still obtaining no reply, he goes into the next room. THEODORE *comes to* PETER.

Theodore [*to* PETER]. Some game up, hey?

Peter. Sssh, sssh!

Theodore. What is it? What trick is she up to now, hey?

LEONARD *reappears.*

Leonard [*standing in the doorway, bewildered*]. I—I can't make it out.

Peter. What?

Leonard. She—she's not there.

Theodore. Ha! Hooked it?

Leonard [*looking toward the balcony*]. She must have gone along the balcony without our noticing her, and through the kitchen. [*Looking at* PETER.] She must have done so.

Peter. Why?

Leonard. You know there's no other door. . . .

He crosses to the door on the left. As he gets to it, it opens and RIDEOUT *presents himself.*

Rideout [*in an odd voice*]. Sir . . .

Leonard [*to* RIDEOUT]. Has anybody passed through your kitchen?

Rideout. N-no, sir.

Leonard [*after a pause, sharply*]. What d'ye want?

Rideout. There—there's been an accident, sir.

Leonard. Accident . . . ?

At this moment THEODORE *and* PETER *turn their heads toward the balcony as if they are listening to some sounds reaching them from a distance. Giving* LEONARD *a frightened look,* RIDEOUT *withdraws quickly.* LEONARD *turns to* THEODORE *and* PETER *in time to see them hurrying on to the balcony through the left-hand window. He follows them as far as the window and recoils before them as they come back into the room after looking over the balustrade.*

Theodore [*staggering to the door on the left*]. Oh, my God; oh, my God; oh, my God! [*He disappears.*]

Leonard [*to* PETER, *shaking a trembling hand at him*]. An accident! It's an accident! [*Coming to* PETER, *appealingly.*] An accident!

Peter. Yes—an accident. . . . [*Gripping* LEONARD'S *arm.*] She told me once it would be in the wintertime! [*They go out together.*]

THE MADRAS HOUSE
A Comedy in Four Acts

by
HARLEY GRANVILLE-BARKER

The Madras House is published by kind permission of the Trustees of Granville-Barker Estates and permission to perform this play may be obtained from Curtis Brown, Ltd., 575 Madison Avenue, New York 22, New York.

CHARACTERS

Henry Huxtable

Katherine Huxtable

Laura Huxtable

Minnie Huxtable

Clara Huxtable

Julia Huxtable

Emma Huxtable

Jane Huxtable

Major Hippisly Thomas

Philip Madras

Jessica Madras

Amelia Madras

Constantine Madras

Eustace Perrin State

Marion Yates

Mr. Brigstock

Mrs. Brigstock

Miss Chancellor

Mr. Windlesham

Mr. Belhaven

Three Mannequins

A Maid at Denmark Hill

A Maid at Phillimore Gardens

THE MADRAS HOUSE

ACT ONE

The Huxtables live at Denmark Hill, for MR. HUXTABLE *is
the surviving partner in the well-known Peckham drapery
establishment of Roberts & Huxtable, and the situation, besides being salubrious, is therefore convenient. It is a new
house.* MR. HUXTABLE *bought it half finished, so that the
interior might be to his liking; its exterior the builder said
one might describe as of a Free Queen Anne Treatment; to
which* MR. HUXTABLE *rejoined, after blinking at the red brick
spotted with stone ornament, that After all it was inside they
were going to live, you know.*

*Through the stained, grained front door, rattling with col-
ored glass, one reaches the hall, needlessly narrow, needlessly dark, but with its black and white tessellated pave-
ment making for cleanliness. On the left is the stained and
grained staircase, with its Brussels carpet and twisted brass
stair rods, on the right the drawing room. The drawing room
can hardly be said to express the personality of* MR. HUX-
TABLE. *The foundations of its furnishings are in the taste of*
MRS. HUXTABLE. *For fifteen years or so additions to this family museum have been disputed into their place by the six Miss
Huxtables:* LAURA *(aged thirty-nine),* MINNIE, CLARA, JULIA,
EMMA, JANE *(aged twenty-six). The rosewood cabinets, the
picture from some academy of the early seventies, entitled
In Ye Olden Time (this was a wedding present, most
likely), the gilt clock, which is a Shakespeare, narrow-headed,
but with a masterly pair of legs, propped pensively against a
dial and enshrined beneath a dome of glass, another wedding present. These were the treasures of* MRS. HUXTABLE's
*first drawing room, her solace in the dull post-honeymoon
days. She was the daughter of a city merchant, wholesale as
against her husband's retail; but even in the seventies retail
was lifting its head. It was considered, though, that Katherine
Tombs conferred some distinction upon young* HARRY HUX-
TABLE *by marrying him, and even now, as a portly lady near-
ing sixty, she figures by the rustle of her dress, the measure
of her mellow voice, with its carefully chosen phrases, for
the dignity of the household.*

*The difference between one Miss Huxtable and another is,
to a casual eye, the difference between one lead pencil and*

321

another, as these lie upon one's table, after some weeks' use; a matter of length, of sharpening, of wear. LAURA's *distinction lies in her being the housekeeper; it is a solid power, that of ordering the dinner. She is very silent. While her sisters are silent with strangers, she is silent with her sisters. She doesn't seem to read much, either; one hopes she dreams, if only of wild adventures with a new carpet sweeper. When there was some family bitterness as to whether the fireplace, in summer, should hold ferns or a Chinese umbrella, it was* LAURA's *opinion that an umbrella gathers less dust, which carried the day.* MINNIE *and* CLARA *are inclined to religion; not sentimentally; works are a good second with them to faith. They have veered, though, lately, from district visiting to an interest in missions—missions to Poplar or China (one is almost as far as the other); good works, the results of which they cannot see. Happily, they forbear to ask why this proves the more soul-satisfying sort.*

JULIA *started life—that is to say, left school—as a genius. The headmistress had had two or three years of such dull girls that really she could not resist this excitement. Water-color sketches were the medium. So* JULIA *was dressed in brown velveteen, and sent to an art school, where they wouldn't let her do water-color drawing at all. And in two years she learned enough about the trade of an artist not ever to want to do those water-color drawings again.* JULIA *is now over thirty, and very unhappy. Three of her water colors (early masterpieces) hang on the drawing-room wall. They shame her, but her mother won't have them taken down. On a holiday she'll be off now and then for a solitary day's sketching, and as she tears up the vain attempt to put on paper the things she has learned to see, she sometimes cries. It was* JULIA, EMMA, *and* JANE *who, some years ago, conspired to present their mother with that intensely conspicuous cosy corner. A cosy corner is apparently a device for making a corner just what the very nature of a corner should forbid it to be. They beggared themselves; but one wishes that* MR. HUXTABLE *were more lavish with his dress allowances, then they might at least have afforded something not quite so hideous.*

EMMA, *having* JULIA *in mind, has run rather to coats and skirts and common sense. She would have been a success in an office, and worth, perhaps, thirty shillings a week. But the Huxtables don't want another thirty shillings a week, and this*

gift, such as it is, has been wasted, so that EMMA *runs also to
a brusque temper.*

JANE *is meekly enough a little wild.* MRS. HUXTABLE'S *power
of applying the brake of good breeding, strong enough over
five daughters, waned at the sixth attempt in twelve years,
and* JANE *has actually got herself proposed to twice by not
quite desirable young men. Now the fact that she was old
enough to be proposed to at all came as something of a shock
to the family. Birthdays pass, their celebration growing less
emphatic. No one likes to believe that the years are passing;
even the birthday's owner, least able to escape its significance,
laughs, and then changes the subject. So the Miss Huxtables
never openly asked each other what the marriage of the
youngest of them might imply; perhaps they never even asked
themselves. Besides,* JANE *didn't marry. But if she does, unless, perhaps, she runs away to do it, there will be heart
searchings, at least.* MR. HUXTABLE *asked, though, and* MRS.
HUXTABLE'S *answer—given early one morning; before the
hot water came—scarcely satisfied him.* "For," *said* MR.
HUXTABLE, "*if the girls don't marry some day, what are they
to do! It's not as if they had to go into the shop.*" "*No, thank
heaven!*" *said* MRS. HUXTABLE.

Since his illness MR. HUXTABLE *has taken to asking questions
—of anybody and about anything; of himself oftenest of all.
But for that illness he would have been a conventional enough
type of successful shopkeeper, coarsely fed, whiskered, podgy.
But eighteen months' nursing and dieting and removal from
the world seem to have brought a gentleness to his voice, a
spark of humor to his eye, a childishness to his little bursts
of temper—they have added, in fact, a wistfulness which
makes him rather a lovable old buffer on the whole.*

*This is a Sunday morning, a bright day in October. The
family are still at church, and the drawing room is empty.
The door opens, and the* PARLORMAID—*much becapped and
aproned—shows in* PHILIP MADRAS *and his friend* MAJOR
HIPPISLY THOMAS. THOMAS, *long-legged and deliberate, moves
across the room to the big French windows, which open onto
a balcony and look down on the garden and to many gardens
beyond.* THOMAS *is a good fellow.*

PHILIP MADRAS *is more complex than that. To begin with,
it is obvious he is not wholly English. A certain likeness of
figure, the keenness and color of his voice, and a liking for*

*metaphysical turns of speech show an Eastern origin, per-
haps. He is kind in manner, but rather cold, capable of that
least English of dispositions—intellectual passion. He is about
thirty-five, a year or two younger than his friend. The*
PARLORMAID *has secured* MAJOR THOMAS' *hat, and stands
clutching it. As* PHILIP *passes her into the room he asks* . . .

PHILIP. About how long?
    The Maid. In just a few minutes now, I should say, sir. Oh,
I beg pardon, does it appen to be the third Sunday in the
month?
    Philip. I don't know. Tommy, does it?
    Thomas [from the window]. Don't ask me. Well, I sup-
pose I can tell you. [*And he vaguely fishes for his diary.*]
    The Maid. No, I don't think it does, sir. Because then some
of them stop for the Oly Communion, and that may make
them late for dinner, but I don't think it is, sir.

She backs through the door, entangling the hat in the handle.

    Philip. Is my mother still staying here?
    The Maid. Mrs. Madras, sir? Yes, sir.

Then, having disentangled the hat, the PARLORMAID *vanishes.*
PHILIP *thereupon plunges swiftly into what must be an interrupted argument.*

    Philip. Well, my dear Tommy, what are the two most im-
portant things in a man's character? His attitude towards
money and his attitude towards women.
    Thomas [ponderously slowing him up]. Yes, you're full up
with moral precepts. Why behave about money as if it didn't
exist? I never said don't join the County Council.
    Philip [deliberately, but in a breath]. It is quite impossible
for any decent man to walk with his eyes open from Waterloo to Denmark Hill on a Sunday morning without wishing
me to stand for the County Council.

THOMAS *entrenches himself on a sofa.*

    Thomas. You've got what I call the reformer's mind. I
shouldn't cultivate it, Phil. It makes a man unhappy and dis-
contented, not with himself, but with other people, mark
you . . . so it makes him conceited, and puts him out of
condition both ways. Don't you get to imagine you can make
this country better by tidying it up.
    Philip [whimsically]. But I'm very interested in England,
Tommy.

Thomas [*not without some answering humor*]. We all are. But we don't all need to go about saying so. Even I can be interested in England, I suppose, though I have had to chuck the Army and take to business to earn bread and treacle for a wife and four children . . . and not a bad thing for me, either. I tell you if every chap would look after himself and his family, and lead a godly, righteous, and sober life—I'm sorry, but it is Sunday—England would get on a damn sight better than it will with all your interference.

He leans back. PHILIP's *eyes fix themselves on some great distance.*

Philip. It's a muddled country. One's first instinct is to be rhetorical about it . . . to write poetry and relive one's feelings. I once thought I might be self-sacrificing—give my goods to the poor, and go slumming—keeping my immortal soul superior still. There's something wrong with a world, Tommy, in which it takes a man like me all his time to find out that it's bread people want, and not either cake or crumbs.

Thomas. There's something wrong with a man while he will think of other people as if they were ants on an ant heap.

Philip [*relaxing to a smile*]. Tommy, that's perfectly true. I like having a good talk with you: sooner or later you always say one sensible thing.

Thomas. Thank you; you're damn polite. And, as usual, we've got right off the point.

Philip. The art of conversation!

Thomas [*shying at the easy epigram*]. Go on six County Councils, if you like. But why chuck up seven hundred a year and a directorship, if State wants you to keep 'em? And you could have double or more, and manage the place, if you'd ask for it.

Philip [*almost venomously*]. Tommy, I loathe the Madras House. State may buy it, and do what he likes with it.

JULIA *and* LAURA *arrive. They are the first from church. Sunday frocks, Sunday hats, best gloves, umbrellas and prayer books.*

Julia. Oh, what a surprise!

Philip. Yes, we walked down. Ah, you don't know . . . Let me introduce Major Hippisly Thomas . . . my cousin, Miss Julia Huxtable . . . and Miss Huxtable.

Julia. How do you do?

Thomas. How do you do?

Laura. How do you do?

Julia. Have you come to see Aunt Amy?

Philip. No, your father.

Julia. He's walking back with her. They'll be last, I'm afraid.

Laura. Will you stay to dinner?

Philip. No, I think not.

Laura. I'd better tell them you won't. Perhaps they'll be laying for you.

LAURA *goes out, decorously avoiding a collision with* EMMA, *who, panoplied as the others, comes in at the same moment.*

Philip. Hello, Emma!

Emma. Well, what a surprise!

Philip. You don't know . . . Major Hippisly Thomas . . . Miss Emma Huxtable.

Thomas. How do you do?

Emma. How do you do? Will you stay to dinner?

Philip. No, we can't. [*That formula again completed, he varies his explanation.*] I've just brought Thomas a Sunday morning walk to help me tell Uncle Henry a bit of news. My father will be back in England tomorrow.

Emma [*with a round mouth*]. Oh!

Julia. It's a beautiful morning for a walk, isn't it?

Thomas. Wonderful for October.

These two look first at each other, and then out of the window. EMMA *gazes quizzically at* PHILIP.

Emma. I think he knows.

Philip. He sort of knows.

Emma. Why are you being odd, Philip?

PHILIP *is more hail-fellow-well-met with* EMMA *than with the others.*

Philip. Emma . . . I have enticed a comparative stranger to be present so that your father and mother cannot, in decency, begin to fight the family battle over again with me. I know it's very cunning, but we did want a walk. Besides, there's a meeting tomorrow. . . .

JANE *peeps through the door.*

Jane. You? Mother!

She has turned to the hall, and from the hall comes MRS. HUXTABLE'S *rotund voice.*

Mrs. Huxtable. Yes, Jane.

Jane. Cousin Philip!

MRS. HUXTABLE *sails in, and superbly compresses every family greeting into one.*

Mrs. Huxtable. What a surprise! Will you stay to dinner?
Emma [*alive to a certain redundancy*]. No, Mother, they can't.
Philip. May I introduce my friend . . . Major Hippisly Thomas . . . my aunt, Mrs. Huxtable.
Mrs. Huxtable [*stately and gracious*]. How do you do, Major Thomas?
Philip. Thomas is Mr. Eustace State's London manager.
Thomas. How do you do?

MRS. HUXTABLE *takes an armchair with the air of one mounting a throne, and from that vantage point begins polite conversation. Her daughters distribute themselves, so do* PHILIP *and* HIPPISLY THOMAS.

Mrs. Huxtable. Not in the Army, then, Major Thomas?
Thomas. I was in the Army.
Emma. Jessica quite well, Philip?
Philip. Yes, thanks.
Emma. And Mildred?
Philip. I think so. She's back at school.
Mrs. Huxtable. A wonderfully warm autumn, is it not?
Thomas. Quite.
Mrs. Huxtable. Do you know Denmark Hill well?
Thomas. Not well.
Mrs. Huxtable. We have always lived here. I consider it healthy. But London is a healthy place, I think. Oh, I beg your pardon . . . my daughter Jane.
Jane. How do you do?

They shake hands with ceremony. EMMA, *in a mind to liven things up, goes to the window.*

Emma. We've quite a good garden, that's one thing.
Thomas [*not wholly innocent of an attempt to escape from his hostess, makes for the window, too*]. I noticed it. I am keen on gardens.
Mrs. Huxtable [*her attention distracted by* JULIA's *making for the door*]. Julia, where are you going?
Julia. To take my things off, Mother.

JULIA *departs. When they were quite little girls* MRS. HUXTABLE *always did ask her daughters where they were going*

*when they left the room, and where they had been when they
entered it, and she has never dropped the habit. They resent
it only by the extreme patience of their replies.*

Emma [*entertainingly*]. That's the Crystal Palace.
Thomas. Is it?

*They both peer appreciatively at that famous landmark. In
the Crystal Palace and the sunset the inhabitants of Denmark
Hill have acquired almost proprietary interest. Then* MRS.
HUXTABLE *speaks to her nephew with a sudden severity.*

Mrs. Huxtable. Philip, I don't consider your mother's
health is at all the thing.
Philip [*amicably*]. It never is, Aunt Kate.
Mrs. Huxtable [*admitting the justice of the retort*]. That's
true.
Philip. Uncle Henry keeps better, I think.
Mrs. Huxtable. He's well enough now. I have had a slight
cold. Is it true that your father may appear in England again?
Philip. Yes, he has only been on the Continent. He arrives
tomorrow.
Mrs. Huxtable. I'm sorry.
Jane. Mother!

MRS. HUXTABLE *has launched this with such redoubled
severity that* JANE *had to protest. However, at this moment
arrives* MR. HUXTABLE *himself, one glad smile.*

Mr. Huxtable. Ah, Phil . . . I ad an idea you might come
over. You'll stay to dinner. Jane, tell your aunt . . . she's
taking er bonnet off.

JANE *obeys. He sights on the balcony* MAJOR THOMAS' *back.*

Mr. Huxtable. Who's that outside?
Philip. Hippisly Thomas. We wanted a walk; we can't stay.
Mr. Huxtable. Oh!
Mrs. Huxtable. Have you come on business?
Philip. Well . . .
Mrs. Huxtable. On Sunday?
Philip. Not exactly.

She shakes her head, gravely deprecating. THOMAS *comes
from the balcony.*

Mr. Huxtable. How are you?
Thomas. How are you?
Mr. Huxtable. Fine morning, isn't it? Nice prospect, this
. . . see the Crystal Palace?

While THOMAS *turns, with perfect politeness, to view again this phenomenon,* PHILIP *pacifies his aunt.*

Philip. You see, Aunt Katherine, tomorrow afternoon we have the first real conference with this Mr. State about buying up the two firms, and my father is passing through England again to attend it.

Mrs. Huxtable. Of course, Philip, if it's business, I know nothing about it. But is it suggested that your uncle should attend, too?

Her voice has found a new gravity. PHILIP *becomes very airy; so does* MR. HUXTABLE, *who comes back to rejoin the conversation.*

Philip. My dear aunt, naturally.

Mr. Huxtable. What's this?

Mrs. Huxtable [*the one word expressing volumes*]. Constantine.

Mr. Huxtable [*with elaborate innocence*]. That's definite now, is it?

Mrs. Huxtable. You dropped a hint last night, Henry.

Mr. Huxtable. I dessay. I dessay I did. [*His eye shifts guiltily.*]

Mrs. Huxtable. Quite out of the question, it seems to me.

JANE *comes back.*

Jane. Aunt Mary's coming.

Mr. Huxtable [*genial again*]. Oh! My daughter Jane . . . Major Thomas, Major Hippisly Thomas.

Jane [*with discretion*]. Yes, Father.

Mrs. Huxtable [*tactfully*]. You are naturally not aware, Major Thomas, that for family reasons, into which we need not go, Mr. Huxtable has not spoken to his brother-in-law for a number of years.

PHILIP'S *eye meets* THOMAS' *in comic agony. But* MR. HUXTABLE, *too, plunges delightedly into the forbidden subject.*

Mr. Huxtable. Thirty years, very near. Wonderful, isn't it? Interested in the same business. Wasn't easy to keep it up.

Thomas. I had heard.

Mr. Huxtable. Oh, yes, notorious.

Mrs. Huxtable [*in reprobation*]. And well it may be, Henry.

MRS. MADRAS *comes in. It is evident that* PHILIP *is his father's son. He would seem so wholly but for that touch of "self-worship which is often self-mistrust"; his mother's gift,*

*appearing nowadays less lovably in her as a sort of querulous
assertion of her rights and wrongs against the troubles which
have been too strong for her. She is a pale old lady, shrunk
a little, the life gone out of her.*

Mrs. Huxtable [some severity remaining]. Amy, your husband is in England again.

PHILIP *presents a filial cheek. It is kissed.*

Philip. How are you, Mother?
Mr. Huxtable [sotto voce]. Oh, tact, Katherine, tact!
Philip. Perhaps you remember Reggie Thomas?
Thomas. I was at Marlborough with Philip, Mrs. Madras.
Mrs. Madras. Yes. Is he, Katherine?

Having given THOMAS *a limp hand, and her sister this coldest
of responses, she finds her way to a sofa, where she sits silent,
thinking to herself.* MRS. HUXTABLE *keeps majestic hold
upon her subject.*

Mrs. Huxtable. I am utterly unable to see, Philip, why your
uncle should break through his rule now.
Mr. Huxtable. There you are, Phil!
Philip. Of course it is quite for Uncle Henry to decide.
Mr. Huxtable. Naturally . . . naturally. *[Still he has an
appealing eye on* PHILIP, *who obliges him.]*
Philip. But since Mr. State's offer may not be only for the
Madras House, but Roberts and Huxtable into the bargain
. . . if the two principal proprietors can't meet him round a
table to settle the matter . . .
Thomas [ponderously diplomatic]. Yes . . . a little awk-
ward . . . if I may say so . . . as Mr. State's representative,
Mrs. Huxtable.
Mrs. Huxtable. You don't think, do you, Major Thomas,
that any amount of awkwardness should induce us to pass
over wicked conduct?

This reduces the assembly to such a shamed silence that poor
MR. HUXTABLE *can only add——*

Mr. Huxtable. Oh, talk of something else . . . talk of something else.

After a moment MRS. MADRAS' *pale voice steals in, as she
turns to her son.*

Mrs. Madras. When did you hear from your father?
Philip. A letter from Marienbad two or three days ago,
and a telegram yesterday morning.

MRS. HUXTABLE, *with a hostess' authority, now restores a polite and easy tone to the conversation.*

Mrs. Huxtable. And have you left the Army long, Major Thomas?

Thomas. Four years.

Mrs. Huxtable. Now what made you take to the drapery trade?

Philip [*very explanatory*]. Mr. State is an American financier, Aunt Kitty, who has bought up Burrow's, the big mantle place in the city, and is about to buy us up, too, perhaps.

Mrs. Huxtable. We are not in difficulties, I hope.

Philip. Oh, no.

Mrs. Huxtable. No. No doubt Henry would have told me if we had been.

As she thus gracefully dismisses the subject there appear up the steps and along the balcony the last arrivals from church, MINNIE *and* CLARA. *The male part of the company unsettles itself.*

Mr. Huxtable. Ullo! Where have you been?

Minnie. We went for a walk.

Mrs. Huxtable [*in apparently deep surprise*]. A walk, Minnie! Where to?

Minnie. Just the long way home. We thought we'd have time.

Clara. Did you notice what a short sermon?

Mr. Huxtable. Oh, may I . . . My daughter Clara . . . Major Ippisly Thomas. My daughter Minnie . . . Major Thomas.

The conventional chant begins.

Minnie. How d' you do?
Thomas. How d' you do?
Clara. How d' you do?
Minnie. How d' you do, Philip?
Philip. How d' you do?
Clara. How d' you do?
Philip. How d' you do?

The chant over, the company resettles; MR. HUXTABLE *buttonholing* PHILIP *in the process with an air of some mystery.*

Mr. Huxtable. By the way, Phil, remind me to ask you something before you go . . . rather important.

Philip. I shall be at your place in the morning. Thomas is coming to go through some figures.

Mr. Huxtable [*with a regular snap*]. Yes . . . I shan't.

Philip. The State meeting is in Bond Street, three o'clock.

Mr. Huxtable. I know, I know. [*Then, finding himself prominent, he captures the conversation.*] I'm slacking off, Major Thomas, slacking off. Ever since I was ill I've been slacking off.

Mrs. Huxtable. You are perfectly well now, Henry.

Mr. Huxtable. Not the point. I want leisure, you know, leisure. Time for reading . . . time to think a bit.

Mrs. Huxtable. Nonsense! [*She adds, with correctness.*] Major Thomas will excuse me.

Mr. Huxtable [*on his hobby*]. Oh, well . . . a man must . . . some portion of his life . . .

Thomas. Quite. I got most of my reading done early.

Mrs. Huxtable. The natural time for it.

Mr. Huxtable. Ah, lucky feller! Educated, I suppose. Well, I wasn't. I've been getting the books for years—good editions. I'd like you to see my library. But these geniuses want settling down to . . . if a man's to keep pace with the thought of the world, y' know. Macaulay, Erbert Spencer, Grote's Istory of Greece! I've got em all there.

He finds no further response. MRS. HUXTABLE *fills the gap.*

Mrs. Huxtable. I thought the sermon dull this morning, Amy, didn't you?

Mrs. Madras [*unexpectedly*]. No, I didn't.

Minnie [*to do her share of the entertaining*]. Mother, somebody ought to speak about those boys . . . it's disgraceful. Mr. Vivian had actually to turn round from the organ at them during the last hymn.

JULIA, *her things taken off, reappears.* MR. HUXTABLE *is on the spot.*

Mr. Huxtable. Ah, my daughter Julia . . . Major——

Julia. We've been introduced, Father.

She says this with a hauteur which really is pure nervousness, but MR. HUXTABLE *is sufficiently crushed.*

Mr. Huxtable. Oh, I beg pardon.

But MRS. HUXTABLE *disapproves of any self-assertion, and descends upon the culprit; who is, for some obscure reason (or for none), more often disapproved of than the others.*

Mrs. Huxtable. Close the door, please, Julia.

Julia. I'm sorry, Mother.

PHILIP *closes the offending door.* JULIA *obliterates herself in a chair, and the conversation, hardly encouraged by this little affray, comes to an intolerable standstill. At last* CLARA *makes an effort.*

Clara. Is Jessica quite well, Philip?

Philip. Yes, thank you, Clara.

Mrs. Huxtable. And dear little Mildred?

Philip. Yes, thank you, Aunt Kate.

Further standstill. Then MINNIE *contrives a remark.*

Minnie. Do you still like that school for her?

Philip [*with finesse*]. It seems to provide every accomplishment that money can buy.

MRS. HUXTABLE *discovers a sure opening.*

Mrs. Huxtable. Have you been away for the summer, Major Thomas?

Thomas [*vaguely—he is getting sympathetically tongue-tied*]. Oh . . . yes . . .

Philip. Tommy and Jessica and I took our holidays motoring around Munich and into it for the operas.

Mrs. Huxtable. Was that pleasant?

Philip. Very.

Mrs. Huxtable. And where was dear Mildred?

Philip. With her aunt most of the time . . . Jessica's sister-in-law, you know.

Minnie. Lady Ames?

Philip. Yes.

Mrs. Huxtable [*innocently, genuinely snobbish*]. Very nice for her.

Mr. Huxtable. We take a ouse at Weymouth, as a rule.

Mrs. Huxtable. Do you know Weymouth, Major Thomas?

Thomas. No, I don't.

Mrs. Huxtable. George III used to stay there, but that is a hotel now.

Mr. Huxtable. Keep your spare money in the country, y' know.

Mrs. Huxtable. Oh, there is everything one wants at Weymouth.

But even this subject flags.

Mrs. Huxtable. You think more of Bognor, Amy, I know.

Mrs. Madras. Only to live in, Katherine.

They have made their last effort. The conversation is dead.
MR. HUXTABLE's *discomfort suddenly becomes physical.*

Mr. Huxtable. I'm going to change my coat.

Philip. I think perhaps we ought to be off.

Mr. Huxtable. No, no, no, no, no! I shan't be a minute. Don't go, Phil; there's a good fellow.

And he has left them all to it. The Huxtable conversation, it will be noticed, consists mainly of asking questions. Visitors, after a time, fall into the habit, too.

Philip. Do you like this house better than the old one, Clara?

Clara. It has more rooms, you know.

Mrs. Huxtable. Do you live in London, Major Thomas?

Thomas. No, I live at Woking. I come up and down every day. I think the country's better for the children.

Mrs. Huxtable. Not a cheerful place, is it?

Thomas. Oh, very cheerful.

Mrs. Huxtable. I had thought not, for some reason.

Emma. The cemetery, Mother.

Mrs. Huxtable [*accepting the suggestion with dignity*]. Perhaps.

Clara. And of course there's a much larger garden. We have the garden of the next house as well.

Jane. Not all the garden of the next house.

Clara. Well, most of it.

This stimulating difference of opinion takes them to the balcony. PHILIP *follows.* JULIA *follows* PHILIP. MINNIE *departs to take her things off.*

Julia. Do you notice how near the Crystal Palace seems? That means rain.

Philip. Of course . . . you can see the Crystal Palace.

Mrs. Huxtable. Julia, do you think you won't catch cold on the balcony without a hat?

Julia [*meek, but, before the visitor, determined*]. I don't think so, Mother.

MRS. HUXTABLE *turns, with added politeness, to* MAJOR THOMAS.

Mrs. Huxtable. Yes, we used to live not so far along the hill; it certainly was a smaller house.

PHILIP *is now on the balcony, receiving more information.*

Philip. That's Ruskin's house, is it? Yes, I see the chimney pots.

Mrs. Huxtable. I should not have moved, myself, but I was overruled.

Emma. Mother, we had grown out of Hollybank.

Mrs. Huxtable. I was overruled. Things are done on a larger scale than they used to be. Not that I approve of that.

Thomas. Of course one's family will grow up.

Mrs. Huxtable. People spend their money nowadays. I remember my father's practice was to live on half his income. However, he lost the greater part of his money by unwise investments in lead, I think it was. I was at school at the time, in Brighton. And he educated me above my station in life.

At this moment CLARA *breaks out of the conservatory. Something has happened.*

Clara. Jane, the Agapanthus is out at last!

Jane. Oh!

They crowd in to see it. PHILIP *crowds in, too.* MRS. HUXTABLE *is unmoved.*

Mrs. Huxtable. We are told that riches are a snare, Major Thomas.

Thomas. It is one I have always found easy to avoid, Mrs. Huxtable.

Mrs. Huxtable [*oblivious of the joke, which, indeed, she would not have expected on such a subject*]. And I have noticed that their acquisition seldom improves the character of people in my station of life. I am, of course, ignorant of my husband's affairs . . . that is to say, I keep myself as ignorant as possible . . . but it is my wish that the ordering of our household should remain as it was when we were first married.

Thomas [*forestalling a yawn*]. Quite so. Quite so.

MRS. HUXTABLE *takes a breath.*

Mrs. Huxtable. A family of daughters, Major Thomas . . .

Emma [*a little agonized*]. Mother!

Mrs. Huxtable. What is it, Emma?

But EMMA *thinks better of it, and goes to join the Agapanthus party, saying——*

Emma. Nothing, Mother. I beg your pardon.

MRS. HUXTABLE *retakes her breath.*

Mrs. Huxtable. What were we saying?

Thomas [*with resigned politeness*]. A family of daughters.

Mrs. Huxtable. Yes. Were you in the war?

The inexplicable but characteristic suddenness of this rouses the MAJOR *a little.*

Thomas. I was.

Mrs. Huxtable. I find that people look differently on family life to what they used. A man no longer seems prepared to marry and support a wife and family by his unaided exertions. I consider that a pity.

Thomas [*near another yawn*]. Quite . . . quite so.

Mrs. Huxtable. I have always determined that my daughters should be sought after for themselves alone. That should insure their happiness. Any eligible gentleman who visits here constantly is always given to understand, delicately, that nothing need be expected from Mr. Huxtable beyond his approval. You are married, I think you said, Major Thomas.

This quite wakes him up, though MRS. HUXTABLE *is really innocent of her implication.*

Thomas. Yes. Oh, dear me, yes.

Mrs. Huxtable. And a family?

Thomas. Four children . . . the youngest is only three.

Mrs. Huxtable. Pretty dear!

Thomas. No; ugly little beggar, but has character.

Mrs. Huxtable. I must take off my things before dinner. You'll excuse me. If one is not punctual oneself . . .

Thomas. Quite.

Mrs. Huxtable. We cannot induce you to join us?

Thomas. Many thanks, but we have to meet Mrs. Phil for lunch in town at two.

Mrs. Huxtable. I am sorry.

THOMAS *opens the door for her with his best bow, and she graciously departs, conscious of having properly impressed him.* CLARA, *who has now her things to take off, crosses the room, saying to* PHILIP, *who follows her from the balcony——*

Clara. Yes, I'll tell Father, Philip. I'm going upstairs.

THOMAS *opens the door for her, but only with his second best bow, and then turns to* PHILIP *with a sigh.*

Thomas. Phil, we ought to be going.

Philip. Wait till you've seen my uncle again.

Thomas. All right.

He heaves another sigh and sits down. All this time there has been MRS. MADRAS *upon her sofa, silent, as forgotten as any other piece of furniture for which there is no immediate use.* PHILIP *now goes to her. When she does speak it is unresponsively.*

Philip. How long do you stay in town, Mother?

Mrs. Madras. I have been here a fortnight. I generally stay three weeks.

Philip. Jessica has been meaning to ask you to Phillimore Gardens again.

Mrs. Madras. Has she?

Philip [*a little guiltily*]. Her time's very much occupied . . . with one thing and another.

Suddenly MRS. MADRAS *rouses herself.*

Mrs. Madras. I wish to see your father, Philip.

Philip [*in doubt*]. He won't be here long, Mother.

Mrs. Madras. No, I am sure he won't.

With three delicate strides THOMAS *lands himself onto the balcony.*

Philip. Tommy being tactful! Well, I'll say that you want to see him.

Mrs. Madras. No, please don't. Tell him that I think he ought to come and see me.

Philip. He won't come, Mother.

Mrs. Madras. No, I know he won't. He came to England in May, didn't he? He was here till July, wasn't he? Did he so much as send me a message?

Philip [*with unkind patience*]. No, Mother.

Mrs. Madras. What was he doing all the while, Philip?

Philip. I didn't see much of him. I really don't know what he came back for at all. We could have done this business without him, and anyway it hasn't materialized till now. This is why he's passing through England again. I don't think there's much to be gained by your seeing him, you know.

Mrs. Madras. You are a little heartless, Philip.

This being a little true, PHILIP *a little resents it.*

Philip. My dear Mother, you and he have been separated for . . . how long is it?

Mrs. Madras [*with withered force*]. I am his wife still, I should hope. He went away from me when he was young. But I have never forgotten my duty. And now that he is an old man, and past such sin, and I am an old woman, I am still ready to be a comfort to his declining years, and it's right that I should be allowed to tell him so. And you should not let your wife put you against your own mother, Philip.

Philip [*bewildered*]. Really!

Mrs. Madras. I know what Jessica thinks of me. Jessica is very clever, and has no patience with people who can only do their best to be good . . . I understand that. Well, it isn't her duty to love me . . . at least it may not be her duty to love her husband's mother, or it may be, I don't say. But it is your duty. I sometimes think, Philip, you don't love me any longer, though you're afraid to say so.

The appeal ends so pathetically that PHILIP *is very gently equivocal.*

Philip. If I didn't love you, my dear Mother, I should be afraid to say so.

Mrs. Madras. When are you to see your father?

Philip. We've asked him to dinner tomorrow night.

At this moment EMMA *comes in with a briskness so jarring to* MRS. MADRAS' *already wrought nerves, that she turns on her.*

Mrs. Madras. Emma, why do you come bouncing in like that when I'm trying to get a private word with Philip?

Emma. Really, Aunt Amy, the drawing room belongs to everyone.

Mrs. Madras. I'm sure I don't know why I come and stay here at all. I dislike your mother intensely.

Emma. Then kindly don't tell me so. I've no wish not to be polite to you.

Philip [*pacifically*]. Emma, I think Uncle Henry ought to attend this meeting tomorrow.

Mrs. Madras [*beginning to cry*]. Of course he ought. Who is he, to go on like this about Constantine! My handkerchief's upstairs.

Emma [*contritely*]. Shall I fetch it for you, Aunt Amy?

Mrs. Madras. No. I'll be a trouble to no one.

She retires, injured. PHILIP *continues, purposely placid.*

Philip. What's more, he really wants to attend it.

Emma. I'm sorry I was rude . . . but she does get on our nerves, you know.

Philip. Why do you invite her?

Emma [*quite jolly with him*]. Oh, we're all very fond of

Aunt Amy, and anyhow, Mother would think it our duty. I
don't see how she can enjoy coming, though. She never goes
out anywhere . . . never joins in the conversation . . . just
sits nursing herself.

Philip [*quizzically*]. You're all too good, Emma.

Emma. Yes. I heard you making fun of Julia in the conservatory. But if one stopped doing one's duty how upside
down the world would be! [*Her voice now takes that tone
which is the well-bred substitute for a wink.*] I say . . . I
suppose I oughtn't to tell you about Julia, but it is rather a
joke. You know, Julia gets hysterical sometimes, when she
has her headaches.

Philip. Does she?

Emma. Well, a collar marked Lewis Waller came back
from the wash in mistake for one of Father's. I don't think
he lives near here, but it's one of these big steam laundries.
And Morgan the cook got it, and she gave it to Julia . . . and
Julia kept it. And when Mother found out she cried for a
whole day. She said it showed a wanton mind.

PHILIP'S *mocking face becomes grave.*

Philip. I don't think that's at all amusing, Emma.

Emma [*in genuine surprise*]. Don't you?

Philip. How old is Julia?

Emma. She's thirty-four. [*Her face falls, too.*] No . . . it
is rather dreadful, isn't it? [*Then wrinkling her forehead, as
at a puzzle.*] It isn't exactly that one wants to get married. I
dare say Mother is right about that.

Philip. About what?

Emma. Well, some time ago a gentleman proposed to Jane.
And Mother said it would have been more honorable if he
had spoken to Father first, and that Jane was the youngest,
and too young to know her own mind. Well, you know, she's
twenty-six. And then they heard of something he'd once done,
and it was put a stop to. And Jane was very rebellious, and
Mother cried. . . .

Philip. Does she always cry?

Emma. Yes, she does cry, if she's upset about us. And I
think she was right. One ought not to risk being unhappy for
life, ought one?

Philip. Are you all happy now, then?

Emma. Oh, deep down, I think we are. It would be so ungrateful not to be. When one has a good home and . . . !
But of course living together, and going away together, and
being together all the time, one does get a little irritable now

and then. I suppose that's why we sit as mum as maggots when people are here; we're afraid of squabbling.

Philip. Do you squabble?

Emma. Not like we used. You know, till we moved into this house, we had only two bedrooms between us, the nursery and the old night nursery. Now Laura and Minnie have one each, and there's one we take by turns. There wasn't a bigger house to be got here, or I suppose we could have had it. They hated the idea of moving far. And it's rather odd, you know, Father seems afraid of spending money, though he must have got lots. He says if he gave us any more we shouldn't know what to do with it, . . . and of course that's true.

Philip. But what occupations have you girls?

Emma. We're always busy. I mean there's lots to be done about the house, and there's calling and classes and things. Julia used to sketch quite well. You mustn't think I'm grumbling, Philip. I know I talk too much. They tell me so.

PHILIP's *comment is the question, half-serious.*

Philip. Why don't you go away, all six of you, or say five of you?

Emma [*wide-eyed*]. Go away!

Philip [*comprehensively*]. Out of it.

Emma [*wider-eyed*]. Where to?

Philip [*with a sigh—for her*]. Ah, that's just it.

Emma. How could one! And it would upset them dread-fully. Father and Mother don't know that one feels like this at times . . . they'd be very grieved.

PHILIP *turns to her with kindly irony.*

Philip. Emma, people have been worrying your father at the shop lately about the drawbacks of the living-in system. Why don't you ask him to look at home for them?

MR. HUXTABLE *returns, at ease in a jacket. He pats his daughter kindly on the shoulder.*

Mr. Huxtable. Now run along, Jane . . . I mean Emma . . . I want a word with your cousin.

Emma. Yes, Father.

EMMA—*or* JANE—*obediently disappears.* PHILIP *then looks sideways at his uncle.*

Philip. I've come over, as you asked me to.

Mr. Huxtable. I didn't ask you.

Philip. You dropped a hint.

Mr. Huxtable [*almost with a blush*]. Did I? I dessay I did.

Philip. But you must hurry up and decide about the meeting tomorrow. Thomas and I have got to go.

Mr. Huxtable. Phil, I suppose you're set on selling.

Philip. Quite.

Mr. Huxtable. You young men! The Madras Ouse means nothing to you.

Philip [*antisentimental*]. Nothing unsaleable, Uncle.

Mr. Huxtable. Well, well, well! [*Then, in a furtive fuss.*] Well, just a minute, my boy, before your aunt comes down . . . she's been going on at me upstairs, y'know! Something you must do for me tomorrow, like a good feller, at the shop in the morning. [*He suddenly becomes portentous.*] Have you heard this yet about Miss Yates?

Philip. No.

Mr. Huxtable. Disgraceful! Disgraceful!

Philip. She got on very well in Bond Street . . . learned a good deal. She has only been back a few weeks.

Mr. Huxtable [*snorting derisively*]. Learned a good deal! [*Then he sights* THOMAS *on the balcony, and hails him.*] Oh, come in, Major Thomas. [*And dropping his voice again ominously.*] Shut the window, if you don't mind; we don't want the ladies to hear this.

THOMAS *shuts the window, and* MR. HUXTABLE *spreads himself to the awful enjoyment of imparting scandal.*

Mr. Huxtable. I tell you, my boy, up at your place, got hold of she's been by some feller . . . some West End Club feller, I dessay . . . and he's put her in the . . . well, I tell you!! Major Thomas will excuse me. Not a chit of a girl, mind you, but first hand in our costume room. Buyer we were going to make her, and all!

PHILIP *frowns, both at the news and at his uncle's manner of giving it.*

Philip. What do you want me to do?

Mr. Huxtable [*more portentous than ever*]. You wait; that's not the worst of it. You know Brigstock.

Philip. Do I?

Mr. Huxtable. Oh, yes; third man in the osiery.

Philip. True.

Mr. Huxtable. Well . . . it seems that more than a week ago Miss Chancellor had caught them kissing.

Philip [*his impatience of the display growing*]. Caught who kissing?

Mr. Huxtable. I know it ain't clear. Let's go back to the beginning . . . Major Thomas will excuse me.

Thomas [*showing the properest feeling*]. Not at all.

Mr. Huxtable. Wednesday afternoon, Willoughby, that's our doctor, comes up as usual. Miss Yates goes in to see him. Miss Chancellor—that's our housekeeper, Major Thomas— over'ears, quite by accident, so she says, and afterwards taxes her with it.

Philip. Unwise.

Mr. Huxtable; No! no! Her plain duty . . . she knows my principle about such things. But then she remembers about the kissing and that gets about among our young ladies. Somebody stupid there, I grant you, but you know what these things are. And then it gets about about Miss Yates . . . all over the shop. And then it turns out that Brigstock's a married man . . . been married two years . . . secret from us, you know, because he's living in and on promotion and all the rest. And yesterday morning his wife turns up in my office, and has hysterics, and says her husband's been slandered.

Philip. I don't see why Miss Yates should come to any particular harm at our place. A girl's only out of our sight at weekends, and then we're suppose to know where she is.

Mr. Huxtable [*still instinctively spreading himself, but with that wistful look creeping on him now*]. Well . . . I had er up the day before. And I don't know what's coming over me. I scolded her well. I was in the right in all I said . . . but . . . ! Have you ever suddenly eard your own voice saying a thing? Well, I did . . . and it sounded more like a dog barking than me. And I went funny all over. So I told her to leave the room. [*He grows distressed and appealing.*] And you must take it on, Phil, . . . it ought to be settled tomorrow. Miss Yates must have the sack, and I'm not sure Brigstock hadn't better have the sack. We don't want to loss Miss Chancellor, but really if she can't hold er tongue at her age . . . well, she'd better have . . .

Philip [*out of patience*]. Oh, nonsense, Uncle!

Mr. Huxtable [*his old unquestioning self asserted for a moment*]. No, I will not have these scandals in the shop. We've always been free of em . . . almost always. I don't want to be hard on the girl. If the man's in our employ, and you can find im out . . . punish the guilty as well as the innocent . . . I'm for all that. [*That breath exhausted, he continues, quite pathetically, to* THOMAS.] But I do not know what's coming over me. Before I got ill I'd have tackled this business like winking. But when you're a long time in bed

. . . I'd never been ill like that before . . . I dunno how it
is . . . you get thinking . . . and things which used to be
quite clear don't seem nearly so clear . . . and then after,
when you start to do and say the things that used to come
natural . . . they don't come so natural as they did, and that
puts you off something . . .

This is interrupted by the reappearance of MRS. HUXTABLE,
*lace-capped, and ready for dinner. She is at the pitch to which
the upstairs dispute with her husband evidently brought her.
It would seem he bolted in the middle of it.*

Mrs. Huxtable. Is it the fact, Philip, that if your uncle
does not attend the meeting tomorrow that this business transaction with Mr.—I forget his name—the American gentleman
. . . and which I, of course, know nothing about, will be seriously upset?

Mr. Huxtable [*joining battle*]. Kitty, I don't see why I
shouldn't go. If Constantine chooses to turn up . . . that is
his business. I needn't speak directly to him . . . so to say.

Mrs. Huxtable [*hurling this choice bolt from her vocabu-
lary*]. A quibble, Henry.

Mr. Huxtable. If he's leaving England now for good . . .

Mrs. Huxtable. But you do as you like, of course.

Mr. Huxtable [*wistful again*]. I should so like you to be
convinced.

Mrs. Huxtable. Don't prevaricate, Henry. And your sister
is just coming into the room. We had better drop the subject.

And in MRS. MADRAS *does come, but what with one thing and
another* MR. HUXTABLE *is now getting what he would call
thoroughly put out.*

Mr. Huxtable. Now if Amelia here was to propose seeing
im——

Mrs. Huxtable. Henry . . . a little consideration!

Mr. Huxtable [*goaded to the truth*]. Well, I want to go,
Kitty, and that's all about it. And I dropped a int, I did, to
Phil to come over and help me through it with you. I
thought he'd make it seem as if it was most pressing business
. . . only he hasn't . . . so as to hurt your feelings less. Because I'd been bound to have told you afterwards, or it
might have slipped out somehow. Goodness gracious me, here's
the Madras House, which I've sunk enough money in these
last ten years to build a battleship, very nearly . . . a small
battleship, y'know . . . it's to be sold because Phil won't
stand by me, and his father don't care a button now. Not but

what that's Constantine all over! Marries you, Amelia, behaves like a duke and an archangel, mixed, for eighteen
months, and then——

Mrs. Huxtable [*scandalized, "Before visitors, too!"*].
Henry!

Mr. Huxtable. All right, all right. And I'm not to attend this
meeting, if you please!

The little storm subsides.

Mrs. Madras. It's to be sold, is it?

Philip. Yes, Mother.

Mrs. Madras [*at her brother*]. It was started with my
money as well as yours.

MR. HUXTABLE *is recovering, and takes no notice.*

Philip. Yes, Mother, we know.

Mrs. Madras. And if that's all you've lost by Constantine,
I don't see you've a right to be so bitter against him.

She is still ignored. MR. HUXTABLE, *quite cheery again, goes
on affably.*

Mr. Huxtable. D'you know, Major Thomas, that twenty
years ago, when that shop began to be the talk of London,
duchesses have been known to go, to all intents and purposes,
on their knees to him to design them a dress. Wouldn't do it
unless he pleased—not unless he approved their figure. Ad
Society under his thumb.

Mrs. Huxtable [*from the height of respectability*]. No
doubt he knew his business.

Mr. Huxtable [*in an ecstasy*]. Knew his business! Knew
his business!! My boy, in the old days . . . asked everywhere, like one of themselves, very nearly! First of his sort
to break that barrier. D'you know, it's my belief that if
Mrs. Gladstone had been thirty years younger, and a fashionable woman . . . he could have had a knighthood.

Mrs. Huxtable [*explicitly*]. He was untrue to his wife,
Henry.

At this MR. HUXTABLE *is the moral man again. These sudden
changes are so like him. They are genuine; he is just half-
conscious of their suddenness.*

Mr. Huxtable. Yes, I know, and Amy did what she should
have done. You see, it wasn't an ordinary case, Major Thomas.
It was girls in the shop. And even though he took em out of

the shop . . . that's a slur on the whole trade. A man in his position . . . you can't overlook that.

Mrs. Madras [*palely asserting herself*]. I could have overlooked it if I had chosen.

Philip [*to whom this is all so futile and foolish*]. My dear Mother, you were unhappy with my father, and you left him . . . the matter is very simple.

Mrs. Madras. I beg your pardon, Philip . . . I was not unhappy with him.

Mrs. Huxtable. Amy, how could you be happy with a man who was unfaithful to you? What nonsense!

JANE *and* JULIA, *from the balcony, finding the window locked, tap with their fingernails upon the pane. The very sharpness of the sound begins to put out* MR. HUXTABLE *again.*

Mr. Huxtable. No, no! They can't come in! [*He mouths at them through the window.*] You can't come in.

JANE *mouths back.*

Mr. Huxtable. What? [*Then the sense of it coming to him, he looks at his watch.*] No, it isn't . . . two minutes yet.

And he turns away, having excluded the innocent mind from this unseemly discussion. But at the very moment LAURA *comes in by the door. His patience flies.*

Mr. Huxtable. Oh, damn! Well, I beg pardon. [*Then in desperate politeness.*] Let me introduce . . . my daughter Laura . . . Major Thomas.

Laura [*collectedly*]. We have met, Father.

Mr. Huxtable [*giving it all up*]. Well . . . how can I tell . . . there are so many of you!

Mrs. Huxtable [*severely*]. I think, Henry, you had better go to this meeting tomorrow.

Mr. Huxtable [*wistful for a moment*]. You think I ought?

Mrs. Huxtable. You know you ought not.

Mr. Huxtable [*disputing it manfully*]. No . . . I don't know I ought not. It isn't so easy to know what ought and ought not to be done as you always make out, Kitty. And suppose I just do something wrong for once, and see what happens.

Mrs. Huxtable. Henry, don't say such things.

Mr. Huxtable [*very reasonably to Major Thomas*]. Well, since I've been ill——

But EMMA *and* MINNIE *have come in now, and* JANE *and* JULIA, *finding their exile a little unreasonable, rattle hard at the window.* MR. HUXTABLE *gives it all up again.*

Mr. Huxtable. Oh, let em in, Phil . . . there's a good feller.

Thomas. Allow me. [*And he does so.*]

Emma [*crisply*]. Oh! what's it all been about?

Mrs. Huxtable. Never mind, Emma.

She says this to EMMA *as she would have said it to her at the age of four. Meanwhile,* MR. HUXTABLE *has recovered.*

Mr. Huxtable. You know, Major Thomas, Constantine could always get the better of me in little things.

JANE *has sighted* MINNIE, *and callously, across the breadth of the room, imparts a tragedy.*

Jane. Minnie, your frog's dead . . . in the conservatory.

MINNIE *pales.*

Minnie. Oh, dear!

Mr. Huxtable. . . . After the difference I began to write to him as Dear Sir; to this day he'll send me business letters beginning Dear Arry.

MINNIE *is hurrying to the glass house of death.*

Jane. I buried it.

Mr. Huxtable. . . . Always at his ease, you know.

THOMAS *escapes from him.* PHILIP *is bending over his mother a little kindlier.*

Philip. I'll try to see you again before you go back to Bognor, Mother.

At this moment the gong rings. A tremendous gong, beloved of the English middle class, which makes any house seem small. A hollow sound; the dinner hour striking its own empty stomach. JANE, *whose things are not taken off, gives a mitigated yelp and dashes for the door, dashes into the returning, tidy* CLARA. MRS. HUXTABLE *shakes a finger.*

Mrs. Huxtable. Late again, Jane.

Philip. We'll be off, Aunt Katherine.

Mrs. Huxtable [*with a common humanity she has not shown before*]. Philip . . . never think I mean to be self-righteous about your father. But he made your mother most unhappy when you were too young to know of it . . . and there is the example to others, isn't there?

Philip. Yes . . . of course, Aunt Kate. I know just how you feel about it . . . I'm not fond of him, either.

PHILIP *must be a little mischievous with his aunt. She responds by returning at once to her own apparent self again.*

Mrs. Huxtable. My dear boy . . . and your own father!

From the balcony one hears the tag of JULIA'S *entertaining of* MAJOR THOMAS. *They have been peering at the horizon.*

Julia. Yes, it means rain . . . when you see it so clearly.

A general-post of leave-taking now begins.

Philip. Well, see you tomorrow, Uncle Henry.

Mr. Huxtable. Yes, I suppose so. Oh, and about that other matter. . . .

Philip. What can I do?

Mr. Huxtable. I'll telephone you in the morning.

Philip. Good-by, Mother.

Thomas. Good-by, Mrs. Huxtable.

Mrs. Huxtable [*with a final flourish of politeness*]. You have excused this domestic discussion, I hope, Major Thomas . . . it will happen sometimes.

Thomas. I've been most interested.

MINNIE *comes back sadly from the frog's grave.*

Philip. Good-by, Clara.

Clara. Good-by, Philip.

Mr. Huxtable. You really won't stay to dinner?

Philip. Good-by, Laura.

Thomas. Thanks, no. We meet tomorrow.

The general-post quickens, the chorus grows confused.

Laura. Good-by.

Thomas. Good-by.

Jane. Good-by.

Thomas. Good-by.

Philip. Good-by, Emma—oh, pardon.

There has been confusion of crossed hands. Apologies, withdrawals, a treading on toes, more apologies.

Emma. Good-by, Major Thomas.

Philip. Now good-by, Emma.

Thomas. Good-by, Mrs. Madras.
Philip. Good-by.
Thomas. Good-by.

The chorus and the general-post continue, until at last
PHILIP *and* THOMAS *escape to a tram and a tube and their
lunch, while the Huxtables sit down in all ceremony to Sunday
dinner: roast beef, horse-radish, Yorkshire pudding, brown
potatoes, Brussels sprouts, apple tart, custard and cream,
Stilton cheese, desert.*

ACT TWO

*The business offices of Roberts & Huxtable are tucked away
upon the first floor somewhere at the back of that large
drapery establishment. The waiting room—the one in which
employee sits in shivering preparation for interviews with
employer—besides thus having been the silent scene of more
misery than most places on earth, is one of the very ugliest
rooms that ever entered into the mind of a builder and deco-
rator. Four plain walls of brick or plaster, with seats round
them, would have left it a waiting room pure and simple. But
the ugly hand of the money-maker was upon it. In the person
of a contractor he thrust upon the unfortunate room—as on
all the others—everything that could excuse his price and dis-
guise his profit. The walls, to start with, were distempered an
unobjectionable green, but as that might seem too plain and
cheap, a dado of a nice stone color was added, topped with
stenciling in dirty red of a pattern that once was Greek.*

*The fireplace is apparently designed to provide the maximum
amount of work possible for the wretched boy who cleans it
every morning, retiring from the contest well black-leaded
himself. The mantelpiece above—only an expert in such
abominations knows what it is made of; but it pretends, with
the aid of worm-shaped dashes of paint, to be brown marble.
It is too high for comfort, too low for dignity. It has to be
dusted, and usually isn't.*

*The square lines of the two long windows, which look upon
some sanitary brick airshaft, have been carefully spoiled by
the ovaling of their top panes. The half-glazed door, that*

*opens from the passage, is of the wrong shape; the green baize
door, that admits to* MR. PHILIP's *room, is of the wrong
color.*

*And then the furnishing! Those yellow chairs upholstered in
red-cotton goose-flesh plush; that plush-seated, plush-backed
bench, placed draftily between the windows! There is a
reasonable office table in the middle of the room. On the walls
are, firstly, photographs of Roberts and Huxtable. Roberts
was a Welshman, and looks it. No prosperous drapery business in London but has its Welshman. There is also a photograph of the premises—actual; and an advertisement sketch
of them—ideal. There is a ten-year-old fashion plate: twenty
faultless ladies engaged in ladylike occupations or serene in
the lack of any. There is an insurance almanac, the one thing
of beauty in the room. On the mantelpiece lies a London Di-
rectory, the one piece of true color.*

*The hand of the money-maker that has wrenched awry the
Greek pattern on the wall has been laid also on all the four
people who sit waiting for* MR. PHILIP *at noon on this Monday; and to the warping more or less of them all.*

MRS. BRIGSTOCK, *sitting stiffly on the plush bench, in brown
quilled hat and coat and skirt, is, one would guess, a clerk of
some sort. She lacks color; she lacks repose; she lacks—one
stops to consider that she might possibly be a beautiful woman
were it not for the thing she lacks. But she is the product of
fifteen years or so of long hours and little lunch. Certainly
at this moment she is not seen at her best. She sits twisting
her gloved hands, pulling at a loose thread, now and then biting it. Otherwise she bites her lips; her face is drawn, and she
stares in front of her with only a twist of the eye now and
then toward her husband, who is uncomfortable upon a chair
a few feet away.*

If one were asked to size up MR. BRIGSTOCK, *one would say:
Nothing against him. The position of Third Man in the
Hosiery does not require any special talents, and it doesn't
get them; or if it does, they don't stay there. And* MR. BRIG-
STOCK *stays there—just stays there. It sums him up—sums
up millions of him—to say that in their youth they have
energy enough to get into a position; afterwards, in their terror—or sometimes only because their employers have not the
heart to dismiss them—they stay there. Sometimes, though,
the employers have the heart, and do. And then what hap-*

*pens? Considered as a man rather than a wage earner—not
that it is usual for us so to consider him—he is one of those
who, happily for themselves, get married by women whom
apparently no other man much wants to marry. Subdued to
what he works in, he is dressed as a Third Man in the Hosiery
should be. He is, at the moment, as agitated as his wife, and
as he has no nervous force to be agitated with, is in a state
of greater wretchedness.*

On the other side of the room sits MISS CHANCELLOR. *Every
large living-in draper's should have as housekeeper a lady of a
certain age, who can embody in her own person the virtues
she will expect in the young ladies under her. Decorum, sobriety of thought, tidiness, respect of persons—these are the
qualities generally necessary to a shop assistant's salvation.*
MISS CHANCELLOR *radiates them. They are genuine in her,
too. She is now planted squarely on her chair, as it might be,
in easy authority, but looking closely, one may see that it is
a dignified resentment keeping her there unmovable.*

In the middle of the room, by the table, sits MISS YATES.
*While they wait this long time the other three try hard to
keep their eyes off her. It isn't easy; partly because she is in
the middle of the room and they are not. But anyhow and
anywhere* MISS YATES *is a person that you look at, though
you may ignorantly wonder why. She is by no means pretty,
nor does she try to attract you. But look at her as you look
at a fire or a light in an otherwise empty room. She is not a
lady, nor is she well educated, and ten years' shop assisting
has left its marks on her. But there it is. To the seeing eye she
glows in that room like a live coal. She has genius—she has
life, to however low a use she—or the world for her—may put
it. And commoner people are lusterless beside her.*

*They wait silently, and the tension increases. At last it is
slightly relieved by* PHILIP's *arrival. He comes in briskly, his
hat on, a number of unopened letters in his hand. They get
up to receive him with varying degrees of respect and appre-
hension.*

PHILIP. Good morning, Miss Chancellor. Good morning, Miss
Yates. Good morning, Mr. Brigstock.
    Mr. Brigstock [introducing her]. Mrs. Brigstock.

PHILIP *nods pleasantly to* MRS. BRIGSTOCK, *who purses her
lips in a half-frightened, half-vengeful way, and sits down
again. Then he puts his hat on the mantelpiece and settles
himself in the master position at the table.*

Philip. I'm afraid I've kept you waiting a little. Well, now——

There is a sharp knock at the door.

Philip. Come in.

It is BELHAVEN. BELHAVEN *is seventeen, perhaps, on the climb from office boy to clerk, of the usual pattern.* PHILIP *greets him pleasantly.*

Philip. Oh, good morning, Belhaven.

Belhaven. I've put Major Thomas in your room, sir, as the papers were there, but Mr. Huxtable's is empty, if you'd like . . .

Philip. No, this'll do.

Belhaven. Major Thomas said would you speak to him for a minute, as soon as you came.

Philip. I'll go in now.

Belhaven. Thank you, sir.

Philip [*to the waiting four*]. Excuse me one minute, please.

BELHAVEN *bolts back to his outer office by one door—his way of opening and getting through it is a labor-saving invention; and* PHILIP *goes to find* THOMAS *through the other. There is silence again, held by these four at a greater tension than ever. At last* MRS. BRIGSTOCK, *least able to bear it, gives one desperate wriggle-fidget.* BRIGSTOCK *looks at her deprecatingly and says* . . .

Mr. Brigstock. Will you sit here, Freda, if you feel the draft?

Mrs. Brigstock [*just trusting herself to answer*]. No, thank you.

Silence again, but soon broken by PHILIP, *who comes from the other room, throwing over his shoulder the last of his few words with* THOMAS.

Philip. All right, Tommy. [TOMMY, *even at the dullest business, always pleasantly amuses him. Then he settles himself at the table for the second time, conciliatory, kind.*] Well, now . . .

MRS. BRIGSTOCK, *determined to be first heard, lets slip the torrent of her wrath.*

Mrs. Brigstock. It's slander, Mr. Madras, and I request that it shall be retracted immediately . . . before everybody . . . in the public press . . . by advertisement.

Mr. Brigstock [*in an agonized whisper*]. Oh, Freda . . .
not so eadstrong.

PHILIP *is elaborately cool and good-tempered.*

Philip. Miss Chancellor.

MISS CHANCELLOR *is even more elaborately cold and dignified.*

Miss Chancellor. Yes, sir.
Philip. I think we might inform Mrs. Brigstock that we're
sorry the accusation has become so public . . . it has nat-
urally caused her some pain.
Mrs. Brigstock [*ascending the scale*]. I don't believe it
. . . I didn't believe it . . . if I'd have believed it——
Mr. Brigstock [*interposing*]. Oh, Freda!
Miss Chancellor [*very definitely*]. I saw them kissing. I
didn't know Mr. Brigstock was a married man. And even if
I had known it . . . I saw them kissing.

MISS YATES, *opening her mouth for the first time, shows an
easy impatience of their anger and their attitudes, too.*

Miss Yates. Oh . . . what sort of a kiss?
Miss Chancellor. Are there different sorts of kisses, Miss
Yates?
Miss Yates. Well . . . aren't there?
Mrs. Brigstock [*growing shrill now*]. He owns he did that,
and he knows he shouldn't have, and he asked my pardon . . .
and whose business is it, but mine . . . ?
Mr. Brigstock [*vainly interposing this time*]. Oh, Freda!
Mrs. Brigstock [*climbing to hysterics*]. Hussy to let him
. . . hussy . . . hussy!

PHILIP *adds a little severity to his coolness.*

Philip. Mrs. Brigstock.
Miss Yates [*as pleasant as possible*]. All right . . . Mr.
Madras, I don't mind.
Philip. But I do. Mrs. Brigstock, I shall not attempt to
clear up this business unless we can all manage to keep our
tempers.

MISS YATES *collectedly explains.*

Miss Yates. I've been friends with Mr. Brigstock these
twelve years. We both came into the firm together . . . and
I knew he was married . . . p'raps I'm the only one that
did. And when I told him . . . all I chose to tell him as to

what had happened to me . . . I asked him to kiss me just to show he didn't think so much the worse of me. And he gave me one kiss . . . here. [*She dabs with one finger the left top corner of her forehead.*] And that is the truth of that.

Philip. You might have given this explanation to Miss Chancellor.

Miss Yates. She wouldn't have believed it.

Miss Chancellor. I don't believe it.

Mrs. Brigstock [*with gathering force*]. William! William!! William!!!

BRIGSTOCK *desperately musters a little authority.*

Mr. Brigstock. Freda, be quiet . . . haven't I sworn it to you on the Bible?

MISS CHANCELLOR *now puts her case.*

Miss Chancellor. I may say I have known other young ladies in trouble and whether they behaved properly or improperly under the circumstances . . . and I've known them behave both . . . they did not confide in their gentlemen friends . . . without the best of reasons.

Philip. There is no reason that they shouldn't, Miss Chancellor.

Miss Chancellor. They didn't.

Miss Yates. Well . . . I did.

Miss Chancellor. I had no wish for the scandal to get about. I don't know how it happened.

Miss Yates. Ask your little favorite, Miss Jordan, how it happened.

This shot tells. MISS CHANCELLOR's *voice sharpens.*

Miss Chancellor. Mr. Madras, if I am to be accused of favoritism——

Philip. Yes, yes . . . we'll keep to the point, I think.

Miss Chancellor. If Mr. Brigstock wasn't the man——

Mrs. Brigstock [*the spring touched*]. William!

Miss Chancellor. Why shouldn't she tell me who it was?

Miss Yates. Why should I?

Miss Chancellor. Am I here to look after the morals of these young ladies, or am I not?

Mrs. Brigstock. A set of hussies.

Mr. Brigstock [*in agony*]. Freda, you'll get me the sack.

Philip. Brigstock, if I wished to give anyone the sack, I should not be taking the trouble to discuss this with you all in—I hope—a reasonable way.

MRS. BRIGSTOCK, *much resenting reasonableness, stands up now to give battle.*

Mrs. Brigstock. Oh, give him the sack, if you please, Mr. Madras. It's time he had it for his own sake.

Mr. Brigstock. No, Freda!

Mrs. Brigstock. You've got your way to make in the world, haven't you? He's got to start on his own like other people, hasn't he?

Mr. Brigstock [*feeling safety and his situation slipping*]. In time, Freda.

Mrs. Brigstock. Now's the time. If you're not sick of the life you lead . . . seeing me once a week for an hour or two . . . then I am. And this libel and slander makes about the last straw, I should think.

Philip. How long have you been married, Mrs. Brigstock?

Mrs. Brigstock. Four years.

Philip. Four years!

Mrs. Brigstock [*a little quelled by his equable courtesy*]. Four years!

Philip [*in amazed impatience*]. My dear Brigstock, why not have come to the firm and told them? It could have been arranged for you to live out with your wife.

Mr. Brigstock. Well, I have been thinking of it lately, sir, but I never seem to happen on a really likely moment. I'm afraid I'm not a favorite in my department.

Mrs. Brigstock. No fault of his!

Mr. Brigstock. And it's sometimes a very little thing makes the difference between a feller's going and staying . . . when all those that aren't wanted are cleared out after sale time, I mean, for instance. And, of course, the thirty pound a year they allow you to live out on does not keep you . . . it's no use my saying it does. And when you're married . . .

Mrs. Brigstock [*who has gathered her grievances again*]. I agreed to it. I have my profession, too. We've been saving quicker. It's three hundred pounds now, all but a bit . . . that's enough to start on. I've got my eye on the premises. It's near here, I don't mind telling you. Why shouldn't we do as well as others . . . and ride in our carriages when we're fifty!

Mr. Brigstock [*deprecating such great optimism*]. Well, I've asked advice . . .

Mrs. Brigstock. You think too much of advice. If you'd value yourself higher! Give him the sack, if you please, Mr. Madras, and I'll say thank you.

THE MADRAS HOUSE

She finishes, and suddenly Miss Yates *takes up this part of the tale quite otherwise.*

Miss Yates. He has asked my advice, and I've told him to stay where he is.

Mrs. Brigstock [*her breath leaving her*]. Oh, indeed!

Miss Yates. He's as steady as can be. But his appearance is against him.

Mrs. Brigstock [*hardly recovering it*]. Well, I never!

Mr. Brigstock. A feller does think of the future, Marion.

Miss Yates. I wouldn't if I were you. I don't know where we all get to when we're fifty, and I've never met anyone who did. We're not in the shop any longer, most of us, are we? And we're not all in our carriages.

Mr. Brigstock [*meekly*]. I suppose it can be done.

Miss Yates. Oh . . . premises near here and three hundred pounds. Perfect foolery, and William ought to know it is. This firm'll undersell you and eat you up and a dozen more like you . . . and the place that's trusted you for your stock will sell up every stick, and there you'll be in the gutter. I advised him to own up to you [*She nods at* Mrs. Brigstock.] and live out and do the best he could.

Mrs. Brigstock [*more drenched with the cold water than she'll own*]. I'm much obliged, I'm sure . . . I've my own opinion. . . .

Philip [*who has been studying her rather anxiously*]. You've no children, Mrs. Brigstock?

Mrs. Brigstock *goes white.*

Mrs. Brigstock. No, I've no children. How can you save when you have children? But if it was his child this hussy was going to have, and I thought God wouldn't strike him dead on the spot, I'd do it myself, so I would . . . and he knows I would.

Mr. Brigstock. Haven't I taken my oath to you, Freda?

Mrs. Brigstock. How can I tell if he's speaking the truth . . . I ask you how can I tell? I lie awake at night away from him till I could scream with thinking about it. And I do scream as loud as I dare . . . not to wake the house. And if somebody don't open that window, I shall go off.

Philip. Open the window, please, Mr. Brigstock.

Philip's *voice is serious, though he says but a simple thing.* Mr. Brigstock *opens the window as a man may do in a sick room, helpless, a little dazed. Then he turns back to his wife, who is sitting, head tilted against the sharp back of the plush bench, eyes shut, mouth open. Only* MISS YATES *is ready with her bit of practical comfort.*

Miss Yates. Look here, don't you worry. I could have married William if I'd wanted to. That ought to be proof enough.

Mr. Brigstock. There you are, Freda.

Miss Yates. Before he knew you.

Mrs. Brigstock [*opening her eyes*]. Did you ask her?

Miss Yates. No, he never asked me . . . but you know what I mean.

MISS YATES *gives emphasis to this with what one fears must be described as a wink.* MRS. BRIGSTOCK *looks at the acquiescent* BRIGSTOCK *and acknowledges the implication.*

Mrs. Brigstock. Yes, I know. Oh, I don't believe it really.

Comforted, she discovers her handkerchief and blows her nose, after which MISS CHANCELLOR, *who has been sitting all this while still, silent, and scornful, inquires in her politest voice.*

Miss Chancellor. Do you wish me still to remain, Mr. Madras?

Philip. One moment.

Miss Yates. Oh, you'll excuse my back, sir. [*And she turns to the table again.*]

Philip. I don't think I need detain you any longer, Mr. and Mrs. Brigstock. Your character is now quite clear in the firm's eyes, Brigstock, and I shall see that arrangements are made for you to live out in the future. I apologize to you both for all this unpleasantness.

They have both risen at this, and now BRIGSTOCK *begins, hesitatingly.*

Mr. Brigstock. Well . . . thank you . . . sir . . . and . . .

Mrs. Brigstock. No, William.

Mr. Brigstock. All right, Freda! [*He struggles into his prepared speech.*] We are very much obliged to you, sir, but I do not see how I can remain with the firm unless there has been, with regard to the accusation, some definite retraction.

Philip [*near the end of his patience*]. My good man, it is retracted.

Mrs. Brigstock. Publicly.

Philip. Nonsense, Mrs. Brigstock.

Mrs. Brigstock [*quite herself again*]. Is it indeed . . . how would you like it? [*Then becoming self-conscious.*] Well, I beg pardon. I'm sure we're very sorry for Miss Yates, and I wish she were married.

Miss Yates [with some gusto]. So do I!

Suddenly MISS CHANCELLOR *bursts out.*

Miss Chancellor. Then you wicked girl, why didn't you say so before . . . when I wished to be kind to you? And we shouldn't all be talking in this outrageous, indecent way. I never did in all my life. I don't know how I manage to sit here. Didn't I try to be kind to you?

Miss Yates [unconquerable]. Yes, and you tried to cry over me. No, I don't wish I were married.

Mr. Brigstock. Of course, it's not for me to say, Marion, but will the way you're going on now stop the other young ladies tattling?

The tone of the dispute now sharpens rather dangerously.

Mrs. Brigstock. How's Mr. Brigstock to remain in the firm if Miss Chancellor does?

Philip. That is my business, Mrs. Brigstock.

Miss Chancellor. What . . . when I saw him kissing her . . . kissing her!

Mrs. Brigstock. William!

Philip. That has been explained.

Miss Chancellor. No, Mr. Madras, while I'm housekeeper here I will not countenance loose behavior. I don't believe one word of these excuses.

Philip. This is just obstinacy, Miss Chancellor.

Miss Chancellor. And personally I wish to reiterate every single thing I said.

And now it degenerates into a wrangle.

Mrs. Brigstock. Then the law shall deal with you.

Miss Chancellor. You can dismiss me at once, if you like, Mr. Madras.

Mrs. Brigstock. It's libelous . . . it's slander . . . !

Mr. Brigstock. Oh, Freda, don't!

Mrs. Brigstock. Yes, and she can be put in prison for it.

Miss Chancellor. If Miss Yates and Mr. Brigstock stay with this firm, I go.

Mrs. Brigstock. And she shall be put in prison . . . the cat!

Mr. Brigstock. Don't, Freda!

Mrs. Brigstock. The heartless cat! Do you swear it isn't true, William?

Philip. Take your wife away, Brigstock.

PHILIP'*s sudden vehemence causes* MRS. BRIGSTOCK *to make straight for the edge of her self-control—and over it.*

Mrs. Brigstock. Yes, and he takes himself away . . . leaves the firm, I should think so, and sorry enough you'll be before we've done. I'll see what the law will say to her . . . and they're not a hundred yards off . . . on the better side of the street, too, and a plate glass window as big as yours.

Mr. Brigstock. Do be quiet, Freda!

Mrs. Brigstock [*in hysterics now*]. Three hundred pounds, and how much did Maple have when he started . . . or Whiteley . . . and damages, what's more . . . And me putting up with the life I've led . . . !

*They wait till the fit subsides—*PHILIP *with kindly impatience,* BRIGSTOCK *in mute apology—and* MRS. BRIGSTOCK *is a mass of sobs. Then* BRIGSTOCK *edges her towards the door.*

Philip. Wait . . . wait . . . wait. You can't go into the passage making that noise.

Mr. Brigstock. Oh, Freda, you don't mean it.

Mrs. Brigstock [*relieved and contrite*]. I'm sure I hope I've said nothing unbecoming a lady . . . I didn't mean to.

Philip. Not at all . . . it's natural you should be upset.

Mrs. Brigstock. And we're very much obliged for your kind intentions to us . . .

Philip. Wait till you're quite calm.

Mrs. Brigstock. Thank you.

Then with a final touch of injury, resentment, dignity, she shakes off BRIGSTOCK'*s timid hold.*

Mrs. Brigstock. You needn't hold me, William.

WILLIAM *follows her out to forget and make her forget it all as best he can.* PHILIP *comes back to his chair, still good-humored, but not altogether pleased with his own part in the business so far.*

Philip. I'm afraid you've put yourself in the wrong, Miss Chancellor.

Miss Chancellor. One often does, sir, in doing one's duty. [*Then her voice rises to a sort of swan song.*] Thirty years have I been with the firm . . . only thirty years. I will leave tomorrow.

Philip. I hope you recognize it will not be my fault if you have to.

Miss Chancellor. Miss Yates can obviate it. She has only to speak the truth.

PHILIP *now makes another effort to be frank and kindly.*

Philip. Miss Chancellor, are we quite appreciating the situation from Miss Yates's point of view? Suppose she were married?

Miss Yates. I'm not married.

Philip. But if you told us you were, we should have to believe you.

Miss Chancellor. Why, Mr. Madras?

Philip [*with a smile*]. It would be good manners to believe her. We must believe so much of what we're told in this world.

Miss Yates [*who has quite caught on*]. Well, I did mean to stick that up on you . . . if anyone wants to know. I bought a wedding ring, and I had it on when I saw Dr. Willoughby. But when she came in with her long face and her What can I do for you, my poor child? . . . well, I just couldn't . . . I suppose the Devil tempted me, and I told her the truth.

Philip. That's as I thought, so far. Miss Yates, have you that wedding ring with you?

Miss Yates. Yes, I have . . . it's not real gold.

Philip. Put it on.

MISS YATES, *having fished it out of a petticoat pocket, rather wonderingly does so, and* PHILIP *turns, maliciously humorous, to* MISS CHANCELLOR.

Philip. Now where are we, Miss Chancellor?

Miss Chancellor. I think we're mocking at a very sacred thing, Mr. Madras.

Miss Yates. Yes . . . and I won't now.

With a sudden access of emotion she slams the ring upon the table. PHILIP *meditates for a moment on the fact that there are some things in life still inaccessible to his light-hearted logic.*

Philip. True . . . true . . . I beg both your pardons. But suppose the affair had not got about, Miss Yates?

Miss Yates. Well . . . I should have had a nice long illness. It'd all depend on whether you wanted me enough to keep my place open.

Philip. You are an employee of some value to the firm.

Miss Yates. I reckoned you would. Miss McIntyre'd be pleased to stay on a bit now she's quarreled with her fiancé. Of course, if I'd only been behind the counter . . .

Miss Chancellor [*who has drawn the longest of breaths at this calculated immodesty*]. This is how she brazened it out to me, Mr. Madras. This is just what she told Mr. Huxtable

. . . and you'll pardon my saying he took a very different view of the matter to what you seem to be taking.

Miss Yates. Oh, I've got to go, now I'm found out . . . I'm not arguing about it.

Miss Chancellor [*severely*]. Mr. Madras, what sort of notions are you fostering in this wretched girl's mind?

Philip [*gently enough*]. I was trying for a moment to put myself in her place.

Miss Chancellor. You will excuse me saying, sir, that you are a man . . .

Philip. Not at all!

A poor joke, but MISS CHANCELLOR *remains unconscious of it.*

Miss Chancellor. Because a woman is independent, and earning her living, she's not to think she can go on as she pleases. If she wishes to have children, Providence has provided a way in the institution of marriage. Miss Yates would have found little difficulty in getting married, I gather.

Miss Yates. Living in here for twelve years!

Miss Chancellor. Have you been a prisoner, Miss Yates? Not to mention that there are two hundred and thirty-five gentlemen employed here.

Miss Yates. Supposing I don't like any of em?

Miss Chancellor. My dear Miss Yates, if you are merely looking for a husband as such . . . well . . . we're all God's creatures, I suppose. Personally, I don't notice much difference in men, anyway.

Miss Yates. Nor did I.

Miss Chancellor. Lack of self-control . . .

Miss Yates. Is it!

Miss Chancellor. . . . And self-respect. That's what the matter is. Are we beasts of the field, I should like to know? I simply do not understand this unladylike attitude towards the facts of life. Is there nothing for a woman to do in the world but to run after men . . . or pretend to run away from them? I am fifty-eight . . . and I have passed, thank God, a busy and a happy and I hope a useful life . . . and I have never thought any more or less of men than I have of any other human beings . . . or any differently. I look upon spinsterhood as an honorable state, as my Bible teaches me to. Men are different. But some women marry happily and well . . . and all women can't . . . and some can't marry at all. These facts have to be faced, I take it.

Philip. We may take it that Miss Yates has been facing them.

Miss Chancellor. Yes, sir, and in what spirit? I have always endeavored to influence the young ladies under my control toward the virtues of modesty and decorum . . . so that they may regard either state with an indifferent mind. If I can no longer do that, I prefer to resign my charge. I will say before this young person that I regret the story should have got about. But when anyone has committed a fault it seems to me immaterial who knows of it.

Philip [*reduced to irony*]. Do you really think so?

Miss Chancellor. Do you require me any more now?

Philip. I am glad to have had your explanation. We'll have a private talk tomorrow.

Miss Chancellor. Thank you, sir. I think that will be more in order. Good morning.

Philip. Good morning.

MISS CHANCELLOR *has expressed herself to her entire satisfaction, and retires in good order.* MISS YATES, *conscientiously brazen until the enemy has quite disappeared, collapses pathetically. And* PHILIP, *at his ease at last, begins to scold her in a most brotherly manner.*

Miss Yates. I'm sure she's quite right in all she says.

Philip. She may not be. But are you the sort of woman to have got yourself into a scrape of this kind, Miss Yates?

Miss Yates. I'm glad you think I'm not, sir.

Philip. Then what on earth did you go and do it for?

Miss Yates. I don't know. I didn't mean to.

Philip. Why aren't you married?

Miss Yates. That's my business. [*Then, as if making amends for the sudden snap.*] Oh . . . I've thought of getting married any time these twelve years. But look what happens . . . look at the Brigstocks . . .

Philip. No, no, no . . . that's not what I mean. Why aren't you to be married even now?

Miss Yates. I'd rather not say.

MISS YATES *assumes an air of reticence natural enough; but there is something a little peculiar in the manner of it, so* PHILIP *thinks.*

Philip. Very well.

Miss Yates. I'd rather not talk about that part of it, sir, with you, if you don't mind. [*Then she bursts out again.*] I took the risk. I knew what I was about. I wanted to have my fling. And it was fun for a bit. That sounds horrid, I know, but it was.

PHILIP *is watching her.*

Philip. Miss Yates, I've been standing up for you, haven't I?

Miss Yates. Yes.

Philip. That's because I have unconventional opinions. But I don't do unconventional things.

Miss Yates [*naïvely*]. Why don't you?

Philip. I shouldn't do them well. Now you start on this adventure believing all the other people say, so I'm not happy about you. As man to man, Miss Yates . . . were you in a position to run this risk?

MISS YATES *honestly thinks before she speaks.*

Miss Yates. Yes . . . I shall be getting a hundred and forty a year living-out. I've planned it all. [*She grows happily confidential.*] There's a maisonette at Raynes Park, and I can get a cheap girl to look after it and to take care of . . . I shall call him my nephew, like the Popes of Rome used to . . . or why can't I be a widow? I can bring him up and do him well on it. Insurance'll be a bit stiff in case anything happens to me. But I've got nearly two hundred saved in the bank to see me through till next summer.

Philip. Where are you going when you leave here? What relations have you?

Miss Yates. I have an aunt. I hate her.

Philip. Where are you going for the winter?

Miss Yates. Evercreech.

Philip. Where's that?

Miss Yates. I don't know. You get to it from Waterloo. I found it in the A. B. C.

Philip [*in protest*]. But my dear girl . . . !

Miss Yates. Well, I want a place where nobody knows me, so I'd better go to one which I don't know, hadn't I? I always make friends. I'm not afraid of people. And I've never been in the country in the winter. I want to see what it's like.

PHILIP *surrenders, on this point beaten; but takes up another more seriously.*

Philip. Well . . . granted that you don't want a husband . . . it's your obvious duty to make the man help you support his child.

Miss Yates *is ready for it; serious, too.*

Miss Yates. I dare say. But I won't. I've known other girls in this sort of mess—one or two . . . with everybody being kind to them and sneering at them. And there they sat and cried, and were ashamed of themselves! What's the good of that? And the fellows hating them. Well, I don't want him to hate me. He can forget all about it if he likes . . . and of course he will. I started by crying my eyes out. Then I thought that if I couldn't buck up and anyway pretend to be pleased and jolly-well proud, I might as well die. And d'you know when I'd been pretending a bit I found that I really was pleased and proud. . . . And I am really proud and happy about it now, sir . . . I am not pretending. I dare say I've done wrong . . . perhaps I ought to come to grief altogether, but——

At this moment a telephone in the table rings violently, and Miss Yates *apologizes—to it, apparently.*

Miss Yates. Oh, I beg pardon.
Philip. Excuse me. [*Then answering.*] Yes. Who? No, no, no . . . State. Mr. State. Put him through. [*He is evidently put through.*] Morning! Who? My father . . . not yet. Yes, from Marienbad.

Miss Yates *gets up, apparently to withdraw tactfully, but looking a little startled, too.*

Miss Yates. Shall I . . .
Philip. No, no; it's all right.

Belhaven *knocks, comes in, and stands waiting by* Philip, *who telephones on.*

Philip. Yes? Well? . . . Who? . . . Mark who? . . . Aurelius. No. I've not been reading him lately . . . Certainly I will . . . Thomas is here doing figures . . . d'you want him . . . I'll put you through. . . . No, wait. I'll call him here, if it's not private. [*Then calling out.*] Tommy!
Belhaven. Major Thomas is in the countinghouse, sir.
Philip. Oh. [*Then through the telephone.*] If you'll hold the line I can get him in a minute. Say Mr. State's on the telephone for him, Belhaven.
Belhaven. Yes, sir . . . and Mrs. Madras is below in a taxicab, sir, and would like to speak to you. Shall she come up, or, if you're too busy to be interrupted, will you come down to her?

Philip. My mother?

Belhaven. No, not Mrs. Madras . . . your Mrs. Madras, sir.

Philip. Bring her up. And tell Major Thomas.

Belhaven. Yes, sir.

BELHAVEN *achieves a greased departure, and* PHILIP *turns back to* MISS YATES.

Philip. Where were we?

Miss Yates [*inconsequently*]. It is hot in here, isn't it?

Philip. The window's open.

Miss Yates. Shall I shut it?

She turns and goes up to the window; one would say to run away from him. PHILIP *watches her steadily.*

Philip. What's the matter, Miss Yates?

She comes back more collectedly.

Miss Yates. Oh, I'm sure Miss Chancellor can't expect me to marry one like that now . . . can she?

Philip. Marry who?

Miss Yates. Not that I say anything against Mr. Belhaven . . . a very nice young man. And, indeed, I rather think he did try to propose last Christmas. The fact is, y'know, it's only the very young men that ever do ask you to marry them here. When they get older they seem to lose heart . . . or they think it'll cost too much . . . or . . . but anyway, I'm sure it's not important . . .

This very out-of-place chatter dies away under PHILIP'*s sternly inquiring gaze.*

Philip. There's one more thing I'm afraid I ought to ask you. This trouble hasn't come about in any way by our sending you up to Bond Street, has it?

Miss Yates [*diving into many words again*]. Oh, of course it was most kind of you to send me to Bond Street to get a polish on one's manners . . . but I tell you . . . I couldn't have stood it for long. Those ladies that you get coming in there . . . well, it does just break your nerve. What with following them about, and the things they say you've got to hear, and the things they'll say . . . about you half the time . . . that you've got not to hear . . . and keep your voice low and sweet, and let your arms hang down straight. You may work more hours in this place, and I daresay it's commoner, but the customers are friendly with you.

Philip. . . . Because, you see, Mr. Huxtable and I would feel a little more responsible if it was anyone connected with us who . . .

Miss Yates [quite desperately]. No, you needn't . . . indeed you needn't . . . I will say there's something in that other place that does set your mind going about men. What he saw in me I never could think . . . honestly, I couldn't, though I think a good deal of myself, I can assure you. But it was my own fault, and so's all the rest of it going to be . . . my very own . . .

MAJOR THOMAS' *arrival is to* MISS YATES *a very welcome interruption, as she seems, perhaps by the hypnotism of* PHILIP's *steady look, to be getting nearer and nearer to saying just what she means not to. He comes in at a good speed, glancing back along the passage, and saying . . .*

Thomas. Here's Jessica.
Philip. State on the telephone.
Thomas. Thank you.

And he makes for it as JESSICA *comes to the open door.* PHILIP's *wife is an epitome of all that aesthetic culture can do for a woman. More: She is the result—not of thirty-three years—but of three or four generations of cumulative refinement. She might be a race horse! Come to think of it, it is a very wonderful thing to have raised this crop of ladyhood. Creatures, dainty in mind and body, gentle in thought and word, charming, delicate, sensitive, graceful, chaste, credulous of all good, shaming the world's ugliness and strife by the very ease and delightsomeness of their existence; fastidious—fastidious—fastidious; also in these latter years with their attractions more generally salted by the addition of learning and humor. Is not the perfect lady perhaps the most wonderful achievement of civilization, and worth the cost of her breeding, worth the toil and the helotage of—all the others?* JESSICA MADRAS *is even something more than a lady, for she is conscious of her ladyhood. She values her virtue and her charm: she is proud of her culture, and fosters it. It is her weapon; it justifies her. As she floats now into the ugly room, exquisite from her eyelashes to her shoes, it is a great relief —just the sight of her.*

Jessica. Am I interrupting?
Philip. No, come in, my dear.
Thomas [into the telephone]. Hello!
Philip. Well, Miss Yates, I want to see, if I can, that you

are not more unfairly treated than people with the courage
of their opinions always are.

Thomas. Hello!

Philip. Oh, you don't know my wife. Jessica, this is Miss
Yates, who is in our costume room. You're not actually working in your department now, I suppose?

Miss Yates [*as defiant of all scandal*]. I am.

Thomas [*still to the unresponsive telephone*]. Hello! Hello!

Philip [*finding* MISS YATES *beyond—possibly above him*].
Very well. That'll do now.

But MISS YATES, *by the presence of* JESSICA, *is now brought
to her best costume department manner. She can assume at
will, it seems, a new face, a new voice; can become, indeed,
a black-silk being of another species.*

Miss Yates. Thank you, sir. I'm sure I hope I've not
talked too much. I always was a chatterbox, madam.

Philip. You had some important things to say, Miss Yates.

Miss Yates. Not at all, sir. Good morning, madam.

Jessica. Good morning.

And there is an end of MISS YATES. *Meanwhile, the telephone is reducing* THOMAS *to impotent fury.*

Thomas. They've cut him off.

While he turns the handle, fit to break it, JESSICA *produces
an opened telegram, which she hands to* PHILIP.

Jessica. This . . . just after you left.

Philip. My dear, coming all this way with it! Why didn't
you telephone?

Thomas [*hearing something at last*]. Hello . . . is that
Mr. State's office? No! Well . . . Countinghouse, are you
still through to it?

JESSICA *is watching, with an amused smile.*

Jessica. I hate the telephone, especially the one here. Hark
at you, Tommy, poor wretch! They put you through from
office to office . . . six different clerks . . . all stupid, and
all with hideous voices.

PHILIP *has now read his telegram, and is making a face.*

Philip. Well, I suppose she must come, if she wants to.

Jessica. What'll your father say?

Philip. My dear girl . . . she has a right to see him if she
insists . . . it's very foolish. Here, Tommy! [*He ousts him*

from the telephone and deals expertly with it.] I want a telegram sent. Get double three double O Central, and plug through to my room . . . not here . . . my room.

Thomas [*fervently*]. Thank yer.

Jessica. Got over your anger at the play last night?

Thomas. Oh, sort of play you must expect if you go to the theatre on a Sunday. Scuse me.

Having admiringly sized up JESSICA *and her costume, he bolts.* PHILIP *sits down to compose his telegram in reply.* JESSICA, *discovering that there is nothing attractive to sit on, hovers.*

Philip. Can you put her up for the night?

Jessica. Yes.

Philip. Shall I ask her to dinner?

Jessica. She'll cry into the soup . . . but I suppose it doesn't matter.

Philip. Dinner at eight?

Jessica. I sound inhospitable.

Philip. Well, I've only said we shall be delighted.

Jessica. But your mother dislikes me so. It's difficult to see much of her.

Philip. You haven't much patience with her, have you, Jessica?

Jessica. Have you?

Philip [*whimsically*]. I've known her longer than you have.

Jessica [*with the nicest humor*]. I only wish she wouldn't write Mildred silly letters about God.

Philip. A grandmother's privilege.

Jessica. The child sends me on another one this morning . . . did I tell you?

Philip. No.

Jessica. Miss Gresham writes, too. She puts it quite nicely. But it's an awful thing for a school to get religion into it.

BELHAVEN *slides in.*

Belhaven. Yessir.

Philip. Send this at once, please.

Belhaven. Yessir.

BELHAVEN *slides out. Then* PHILIP *starts attending to the little pile of letters he brought in with him.* JESSICA, *neglected, hovers more widely.*

Jessica. Will you come out to lunch, Phil?

Philip. Lord! is it lunchtime?

Jessica. It will be soon. I'm lunching with Margaret Inman and Walter Muirhead at the Dieudonné.

Philip. Then you won't be lonely.

Jessica [*mischievous*]. Margaret may be if you don't come.

Philip. I can't, Jessica. I'm not nearly through.

She comes to rest by his table, and starts to play with the things on it, finding at last a blotting roller that gives satisfaction.

Jessica. Phil, you might come out with me a little more than you do.

Philip [*humorously final*]. My dear, not at lunchtime.

Jessica. Ugly little woman you'd been scolding when I came in.

Philip. I didn't think so.

Jessica. Are ugly women as attractive as ugly men?

Philip. D'you know . . . I don't find that women attract me.

Jessica. What a husband!

Philip. D'you want them to?

Jessica. Yes . . . in theory.

Philip. Why, Jessica?

Jessica [*with charming finesse*]. For my own sake. Last day of Walter's pictures. He has sold all but about five . . . and there's one I wish you'd buy.

Philip. Can't afford it.

Jessica. I suppose, Phil, you're not altogether sorry you married me?

Although PHILIP *is used enough to her charming and reasoned inconsequence, he really jumps.*

Philip. Good heavens, Jessica! Well, we've got through eleven years, haven't we?

JESSICA *puts her head on one side and is quite half-serious.*

Jessica. Are you in the least glad you married me?

Philip. My dear . . . I don't think about it. Jessica, I cannot keep up this game of repartee.

She floats away at once, half-seriously snubbed and hurt.

Jessica. I'm sorry. I know I'm interrupting.

Philip [*remorseful at once, for she is so pretty*]. No, no! I didn't mean that. These aren't important.

But he goes on with his letters, and JESSICA *stands looking at him, her face hardening a little.*

Jessica. But there are times when I get tired of waiting for you to finish your letters.

Philip. I know . . . I never quite finish my letters nowadays. You've got a fit of the idle fidgets this morning . . . that's what brings you after me. Shall we hire a motorcar for the week end?

THOMAS *bundles into the tête-à-tête, saying as he comes . . .*

Thomas. He'll make you an offer for the place here, Phil.
Philip. Good!

JESSICA *stands there, looking her prettiest.*

Jessica. Tommy, come out and lunch . . . Phil won't.
Thomas. I'm afraid I can't.
Jessica. I've got to meet Maggie Inman and young Muirhead. He'll flirt with her all the time. If there isn't a fourth I shall be fearfully in the cold.
Philip [*overcome by such tergiversation*]. Oh, Jessica!

THOMAS *is nervous, apparently; at least he is neither ready nor gallant.*

Thomas. Yes, of course you will. But I'm afraid I can't.
Jessica [*in cheerful despair*]. Well, I won't drive to Peckham again of a morning. Wednesday, then, will you call for me?
Thomas. Wednesday?
Jessica. Symphony concert.
Thomas [*with sudden seriousness*]. D'you know, I'm afraid I can't on Wednesday, either.
Jessica. Why not?
Thomas [*though the pretense withers before a certain sharpness in her question*]. Well . . . I'm afraid I can't.

It is evident that JESSICA *has a temper bred to a point of control which makes it nastier, perhaps. She now becomes very cold, very civil, very swift.*

Jessica. We settled it only last night. What's the time?
Philip. Five to one.
Jessica. I must go. I shall be late.
Thomas [*with great concern*]. Have you got a cab?
Jessica. I think so.

Thomas. We might do the next, perhaps.

Jessica. All right, Tommy . . . don't be conscience-stricken. But when you change your mind about going out with me it's pleasanter if you'll find some excuse. Good-by, you two.

And she is gone; PHILIP *calling after her——*

Philip. I shall be in by seven, my dear.

THOMAS *looks a little relieved, and then considerably worried; in fact, he frowns portentously.* PHILIP *disposes of his last letter.*

Philip. We've so organized the world's work as to make companionship between men and women a very artificial thing.

Thomas [*without interest*]. Have we?

Philip. I think so. What have we got to settle before this afternoon?

Thomas. Nothing much. [*Then seeming to make up his mind to something.*] But I want three minutes' talk with you, old man.

Philip. Oh!

And he gets up and stretches.

Thomas. D'you mind if I say something caddish?

Philip. No.

Thomas. Put your foot down and don't have me asked to your house quite so much.

PHILIP *looks at him for half a puzzled minute.*

Philip. Why not?

Thomas. I'm seeing too much of your wife.

He is so intensely solemn about it that PHILIP *can hardly even pretend to be shocked.*

Philip. My dear Tommy!

Thomas. I don't mean one single word more than I say.

Philip [*good-naturedly*]. Tommy, you always have flirted with Jessica.

Thomas. I don't want you to think that I'm the least bit in love with her.

Philip. Naturally not . . . you've got a wife of your own.

Thomas [*in intense brotherly agreement*]. Right. That's good horse sense.

Philip. And though, as her husband, I'm naturally obtuse in

the matter . . . I really don't think that Jessica is in love
with you.

Thomas [*most generously*]. Not for a single minute.

Philip. Then what's the worry, you silly old ass?

THOMAS *starts to explain, a little tortuously.*

Thomas. Well, Phil, this is such a damned subtle world. I
don't pretend to understand it, but in my old age I have got
a sort of rule of thumb experience to go by . . . which,
mark you, I've paid for.

Philip. Well?

Thomas. Phil, I don't like women, and I never did . . .
but I'm hardly exaggerating when I say I married simply to
get out of the habit of finding myself once every six months
in such a position with one of them that I was supposed to
be making love to her.

PHILIP *is enjoying himself.*

Philip. What do they see in you, Tommy?

Thomas. God knows, old man . . . I don't. And the time
it took up! Of course I was as much in love with Mary as
you like, or I couldn't have asked her to marry me. And I
wouldn't be without her and the children now for all I ever
saw. But I don't believe I'd have gone out of my way to get
them if I hadn't been driven to it, old man, . . . driven to it.
I'm not going to start the old game again now. [*And he wags
his head wisely.*]

Philip. What's the accusation against Jessica? Let's have it
in so many words.

THOMAS *gathers himself up to launch the vindicating compliment effectively.*

Thomas. She's a very accomplished and a very charming
and a very sweet-natured woman. I consider she's an ornament to society.

Philip [*with equal fervor*]. You're quite right, Tommy,
. . . what are we to do with them?

Thomas [*it's his favorite phrase*]. What d'you mean?

Philip. Well . . . what's your trouble with her?

Thomas [*tortuously still*]. There ain't any yet . . . but
. . . well . . . I've been dreading for the last three weeks
that Jessica would begin to talk to me about you. That's why
I'm talking to you about her. [*Then, with a certain enjoyment of his shocking looseness of behavior.*] I am a cad!

Philip [*still amused—but now rather sub-acidly*]. My standing for the County Council must be a most dangerous topic.

Thomas. But that's just how it begins. Then there's hints . . . quite nice ones . . . about how you get on with each other. Last night in the cab she was talking about when she was a girl . . .

Philip. I walked home. Tactful husband!

Thomas. Phil . . . don't you be French.

PHILIP, *suddenly serious, turns to him*.

Philip. But, Tommy, do you imagine that she is unhappy with me?

Thomas. No, I don't. But she thinks a lot . . . when she's bored with calling on people, and her music and her pictures. And once you begin putting your feelings into words . . . why, they grow.

Philip. But if she were, I'd rather that she did confide in you.

THOMAS *shakes his head vehemently*.

Thomas. No.

Philip. Why shouldn't she? You're friends.

Thomas. Yes . . . there's no reason . . . but I tell you it always begins that way.

Philip. You silly ass . . . can't you let a woman talk seriously to you without making love to her?

Thomas. Damn it, that's what they say . . . but it never made any difference.

Philip. Tommy, you're a perfect child!

Thomas. I remember when I was twenty-four . . . there was one woman . . . years older than me . . . had a grown-up son. She took to scolding me for wasting my time flirting. Told me she'd done it herself once . . . then told me why she'd done it. I kept off kissing her for six weeks, and I'll swear she never wanted me to kiss her. But I did.

Philip. Did she box your ears?

Thomas. No . . . she said she couldn't take me seriously. Well . . . if I'd gone away that would have been priggish. And if I'd stayed I'd have done it again.

Philip [*mischievously*]. Which did you do?

Thomas. Oh . . . never you mind.

Philip [*with the utmost geniality*]. Well . . . you have my permission to kiss Jessica, if you think she wants you to.

Thomas. Thanks, old man . . . that's very clever and up

to date, and all the rest of it . . . but I asked you to chuck me out of the house to some extent.

Philip. I'm not going to.

Thomas. Then you're no friend of mine.

Philip. Let us put it quite brutally. If Jessica chooses to be unfaithful to me how am I to stop her . . . even if I've the right to stop her?

Thomas. If you're not prepared to behave like a decent married man you've no right to be married . . . you're a danger.

Philip. Also, Tommy, if you caught me making love to your wife you might talk to me . . . but you wouldn't talk to her about it.

Thomas [*with a touch of sentiment*]. Mary's different. [*Then protesting again.*] And I'm not making love to your wife. I told you so.

Philip. Then if she's making love to you, run away for yourself.

Thomas. She isn't making love to me. But if you can't take a hint——

Philip. A *hint!* Well . . . I'm dashed!

Thomas. Well, old man, I give you fair warning of the sort of fool I am . . . and I'll take no more responsibility in the matter.

Philip [*in comic desperation*]. Don't warn me . . . warn Jessica. Tell her you're afraid of making a fool of yourself with her . . .

Thomas [*his eyebrows up*]. But that'd be as good as doing it. Good Lord, you can't behave towards women as if they were men!

Philip. Why not?

Thomas. You try it.

Philip. I always do.

Thomas. No wonder she wants to grumble about you to me.

PHILIP *takes him seriously again.*

Philip. Look here, Tommy, I know Jessica pretty well. She doesn't want to be made love to.

Thomas [*positively and finally*]. Yes, she does. [*Then with real chivalry.*] I don't mean that unpleasantly . . . but all women do. Some of em want to be kissed and some want you to talk politics . . . but the principle's the same.

Philip [*finely contemptuous*]. What a world you live in!

Thomas. . . . And the difficulty with me is that if I try to talk politics I find they don't know enough about it . . .

or else that they know too much about it . . . and it's simpler
to kiss em and have done.

Philip. Oh, much simpler!

Thomas [*back to his starting point—pathetic*]. But I'm
married now, and I want a quiet life . . .

A knock at the door interrupts him.

Philip. Come in.

It is BELHAVEN.

Belhaven. Will you lunch, sir?

Philip. What is there?

Belhaven. I'm afraid only the usual, sir.

Philip. Can you manage the usual, Tommy? What is it,
Belhaven?

Belhaven. Boiled mutton and a jam pudding, I think, sir.
[*Then, as confessing to a vulgarity.*] Roly-poly.

Thomas [*with great approval*]. Right. I hope it's strawberry
jam.

Philip. Sure to be. Put it in Mr. Huxtable's room, will you
. . . that's airy.

Belhaven. Yessir.

BELHAVEN *vanishes.*

Thomas [*as on reflection*]. Not plum, y'know . . . plum's
no use.

PHILIP *gathers up his papers.*

Philip. I'll give the wicked woman your message.

THOMAS *takes alarm. He hadn't thought of this.*

Thomas. No . . . do it off your own bat. She won't mind,
then.

Philip. Tommy, I cannot assume the turban of the Turk.
My sense of humor and my sense of decency toward women
won't let me.

Thomas [*frowning*]. I believe I'd better not have told you.

Philip [*unsympathetic*]. Why not? Next to telling her, the
most common-sense thing to do.

Thomas. She won't think so.

Philip. She'll have to.

There is something so like cruelty in these three words that
THOMAS *stares at him. Then he says, reflectively.*

Thomas. Phil, d'you ever thank God you're not a woman?

Philip. No.

Thomas. When I think what most of em have to choose between is soft-hearted idiots like me and hard-headed devils like you . . . I wonder they put up with us as they do.

PHILIP *stares at him in turn with a queer smile. Then, as he turns to go . . .*

Philip. You've made it again, Tommy.
Thomas. What?
Philip. Your one sensible remark. Come along.

And he is gone. THOMAS *follows, protesting.*

Thomas. Look here . . . what d'you mean by One Sensible Remark? It's like your infernal . . .

He pulls the door to after him. The room is alone with its ugliness.

ACT THREE

In 1884 the Madras House was moved to its present prem- ises in Bond Street. In those days decoration was mostly a matter of paint and wallpaper, but MR. CONSTANTINE MADRAS, *ever daring, proceeded to beautify the home of his profes- sional triumphs. He could neither draw nor color, but he designed and saw to it all himself, and being a man of great force of character, produced something which, though ex- traordinarily wrong, was yet, since it was sincere, in a way effective. It added to his reputation and to the attractiveness of the Madras House.*

In twenty-six years there have been changes, but one room remains untouched from then till now. This is the rotunda, a large, lofty, skylighted place, done in the Moorish style. The walls are black marble to the height of a man, and from there to the ceiling the darkest red. The ceiling is of a cerulean blue, and in the middle of the skylight a golden sun, with spiked rays proceeding from its pleasant human countenance, takes credit for some of the light it intercepts. An archway with fretted top leads from the rest of the establishment. Another has behind it a platform, a few steps high, hung with black velvet. The necessary fireplace (were there hot-water

*pipes in 1884?) is disguised by a heavy multicolored canopy,
whose fellow hangs over a small door opposite. On the floor
is a Persian carpet of some real beauty. On the walls are gas
brackets (1884 again!) the oriental touch achieved in their
crescent shape. Round the wall are divans, many cushioned;
in front of them little coffee stools. It is all about as Moorish
as Baker Street Station, but the general effect is humorous,
pleasant, and even not undignified.*

*In the old, grand days of the Madras House the rotunda
was the happy preserve of very special customers, those on
whom the great man himself would keep an eye. If you had
been there you spoke of it casually; indeed, to be free of the
rotunda was to be a well-dressed woman and recognized by
all society as such. Ichabod! Since* MR. CONSTANTINE MADRAS
*retired, the Madras House is on the way to becoming almost
like any other shop; the special customers are nobody in
particular, and the rotunda is where a degenerate management
meet to consider the choice of ready-made models from Paris.
A large oval table had to be imported and half a dozen Moorish chairs. It seemed, to the surprise of the gentleman who
went innocently ordering such things, that there were only
that number in existence. Scene of its former glories, this is
now to be the scene, perhaps, of the passing of the Madras
House into alien hands.*

*Three o'clock on the Monday afternoon is when the deal is
to be put through, if possible, and it is now five minutes to.*
MAJOR THOMAS *is there, sitting at the table; papers spread
before him, racking his brains at a few final figures.* PHILIP
*is there, in rather a schoolboyish mood. He is sitting on the
table, swinging his legs.* MR. HUXTABLE *is there, too, dressed
in his best, important and nervous, and he is talking to* MR.
EUSTACE PERRIN STATE.

MR. STATE *is an American, and if American magazine literature is anything to go by, no American is altogether unlike
him. He has a rugged, blood and iron sort of face, utterly
belied by his soft, smiling eyes; rightly belied, too, for he has
made his thirty or forty millions in the gentlest way—as far
as he knows. You would not think of him as a money-maker.
As a matter of fact, he has no love of money, and little use
for it, for his tastes are simple. But money-making is the
honorable career in his own country, and he has the instinct
for turning money over and the knack of doing so on a big
scale. His shock of gray hair makes him look older than he*

probably is; his voice is almost childlike in its sweetness. He has the dignity and aptitude for command that power can give.

From the little canopied dome comes MR. WINDLESHAM, *present manager of the establishment. He is a tailor-made man; and the tailor only left off for the wax modeler and wig-maker to begin. For his clothes are too perfect to be worn by anything but a dummy, and his hair and complexion are far from human. Not that he dyes or paints them; no, they were made like that. His voice is a little inhuman, too, and as he prefers the French language, with which he has a most unripe acquaintance, to his own, and so speaks English as much like French as his French is like English, his conversation seems as unreal as the rest of him. Impossible to think of him in any of the ordinary relations of life. He is a functionary. Nature, the great inventor, will evolve, however roughly, what is necessary for her uses. Millinery has evolved the man-milliner. As he comes in—and he has the gait of a water-wagtail—*MR. HUXTABLE *is making conversation.*

MR. HUXTABLE. A perfect barometer, as you might say—when your eye gets used to it.

Windlesham [to PHILIP, *and with a wag of his head back to the other room].* They're just ready.

Mr. State [smiling benevolently at MR. HUXTABLE]. Is it really? The Crystal Palace! But what a sound that has!

Mr. Huxtable [with modest pride]. And a very ealthy locality!

Philip. Come along and meet State. [*He jumps off the table, capturing* WINDLESHAM'S *arm.*]

Mr. State [enthusiastic]. Denmark Hill. Compliment to Queen Alexandra!

Mr. Huxtable [struck by the information]. Was it, now?

Mr. State. Herne Hill . . . Herne the Hunter! That's the charm of London to an American. Association. Every spot speaks.

Philip [as he joins them]. This is Mr. Windlesham . . . our manager. He's going to show us some new models.

MR. STATE *impressively extends a hand and repeats the name.*

Mr. State. Mr. Windlesham.

Windlesham. Most happy. I thought you'd like to see the very latest . . . brought them from Paris only yesterday.

Mr. State. Most opportune! [*Then with a sweeping ges-*

ture.] Mr. Philip, this room inspires me. Your father's design?

Philip. Yes.

Mr. State. I thought so.

Philip. That used to be his private office.

Mr. State [*reverently*]. Indeed! Where the Duchess went on her knees! An historic spot. Interesting to me!

Philip. Something of a legend, that.

MR. STATE, *intensely solemn, seems now to ascend the pulpit of some philosophic conventicle.*

Mr. State. I believe in legends, sir . . . they are the spiritual side of facts. They go to form tradition. And it is not given to man to found his institutions in security of mind except upon tradition. That is why our eyes turn eastward to you from America, Mr. Huxtable.

Mr. Huxtable [*in some awe*]. Do they, now?

Mr. State. Has it never struck you that while the progress of man has been in the path of the sun, his thoughts continually go back to the place of its rising? I have at times found it a very illuminating idea.

Philip [*not indecently commonplace*]. Well, have them in now, Windlesham, while we're waiting.

Windlesham. You might cast your eyes over these new girls, Mr. Philip . . . the very best I could find, I do assure you. Faces are hard enough to get, but figures . . . Well, there! [*Reaching the little door, he calls through.*] Allons mes'moiselles! Non . . . non . . . par l'autre porte et à la gauche. [*Then back again.*] You get the best effect through a big doorway. [*He further explains this by sketching one in the air.*] One, two, and four first.

He exhibits some costume drawings he has been carrying, distributes one or two, and then vanishes into the other room, from which his voice vibrates.

Windlesham. En avant s'il vous plaît. Numéro un! Eh bien . . . numéro trois. Non, ma'moiselle, ce n'est pas commode . . . regardez ce corsage là . . .

Mr. Huxtable [*making a face*]. What I'm always thinking is, why not have a manly chap in charge of the place up here.

Mr. State [*with perfect justice*]. Mr. Windlesham may be said to strike a note. Whether it is a right note . . . ?

Through the big doorway WINDLESHAM *ushers in a costume from Paris, the very last word in discreet and costly finery, delicate in color, fragile in texture; a creation. This is hung upon a young lady of pleasing appearance, preoccupied with its exhibition, which she achieves by slow and sinuous, never-ceasing movements. She glides into the room. She wears a smile also.*

Windlesham. One and two are both Larguillière, Mr. Philip. He can't get in the Soupçon Anglais, can he? Won't . . . I tell him. Promenez et sortez, ma'moiselle.

The young lady, still smiling and sinuous, begins to circle the room. She seems to be unconscious of its inhabitants, and they, in return, rather dreadfully pretend not to notice her, but only the costume.

Windlesham. Numéro deux.

Another costume, rakishly inclined, with a hat deliberately hideous. The young lady contained in them is again slow and sinuous and vacantly smiling.

Windlesham. But this is chic, isn't it? Promenez.
Mr. State [in grave inquiry]. What is the Soupçon Anglais?
Philip. A Frenchman will tell you that for England you must first make a design and then spoil it.
Thomas [whose attention has been riveted]. Don't they speak English?
Windlesham. Oh, pas un mot . . . I mean, not a word. Only came over with me yesterday . . . these three.
Thomas. Because this frock's a bit thick, y'know.
Windlesham. Numéro trois!

A third costume, calculated to have an innocent effect. The accompanying young lady, with a sense of fitness, wears a pout instead of a smile.

Philip. What's this? [His eye is on the surmounting hat of straw.]
Windlesham [with a little crow of delight]. That's the new hat. La belle Hélène again!
Mr. State [interested, still grave]. La belle Hélène. A Parisian firm?
Windlesham [turning this to waggish account]. Well . . . dear me . . . you can almost call her that, can't you? [Suddenly he dashes at the costume and brings it to a standstill.] Oh, mon dieu, ma'moiselle! La gorgette . . . vous l'avez derangé.

He proceeds to arrange la gorgette *to his satisfaction, also some other matters which seem to involve a partial evisceration of the underclothing. The young lady, passive, pouts perseveringly. He is quite unconscious of her separate existence. But* THOMAS *is considerably shocked, and whispers violently to* PHILIP.

Thomas. I say, he shouldn't pull her about like that.

Windlesham [skipping back to admire the result]. Là . . . comme ça.

The costume continues its round; the others are still circling, veering and tacking, while WINDLESHAM *trips admiringly around and about them. It all looks like some dance of modish dervishes.*

Philip [heartlessly]. La belle Hélène, Mr. State, is a well-known Parisian cocotte . . . who sets many of the fashions which our wives and daughters afterward assume.

Mr. Huxtable [scandalized]. Don't say that, Phil; it's not nice.

Philip. Why?

Mr. Huxtable. I'm sure no ladies are aware of it.

Philip. But what can be more natural and right than for the professional charmer to set the pace for the amateur!

Windlesham [pausing in the dance]. Quite la haute cocotterie, of course.

Mr. State [solemnly]. Do you infer, Mr. Madras, a difference in degree, but not in kind?

Philip [courteously echoing his tone]. I do.

Mr. State. That is a very far-reaching observation, sir.

Philip. It is.

Thomas. Do you know the lady personally, Mr. Windlesham?

WINDLESHAM *turns, with some tag of a costume in his hand, thus unconsciously detaining the occupier.*

Windlesham. Oh, no . . . oh, dear me, no . . . quite the reverse, I do assure you. There's nothing gay in Paris to me. I was blasé long ago.

Mr. State. But touching that hat, Mr. Windlesham.

Windlesham. Oh, to be sure. Attendez, mademoiselle.

Tiptoeing, he dexterously tilts the straw hat from the elaborate head it is perched on.

Windlesham. It's not a bad story. Sortez.

By this two costumes have glided out. The third follows.
STATE, *who has found it hard to keep his eyes off them, gives
something of a sigh.*

Mr. State. If they'd only just smile or wink, I might get
over the extraordinary feeling it gives me.

WINDLESHAM, *caressing the hat, takes up an attitude for his
story.*

Windlesham. Well . . . it appears that a while ago, out at
the Pré Cathelan . . . there was Hélène, taking her afternoon cup of buttermilk. What should she see but Madame
Erlancourt . . . one knows enough about that lady, of course
. . . in a hat the very twin of hers . . . the very twin.
Well . . . you can imagine! Someone had blundered.

Mr. State [*absorbed*]. No, I don't follow.

Philip. Some spy in the service of that foreign power had
procured and parted with the plans of the hat.

Mr. State. Madame what's-her-name might have seen it on
her before, and copied it.

Philip. Mr. State, Hélène doesn't wear a hat twice.

Mr. State. My mistake!

Windlesham. So there was a terrible scene . . .

Thomas. With madame . . . ?

Windlesham [*repudiating any such vulgarity*]. Oh, no.
Hélène just let fly at her chaperon, she being at hand, so to
speak.

Mr. State [*dazzled*]. Her *what!* [*Then with humorous
awe.*] No, I beg your pardon . . . go on . . . go on.

Windlesham. She took off her own hat . . . pinned it on
the head of the ugliest little gamine she could find, and sent
the child walking along the grass in it. Then she sent to the
kitchens for one of those baskets they bring the fish in . . .
[*He twirls the hat.*] . . . you see. Then she ripped a yard of
lace off her underskirt and twisted it round. Then she took
off both her . . . well . . . la belle France, you know . . .
there is something in the atmosphere! It was her garters she
took off . . . blue silk.

Mr. State [*puritan*]. In public?

Windlesham [*professional*]. Oh, . . . it can be done.
Hooked them together and fastened the bit of lace round
the basket this way. Très simple! That's what she wore the
rest of the afternoon and back to Paris. This is what's going
to be the rage.

Having deftly pantomimed this creation of a fashion, he hands the hat, with an air, to MR. STATE, *who examines it.* PHILIP *is smilingly caustic.*

Philip. La belle Hélène has imagination, Mr. State. She is also, I am told, thrifty, inclined to religion, a vegetarian, Vichy water her only beverage; in fact, a credit to her profession and externally . . . to ours.

MR. STATE *hands back the hat, with the solemnest humor.*

Mr. State. Mr. Windlesham, I am much obliged to you for this illuminating anecdote.
Windlesham. Not at all. . . . Will you see the other three?
Mr. State. By all means.
Windlesham. They won't be long in changing . . . but there's one I must just pin on.
Mr. State. No hurry.

He has acquired a new joy in WINDLESHAM, *whom he watches dance away. Then a song is heard from the next room* . . .

Windlesham. Allons . . . numéro cinq . . . numéro sept . . . numéro dix. Ma'moiselle Ollivier . . . vous vous mettrez . . .

And the door closes. PHILIP *looks at his watch.*

Philip. But it's ten past three. We'd better not wait for my father.

They surround the table and sit down.

Mr. State. Major Thomas, have you my memoranda?
Thomas. Here.

He hands them to STATE, *who clears his throat, refrains from spitting, and begins the customary American oration.*

Mr. State. The scheme, gentlemen, for which I desire to purchase the Madras House and add it to the interest of the Burrows enterprise, which I already control, is—to put it shortly—this. The Burrows provincial scheme—you are aware of its purpose—goes well enough as far as the shareholding by the local drapery stores is concerned. It has been interesting to me to discover which aspects of the Burrows scheme suit which cities . . . and why. An absorbing problem in the psychology of local conditions! Now, we have eliminated from the mass a considerable number of cases where the local people will not join with us. And in your Leicesters and Nor-

wiches and Plymouths and Coventrys . . . there the unknown
name, the uninspiring name of Burrows, upon a fire-new
establishment next door might anyhow be ineffective. But
beyond that I have a reason . . . and I hope a not uninteresting reason, to put before you gentlemen . . . why it is in
these provincial centers that we should look to establish our
Madras Houses . . . New Edition. Is that clear so far?

During this MR. CONSTANTINE MADRAS *has arrived. He turned
aside for a moment to the door that the models came from,
now he joins the group. A man of sixty, to whom sixty is the
prime of life. Tall, quite dramatically dignified, suave, a little
remote; he is one of those to whom life is an art of which
they have determined to be master. It is a handsome face,
Eastern in type, the long beard only streaked with gray. He
does not dress like the ruck of men, because he is not of
them. The velvet coat, brick-red tie, shepherd's-plaid trousers,
white spats and patent boots, both suit him and express him
subtly and well—the mixture of sensuous originality and tradition which is the man.* PHILIP *is purposely casual in greeting
him; he has sighted him first. But* MR. STATE *gets up, impressed. It is part of his creed to recognize greatness; he
insists on recognizing it.*

Philip. Hello, Father!

Mr. State. Mr. Madras! Proud to meet you again.

Constantine [*graciously, without emotion*]. How do you do,
Mr. State.

Philip. You know everyone, Father. Oh . . . Hippisly
Thomas.

Constantine [*just as graciously*]. How do you do, sir.
[*Then, with a mischievous smile, he pats* HUXTABLE *on the
shoulder.*] How are you, my dear Harry?

MR. HUXTABLE *had heard him coming, and felt himself turn
purple. This was the great meeting after thirty years! He had
let it come upon him unawares; purposely let it, for indeed he
had not known what to say or do. He had dreaded having
the inspiration to say or do anything. Now, alas, and thank
goodness! it is too late. He is at a suitable disadvantage. He
need only grunt out sulkily . . . .*

Mr. Huxtable. I'm quite well, thank you.

CONSTANTINE, *with one more pat in pardon for the rudeness,
goes to his chair.*

Mr. State. A pleasant trip on the Continent?

Constantine. Instructive. Don't let me interrupt business. I shall pick up the thread.

Mr. State [*serving up a little rewarmed oration*]. I was just proceeding to place on the tablecloth some preliminary details of the scheme that has been elaborating since our meeting in June last to consolidate your name and fame in some of the most important cities of England. We had not got far.

He consults his notes. CONSTANTINE *produces from a case a slender cigarette holder of amber.*

Constantine. You've some new models, Phil.
Philip. Yes.
Constantine. The tall girl looks well enough. May I smoke?
Mr. State. Allow me. [*Whipping out his cigar case.*]
Constantine. A cigarette, thank you, of my own.

He proceeds to make and light one. MR. STATE *offers cigars generally, and then places one to his own hand.*

Mr. State. I occasionally derive some pleasure from a cold cigar. I was not for the moment entering upon the finance of the matter because I entertain no doubt that . . . possibly with a little adjustment of the proportion of shares and cash . . . that can be fixed.

Mr. Huxtable [*in emulation of all this ease and grace*]. I'll ave a cigarette, Phil . . . if you've got one.

PHILIP *has one. And everyone makes himself comfortable, while* MR. STATE *continues enjoyably . . .*

Mr. State. And I suspect that you are no more interested in money than I am, Mr. Madras. Anyone can make money, if he has capital enough. The little that I have came from lumber and canned peaches. Now, there was poetry in lumber. The virgin forest . . . I'd go sit in it for weeks at a time. There was poetry in peaches . . . before they were canned. Do you wonder why I bought that mantle establishment in the city?

Philip [*who is only sorry that some time he must stop*]. Why, Mr. State?

Mr. State. Because, Mr. Philip, I found myself a lonely man. I felt the need of getting into touch with what Goethe refers to as the woman-spirit . . . drawing us ever upward and on. That opportunity occurred, and it seemed a businesslike way of doing the trick.

Constantine [*through a little cloud of smoke*]. And satisfying?

Mr. State. I beg your pardon?

Constantine. Has the ready-made skirt business satisfied your craving for the eternal feminine?

Mr. State. Mr. Madras . . . that sarcasm is deserved . . . No, sir, it has not. The Burrows business, I discover, lacks all inner meaning . . . it has no soul. A business can no more exist without a soul than a human being can. I'm sure I have you with me there, Mr. Huxtable.

Poor MR. HUXTABLE *quite chokes at the suddenness of this summons, but shines his best.*

Mr. Huxtable. I should say so, quite.

MR. STATE *begins to glow.*

Mr. State. There was fun, mind you . . . there still is . . . in making these provincial milliners hop . . . putting a pistol to their heads . . . saying buy our goods or be froze out. That keeps me lively and it wakes them up . . . does them good. But Burrows isn't in the movement. The woman's movement. The great modern woman's movement. It has come home to me that the man, who has as much to do with woman as manufacturing the bones of her corsets and yet is not consciously in that movement, is outside history. Shoveling goods over a counter and adding up profits . . . that's no excuse for cumbering the earth . . . nothing personal, Mr. Huxtable.

MR. HUXTABLE *is ready this time.*

Mr. Huxtable. No, no . . . I'm listening to you. I'm not too old to learn.

Mr. State. Mind, I don't say I haven't taken pleasure in Burrows. We've had notions . . . caused two ideas to spring where one sprung before. There was Nottingham.

Mr. Huxtable. I know Nottingham . . . got a shop there?

Mr. State [*with wholesome pride*]. In two years the Burrows establishment in Nottingham has smashed competition. I've not visited the city myself. The notion was our local manager's. Simple. The ladies' department served by gentlemen . . . the gentlemen's by ladies. Always, of course, within the bounds of delicacy. Do you think there is nothing in that, Mr. Huxtable?

Mr. Huxtable [*round-eyed and open-mouthed*]. Oh . . . well . . .

Mr. State. But are you the mean sensual man?

Mr. Huxtable [*whose knowledge of the French language*

hardly assists him to this startling translation]. No . . . I
hope not.

Mr. State. Put yourself in his place. Surrounded by pretty
girls . . . good girls, mind you . . . high class. Pay them
well . . . let them live out . . . pay for their mothers and
chaperons, if necessary. Well . . . surrounded by gracious
womanhood, does the sensual man forget how much money he
is spending or does he not? Does he come again? Is it a little
oasis in the desert of his business day? Is it a better attraction
than alcohol, or is it not?

Philip [*bitingly*]. Is it?

Mr. State. Then, sir . . . *audi alteram partem.* I should
like you to see our Ladies' Fancy Department at its best . . .
just before the football season.

Philip. I think I do!

Mr. State. Athletes everyone of em . . . not a man under
six foot . . . bronzed, noble fellows! And no flirting allowed
. . . no making eyes . . . no pandering to anything depraved.
Just the ordinary courtesies of our modern civilization from
pure, clean-minded gentlemen towards any of the fair sex who
step in to buy a shilling sachet or the like. And pay, sir . . .
The women come in flocks!

Mr. Huxtable [*bereft of breath*]. Is this how you mean to
run your new Madras Houses?

Mr. State. Patience, Mr. Huxtable. It's but six months ago
that I started to study the woman question from the point of
view of Burrows and Co. I attended women's meetings in
London, in Manchester, and in one-horse places as well. Now,
political claims were but the narrowest, drabbest aspect of the
matter as I saw it. The woman's movement is woman expressing herself. Let us look at things as they are. What are a
woman's chief means . . . how often her only means of expressing herself? Anyway . . . what is the first thing that
she spends her money on? Clothes, gentlemen, clothes. Therefore, I say . . . though at Cannon Street we may palp with
good ideas . . . the ready-made skirt is out of date . . .

WINDLESHAM, *pins in his mouth, fashion plates under his arm,
and the fish-basket hat in his hand, shoots out of the other
room.*

Windlesham. Will you have the others in now? [*Then back
through the door.*] Allons, mesmoiselles, s'il vous plaît.
Numéro cinq le premier. [*Then he turns the hat upside down
on the table.*] I thought you'd like to see that they've actually

left the handles on. But I don't think we can do that here,
do you?

*There comes in as before the most elaborate evening gown
that ever was.*

Windlesham [as he searches for the design]. Numéro cinq
. . . number five.

THOMAS *is much struck.*

Thomas. I say . . . by Jove!

*But the cold, searching light seems to separate from the
glittering pink affair the poor, pretty, smiling creature ex-
hibiting it, until, indeed, she seems half-naked.* MR. WINDLE-
SHAM's *aesthetic sense is outraged.*

Windlesham. Mais non, mais non . . . pas en plein jour.
Mettez vous par là dans le . . . dans l'alcove . . . à côté du
velours noir.

The costume undulates towards the black velvet platform.
THOMAS *is lost in admiration.*

Thomas. That gives her a chance, don't it? Damn pretty
girl!
Philip [his eye twinkling]. She'll understand that, Tommy.
Thomas [in good faith]. She won't mind.
Mr. State [who has been studying the undulations]. How
they learn to walk like it . . . that's what beats me!

MR. WINDLESHAM *turns on the frame of lights which bear
upon the velvet platform. The vision of female loveliness is
now complete.*

Windlesham. There . . . that's the coup d'oeil.

*The vision turns this way and that to show what curves of
loveliness there may be. They watch, all but* CONSTANTINE,
*who has sat silent and indifferent, rolling his second cigarette,
which he now smokes serenely. At last* PHILIP's *voice breaks
in, at its coolest, its most ironic.*

Philip. And are we to assume, Mr. State, that this piece of
self-decoration really expresses the nature of any woman?
Rather an awful thought!
Thomas [in protest]. Why?
Philip. Or if it expresses a man's opinion of her . . . that's
rather worse.

Thomas. It's damned smart. Ain't it, Mr. Huxtable?

Mr. Huxtable [*who is examining closely*]. No use to us, of course. We couldn't imitate that under fifteen guineas. Look at the . . . what d'you call it?

Windlesham [*loving the very word*]. Diamanté.

Thomas [*with discretion*]. Just for England, of course, you might have the shiny stuff marking a bit more definitely where the pink silk ends and she begins.

Mr. Huxtable [*not to be sordid*]. But it's a beautiful thing.

Mr. State [*sweepingly*]. Fitted to adorn the presiding genius of some intellectual and artistic salon. More artistic than intellectual, perhaps . . . more likely to be the center of emotion than thought!

Windlesham. I could almost tell you who we shall sell that to. Mrs. . . . Mrs. . . . dear me . . . you'd all know the name. Assez, mamoiselle . . . sortez.

He turns off the light. The vision becomes once more a ridiculously expensive dress, with a rather thin and shivering young person half inside it, who is thus unceremoniously got rid of.

Windlesham. Numéro sept.

Another costume.

Mr. State. Now here again. Green velvet. Is it velvet?

Windlesham. Panne velvet. Promenez, s'il vous plaît.

Mr. State. And ermine.

Mr. Huxtable. Good Lord . . . more buttons!

Mr. State. The very thing, no doubt, in which some peeress might take the chair at a drawing-room meeting.

Philip [*as he eyes the buttons and the ermine*]. Either of Humanitarian or of the Anti-Sweating League. Indeed, no peeress could dream of taking a chair without it.

Mr. State [*in gentle reproof*]. Sarcasm, Mr. Philip.

Philip [*won by such sweetness*]. I really beg your pardon.

Windlesham. Numéro dix.

A third costume.

Philip. What about this?

Mr. State. Gray with a touch of pink . . . severely soft. An Anti-Suffrage Platform.

Philip [*in tune with him*]. No . . . it's cut square in the neck. Suffrage, I should say.

Mr. State [*rubbing his hands*]. Good! There is purpose in this persiflage, Major Thomas. Woman allures us along many paths. Be it ours to attend her, doing what service we may.

Constantine. You are a poet, Mr. State.

Mr. State. I never wrote one in my life, sir.

Constantine. How many poets should cease scribbling and try to live such perfect epics as seems likely to be this purchase of yours of the Madras House!

Mr. State [*much gratified*]. I shall be proud to be your successor. [*Then he soars.*] But it is the middle-class woman of England that is waiting for me. The woman who still sits at the parlor window of her provincial villa, pensively gazing through the laurel bushes. I have seen her on my solitary walks. She must have *her* chance to dazzle and conquer. That is every woman's birthright . . . be she a duchess in Mayfair or a doctor's wife in the suburbs of Leicester. And remember, gentlemen, that the middle-class women of England . . . think of them in bulk . . . they form one of the greatest money-spending machines the world has ever seen.

Mr. Huxtable [*with a wag of the head; he is more at his ease now*]. Yes . . . their husbands' money.

Mr. State [*taking a long breath and a high tone*]. All our most advanced thinkers are agreed that the economic independence of women is the next step in the march of civilization.

Mr. Huxtable [*overwhelmed*]. Oh . . . I beg pardon.

Mr. State [*soaring now more than ever*]. And now that the seed of freedom is sown in their sweet natures . . . what mighty forest . . . what a luxuriant, tropical, scented growth of womanhood may not spring up around us. For we live in an ugly world. Look at my tie! Consider your vest, Major Thomas! [*His eye searches for those costumes, and finds one.*] This is all the living beauty that there is. We want more of it. I want to see that poor provincial lady burst through the laurel bushes and dash down the road . . . clad in colors of the rainbow.

WINDLESHAM *has indeed detained the severely soft costume and its young lady, and there she has stood for a while, still smiling, but wondering, perhaps, behind the smile, into what peculiar company of milliners she has fallen.* THOMAS, *suddenly noticing that she is standing there, with the utmost politeness jumps up to hand his chair.*

Thomas. I say, though . . . allow me.

Windlesham. Thank you . . . but she can't. Not in that corset.

Mr. State. Dear me, I had not meant to detain mademoi-

selle. [*Then to amend his manners, and rather as if it were
an incantation warranted to achieve his purpose.*] Bonjour.

The young lady departs, a real smile quite shaming the unreal.

Mr. State. You clean forget they're there. We gave some
time and money to elaborating a mechanical moving figure to
take the place of . . . a real automation, in fact. But sometimes it stuck and sometimes it ran away . . .

Thomas. And the cost!

Philip [*finely*]. Flesh and blood is always cheaper.

Mr. State. You approve of corsets, Mr. Windlesham?

Windlesham. Oh, yes . . . the figure is the woman, as we
say.

Mr. State. Have you ever gone deeply into the psychology
of the question? A while ago I had a smart young historian
write Burrows a little monograph on corsets . . . price one
shilling. Conservative, summing up in their favor. And we
made up a little museum of them . . . at Southampton, I
think . . . but that was not a success. Major Thomas . . .
we must send Mr. Windlesham a copy of that monograph.
You will find it very interesting.

Windlesham. I'm sure I shall. Can I do any more for you?

Philip. See me before I go, will you?

Windlesham. Then it's au'voir.

*And he flutters away. There is a pause as if they had to recol-
lect where they were. It is broken by* PHILIP *saying, meditatively.*

Philip. I sometimes wonder if we realize what women's
clothes are like . . . or our own, for that matter.

Mr. Huxtable. What's that?

Philip. Have you ever tried to describe a costume as it
would appear to a strange eye? Can you think of this last?
A hat as little like a hat as anything on a creature's head
may be. Lace. Flowers of a color it never pleases God to grow
them. And a jeweled feather . . . a feather with stones in it.
The rest might be called a conspiracy in three colors on the
part of a dozen sewing women to persuade you that the creature they have clothed can neither walk, digest her food, nor
bear children. Now . . . can that be beautiful?

Mr. State [*to whom this is the real conversational thing*].
Mr. Philip, that notion is a lever thrust beneath the very
foundations of society.

Mr. Huxtable [*showing off a little*]. Oh . . . trying to
upset people's ideas for the sake of doing it . . . silly.

Thomas [*with solid sense*]. I think a crowd of well-dressed women is one of the most beautiful things in the world.

Philip. Have you ever seen an Eastern woman walk into a Bond Street tea shop?

Thomas. No.

Philip [*forcefully*]. I have.

Constantine. Ah!

With one long, meditative exhalation he sends a little column of smoke into the air. MR. STATE *turns to him deferentially.*

Mr. State. We are boring you, Mr. Madras, I'm afraid. You were Facile Princeps upon all these questions so long ago.

CONSTANTINE *speaks in the smoothest of voices.*

Constantine. No, I am not bored, Mr. State . . . only a little horrified.

Mr. State. Why so?

Constantine. You see . . . I am a Mahommedan . . . and this attitude toward the other sex has become loathsome to me.

This bombshell, so delicately exploded, affects the company very variously. It will be some time before MR. HUXTABLE *grasps its meaning at all.* THOMAS *simply opens his mouth.* MR. STATE *has evidently found a new joy in life.* PHILIP, *to whom it seems no news, merely says in light protest* . . .

Philip. My dear Father!

Mr. State [*as he beams round*]. A *real* Mahommedan?

Constantine. I have become a Mahommedan. If you were not, it would be inconvenient to live permanently at Hit . . . a village upon the borders of Southern Arabia . . . that is my home. Besides, I was converted.

Thomas [*having recovered enough breath*]. I didn't know you could become a Mahommedan.

Constantine [*with some severity*]. You can become a Christian, sir.

Thomas [*a little shocked*]. Ah . . . not quite the same sort of thing.

Mr. State [*who feels that he really is rediscovering the old world*]. But how very interesting! To a broadminded man . . . how extraordinarily interesting! Was it a sudden conversion?

Constantine. No . . . I had been searching for a religion

. . . a common need in these times . . . and this is a very fine one, Mr. State.

Mr. State. Is it? I must look it up. The Koran! Yes, I've never read the Koran . . . an oversight.

He makes a mental note. And slowly, slowly, the full iniquity of it has sunk into MR. HUXTABLE. *His face has gone from red to white and back again to red. He becomes articulate and vehement. He thumps the table.*

Mr. Huxtable. And what about Amelia?

Mr. State [*with conciliatory calm*]. Who is Amelia?

Philip. Afterwards, Uncle.

Mr. Huxtable [*thumping again*]. What about your wife? No, I won't be quiet, Phil! It's illegal.

Constantine [*with a half-cold, half-kindly eye on him*]. Harry . . . I dislike to see you make yourself ridiculous.

Only this was needed.

Mr. Huxtable. Who cares if I'm ridiculous? I've not spoken to you for thirty years . . . have I? That is . . . I've not taken more notice of you than I could help. And I come here today full of forgiveness . . . and curiosity . . . to see what you're really like now . . . and whether I've changed my mind . . . or whether I never really felt all that about you at all . . . and damned if you don't go and put up a fresh game on me! What about Amelia? Religion this time! Mahommedan, indeed . . . at your age! Can't you ever settle down? I beg your pardon, Mr. State. All right, Phil, afterwards! I've not done . . . but you're quite right . . . afterwards.

The gust over, MR. STATE, *who is a little be-blown by it at such close quarters, says, partly with a peace-making intention, partly in curiosity . . .*

Mr. State. But do you indulge in a harem?

MR. HUXTABLE *is on his feet, righteously strepitant.*

Mr. Huxtable. If you insult my sister by answering that question . . .

With a look and a gesture CONSTANTINE *can silence him. Then with the coldest dignity he replies . . .*

Constantine. My household, sir, is that of the ordinary Eastern gentleman of my position. We do not speak of our women in public.

Mr. State. I'm sure I beg your pardon.

Constantine. Not at all. It is five years since I definitely retired from business and decided to consummate my affection for the East by settling down there. This final visit to Europe . . . partly to see you, Mr. State . . . was otherwise only to confirm my judgment on the question.

Mr. State. Has it?

Constantine. It has. I was always out of place amongst you. I was sometimes tempted to regret my scandalous conduct . . . [*A slight stir from* MR. HUXTABLE.] Hush, Harry . . . hush! But I never could persuade myself to amend it. It is some slight personal satisfaction to me to discover . . . with a stranger's eye . . . that Europe in its attitude toward women is mad.

Mr. State. Mad!

Constantine. Mad.

Thomas [*who is all ears*]. I say!

Constantine. You possibly agree with me, Major Thomas.

Thomas [*much taken aback*]. No . . . I don't think so.

Constantine. Many men do, but—poor fellows—they dare not say so. For instance, Mr. State, what can be said of a community in which five men of some ability and dignity are met together to traffic in . . . what was the numéro of that aphrodisiac that so particularly attracted Major Thomas?

THOMAS *is shocked even to violence.*

Thomas. No . . . really. I protest——

Mr. State [*utterly calm*]. Easy, Major Thomas. Let us consider the accusation philosophically. [*Then with the sweetest smile.*] Surely that is a gross construction to put on the instinct of every beautiful woman to adorn herself.

Constantine. Why gross? I delight in pretty women, prettily adorned. To come home after a day's work to the welcome of one's women folk . . . to find them unharassed by notions of business or politics . . . ready to refresh one's spirit by attuning it to the gentler, sweeter side of life . . .

Thomas [*making hearty atonement*]. Oh! Quite so . . . quite so.

Constantine. I thought you would agree with me, Major Thomas. That is the Mahommedan gentleman's domestic ideal.

Thomas [*brought up short*]. Is it?

Constantine. But you don't expect to find your wife dressed like that . . . the diamanté and the . . .

Thomas [*mental discomfort growing on him*]. No . . . that was a going-out dress.

Philip [*greatly enjoying this contest*]. Oh . . . Tommy! Tommy!

Thomas [*in tortuosity of mind—and conscience*]. But I tell you if my wife would . . . that is, if any chap's wife will . . . I mean . . . [*Then he gets it out.*] If a woman always kept herself smart and attractive at home then a man would have no excuse for gadding about after other women.

MR. HUXTABLE *joins the fray, suddenly, snappily.*

Mr. Huxtable. She sits looking after his children . . . what more does he want of her?

Constantine. Harry is a born husband, Major Thomas.

Mr. Huxtable. I'm not a born libertine, I hope.

Thomas. Libertine be damned.

Mr. State [*pacifically*]. Gentlemen, gentlemen . . . these are abstract propositions.

Mr. Huxtable. Gadding after another man's wife, perhaps! Though I don't think you ever did that, Constantine . . . I'll do you justice . . . I don't think you ever did.

Constantine. I never did.

Philip [*with intense mischief*]. Oh, Tommy, Tommy . . . can you say the same?

THOMAS *is really flabbergasted at the indecency.*

Thomas. Phil, that ain't nice . . . that ain't gentlemanly. And I wasn't thinking of that, and you know I wasn't. And . . . we ain't all so unattractive to women as you are.

MR. STATE *loses himself in enjoyment of this repartee.*

Mr. State. Ah . . . sour grapes, Mr. Philip. We mustn't be personal . . . but is it sour grapes?

Philip [*very coolly on his defense*]. Thank you, Tommy . . . I can attract just the sort of woman I want to attract. But as long as it's numéro cinq, six, or sept that attracts you . . . well . . . so long will Madras House be an excellent investment for Mr. State.

That is the end of that little breeze, and CONSTANTINE'S *voice completes the quieting.*

Constantine. Phil is a cold-blooded egotist, and if women like him that is their misfortune. I know his way with a woman . . . coax her on to the intellectual plane, where he thinks he can better her. You have my sympathy, Major Thomas. I also am as susceptible as nature means a man to be . . . as all women must wish him to be. And I referred to these going-out dresses because—candidly—I found myself obliged to leave a country where women are let loose with money to spend and time to waste. Encouraged to flaunt their charms on the very streets . . . proud if they see the busmen wink . . .

Mr. Huxtable. Not busmen. [*He is only gently deprecating now.*]

Constantine. Proud, my dear Harry, if they see a cabman smile.

MR. HUXTABLE *looks around, and then nods solemnly and thoughtfully.*

Mr. Huxtable. Yes, it's true. I'd deny it any other time, but I've been thinking a bit lately . . . and the things you think of once you start to think! And it's true. [*But with great chivalry.*] Only they don't know they do it. They don't know they do it. [*Then a doubt occurring.*] D'you think they know they do it, Phil?

Philip. Some of them suspect, Uncle.

Mr. Huxtable [*his faith unspoiled*]. No, what I say is it's instinct . . . and we've just got to be as nice-minded about it as we can. There was Julia, this summer at Weymouth . . . that's one of my daughters. Bought herself a dress . . . not one of the numéro sort, of course . . . but very pretty . . . orange color, it was . . . stripes. But you could see it a mile off on the parade . . . and her sisters all with their noses out of joint. I said to myself . . . instinct . . .

Suddenly MR. STATE *rescues the discussion.*

Mr. State. Yes, sir . . . the noblest instinct of all . . . the instinct to perpetuate our race. Let us take high ground in this matter, gentlemen.

Constantine [*unstirred*]. The very highest, Mr. State. If you think that to turn Weymouth for a month a year into a cockpit of haphazard love-making, with all the consequences that custom entails, is the best way of perpetuating your race . . . well, I disagree with you . . . but it's a point of view. What I ask is why Major Thomas and myself . . . already perhaps in a creditable state of marital perpetuation . . . should have our busy London lives obsessed by . . . What is this thing?

Philip. La belle Hélène's new hat, Father.

Constantine. Now, that may be ugly . . . I hope I never made anything quite so ugly myself . . . but it's attractive.

Philip [*with a wry face*]. No, Father.

Constantine. Isn't it, Major Thomas?

Thomas [*honestly*]. Well . . . it makes you look at em when you might not otherwise.

Constantine. Yes . . . it's provocative. Its intention is that none of the world's work shall be done while it's about. And when it's always about I honestly confess again that I cannot do my share. It's a terrible thing to be constantly conscious of women. They have their uses to the world . . . as you so happily phrased it, Mr. State . . . their perpetual use . . . and the world's interest is best served by keeping them strictly to it. Are these provocative ladies [*He fingers the hat again.*] remarkable for perpetuation nowadays?

Once more MR. STATE *bursts in—this time almost heart-brokenly.*

Mr. State. I can't bear this, sir . . . I can't bear to take such a view of life . . . no man of feeling could. Besides, it's reactionary . . . you're on the wrong tack. You must come back to us, sir. You gave us joy and pleasure . . . can we do without them? When you find yourself once more among the loveliness you helped us to worship you'll change your mind. What was the end of that little story of the duchess? How, on the appointed night, attired in her Madras creation, she swept into the ballroom with a frou-frou of silk skirt wafting perfume as she came . . . while her younger rivals pale before the intoxication of her beauty, and every man in the room . . . young and old . . . struggles for a glimpse . . . a word . . . a look. [*Once again he starts to soar.*] A ballroom, sir . . . isn't it one of the sweetest sights in the world? When bright the lamps shine o'er fair women and brave men. Music arises with its voluptuous swell. Soft eyes look love to eyes which speak again. And all goes merry as a marriage bell! Byron, gentlemen, taught me at my mother's knee. The poet of love and liberty . . . read in every school in America.

At the end of this recitation, which MR. HUXTABLE *barely refrains from applauding,* CONSTANTINE *goes coolly on.*

Constantine. Mr. State, that is my case. The whole of our upper-class life, which everyone with a say in the government of the country tries to lead . . . is now run as a ballroom is run. Men swaggering before women . . . the women ogling the men. Once a lad got some training in manliness. But now from the very start . . . ! In your own progressive country . . . mixed education . . . oh, my dear sir . . . mixed education!

Mr. State. A softening influence.

Constantine [*unexpectedly*]. Of course it is. And what has it sunk to, moreover . . . all education nowadays? Booklearning. Because woman's a dab at that . . . though it's of quite secondary importance to a man.

Thomas [*feelingly*]. That's so.

Constantine. And moral influence. Woman's morality . . . the worst in the world.

Philip. Slave morality.

Constantine. Yes. Read Nietzsche . . . as my friend Tarleton says. [*All one gathers from this cryptic allusion is that* MR. HUXTABLE, *at any rate, reprobates Tarleton, and, inferentially, Nietzsche.*] At Oxford and Cambridge it grows worse . . . married professors . . . Newnham and Girton . . . suffrage questions . . . purity questions.

Mr. Huxtable. Of course, some of the novels . . .

Constantine. From seventeen to thirty-four . . . the years which a man should consecrate to the acquiring of political virtue . . . wherever he turns he is distracted, provoked, tantalized by the barefaced presence of women. How's he to keep a clear brain for the larger issues of life? Why do you soldiers, Major Thomas, volunteer with such alacrity for foreign service?

Thomas [*with a jump*]. Good God . . . I never thought of that.

Constantine. What's the result? Every great public question . . . all politics, all religion, all economy is being brought down to the level of women's emotion. Admirable in its way, . . . charming in its place! But softening, sentimentalizing, enervating . . . lapping the world, if you let it, in the nursery cotton wool of prettiness and pettiness. Men don't realize how far rotted by the process they are . . . that's what's so fatal. We're used to a whole nation's anger being vented in scoldings . . . or rather we're getting used to the thought that it's naughty to be angry at all. Justice degenerates into kindness . . . that doesn't surprise us. Religion is a pretty hymn tune to keep us from fear of the dark. You four unfortunates might own the truth just for once . . . you needn't tell your wives.

Mr. State. I am not married.

Constantine. I might have known it.

Mr. State [*a little astonished*]. But no matter.

Constantine [*with full appreciation of what he says*]. Women haven't morals or intellect in our sense of the words. They have other incompatible qualities quite as important, no doubt. But shut them away from public life and public exhibition. It's degrading to compete with them . . . it's as degrading to compete for them. Perhaps we're too late already . . . but oh, my dear sentimental sir [*He addresses the pained though admiring* MR. STATE.], if we could replant the laurel bushes thick enough we might yet rediscover the fine manly world we are losing.

Except PHILIP, *who sits detached and attentive, they are all rather depressed by this judgment upon them.* THOMAS *recovers sufficiently to ask* . . .

Thomas. Are you advocating polygamy in England?

Constantine. That is what it should come to.

Thomas. Well . . . I call that rather shocking. [*Then with some hopeful interest.*] And is it practical?

Constantine. I did not anticipate the reform in my lifetime . . . so I left for the East.

Philip [*finely*]. You did quite right, Father. I wish everyone of your way of thinking would do the same.

CONSTANTINE *is ready for him.*

Constantine. Are you prepared for so much depopulation? Think of the women who'd be off tomorrow.

MR. HUXTABLE *wakes from stupefaction to say with tremendous emphasis.*

Mr. Huxtable. Never!

Constantine. Wrong, Harry.

Mr. Huxtable. No, I'm not wrong just because you say so! You ought to listen to me a bit sometimes. I always listened to you.

Constantine. Bless your quick temper.

Who could resist CONSTANTINE's *smile* . . . *Well, not* HUXTABLE.

Mr. Huxtable. Oh . . . go on . . . tell me why I'm wrong . . . I dare say I am.

Constantine. Even if you have liked bringing up six daughters and not getting them married . . . how have they liked it? You should have drowned them at birth, Harry . . .

Mr. Huxtable. You must have your joke, mustn't you?

Constantine. Therefore, how much pleasanter for you . . . how much better for them . . . if you'd only to find one man ready, for a small consideration, to marry the lot.

Mr. Huxtable [*with intense delight*]. Now if I was to tell my wife that she wouldn't see the umor of it.

Constantine. The woman emancipator's last ditch, Mr. State, is the trust that women will side with him. Don't make any mistake. This is a serious question to them . . . of health and happiness . . . and sometimes of bread and butter. Quite apart from our customers here . . . kept women, every one of them . . .

Mr. State [*in some alarm*]. You don't say!

Constantine [*gently lifting him from the little trap*]. Economically. Kept by their husbands . . . or if they live on their dividends, kept by society.

Philip. What about men who live on their dividends?

Mr. State. No . . . now don't let us go on to politics.

Constantine. . . . And apart from the prisoners in that chaste little fortress on Denmark Hill . . . we used to employ, Harry, between us . . . what? two or three hundred free and independent women . . . making clothes for the others, the ladies. They are as free as you like . . . free to go . . . free to starve. How much do they rejoice in their freedom to earn their living by ruining their health and stifling their instincts? Answer me, Harry, you monster of good-natured wickedness.

Mr. Huxtable. What's that?

Constantine. You keep an industrial seraglio.

Mr. Huxtable. A what!

Constantine. What else is your Roberts and Huxtable but a harem of industry. Do you know that it would sicken with horror a good Mahommedan? You buy these girls in the open market . . . you keep them under lock and key . . .

Mr. Huxtable. I do?

Constantine. Quite right, Harry, no harm done. [*Then his voice sinks to the utmost seriousness.*] But you coin your profits out of them by putting on exhibition for ten hours a day . . . their good looks, their good manners, their womanhood. Hired out it is to any stranger to hold as cheap for a few minutes as common decency allows. And when you've worn them out you turn them out . . . forget their very names . . . wouldn't know their faces if you met them selling matches at your door. For such treatment of potential motherhood, my Prophet condemns a man to Hell.

Mr. Huxtable [*breathless with amazement*]. Well, I never did in all my born days! They can marry respectably, can't they? We like em to marry.

Philip. Yes, Uncle . . . I went into that question with Miss Yates and the Brigstocks this morning.

Constantine [completing his case]. I ask you all . . . what is to happen to you as a nation? Where are your future generations coming from? What with the well-kept women you flatter and aestheticize till they won't give you children, and the free women you work at market rates till they can't give you children . . .

Mr. Huxtable [half-humorously sulky]. Miss Yates has obliged us, anyhow.

Philip [quickly capping him]. And we're going to dismiss her.

MR. HUXTABLE *flashes again into protestation.*

Mr. Huxtable. What else can we do? But I said you weren't to be hard on the girl. And I won't be upset like this. I want to take things as I find em . . . that is as I used to find em . . . before there was any of these ideas going around . . . and I'm sure we were happier without em. Stifling their instincts . . . it's a horrid way to talk. And I don't believe it. I could send for every girl in the shop, and not one of em would hint at it to me. [*He has triumphed with himself so far, but his new-born intellectual conscience brings him down.*] Not that that proves anything, does it? I'm a fool. It's a beastly world. But I don't make it so, do I?

Philip. Who does?

Mr. Huxtable. Other people. [PHILIP's *eye is on him.*] Oh, I see it coming. You're going to say we're all the other people or something. I'm getting up to you.

Constantine [very carefully]. What is this about a Miss Yates?

Philip. A little bother down at Peckham. I can tell you afterwards if you like.

Constantine. No . . . there is no need.

Something in the tone of this last makes PHILIP *look up quickly. But* MR. STATE, *with a sudden thought, has first dived for his watch, and then, at the sight of it, gets up from the table.*

Mr. State. Gentlemen, are you aware of the time? I may mention that I have a city appointment at four o'clock.

Constantine [polite, but leisurely]. Are we detaining you, Mr. State? Not universal or compulsory polygamy, Major Thomas. That would be nonsense. The very distribution of the sexes forbids it. But its recognition is one of the logical outcomes of the aristocratic method of government. And that's the only ultimate method . . . all others are interim plans for sifting out various aristocracies. The community of the future will specialize its functions. Women will find, I hope, some intellectual companions like my son, who will, besides, take a gentle interest in the County Council. There will be single-hearted men like Harry, content with old-fashioned domesticity. There will be poets like you, Mr. State, to dream about women and to dress them . . . their bodies in silks and their virtues in phrases. But there must also be such men as Major Thomas and myself . . .

THOMAS *rises, yet again, to this piece of chaff.*

Thomas. No, no! I'm not like that . . . not in the least. Because a fellow has been in the Army! Don't drag me in.

Mr. State. As stimulating a conversation as I remember. A little hard to follow at times . . . but worth far more than the sacrifice of any mere business doings.

CONSTANTINE *takes the hint graciously, and is apt for business at once.*

Constantine. My fault! Shall we agree, Mr. State, to accept as much of your offer as you have no intention of altering? We are dealing for both the shops?

Mr. State. Yes. What are we proposing to knock off their valuation, Major Thomas?

Thomas. Eight thousand six hundred.

Constantine. Phil, what were we prepared to come down?

Philip. Nine thousand.

Constantine. A very creditable margin. Your offer is accepted, Mr. State.

MR. STATE *feels he must really play up to such magnificent conducting of business.*

Mr. State. I should prefer to knock you down only eight thousand.

Constantine [*keeping the advantage*]. Isn't that merely romantic of you, Mr. State . . . not in the best form of business art?

Thomas. But the conditions, you know?

Constantine. We accept your conditions. If they won't work you'll be only anxious to alter them. So the business is done.

MR. HUXTABLE'S *eyes are wide.*

Mr. Huxtable. But look here.

Philip. Uncle Harry has something to say . . .

Mr. Huxtable [*assertively*]. Yes.

Constantine. Something different to say, Harry?

Mr. Huxtable [*after thinking it over*]. No.

So CONSTANTINE *returns happily to his subject.*

Constantine. What interests me about this woman question . . . now that I've settled my personal share in it . . . is to wonder how Europe, hampered by such an unsolved problem, can hope to stand up against the Oriental revival.

Thomas. What's that?

Constantine. You'll hear of it shortly. Up from the Persian gulf to where I live we could grow enough wheat to feed the British Empire. Life there is simple and spacious . . . the air is not breathed out. All we want is a happy, hardy race of men, and under a decent government we shall soon beget it. But you Europeans! Is this the symbol you are marching to the future under? [*He has found again, and lifts up, la belle Hélène's new hat.*] A cap of slavery! You are all idolaters of women . . . and they are the slaves of your idolatry.

Mr. State [*with undisguised admiration*]. Mr. Madras, I am proud to have met you again. If I say another word, I may be so interested in your reply that I shall miss my appointment. My coat? Thank you, Mr. Philip. I have to meet a man about a new system of country house drainage that he wants me to finance. I can hardly hope for another transcendental discussion upon that.

Constantine. Why not?

Mr. State. If you were he! Good-by, sir. Good-day, Mr. Huxtable. Till tomorrow, Major Thomas. No, Mr. Philip, don't see me down.

He is off for his next deal. PHILIP *civilly takes him past the door saying* . . .

Philip. Your car's at the Bond Street entrance, I expect.

And then he comes back. CONSTANTINE *is keeping half a friendly eye on* HUXTABLE, *who fidgets under it.* THOMAS *takes breath and expounds a grievance.*

Thomas. That's how he settles business. But leaves us all the papers to do. I shall take mine home. The four-thirty gets me indoors by a quarter to six. Time for a cup of tea! Phil, have you got China tea?

Philip. Downstairs.

Mr. Huxtable. I must be getting back, I think.

Constantine. Harry . . . you're running away from me.

Mr. Huxtable [*in frank amused confession*]. Yes . . . I was. Habit, y'know . . . habit.

Constantine [*with the most friendly condescension*]. Suppose I go with you . . . part of the way. How do you go?

Mr. Huxtable. On a bus.

Constantine. Suppose we go together . . . on a bus.

Mr. Huxtable [*desperately cunning*]. It's all right . . . they won't see me with you. We don't close till seven.

CONSTANTINE'S *face sours.*

Constantine. No, to be sure. Phil, I can't come to dinner, I'm afraid.

Philip. Oh, I was going to tell you. Mother will be there. Tommy, you know the tea room.

Thomas [*all tact*]. Oh, quite!

Philip. Straight downstairs, first to the left and the second passage. I'll follow.

THOMAS *departs.* CONSTANTINE *says, indifferently* . . .

Constantine. Then I'll come in after dinner.

Philip. You don't mind?

Constantine. No.

There stands MR. HUXTABLE, *first on one foot and then on the other, desperately nervous.* CONSTANTINE *smiling at him.* PHILIP *cannot resist it. He says* . . .

Philip. It's afterward now, Uncle. Fire away.

And is off. CONSTANTINE *still smiles. Poor* MR. HUXTABLE *makes a desperate effort to do the proper thing by this reprobate. He forms his face into a frown. It's no use; an answering smile will come. He surrenders.*

Mr. Huxtable. Look here . . . don't let's talk about Amelia.

Constantine. No . . . never rake up the past.

Mr. Huxtable. Lord! What else has a chap got to think of?

Constantine. That's why you look so old.

Mr. Huxtable. Do I, now?

Constantine. What age are you?

Mr. Huxtable. Sixty.

The two sit down together.

Constantine. You should come and stay with me at Hit . . . not far from Hillel . . . Hillel is Babylon, Harry.

Mr. Huxtable [*curiously*]. What's it like there?

Constantine. The house is white, and there are palm trees about it . . . and not far off flows the Euphrates.

Mr. Huxtable. Just like in the Bible. [*His face is wistful.*] Constantine.

Constantine. Yes, Harry.

Mr. Huxtable. You've said odder things this afternoon than I've ever heard you say before.

Constantine. Probably not.

Mr. Huxtable [*wondering*]. And I haven't really minded em. But I believe it's the first time I've ever understood you . . . and p'raps that's just as well for me.

Constantine [*encouragingly*]. Oh . . . why, Harry?

Mr. Huxtable. Because . . . d'you think it's only not being very clever keeps us . . . well behaved?

Constantine. Has it kept you happy?

Mr. Huxtable [*impatient at the petty word*]. Anyone can be happy. What worries me is having got to my age and only just beginning to understand anything at all. And you can't learn it out of books, old man. Books don't tell you the truth . . . at least not any that I can find. I wonder if I'd been a bit of a dog like you . . . ? But there it is . . . you can't do things on purpose. And what's more, don't you go to think I'd have done them if I could . . . knowing them to be wrong. [*Then comes a discovery.*] But I was always jealous of you, Constantine, for you seemed to get the best of everything . . . and I know people couldn't help being fond of you . . . for I was fond of you myself, whatever you did. That was odd to start with. And now here we are, both of us old chaps . . .

Constantine [*as he throws back his head*]. I am not old.

Mr. Huxtable [*with sudden misgiving*]. You don't repent, do you?

Constantine. What of?

Mr. Huxtable. Katherine said this morning that you might have . . . but I wasn't afraid of that. [*Now he wags his head wisely.*] You know . . . you evildoers . . . you upset us all, and you hurt our feelings, and of course you ought to be ashamed of yourself. But . . . well . . . it's like the only time I went abroad. I was sick going . . . I was orribly uncomfortable . . . I ated the cooking . . . I was sick coming back. But I wouldn't have missed it . . . !

Constantine [*in affectionate good fellowship*]. Come to Arabia, Harry.

Mr. Huxtable [*humorously pathetic about it*]. Don't you make game of me. My time's over. What have I done with it, now? Married. Brought up a family. Been master to a few hundred girls and fellows who never really cared a bit for me. I've been made a convenience of . . . that's my life. That's where I envy you. You've had your own way . . . and you don't look now as if you'd be damned for it, either.

Constantine [*in gentlemanly defiance*]. I shan't be.

MR. HUXTABLE *shakes a fist, somewhat, though unconsciously, in the direction of the ceiling.*

Mr. Huxtable. It's not fair, and I don't care who hears me say so.

Constantine. Suppose we shout it from the top of the bus.

As they start, MR. HUXTABLE *returns to his mundane, responsible self.*

Mr. Huxtable. But you know, old man . . . you'll excuse me, I'm sure . . . and it's all very well having theories and being able to talk . . . still, you did treat Amelia very badly . . . and those other ones, too . . . say what you like! Let go my arm, will you!

Constantine. Why?

Mr. Huxtable [*his scruples less strong than the soft touch of* CONSTANTINE'S *hand*]. Well, p'raps you needn't. [*A thought strikes him.*] Are you really going away for good this time?

Constantine. Tomorrow.

Mr. Huxtable [*beaming on him*]. Then come home and see mother and the girls.

MAJOR THOMAS *comes back, looking about him.*

Thomas. Excuse me . . . I left my hat.

Constantine. It will make them very uncomfortable.

Mr. Huxtable [*his smile fading*]. D'you think so? Won't it do em good . . . broaden their minds?

PHILIP *comes back, too.*

Mr. Huxtable. Phil . . . shall I take your father ome to call?

Philip [*after one gasp at the prospect, says with great cheerfulness* . . .]. Certainly.

Constantine. I'll be with you by nine, Phil.

MR. HUXTABLE's *daredevil heart fails once more.*

Mr. Huxtable. I say . . . better not be too friendly through the shop.

CONSTANTINE *smiles still, but does not loose his arm. Off they go.*

Thomas [*still searching*]. Where the devil did I put it?
Philip. Pity you can't take father's place at dinner, Tommy.

THOMAS *stops and looks at him aggrievedly.*

Thomas. Are you chaffing me?
Philip. We might get some further light on the woman question. My mother's opinion and Jessica's upon such men as you and my father.

He picks up some papers and sits to them at the table.

Thomas. Look here, Phil . . . don't you aggravate me into behaving rashly. Here it is. [*He has found his hat on a gas bracket—and he slams it on.*]
Philip. With Jessica?
Thomas [*with ferocious gallantry*]. Yes . . . a damned attractive woman.
Philip. After all . . . as an abstract proposition, Tommy . . . polyandry is just as simple a way . . . and as far as we know, as much nature's way as the other. We ought to have put that point to the gentle Mahommedan.
Thomas [*after vainly considering this for a moment*]. Phil, I should like to see you in love with a woman . . . It'd serve you right.

Suddenly PHILIP *drops his mocking tone and his face grows gentle and grave.*

Philip. Tommy . . . what's the purpose of it all? Apart from the sentimental wallowings of Mr. Eustace Perrin State . . . and putting that Lord of Creation, my father, on one side for a moment . . . what do we slow-breeding, civilized people get out of love . . . and the beauty of women . . . and the artistic setting that beauty demands? For which we do pay rather a big price, you know, Tommy. What do we get for it?
Thomas [*utterly at sea*]. I don't know.
Philip. It's an important question. Think it over in the train.
Thomas. Old chap . . . I beg your pardon . . . the County

Council is the best place for you. It'll stop your addling over these silly conundrums.

Philip [*subtly*]. On the contrary.

Thomas [*his favorite phrase again*]. What do you mean?

Philip. Get out . . . you'll miss that four-thirty.

THOMAS *gets out.* PHILIP *gets desperately to loathed business.*

ACT FOUR

PHILIP, *his mother, and* JESSICA, *are sitting, after dinner, round the drawing-room fire in Phillimore Gardens.* JESSICA, *rather, is away upon the bench of her long, black piano, sorting bound books of music, and the firelight hardly reaches her. But it flickers over* MRS. MADRAS, *and though it marks more deeply the little bitter lines on her face, it leaves a glow there in recompense. She sits, poor, anxious old lady, gazing, not into the fire, but at the shining copper fender, her hands on her lap, as usual. Every now and then she lifts her head to listen.* PHILIP *is comfortable upon the sofa opposite; he is smoking, and is deep, besides, in some weighty volume, the Longman edition of the Minority Report of the Poor Law Commission, perhaps.*

It is a charming room. The walls are gray, the paint is a darker gray. The curtains to the two long windows are of the gentlest pink brocade; the lights that hang on plain little brackets from the walls are a soft pink, too, and there is no other color in the room, but the maziness of some Persian rugs on the floor and the mellowed brilliancy of the Arundel prints on the walls. There is no more furniture than there need be; there is no more light than there need be; yet it is not empty or dreary. There is just nothing to jar, nothing to prevent a sensitive soul finding rest there.

The PARLORMAID *comes in; she is dressed in gray, too, capless, some black ribbons about her.* (*Really,* JESSICA's *home inclines to be a little precious!*) *She brings letters, one for* JESSICA, *two for* PHILIP, *and departs.*

PHILIP. Last post.

Jessica. Half-past nine. I suppose your father means to come?

Philip. He said so.
Mrs. Madras. Is your letter interesting, Jessica?
Jessica. A receipt.
Mrs. Madras. Do you run bills?
Jessica. Lots.
Mrs. Madras. Is that quite wise?
Jessica. The tradesmen prefer it.

With that she walks to her writing table. JESSICA's *manner to
her mother-in-law is overcourteous, an unkind weapon against
which the old lady, but half-conscious of it, is quite defense-
less.* PHILIP *has opened his second letter, and whistles, at its
contents, a bar of a tune that is in his head.*

Jessica. What's the matter, Phil?

*To emphasize his feelings he performs the second bar with
variations.*

Jessica. As bad as that?

*For final comment he brings the matter to a full close on
one expressive note, and puts the letter away.* JESSICA *flicks at
him amusedly.*

Mrs. Madras. How absurd! You can't tell in the least what
he means.
Jessica. No.

With forced patience she wanders back to her piano.

Mrs. Madras. You might play us something, Jessica . . .
just to pass the time.

Unobserved, JESSICA *casts her eyes up to the ceiling.*

Jessica. What will you have?
Mrs. Madras. I am sure you play all the latest things.
Jessica. I'm afraid you don't really like my playing.
Mrs. Madras. I do think it's a little professional. I prefer
something softer.

JESSICA *leaves the piano.*

Jessica. I'm afraid we are giving you a dull evening.
Mr. Madras [*with that suddenness which seems to charac-
terize the Huxtable family*]. Why do you never call me
mother, Jessica?
Jessica. Don't I?
Mrs. Madras [*resenting prevarication*]. You know you
don't.

Jessica. I suppose I don't think of you just like that.

Mrs. Madras. What has that to do with it?

Jessica [more coldly courteous than ever.] Nothing . . . Mother.

Mrs. Madras. That's not a very nice manner of giving way, either, is it?

Jessica [on the edge of an outburst]. It seemed to me sufficiently childish.

Mrs. Madras [parading a double injury]. I don't know what you mean. It's easy to be too clever for me, Jessica.

PHILIP *mercifully intervenes.*

Philip. Mother, what do you think parents gain by insisting on respect and affection from grown-up children?

Mrs. Madras. Isn't it their right?

Philip. But I asked what they gained.

Mrs. Madras. Isn't it natural? When an old woman has lost her husband, or worse, if she's to lose her children, too, what has she left?

Jessica [recovering a little kindness]. Her womanhood, Mother.

Philip. Her old-womanhood. You know, it may be a very beautiful possession.

The PARLORMAID *announces* "MR. CONSTANTINE MADRAS." *There stands* CONSTANTINE *in the bright light of the hall, more dramatically dignified than ever. As he comes in, though, it seems as if there was the slightest strain in his charming manners. He has not changed his clothes for the evening. He goes straight to* JESSICA, *and it seems that he has a curious soft way of shaking hands with women.*

Constantine. How do you do, Jessica? I find you looking beautiful.

JESSICA *acknowledges the compliment with a little disdainful bend of the head and leaves him, then with a glance at* PHILIP *leaves the room.* CONSTANTINE *comes toward his wife. She does not look up, but her face wrinkles pathetically. So he speaks at last.*

Constantine. Well, Amelia?

For MRS. MADRAS *it must be resentment or tears, or both. Resentment comes first.*

Mr. Madras. Is that the way to speak to me after thirty years?

Constantine [amicably]. Perhaps it isn't. But there's not much variety of choice in greetings, is there?

PHILIP, *nodding to his father, has edged to the door, and now edges out of it.*

Constantine. They leave us alone. We might be an engaged couple.

She stays silent, distressfully avoiding his eye. He takes a chair and sits by her. He would say (as JESSICA *no doubt would say of herself) that he speaks kindly to her.*

Constantine. Well, Amelia? I beg your pardon. I repeat myself, and you dislike the phrase. I hope, though, that you are quite well? Don't cry, dear Amelia . . . unless, of course, you want to cry. Well, then . . . cry. And, when you've finished crying . . . there's no hurry . . . you shall tell me why you wished to see me . . . and run the risk of upsetting yourself like this.

Mrs. Madras [dabbing her eyes]. I don't often cry. I don't often get a chance.

Constantine. I fear that is only one way of saying that you miss me.

The handkerchief is put away, and she faces him.

Mrs. Madras. Are you really going back to that country tomorrow?

Constantine. Tomorrow morning.

Mrs. Madras. For good?

Constantine [with thanksgiving]. Forever.

Mrs. Madras [desperately resolute]. Will you take me with you?

It takes CONSTANTINE *just a moment to recover.*

Constantine. No, Amelia, I will not.

Mrs. Madras [reacting a little hysterically]. I'm sure I don't want to go, and I'm sure I never meant to ask you. But you haven't changed a bit, Constantine . . . in spite of your beard. [*Then the voice saddens and almost dies away.*] I have.

Constantine. Only externally, I'm sure.

Mrs. Madras. Why did you ever marry me? You married me for my money.

Constantine [sighting boredom]. It is so long ago.

Mrs. Madras. It isn't . . . it seems like yesterday. Didn't you marry me for my money?

Constantine. Partly, Amelia, partly. Why did you marry me?

Mrs. Madras. I wanted to. I was a fool.

Constantine [*evenly still*]. You were a fool, perhaps, to grumble at the consequence of getting what you wanted. It would have been kinder of me, no doubt, not to marry you. But I was more impetuous then, and, of course, less experienced. I didn't realize you never could change your idea of what a good husband must be, nor how necessary it would become that you should.

Mrs. Madras. How dare you make excuses for the way you treated me?

Constantine. There were two excuses. I was the first. I'm afraid that you ultimately became the second.

Mrs. Madras [*with spirit*]. I only stood up for my rights.

Constantine. You got them, too. We separated, and there was an end of it.

Mrs. Madras. I've never been happy since.

Constantine. That is nothing to be proud of, my dear.

MRS. MADRAS *feels the strangeness between them wearing off.*

Mrs. Madras. What happened to that woman and her son . . . that Flora?

Constantine. The son is an engineer . . . promises very well, his employers tell me. Flora lives at Hitchin . . . quite comfortably, I have reason to believe.

Mrs. Madras. She was older than me.

Constantine. About the same age, I think.

Mrs. Madras. You've given her money?

Constantine [*his eyebrows up*]. Certainly . . . they were both provided for.

Mrs. Madras. Don't you expect me to be jealous?

Constantine [*with a sigh*]. Still, Amelia?

Mrs. Madras. Do you ever see her now?

Constantine. I haven't seen her for years.

Mrs. Madras. It seems to me she has been just as well treated as I have . . . if not better.

Constantine. She expected less.

Mrs. Madras. And what about the others?

Constantine [*his patience giving out*]. No, really, it's thirty years ago . . . I cannot fight my battles over again. Please tell me what I can do for you beyond taking you back with me.

Mrs. Madras [*cowering to the last harshness*]. I didn't mean that. I don't know what made me say it. But it's dreadful seeing you once more and being alone with you.

Constantine. Now, Amelia, are you going to cry again?

Mrs. Madras [*setting her teeth*]. No.

Constantine. That's right.

MRS. MADRAS *really does pull herself together, and becomes intensely reasonable.*

Mrs. Madras. What I really want you to do, if you please, Constantine, is not to go away. I don't expect us to live together . . . after the way you have behaved I could not consent to such a thing. But somebody must look after you when you are ill, and, what's more, I don't think you ought to go and die out of your own country.

Constantine [*meeting reason with reason*]. My dear . . . I have formed other ties.

Mrs. Madras. Will you please explain exactly what you mean by that?

Constantine. I am a Mahommedan.

Mrs. Madras. Nonsense!

Constantine. Possibly you are not acquainted with the Mahommedan marriage laws.

Mrs. Madras. D'you mean to say you're not married to me?

Constantine. No . . . though it was not considered necessary for me to take that into account in conforming to it . . . I did.

Mrs. Madras. Well . . . I never thought you could behave any worse. Why weren't you satisfied in making me unhappy? If you've gone and committed blasphemy as well . . . I don't know what's to become of you, Constantine.

Constantine. Amelia, if I had been a Mahommedan from the beginning you might be living happily with me now.

Mrs. Madras. How can you say such a horrible thing? Suppose it were true?

Constantine. I came from the East.

Mrs. Madras. You didn't.

Constantine. Let us be quite accurate. My grandfather was a Smyrna Jew.

Mrs. Madras. You never knew him. Your mother brought you up a Baptist.

Constantine. I was an unworthy Baptist. As a Baptist I owe you apologies for my conduct. What does that excellent creed owe me for the little hells of temptation and shame and remorse that I passed through because of it?

Mrs. Madras [*in pathetic wonder*]. Did you, Constantine?

Constantine. I did.

Mrs. Madras. You never told me.

Constantine [*with manly pride*]. I should think not.

Mrs. Madras. But I was longing to have you say you were sorry, and let me forgive you. Twice and three times I'd have forgiven you . . . and you knew it, Constantine.

CONSTANTINE *recovers his humor, his cool courtesy, and his inhumanity, which he had momentarily lost.*

Constantine. Yes, it wasn't so easy to escape your forgiveness. If it weren't for Mahomet, the Prophet of God, Amelia, I should hardly be escaping it now.

PHILIP *comes delicately in.*

Philip. I beg pardon . . . only my book. [*Which he takes from the piano.*]

Constantine. Don't go, Phil.

So PHILIP *joins them, and then, as silence supervenes, says, with obvious cheerfulness* . . .

Philip. How are you getting on?

Mrs. Madras [*her tongue released*]. Philip, don't be flippant. It's just as your cousin Ernest said. Your father has gone and pretended to marry a lot of wretched women out in that country you showed me on the map, and I don't know what's to be done. My head's going round.

Constantine. Not a lot, Amelia.

Mrs. Madras. And if anybody had told me, when I was a girl at school, and learning about such things in history and geography, that I should ever find myself in such a situation as this, I wouldn't have believed them. [*She piles up the agony.*] Constantine, how are you going to face me hereafter? Have you thought of that? Wasn't our marriage made in Heaven? I must know what is going to happen to us . . . I simply must. I have always prayed that you might come back to me, and that I might close your eyes in death. You know I have, Philip, and I've asked you to tell him so. He has no right to go and do such wicked things. You're mine in the sight of God, Constantine, and you can't deny it.

Without warning, CONSTANTINE *loses his temper, jumps up and thunders at her.*

Constantine. Woman . . . be silent. [*Then, as in shame, he turns his back on her and says in the coldest voice* . . .]

Philip, I have several things to talk over with you. Suggest to your mother that she should leave us alone.

Philip [*protesting against both temper and dignity*]. I shall do nothing of the sort. While my father's in England, and you're in our house, he can at least treat his wife with politeness.

Mrs. Madras [*with meek satisfaction*]. I'd rather he didn't . . . it's only laughing at me. I'll go to bed. I'd much rather he lost his temper.

She gets up to go. CONSTANTINE'*s bitter voice stops her.*

Constantine. Phil . . . when you were a boy . . . your mother and I once quarreled in your presence.

Philip [*in bitterness, too*]. I remember.

Constantine. I'm ashamed of it to this day.

Mrs. Madras [*quite pleasantly*]. Well . . . I'm sure I don't remember it. What about?

Constantine. Oh . . . this terrible country. Every hour I stay in it seems to rob me of some atom of self-respect.

MRS. MADRAS *joins battle again at this.*

Mrs. Madras. Then why did you come back? And why haven't you been to see me before . . . or written to me?

Constantine [*in humorous despair*]. Amelia, don't aggravate me any more. Go to bed, if you're going.

Mrs. Madras. I wish I'd never seen you again.

Philip. Good night, Mother.

PHILIP *gets her to the door and kisses her kindly. Then* CONSTANTINE *says, with all the meaning possible——*

Constantine. Good-by, Amelia.

She turns, the bright hall light falling on her, looks at him hatefully, makes no other reply, goes. PHILIP *comes back to the fire. All this is bitter to him, too. He eyes his father.*

Constantine. I'm sorry. I'm upset. I was upset when I came here.

Philip. What about? The visit to Denmark Hill?

Constantine [*who has apparently forgotten that*]. No . . . I didn't go there, after all.

Philip. Funked it?

Constantine [*accepting the gibe*]. I dare say. Once we were off the bus, Harry began to mutter about hurting their feelings. I daresay I was funking it, too. I told him to tell them how unbendingly moral he had been with me. He shed three tears as we parted.

Philip. Yes . . . my mother was alone here. She's a disappointed woman . . . peevish with ill health. One has her at a disadvantage. But Aunt Kate . . . unveiled and confident, with six corseted daughters to back her!

Constantine. You think, of course, that I've always treated your mother badly?

Philip. I can't help thinking so. Was it the only way to treat her?

Constantine. Was I meant to pass the rest of a lifetime making her forget that she was as unhappy as people who have outlived their purpose always are?

Philip. Personally, I have this grudge against you both, my dear Father. As the son of a quarrelsome marriage, I have grown up inclined to dislike men and despise women. You're so full of this purpose of getting the next generation born. Suppose you thought a little more of its upbringing.

Constantine. What was wrong with yours?

Philip. I had no home.

Constantine. You spent a Sunday with me every month. You went to the manliest school I could find.

Philip. Never mind how I learned Latin and Greek. Who taught me that every pretty, helpless woman was a man's prey . . . and how to order my wife out of the room?

Constantine [*with a shrug*]. My dear boy . . . they like it.

Philip. Do they?

Constantine. Well . . . how else are you to manage them?

Philip. Father, don't you realize that . . . in decadent England, at least, the manliness of yours is getting a little out of date . . . that you and your kind begin to look foolish at last?

Constantine [*voicing the discomfort that possesses him*]. I dare say. Thank God, I shall be quit of the country tomorrow! I got here late this evening because I traveled three stations too far in that tube, sitting opposite such a pretty little devil. She was so alive . . . so crying out for conquest . . . she had that curve of the instep and the little trick of swinging her foot that I never could resist. How does a man resist it? Yes. That's ridiculous and ignominious and degrading. I escaped from England to escape from it. Old age here . . . a loose lip and a furtive eye. I'd have asked you to shoot me first.

Philip. Was it that upset you?

Constantine. No. [*He frowns; his thoughts are much else-where. There is a moment's silence.* PHILIP *breaks it.*]

Philip. Father, what do you know about this Miss Yates affair?

CONSTANTINE *gives him a sharp look; then carefully casual——*

Constantine. What you've told me.

Philip. No more?

Constantine. Is there more to know?

PHILIP *fishes out and hands across the letter over which he whistled.*

Philip. This has just come from Miss Chancellor.

Constantine. Who's she?

Philip. The housekeeper at Peckham, who rashly accused Brigstock of being the other responsible party.

Constantine. Is he?

Philip. I think not. But she encloses a letter she has just had from Brigstock's solicitors, to the effect that both an apology and compensation is due to him unless the slander is to come into court. Hers faithfully, Meyrick and Hodges.

Constantine. I don't know them.

Philip. We were all still making personal remarks at half-past twelve today . . . so by their expedition I should say they both are and are not a first-class firm. But suppose the whole thing is made public . . . then the question of the parentage must be cleared up. Miss Yates says it's nobody's business but hers. That's an odd idea, in which, if she chooses to have it, the law seems to support her.

The steady eye and the steady voice have seemed to make the tension unbearable, and PHILIP *has meant them to. But he hardly expected this outburst.* CONSTANTINE, *in his own dramatically dignified way, has a fit of hysterics.*

Constantine. Phil, I saw the little baggage when the shop closed. I insisted on her meeting me. You know how I've always behaved over these matters. No one could have been kinder. But she refused money.

Philip [*calling on the gods to witness this occasion*]. Well . . . I might have guessed. Oh . . . you incorrigible old man!

Constantine. She insulted me . . . said she'd done with me . . . denied me the right to my own child. I'd even have taken her away. But you're helpless. I never felt so degraded in my life.

Philip. Serve you right!

Constantine. . . . But the girl's mad! Think of my feelings. What does it make of me? Did she know what she was saying?

Philip [*framing his thoughts at last*]. Possibly not . . . but I'm thankful some woman's been found at last to put you in your place.

These parental-filial passages have brought the two of them face to face, strung to shouting pitch. They become aware of it when JESSICA *walks in very gently*.

Jessica. Your mother gone?

Philip. To bed.

Jessica [*conscious of thunder*]. Am I intruding? I sent Phil in for his book a while ago. He didn't return, so I judged that he was. Perhaps I'm not?

CONSTANTINE *is master of himself again, though the hand holding the letter which* PHILIP *gave him does tremble a little still*.

Constantine. Well . . . what does Miss Chancellor want?

Philip. She asks my advice.

Constantine. Dismiss Baxter.

Philip. D'you mean Brigstock?

Constantine. Brigstock, then. Dismiss him.

Philip. What's he done to deserve it?

Constantine. He seems a nonentity of a fellow, and without grit enough to own up to his wife and risk his place. D'you want to protect a man from the consequences of what he *is?*

Philip. Society conspires to.

Constantine. Then pay him fifty pounds for the damage to his silly little reputation. That'll be a just consequence to you of sentimentalizing over him.

Philip. And stick to Miss Chancellor?

Constantine. Certainly. Thank her from the firm for nosing out such a scandal.

Philip. And what about Miss Yates?

Jessica. The girl in your office this morning?

Philip. Yes.

Jessica. In the usual trouble?

Philip. How d'you know that?

Jessica. By the tone of your voice.

Constantine [*more slowly, more carefully, a little resentfully*]. Dismiss Miss Yates. Keep your eye on her . . . and in a year's time find her a better place . . . if you can . . . in one of these new Madras Houses of State's. He seems to pay very well. [*Then with a breath of relief he becomes his old charming self again.*] Let us change the subject. How is Mildred, Jessica?

Jessica. Growing.

Constantine. I've an appointment with my solicitor tonight . . . ten o'clock. There will be two or three thousand pounds to come to that young lady by my will. I mean to leave it as a dowry for her marriage . . . its interest to be paid to her if she's a spinster at thirty . . . which heaven forbid.

Philip. What are you doing with the rest, Father?

Constantine. There are one or two . . . legacies of honor, shall I call them? What remains will come to you.

Philip. Yes . . . I don't want it, thank you.

Constantine. It isn't much.

Philip. Take it to Hit, that charming village on the borders of Southern Arabia. Stick it in the ground . . . let it breed more corn and oil for you. We've too much of it already . . . it breeds idleness here.

Constantine. Dear me!

They settle into a chat.

Jessica. We're discussing a reduction of our income by a few hundreds a year.

Philip. I'm refusing State's directorship.

Jessica. Though I'm waiting for Phil to tell me where the saving's to come in.

Philip. We ought to change that school of Mildred's, for one thing.

Jessica. Nonsense, Phil!

Philip. My dear Father, I spent a day there with the child, and upon my word, the only thing she's being taught which will not be a mere idle accomplishment is gardening. And even in their gardens . . . No vegetables allowed!

Jessica. Phil, I don't mean to have any nonsense with Mildred about earning her living. Accomplished women have a very good time in this world . . . serious women don't. I want my daughter to be happy.

Philip. If we've only enough life left to be happy with we must keep ourselves decently poor.

CONSTANTINE *gets up.*

Constantine. Could you get me a taxi, I wonder? It had started raining when I came.

Philip. There'll be one on the stand opposite.

Constantine. I mustn't be too late for Voysey. He makes a favor of coming after hours.

Jessica. I frankly cultivate expensive tastes. I like to have things beautiful around me. I don't know what else civilization means.

Constantine. I am sure that Philip can refuse you nothing.

Philip. If I do dismiss Miss Yates, I wonder if I could do it brutally enough to induce her to accept some compensation.

Jessica. What for?

Philip. She won't take money from this gentleman . . . whoever he is . . . that is, she won't be bribed into admitting her shame.

Jessica. When a woman has gone wrong mayn't it be her duty to other women to own up to it?

Constantine [*who has stood still the while, stroking his beard*]. If your auditors won't pass any decent sum, I should be happy to send you a check, Phil.

Philip [*with a wry smile*]. That would be very generous of you, Father.

Constantine. Good-by, Jessica.

Jessica. Good-by.

Constantine. Philip is fortunate in his marriage.

Jessica. So good of you to remind him of that.

Constantine. You have a charming home. I wonder how much of your womanly civilization it would have needed to conquer *me.* Well . . . I leave you to your conversation. A pleasant life to you.

He bends over her hand as if to kiss it. She takes it, as if fastidiously, out of his soft grasp. So he bows again and leaves her.

Constantine. Victoria at eleven o'clock tomorrow, Philip.

Philip. Yes . . . I'll see you off.

Constantine. I have to do a little shopping quite early.

Philip. Shopping! What can the West send the East?

Constantine. I must take back a trinket or two.

Philip. To be sure. We do the same on our travels.

PHILIP *sees him through the hall to the front door, hails a stray cab, and is quit of him.* JESSICA *moves about as if to free the air of this visitation, and when* PHILIP *comes back . . .*

Jessica. Does your father usually scatter checks so generously and carelessly?

Philip. Jessica, while I have every respect for that young lady's independence . . . still two hundred pounds would be all to the good of the child's upbringing . . . and why shouldn't Miss Yates keep her secret?

Jessica. Yes. I don't like your father. And I'm sometimes afraid that you're only an intellectual edition of him. It's very vital, of course, to go about seducing everybody to your own way of thinking. But really it's not quite civilized. You ought to learn to talk about the weather.

Philip. I cannot talk about what can't be helped.

He had settled to a chair and a cigarette, but on the impulse he abandons both and starts a lively argument instead. PHILIP'S *excited arguments are carried on in short dashes about the room and with queer un-English gestures.*

Philip. And I wonder more and more what the devil you all mean by civilization. This room is civilization. Whose civilization? Not ours.

Jessica [*in mock despair*]. Oh, dear!

Philip. Cheer up. Didn't you marry me because I thought more of Bach than Offenbach? Why shouldn't you share a fresh set of convictions? This sort of marriage is worthwhile, you know. Even one's quarrels have a certain dignity.

Jessica. Go ahead . . . bless your heart.

Philip [*shaking his fist at the world in general*]. Whitechapel High Street's our civilization.

Jessica. I don't know it.

Philip. Therefore you don't much matter, my dear . . . any more than my father did with his view of life as a sort of love-chase. [*He surveys the charming room that is his home.*] Persian carpet on the floor. Last supper, by Ghirlandajo, over the mantelpiece. The sofa you're sitting on was made in a forgotten France. This is a museum. And down at that precious school what are they cultivating Mildred's mind into but another museum . . . of good manners and good taste and . . . [*He catches* JESSICA's *half-scornful, half-kindly quizzical look.*] Are we going to have a row about this?

Jessica. If you idealists want Mildred to live in the Whitechapel Road . . . make it a fit place for her.

Philip [*taking the thrust and enjoyably returning it*]. When she lives in it it will become so. Why do I give up designing dresses and running a fashion shop to go on the County Council . . . if I can get on? And not to cut a fine figure there, either. But to be on a committee or committees. Not to talk finely even then . . . Lord keep me from the temptation . . . but to do dull, hard work over drains and disinfectants and . . .

Jessica. Well . . . why, Phil? I may as well know.

Philip. To save my soul alive.

Jessica. I'm sure I hope you may. But what is it we're to cultivate in poor Mildred's soul?

PHILIP *stops in his walk, and then* . . .

Philip. Why not a sense of ugliness? Have you ever really looked at a London street . . . walked slowly up and down it three times . . . carefully testing it with every cultured sense?

Jessica. Yes . . . it's loathsome.

Philip. Then what have you done?

Jessica. What can one do?

Philip. Come home to play a sonata of Beethoven! Does that drown the sights and the sounds and the smell of it?

Jessica. Yes . . . it does.

Philip [*in fierce revolt*]. Not to me . . . my God . . . not to me!

Jessica [*gently bitter*]. For so many women, Phil, art has to make life possible.

Philip. Suppose we teach Mildred to look out of the window at the life outside. We want to make that *impossible*. Neither art nor religion nor good manners have made of the world a place I'll go on living in if I can help it. [*He throws himself into a chair.*] D'you remember in my young days when I used to spend part of a holiday lecturing on Shelley?

Jessica. Yes.

Philip. I remember once traveling in the train with a poor wretch who lived . . . so he told me . . . on what margins of profit he could pick up by standing rather incompetently between the corn field and the baker . . . or the coal mine and the fire . . . or the landowner and the tenant . . . I forget which. And he was weary and irritable and unhealthy. And he hated Jones . . . because Jones had done him out of a half percent on two hundred and fifty pounds . . . and if the sum had been bigger he'd have sued him, so he would. And the end of Prometheus was running in my head . . . This, like thy glory, Titan, is to be good, great and joyous, beautiful and free . . . and I thought him a mean fellow. And then he told me how he dreaded bankruptcy, and how his uncle, who had been a clerk, had come to the workhouse . . . and what a disgrace that was. And I'm afraid he was a little drunk. And I wondered whether it would be possible to interest *him* in the question of Shelley's position as a prosodist . . . or whether even the beauties of Prometheus would comfort him at all. But when he asked me what I was going to Manchester for . . . do you know, I was ashamed to tell him?

There falls a little silence. Their voices hardly break it.

Jessica. Yes . . . a terrible world . . . an ugly, stupid, wasteful world. A hateful world!

Philip. And yet we have to teach Mildred what love of the world means, Jessica. Even if it's an uncomfortable business. Even if it means not adding her to that aristocracy of good feeling and good taste . . . the very latest of class distinctions. I tell you I haven't come by these doubts so easily. Beautiful sounds and sights and thoughts are all of the world's heritage I care about. Giving them up is like giving my carefully created soul out of my keeping before I die.

Jessica [*with a sudden fling of her hands*]. And into whose?

Philip [*shaking his head at the fire*]. I'm afraid into the keeping of everybody we are at present tempted to dislike and despise. For that's public life. That's democracy. But that's the future. [*He looks across at his wife half curiously.*] I know it's even harder for you women. You put off your armor for a man you love. But otherwise you've your honor and dignity and purity . . .

Jessica. Do you want a world without that, either?

Philip. I rather want to know just what the world gets by it. Those six thin girls at my uncle's . . . what do we get from them or they from the world? Little Miss Yates, now . . . her transgressions may be the most profitable thing about her . . .

Jessica. Two wrongs don't make a right.

Philip [*quaintly*]. They often do . . . properly mixed. Of course you women could serve yourselves up to such lords of creation as my father quite profitably, in one sense, if you would.

Jessica [*her lip curling*]. Thank you . . . we're not cattle.

Philip. No. Then there's a price to be paid for free womanhood, I think . . . and how many of you ladies are willing to pay it? Come out and be common women among us common men? [*He leans toward her, and his voice deepens.*] Jessica, do you feel that it was you shot that poor devil six months ago? . . . that it's you who are to be hanged tomorrow?

Jessica. I don't think I do.

Philip. That it's your body is being sold on some street this evening?

She gives a little most genuine shudder.

Jessica. I hate to think about such things.

Philip [*summing up*]. Then there's precious little hope for the Kingdom of Heaven upon earth. I know it sounds mere nonsense, but I'm sure it's true. If we can't love the bad as well as the beautiful . . . if we won't share it all out now . . . fresh air and art . . . and dirt and sin . . . then we good and clever people are costing the world too much. Our brains cost too much if we don't give them freely. Your beauty costs too much if I only admire it because of the uglier women I see . . . even your virtue may cost too much, my dear. Rags pay for finery and ugliness for beauty, and sin pays for virtue. Why can nothing keep for long more beauty in a good man's eyes than the ugliest thing on earth? Why need no man be wiser than the biggest fool on earth? Why does it profit neither man nor woman to be more righteous than the greatest sinner on earth? [*He clenches his hands.*] These are the riddles this Sphinx of a world is asking me. Your artists and scholars and preachers don't answer them . . . so I must turn my back for a bit on artist and scholar and preacher . . . all three.

JESSICA *looks at him as he completes his apologia, sympathetic, if not understanding. Then she rallies him cheerfully.*

Jessica. Meanwhile, my dear Phil, I shall not stop subscribing to the London symphony concerts . . . and I shall expect you to take me occasionally.

Philip [*jumping back from his philosophic world*]. Oh . . . that reminds me . . . I've a message for you from Tommy.

Jessica. Have you? He was really irritating this morning.

Philip. We must take Tommy with a sense of humor. It wasn't so much a message as one of those little bursts of childlike confidence . . . he endears himself to one with them from time to time.

Jessica. About me?

Philip. Yes. What it comes to is this. Will you please not flirt with him any more, because he hasn't the time, and he's too fond both of me and his wife to want to find himself seriously in love with you.

Now PHILIP *has not said this unguardedly, and* JESSICA *knows it. She'll walk into no little trap set for her vanity or the like. Still, it is with hardly a steady voice that she says simply . . .*

Jessica. Thank you for the message.

PHILIP *goes cheerfully on; he is turning the pages of his book.*

Philip. He doesn't at all suppose you are in love with him . . . seriously or otherwise.

Jessica [*steadily*]. Do you?

Philip. No.

Jessica [*her tone sharpening still*]. And is this the first time you've discussed me with Tommy or anyone? Please let it be the last.

Philip. Are you angry, Jessica?

Jessica. I'm more than angry.

Philip. I'm sorry.

Having kept her temper successfully, if not the sense of humor which PHILIP *warned her he was appealing to,* JESSICA *now allows herself a deliberate outburst of indignation.*

Jessica. I despise men. I despised them when I was fifteen . . . the first year I was conscious of them. I've been through many opinions since . . . and I come back to despising them.

Philip. He was afraid you wouldn't be pleased with him. But he has my sympathies, Jessica.

Jessica [*throwing back her head*]. *Has* he!

Philip. Tommy is what the entertaining State called this afternoon the mean sensual man.

Jessica [*with utter contempt*]. Yes. When we're alone, having a jolly talk about things in general, he's all the time thinking I want him to kiss me.

Philip. While what you really want is to have him wanting to kiss you but never to kiss you.

Jessica [*in protest*]. No.

Philip [*fixing her with a finger*]. Oh, yes, Jessica.

JESSICA's *sense of humor returns for a moment.*

Jessica. Well . . . I can't help it if he does.

Philip. You can, of course. And the mean sensual man calls it being made a fool of.

She puts a serious face on it again; not that she can keep one with PHILIP's *twinkling at her.*

Jessica. I give you my word I've never tried to flirt with Tommy . . . except once or twice when he has been boring me. And perhaps once or twice when I was in the dumps . . . and there he was . . . and I was boring him. I know him too well to flirt with him . . . you can't flirt with a man you know well. But he's been boring me lately, and I suppose I've been a bit bored. But suppose I have been flirting with him . . . I thought he was safe enough. [*That attempt failing, there is a tack left, and on this she really manages to work herself back to indignation.*] And a caddish thing to go speaking to you about it.

Philip. So he said . . . so he said.

Jessica. Worse than caddish . . . outrageous! I never heard of such a thing . . . you shouldn't have let him.

Philip. Should I have knocked him down when he mentioned your name?

Jessica. Yes . . . I wish you had.

Philip. Little savage!

Jessica. I can't laugh about this. I'm hurt.

Philip. My dear, if you have any sense at all, you'll ask him to dinner and chaff him about it . . . before me.

Jessica. Have you any understanding of what a woman feels when men treat her like this? Degraded and cheapened.

But the high moral tone PHILIP *will not stand. He drops chaff and tackles her.*

Philip. I can tell you what the man feels. He'll be either my father or me. That's your choice. Tommy's my father when you've put on your best gown to attract him, or he's me when he honestly says that he'd rather you wouldn't. Do you want him to be me or my father? That's the first question for you.

Jessica. I want a man to treat a woman with courtesy and respect.

Philip. And what does that come to? My dear, don't you know that the mean sensual man . . . no, not Tommy for the moment, but say Dick or Harry . . . looks on you all as choice morsels . . . with your prettinesses, your dressings up, your music and art as so much sauce to his appetite. Which only a mysterious thing called your virtue prevents him from indulging . . . almost by force, if it weren't for the police, Jessica. Do you like that?

Jessica. I don't believe it.

Philip. Do you really believe that most men's good manners toward most pretty women are anything else but good manners?

Jessica. I prefer good manners to yours. [*Then, both fine taste and sense of humor to the rescue again.*] No . . . that's rude.

Philip [*with much more affection than the words convey*]. I treat you as a man would treat another man . . . neither better nor worse. Is the compliment quite wasted?

Jessica [*as amazed at this unreasonable world*]. I want to be friends with men. I'd sooner be friends with them. It's they who flirt with me. Why?

Philip [*incurably mischievous*]. Of course I've forgotten what you look like, and I never notice what you have on . . . but I suspect it's because you're rather pretty and attractive.

Jessica. Do you want women not to be?

Philip. No.

Jessica. It's perfectly sickening. Of course, if I had dozens of children, and grew an old woman with the last one, I should be quite out of danger. But we can't all be like that . . . you don't want us to be.

Philip [*purely negative*]. No.

He leaves her free to justify herself.

Jessica. I do my share of things. I make a home for you. I entertain your friends. It may cost your precious world too much . . . my civilization . . . but you want all this done. [*Then with a certainly womanly reserve.*] And Phil . . . suppose I'm not much nicer by nature than some of you men? When I was a baby, if I'd not been fastidious I should have been a sad glutton. My culture . . . my civilization . . . mayn't be quite up to keeping the brilliant Tommy a decent friend to me, but it has its uses.

But PHILIP *means to laugh this out of court, too.*

Philip. Look here, if it's only your culture keeps you from kissing Tommy . . . kiss him.

To be so driven from pillar to post really does exasperate her.

Jessica. Phil . . . I sometimes think I'd sooner have been married to your father.

Philip. Why?

Jessica. If you went on as he did instead of as you do . . . I should be sorry . . . I should despise you . . . but it would string me up and add to my self-respect enormously!

[*Then a little appealingly.*] But it's when you're inhuman, Phil . . . that I'm ever so little tempted.

Philip [*contrite at once*]. I know I am. [*Then he gets up to stand looking into the fire, and what he says is heartfelt.*] But I do so hate that farmyard world of sex . . . men and women always treating each other in this unfriendly way . . . that I'm afraid it hardens me a bit.

Jessica [*from her side, gently, with just a look at him*]. I hate it, too . . . but I happen to love you, Phil.

They smile at each other.

Philip. Yes, my dear. If you'd kindly come over here . . . I should like to kiss you.

Jessica. I won't. You can come over to me.

Philip. Will you meet me halfway?

They meet halfway, and kiss as husband and wife can. They stand together, looking into the fire.

Philip. Do you know the sort of world I want to live in?

Jessica. Should I like it?

Philip. Hasn't humanity come of age at last?

Jessica. Has it?

Philip. Mayn't we hope so? Finery sits so well on children. And they strut and make love absurdly . . . even their quarreling is in all good faith and innocence. But I don't see why we men and women should not find all happiness . . . and beauty, too, . . . in soberer purposes. And with each other . . . why not always some touch of the tranquil understanding which is yours and mine, dear, at the best of moments?

Jessica [*happily*]. Do you mean when we sometimes suddenly want to shake hands?

Philip [*happily, too*]. That's it. And I want an art and a culture that shan't be just a veneer on savagery . . . but it must spring in good time from the happiness of a whole people.

JESSICA *gives herself one little shake of womanly common sense.*

Jessica. Well, what's to be done?

Philip [*nobody more practical than he*]. I've been making suggestions. We must learn to live on a thousand a year . . . put Mildred to a sensible school . . . and I must go on the County Council. That's how these great spiritual revolutions work out in practice, to begin with.

Jessica [*as one who demands a right*]. Where's my share of the job?

Philip [*conscious of some helplessness*]. How is a man to tell you? There's enough to choose from.

Jessica [*the burden of her sex's present fate upon her*]. Ah, you're normal. Nobody sizes you up as a good man or a bad man . . . pretty or plain. There's a trade for bad women and several professions for plain ones. But I've been taught how to be charming and to like dainty clothes. And I dare say I'm excitable and emotional . . . but I can't help it. I'm well off, married to you, I know. You do make me forget I'm a female occasionally.

Philip. Male and female created He them . . . and left us to do the rest. Men and women are a long time in the making . . . aren't they?

Jessica [*enviously*]. Oh . . . you're all right.

Philip [*with some humble knowledge of himself*]. Are we?

Jessica. But I tell you, Phil, it isn't so easy for us. You don't always let us have the fairest of chances, do you?

Philip. No, I grant it's not easy. But it's got to be done.

Jessica. Yes . . .

She doesn't finish, for really there is no end to the subject. But for a moment or two longer, happy together, they stand looking into the fire.

NOTES

Loaves and Fishes (1902) was first produced at the Duke of York's Theatre, London, February 24, 1911, with Robert Loraine as Canon Spratte. In *The Summing Up* (New York, New American Library, 1946, p. 76), Maugham blames the short run on a public that "was uneasy at seeing a clergyman made fun of."

The Return of the Prodigal (1904) was first produced at the Court Theatre, London, September 26, 1905. Granville-Barker directed a cast that included A. E. Matthews as Eustace and Dennis Eadie as Henry. As Desmond MacCarthy says in *The Court Theatre* (London, A. H. Bullen, 1907, pp. 5-6), it was typical of the meticulousness of the Granville-Barker–Vedrenne productions, of the emphasis on every part, however small, that Edmund Gwenn, who had made a hit a few months earlier as Henry Straker in *Man and Superman,* should have been cast as and should have been willing to play Baines, the butler.

Getting Married (1908) was first produced by J. E. Vedrenne and Harley Granville-Barker at the Haymarket Theatre, London, May 12, 1908. It was the last play to be done by the Granville-Barker–Vedrenne partnership. Directed by Granville-Barker, the cast included Fanny Brough as Mrs. George Collins, Henry Ainley as the Bishop of Chelsea and Robert Loraine as St. John Hotchkiss, whose name at least, judging from one of Shaw's letters to Mrs. Campbell (*Bernard Shaw and Mrs. Patrick Campbell, Their Correspondence,* ed. Alan Dent, New York, Knopf, 1952, p. 205), comes from St. John Hankin. The play was first produced in New York at the Booth Theatre, November 6, 1916, by William Faversham, who played the Bishop.

Mid-Channel (1909) was first produced at the St. James's Theatre, London, September 2, 1909, with Irene Vanbrugh as Zoe Blundell. It was first produced in New York by Charles Frohman at the Empire Theatre, January 31, 1910, with Ethel Barrymore as Zoe. The play was more successful in the United States than it was in England. In his "Critical Preface" to the play (*The Social Plays of Arthur Wing Pinero,* Vol. 4, New York, Dutton, 1922, p. 279), Clayton Hamilton quotes Pinero: "Miss Barrymore made Zoe more ladylike and lovable than she actually is. . . . Well, maybe that's another reason why the play did so well in America."

The Madras House (1909) was first produced by Charles Frohman at the Duke of York's Theatre, London, March 9, 1910. It, with John Galsworthy's *Justice* and Bernard Shaw's *Misalliance,* was part of a brief, unsuccessful attempt at a repertory theatre. Granville-Barker directed a cast that included Dennis Eadie as Philip Madras, Mary Jerrold as Marion Yates and Sybil Thorndike as Emma Huxtable. The play was produced in New York at the Neighborhood Playhouse, October 29, 1921. Granville-Barker, who never knew when to quit revising, published a second version of the play in 1925.